THE POLITICAL DISCOURSE OF ANARCHY

SUNY Series in Global Politics

James N. Rosenau, Editor

THE POLITICAL DISCOURSE OF ANARCHY

A DISCIPLINARY HISTORY
OF INTERNATIONAL RELATIONS

BRIAN C. SCHMIDT

STATE UNIVERSITY OF NEW YORK PRESS

Published by
State University of New York Press, Albany

© 1998 State University of New York

For information, address State University of New York Press,
State University Plaza, Albany, N.Y. 12246

Production by M. R. Mulholland
Marketing by Fran Keneston

Library of Congress Cataloging-in-Publication Data

Schmidt, Brian C., 1966–
    The political discourse of anarchy : a disciplinary history of
international relations / Brian C. Schmidt.
        p.   cm.—(SUNY series in global politics)
    Includes bibliographical references and index.
    ISBN 0-7914-3577-6 (hc : acid-free paper).—ISBN 0-7914-3578-4
(pb : acid-free paper)
    1. International relations—Study and teaching.   I. Title.
II. Series.
JX1291.S32   1997
327.1'071—dc21   97-1724
                                                        CIP

10 9 8 7 6 5 4 3 2 1

To Cathleen

CONTENTS

Preface and Acknowledgments

My intellectual interest in the disciplinary history of international relations came about in an indirect manner. As an undergraduate student, I had been exposed to some of the latest theoretical trends in political science and was encouraged by several members of the faculty to pursue my curiosity further. When I entered graduate school, I was most concerned about recent developments in international relations and political theory. Although I was intent on making international relations my major field, I was attracted most to political theory courses and decided to take the unorthodox route of writing my Master's thesis for both an international relations specialist and a political theorist. In the course of writing my thesis on the critical theory of Robert W. Cox, I determined that it was necessary to provide a historical overview of how the field of international relations had developed. The historical account that I offered—one in which academic scholars of international relations were portrayed as the heirs of a great tradition begun by Thucydides and Machiavelli and in which the field progressed through a series of cumulative great debates beginning with that between idealism and realism—is exactly the image of the field's history that this book seeks to put to rest. While the thesis was accepted, I was fortunate that the political theory reader queried if I was certain that the field of international relations had actually developed in the manner that I had depicted. That was the moment at which my interest in the history of the field was kindled and when the idea for this project was born.

John G. Gunnell asked that profound question, and he has provided me with the inspiration and guidance to write this book. Over the years, he has been both my mentor and friend. Gunnell not only commented on and read the entire manuscript more times than I am sure any other person could have possibly endured, but, through the generosity that he displays with his ideas, fostered my discovery of this branch of important research. It would have been impossible to write this book without the support of Professor Gunnell and I hold the deepest sense of heartfelt gratitude to him.

As interest in the history of political science has grown rapidly in the last few years, I have benefited from the work of James Farr, Raymond Seidelman, John Dryzek, and Stephen Leonard. There are a number of similarities between the arguments and concerns advanced in their work, and the historiographical approach adopted in this book. Hopefully, this will be welcomed by the international relations scholarly community, since there is a growing sentiment that the field should no longer remain isolated and detached from the developments occurring within the wider realm of social and political thought. This book aspires to make a contribution to both the disciplinary history of international relations and political science and to promote the effort that is underway to reunite the fields of political theory and international relations.

The first task that I undertook in researching this book was to read the existing accounts of the history of the field. Besides the paucity of material, one of the most striking aspects of these accounts was the tendency to substitute the figures associated with the classic tradition of political thought for the scholars who have institutionally participated in the academic field of international relations. I considered this to be paradoxical, since one of the common assumptions supporting the dichotomy between political theory and international relations theory is that the classic figures of political thought had very little to say about international relations. Nevertheless, in order to reconstruct the disciplinary history of international relations, it was necessary to cast off the various epic accounts of the field's evolution and focus on what can be called the *real history* of the field.

The second, and by far more time consuming, task was to reconstruct the discursive history of the field. This entailed the labor-intensive activity of accumulating and sifting through the numerous isolated artifacts that were located in journals and texts that in most instances had not, for many years, been removed from the shelves on which they were placed. These artifacts, however, are the testimony to an actual conversation that at one time guided inquiry about the subject matter of international relations. Although the effort to locate and read through this material was arduous, the occasional feeling of genuine discovery was enough to sustain my intellectual energies. In recovering this material, I have developed a deep respect for many of the field's long-forgotten individuals who helped to make the field what it is today, and I have attempted to reconstruct their ideas faithfully.

I am deeply grateful to David Brown, Bradley S. Klein, and Sanford F. Schram who each in their own way played a significant role in my undergraduate education. Their sincere commitment to the vocation of political science is evident in the fact that they have all continued to read and comment on my work as well as offer me their devoted support. While work on the history of the field has not yet acquired the same degree of legitimacy as other areas of research, I have received support from a number of international relations scholars who have recognized the importance of disciplinary history. At an early stage, Jeffrey W. Legro read the entire manuscript and not only provided me with some very helpful comments but bolstered my confidence in this project. Richard Little has my deepest appreciation for publishing an initial version of chapter one in the *Review of International Studies:* "The Historiography of Academic International Relations," *Review of International Studies* 20 (1994): 349–367. In my endeavor to interpret theories of international relations, I have greatly benefited from the work of Rob Walker and I value the support and comments that he has provided. Richard Mansbach was very generous in the comments that he offered on the manuscript. I also would like to acknowledge the kind encouragement that I have received from David Campbell, Miles Kahler, Ido Oren, and Robert Vitalis. I would especially like to thank James N. Rosenau, editor of the series in Global Politics, and Clay Morgan of SUNY Press.

There are a number of individuals at the University at Albany—Peter Breiner, Martin Edelman, Walter Goldstein, and Ted Wright—who showed interest in my research and offered their assistance. I am grateful to each of them. I have cherished my friendship with Eric Ziegelmayer with whom I have shared many of my discoveries as well as disappointments over the years. In addition to giving expert computer advice, Damon Knopf has been a dear friend since Potsdam, as have Robert Coats, Eric Pyne, George Perry, Robert Nelson, and the late Dan Spoor. My family has also offered their encouragement throughout this project. I am very thankful to each of them and particularly, my mother, for the help they have provided.

Most importantly, I am forever indebted to my wonderful wife, Cathleen. She greatly supported me in writing this book and was able to tolerate the many hours that I spent alone working on this project. Cathleen shows me the great pleasures of life and I dedicate this book to her.

History without Political Science has no fruit;
Political Science without History has no root.

—John R. Seeley

INTRODUCTION

This study is, most fundamentally, a disciplinary history of academic international relations as a sub-field of American political science. In situating international relations within this context, it offers a general contribution to the history of political science. The basic intention of this work is to provide a detailed account of the history of the academic field of international relations by reconstructing its internal discursive development. By "internal" I mean a focus on the actual conversations about the subject matter of international politics pursued by previous generations of academic practitioners who self-consciously identified themselves with the field of international relations. This approach is offered as an alternative to histories that insist that the development of the field of international relations can be understood primarily in relation to the external events taking place in the realm of international politics.

Chapter 1 delineates a methodological approach that can be described as critical internal discursive history. The intention of such an approach is to reconstruct an actual conversation among political scientists and other professional scholars who institutionally thought of themselves as participating in a formalized academic setting devoted to the study of international politics. The basis of this approach is that the field itself, and not the general political universe, is the most appropriate context for reconstructing these older conversations. Chapter 1 also explicates the political discourse of anarchy which has served as a connecting discursive thread throughout the history of the field of international relations.

Most students of international relations would agree that anarchy, or the interaction of state and non-state actors in the absence of a central authority, is the fundamental condition shaping international politics. Yet what has received little attention is the evolution and discursive transformation of the concept of anarchy. Although reading the recent journal articles in the field might lead one to conclude that anarchy is some newly discovered research puzzle that lends itself to the latest tools of social scientific inquiry, anarchy—and the closely related concept of sovereignty—has served as the core constituent principle throughout the evolution of the field of international relations. The concept of anarchy employed in this book is not an externally or retrospectively imposed theme for purposes of ordering the narrative but instead represents an indigenous construct around which discussions about the subject matter of international relations have continuously revolved.

This investigation is selective but extensive: it begins in the mid-1800s and ends with the outbreak of World War II. This choice may be puzzling for many, since it is a common belief that the field of international relations only began to reach maturity in the late 1940s. Yet the crux of this study is the reconstruction of the earlier and formative periods of the field's history which have either been entirely forgotten or reduced to a caricature that misrepresents the field's early development in the United States. By directing attention to these earlier periods, this book focuses on some of the deep discursive continuities between the early-twentieth-century analyses of international politics and the contemporary field of study. In the process, a number of myths about the field are dispelled, including those about its early development and the alleged shift from "idealism" to "realism." One of the critical purposes of this study is to demonstrate that the characteristic dichotomy between idealist and realist periods in the history of the field is a misrepresentation. This necessitates tracing the descent of the field prior to World War II, and even beyond World War I.

Chapter 2 commences with the emergence of political science from the traditional moral philosophy curriculum in the mid-1800s and proceeds to the end of the nineteenth century. An underlying theme of this chapter is what is described as the theoretical discourse of the state which provided the early paradigmatic framework for both political science and international relations. It was within the context of the theoretical discourse of the state, a conversation that addressed the internal and external dimensions of state sovereignty, that the initial elements of the field of international relations were developed. In addition to examining the central themes that constituted the discourse of the state, attention will be directed toward the conversation that political scientists were pursuing about colonialism and, more specifically, colonial administration and the activities associated with national imperialism, which represented a central dimension of the early study of international politics.

Chapters 3 and 4 deal with different but significant aspects of the academic conversation about international relations between the beginning of the twentieth century and the outbreak of World War I. Chapter 3 reconstructs the discourse that centered on the theoretical issues revolving around the political relations between the important, and mostly European, powers in the international arena. Issues pertaining to state sovereignty, international law, world order reform, and internationalism are addressed in this chapter. More importantly, this chapter describes the manner in which the orthodox juristic conception of the state provided the context for discussing each of these issues and how it, at the same time, constrained the discourse of international relations. The diverse criticisms that were, however, raised against this conception of the state, especially as it related to the subject matter of international law, are addressed, and the chapter concludes by highlighting the liberating effect that alternative conceptions of the state began to have on the field.

Chapter 4 examines more fully the conversation about the relationship between the "uncivilized" or "backward" political territories and the "civilized" states that was introduced in Chapter 2. Unlike the discourse that focused on the political relations between the major actors in world politics, where sovereignty, international law, and the effects of international anarchy were the major issues, the conversation dealing with these "other" entities was devoted to devising the best means of administering order in places plagued by internal disorder. This chapter also explores the variety of meanings that have been given to the pivotal concept of anarchy within the disciplinary history of international relations.

Chapters 5 and 6 focus on the interwar period. These two chapters accentuate the important continuities and discontinuities between the post–World War I discourse of the field and that of the earlier phases. Chapter 5 begins by examining some of the explanations that were put forth to account for the outbreak of World War I. More specifically, it emphasizes the arguments that suggested that the war was, in part, a consequence of the juristic theory of the state and the resulting international anarchy. It was within the contours of this discussion that political scientists attempted to discredit the older conception of the state and offer an alternative conceptualization of sovereignty based on the theory of pluralism. After discussing the modifications in the theoretical understanding of state sovereignty, the focus turns to their important consequences for the discourse of international relations. Most directly, changes in the theoretical conception of the state fostered a revised ontological understanding of the international milieu. This revision, in turn, lent support to those who were attempting to reform the condition of international anarchy that many had concluded facilitated the outbreak of World War I.

Chapter 6 addresses two of the major themes of the interwar period: the study of international organization and of international politics. The formal study of international organization that arose during this period is a central focus, but the examination of this discourse is undertaken in a manner that connects it with earlier themes and issues in the history of the field rather than viewing it as a direct consequence of the institutionalization of the League of Nations. Discussions of international organization were, however, aimed at offering practical knowledge that could be used to ameliorate the negative consequences associated with international anarchy. Specific consideration is devoted to the development of the concept of interdependence and to demonstrating how this led to a different view of the international milieu than that depicted by juristic theory.

The second major theme of this chapter is the transformation that the field began to experience at the end of the interwar period. These changes were initiated by a new group of scholars entering the field who argued that international politics should replace international organization and law as the major focus of the discipline. This transformation has been conventionally understood as representing the field's first "great debate" and as denoting the beginning of the realist phase of development. This period has also been perceived as representing a fundamental rupture with respect to the theories, methods, and concerns of the earlier generation of international relations scholars. In the course of explicating the ideas of those who began to challenge the older assumptions and orientation of the field, this chapter demonstrates the continuity that actually existed between the pre- and post–World War II discourse of international relations.

The concluding chapter recapitulates some of the important themes that have structured the discourse of international relations during the formative years of its history and demonstrates their relevance to the contemporary field. This chapter again questions some of the conventional interpretations of the field's history, and particularly the idea that before World War II the discourse of international relations was distinguished by idealism that was later replaced by a "realist" approach. The general importance of disciplinary history and its critical potential for understanding past and present identities is also confronted.

Although there are a number of intellectual justifications for investigating the history of the field, this study is defended less on the grounds of historical antiquarianism than in terms of the belief that the capacity to examine critically the contemporary nature of the field is inseparable from an understanding of the intellectual roots from which it has evolved. As Miles Kahler has stated, "how we understand the history of international relations will also influence the future contours of the field."[1] The task of accurately comprehending the history of the field is given an added urgency by the fact that the study of international relations has been experiencing a prolonged phase of intellectual ferment as different schools of thought vie for recognition and supremacy. While historical analyses have not been the most favored means of sorting out disciplinary controversy, the present predicament offers an opportunity to reflect on the history of the field. There are, however, several other reasons why an accurate and coherent history of the field is needed.

First, an understanding of the history of the field is crucial for explaining the origin of many of our present assumptions and ideas about the study of international politics. While current intellectual practices and theoretical positions are often evoked as novel approaches to the latest dilemmas confronting international politics, an adequate historical sense reminds us that contemporary approaches often are reincarnations of something quite old and are held captive by past discourses. Second, many of the important insights of our forebears have been erased from memory. Once recalled, these insights can have critical purchase in the present. Third, the history of the field offers a basis for critical reflection on the present. Knowledge of the actual history of the field may force us to reassess some of our dominant understandings of how the field has developed. And this may, in turn, have significant implications for how we study and comprehend international politics today.

There has been, however, very little attention directed toward understanding the history of the field of international relations, and the accounts that have been offered are grossly inadequate. They do little but reinforce entrenched interpretations. Before proceeding, in Chapter 1, to discuss why there have been so few attempts by scholars to examine systematically the history of the field and to explain the inadequacies of attempts that have been made to provide a historical account, it is necessary to situate this study in a broader intellectual context.

Post-Positivism and Disciplinary History

As attested by the burgeoning literature devoted to the history of political science, disciplinary history has recently become an important field of study.[2] Works such as David Easton, Michael Stein, and John G. Gunnell's *Regime and Discipline: Democracy and the Development of Political Science* (1995) and James Farr, John Dryzek, and Stephen Leonard's *Political Science in History: Research Programs and Political Traditions* (1995) indicate that the discipline has "unavoidably become the object of its own inquiries."[3] Research on the history of the discipline has expanded to such an extent that one commentator has claimed that "by the late 1980s, it would not be an exaggeration to suggest that the history of political science is on the threshold of becoming a distinct research specialty."[4] Although there are several possible explanations for this recent attention to the history of the discipline, this introspection is, in large measure, a result of the intellectual atmosphere engendered by what has been termed post-positivism.

Unlike philosophical positivism's claim about the cumulative character of knowledge, the transition to post-positivism has required social scientists to rethink this tale about the unilinear and progressive search for truth. Disciplinary identities mortgaged to positivism have been thrown into disarray by post-positivist philosophers of science, critical theorists, feminists, postmodernists, and other voices of dissent. This is especially true of identities begotten through the conventionally accepted pre- and post-behavioral division in the discipline's history. Within the eclectic atmosphere of the 1990s, however, it increasingly appears that intellectual identity and legitimacy rest upon a more complex understanding of the origins and development of a given research program or tradition. Disciplinary histories, therefore, have become increasingly popular in the social sciences. The renewed importance attached to disciplinary history is in part a consequence of recent work in the philosophy and history of science where post-positivism has sparked a revolution in the historiography of science.

What began as an internal critique of the cumulative progressive image of scientific discourse by philosophers and historians of science such as Thomas Kuhn, Paul Feyerabend, and Karl Popper, has led to a general rethinking of the importance of the history of science. During the reign of logical positivism, writing the history of science was a seemingly straightforward non-controversial activity. This was because of the acceptance of the textbook image of science as the continuous advancement of knowledge and increasing correspondence between theory and fact. Because it was widely believed that there was a fundamental unity of scientific method, social science, while at least temporarily below natural science in the hierarchy of sciences, was, it seemed, destined to mirror the same progressive universalizing trend. All that was required was an emulation of the methods of natural science, which it was thought were mediated by philosophers of science through the medium of the hypothetico-deductive model. Political scientists, in their quest for scientific identity, were "profoundly influenced by the literature of the philosophy of science."[5] During the course of the behavioral revolution, political science increasingly came to understand its past and present history in positivist terms. As long as philosophical positivism was secure about the metatheoretical foundation it attributed to science, political science was equally certain about its scientific identity.

It is not often that a fundamental intellectual break can be attributed to one specific individual, but in the case of the philosophy of science, Thomas Kuhn's *The Structure of Scientific Revolutions* (1970) ushered in a revolution in the philosophy and historiography of science of such proportions that even political scientists were dramatically affected by it. Kuhn directly challenged logical positivism's central premises of the separation of theory from facts, the correspondence theory of truth, and he replaced the textbook account of the history of science with the idea of a discontinuous history marked by scientific revolutions, that is, "those non-cumulative developmental episodes in which an older paradigm is replaced in whole or in part by an incompatible new one."[6] The criteria of scientific knowledge, Kuhn argued, were paradigm specific, and he denied any transcendental metatheoretical vantage point from which to judge the historical progress of science. Kuhn's argument undermined the conventional understanding of scientific inquiry embraced by most philosophers and social scientists, and his work has been a significant catalyst in the post-empiricist philosophy and history of science. Kuhn's debunking of the idea of the progressive development of science has contributed to a renewed interest in disciplinary history. George Orwell's dictum that whoever controls the past controls the future is one that disciplinary historians have taken seriously. Following Kuhn's work, there has been a "recognition of the inseparability of history and philosophy; neither can proceed successfully without the other."[7] Although some philosophers have attempted to defend or reformulate some of the pre-Kuhnian assumptions about the evolution of science and have turned to disciplinary history to demonstrate cumulative scientific progress, the history of science is no longer a neglected field.

There is little doubt that post-positivism has rekindled interest in investigating the past practices of political science, yet it has also created serious theoretical and methodological controversies concerning the manner in which historical research should be conducted. These historiographical issues are addressed in the next chapter; with respect to both the disciplinary history of political science in general, and international relations in particular. But at this point it is important to note the more general intellectual ferment that post-positivist developments have wrought in the field of international relations, since it is within the critical conversation that they have engendered that this book is situated.

International Relations and the Third Debate

For the past decade or more, the field of international relations has been subject to incursions from a proliferating number of voices of dissent.[8] This has sparked a considerable amount of metatheoretical reflection on the current identity and composition of the field which, in turn, has generated an academic controversy the significance of which is best evidenced by the designation that it represents the field's third "great debate."[9] One of the fundamental aims of those who have initiated this debate is to provide an opportunity to think critically about many of the central assumptions of the field. In this manner, it is hoped that marginalized and excluded perspectives can be incorporated into the field. The attempt to form philosophical, epistemological, and theoretical linkages with post-positivist developments in the wider realm of social and political thought and evaluate the potential consequences for traditional approaches in the field is at the forefront of the controversy associated with the third debate. In one of the most lucid descriptions of the third debate, Yosef Lapid declared that "as in other social science disciplines, the current sense of substantial intellectual change in international relations seems to be sustained by a growing sentiment that post-empiricist and anti-foundationalist trends in recent philosophy of science have opened up boundaries of scientific knowledge in general."[10] According to Lapid, "the third debate marks a clear end to the positivist epistemological consensus" and "constitutes a still maturing disciplinary effort to reconsider theoretical options in a 'post-positivist' era."[11]

Many other scholars have concurred with Lapid's claim that the disciplinary controversy associated with the third debate is most essentially attributable to the philosophical transition to post-positivism. This is apparent in the description that Jim George has provided of the major themes characterizing "the agenda of dissent." George maintains that the first major theme "emphasizes the inadequacy of the positivist/empiricist approach to the study of human society and politics." The second theme is concerned with "the process by which knowledge is constituted," which "stresses social, historical, and cultural themes rather than those reliant on 'cognito' rationalism, notions of autonomous individualism, or variants on the 'sense data' or 'correspondence rule' formats." George argues that the third theme, in direct contrast to positivism, is based on a rejection of "the foundationalist search for an objective knowledge external to history and social practice," while the final theme "emphasizes the linguistic construction of reality."[12]

Similarly, Yale H. Ferguson and Richard W. Mansbach contend that "the 'Third Debate' is, indeed, well underway" and that it is "a consequence of a rapidly changing 'reality' and the failure of successive generations of inductionists to fulfill their promise of a genuinely cumulative body of knowledge." They argue that this has led to theoretical disarray, because "although there are widespread doubts about the crude, often ahistorical, empiricism that has dominated scholarship in our field for over three decades, there is little consensus about what to substitute for empiricism."[13] And V. Spike Peterson has argued that there are three reasons why post-positivism is important for the third debate in international relations: first, "developments in the philosophy of science, where positivism has been the target of rigorous critique, compel our attention"; second, "rapidly changing events are not adequately addressed by prevailing theories in international relations"; and third, "post-positivist critiques are already transgressing conventional boundaries and the centre is ill-served by its inattention to the issues raised."[14]

Among those who have embraced the transition to post-positivism, there is the common idea that the latest bout of meta-theoretical controversy has allowed additional "thinking space" within the field. The purpose of the critical voices in the debate, according to George, is "to open space within modern Western theory so that voices otherwise marginalized can be heard; that questions otherwise suppressed can be asked, that points of analytical closure can be opened for debate, that issues and arguments effectively dismissed from the mainstream can be seriously reconsidered and re-evaluated."[15] According to Richard Ashley and R. B. J. Walker, dissident works in the discipline celebrate "difference, not identity; the questioning and transgression of limits, not the assertion of boundaries and frameworks; a readiness to question how meaning and order are imposed, not the search for a source of meaning and order already in place."[16] One of the ways in which "dissident writers" have been attempting to open additional thinking space is by critically reassessing the manner that traditional ontological, epistemological, and theoretical boundaries have been constructed and perpetuated in the field of international relations. Of particular concern are the framing strategies that enable such enduring dichotomies as domestic\international, inside\outside, order\chaos, sovereignty\anarchy, idealist\realist, self\other, subject\object, tradition\science, masculine\feminine, and others to both inform and delimit the range of epistemological and theoretical questions in the field.[17] It is argued that these sorts of binary oppositions, which critical scholars regard as examples of arbitrary academic closure, emanate from the metaphysics of positivism. Deconstructing and transgressing the multiplicity of binary antinomies that can be found in the discourse of international relations is a central concern of dissidents.

One of the tangible results of this search for additional thinking space has been to foster a more pluralistic and tolerant intellectual climate in the field. The condition of enhanced openness has contributed to theoretical pluralism, which has allowed a variety of different voices to be heard. Although the openness in the field is often contrasted with the constricting dominance of realism that prevailed throughout most of the Cold War period, the intellectual merits of pluralism have also become a matter of contention. On the one hand, K. J. Holsti, an advocate of pluralism, writes that "the most obvious and important function of pluralism is based on our Socratic belief that the validity of ideas is enhanced through challenge, debate, and the development of alternatives."[18] But Mark Hoffman, on the other hand, has declared that one of the results of pluralism is that by the early 1980s, "there is no longer any clear sense of what the discipline is about, what its core concepts are, what its methodology should be, what central issues and questions it should be addressing."[19] While older identities are waning, it is unclear what new identity, if any, the field will take in the near future.

Regardless of the opportunities and pitfalls that pluralism brings, it is quite apparent that the current temperament of the field has enabled a number of different paradigms, schools of thought, and research traditions to compete for supremacy. This is one of the reasons why the third debate is often described as being an inter-paradigm debate.[20] Thus, in contrast to the manner in which the two previous debates between idealists and realists during the late 1930s and early 1940s, and between traditionalists and scientists during the late 1950s and early 1960s have been depicted, the third debate is commonly viewed as composed of several competing paradigms: realism, pluralism, globalism, neorealism, and neoliberalism. Even for those who reject this particular characterization of the debate, the controversy is commonly depicted as one that has allowed new concerns, such as normative issues and gender, to enter and contend with other more traditional approaches in the field.[21] Taken together, these new concerns and approaches have contributed to an identity crisis in the field.

Disciplinary History and International Relations

While this study is sympathetic to many of the efforts that are being made by those who are challenging the contemporary identity of the field, this book is, most fundamentally, concerned with redirecting attention to the older identities by which we are still in many respects possessed. Despite the reflection engendered by the third debate, there has been very little attention directed to the field's earlier history. The very designation "third debate" implies that the disciplinary history of international relations contains at least two earlier "great debates," yet the literature and concerns associated with the third debate have not given due attention to this earlier history. The fact that there has been so little focus on the history of the field is unfortunate given the concern of dissident writers to recover marginalized and excluded voices and perspectives.

Not only has there been very little attention directed to the field's history but those histories that have been offered are seriously flawed. Chapter 1 directly takes up these issues and argues that the standard histories of the field are plagued by two pervasive historiographical problems which have greatly influenced the manner in which the development of the field of international relations has been recounted. The first problem involves a fundamental confusion between an "analytical" and a "historical" tradition. The consequence is the mistaken belief that the contemporary configuration of the field can be explained by a continuous tradition that reaches back to classical Athens and extends forward to the present. The second problem arises from the premise that exogenous events in the realm of international politics have had a determinative causal effect upon the development of the field.

These historiographical assumptions have seriously hampered the effort to come to terms with what may be called the *real history* of the field. Reference to "real history" does not imply that there is some pristine neutral methodological vantage point from which to uncover and judge the truth of claims about the field's past. It also does not insinuate the possibility of being able to authoritatively judge one narrative to be more truthful than another. The postmodern age represents the end to the belief in such a possibility or at least, as Jean-Francois Lyotard suggests, "incredulity toward metanarratives."[22] The basic issue is not one of the authenticity of a particular historical account but rather one of focusing on the task of recapitulating the main contours and content of a circumscribed realm of discursive activity conventionally designated as international relations. A principal intention of this study is to recover, and differentiate, the actual discursive realm of disciplinary history from the variety of rhetorical and legitimating histories that currently populate the field.

International Relations as an Academic Field of Study

Before proceeding any further, it is necessary to say something about the extent to which there is a well-defined field of international relations that has a distinct history. Moreover, it is important to be unambiguous at the beginning about the precise meaning that is being conveyed when reference is made to the disciplinary history of the field of international relations.[23] The history being reconstructed in this book is that of the professional academic enterprise of international relations that has, for the most part, resided in the American discipline of political science. This means, almost inevitably, that in reconstructing the history of the field of international relations disciplinary developments within political science will also be discussed and that literature that might more broadly be construed, from various perspectives, as belonging to the field of international relations will not be discussed.

Although it should be self-evident, it is necessary to recognize that this book is not a history of international politics. Rather, it is a history of how the academic field of international relations has attempted to provide authoritative knowledge about the subject matter of international politics. In this respect, there will be references to some of the historical events that shaped international politics during the late nineteenth and early twentieth century, but the predominant focus is on the manner in which scholars of international relations perceived and discussed these events. As to the question of whether the field of international relations has a distinct history, the following chapters are a concrete testimony to the existence of a coherent conversation pursued by scholars who self-consciously understood themselves as participants in this particular field of inquiry.

Although a strong case is made for investigating the disciplinary history of international relations within the institutional matrix of American political science, critics may, nevertheless, charge that this unduly truncates the discourse of international relations and, furthermore, constitutes a parochial American version of what is, at least ostensibly, a broader global discourse. These as well as other contentious issues concerning the identity of the field of international relations arise, first, from the often-noted interdisciplinary character of field's subject matter and, second, from the belief that it is a cosmopolitan discipline devoid of any substantial national distinctions. There are many examples of how these two issues can complicate the task of investigating the history of the field of international relations.

With respect to the first issue, Quincy Wright's *The Study of International Relations* (1955) provides a notable example of the difficulties arising from the multifarious nature of the field's subject matter. Wright argued that a discipline implied "consciousness by writers that there is a subject with some sort of unity." With respect to whether international relations qualified as a discipline, he argued that it had developed synthetically through contributions from other established disciplines, which "militated against its unity." He identified eight "root disciplines" and six disciplines with a "world point of view" that had contributed to the development of international relations, and argued that the scholarly task of synthesizing these largely autonomous fields of inquiry hampered the effort to create a unified coherent discipline of international relations.[24] Other historical surveys that have emphasized the interdisciplinary nature of the field, such as those by S. H. Bailey, Grayson Kirk, William C. Olson, and Harry Howe Ransom, have all questioned the existence of a "singularly ill-defined field" of international relations.[25] Olson, for example, has suggested that "perhaps one of the reasons for the slowness of acceptance of International Relations as a discipline lies in what has been recognized from the beginning, that the subject impinges upon and draws from so many other subjects, each of which has its own disciplinary characteristics."[26] For those who emphasize the interdisciplinary character of the field, the idea of reconstructing its history from the point of view of the context of political science may appear problematical or misguided.

The issue of whether the geographical boundaries of the field of international relations should be demarcated in terms of one particular country or as a more cosmopolitan endeavor without regard to national differences certainly complicates the task of writing a history of the field.[27] For one thing, the infrastructure of the field of international relations varies across national settings, and it is not surprising that some of the dissimilarities among histories of the field stem from differences in national and institutional contexts.[28] This is definitely the case with respect to the different institutional infrastructures found in Great Britain and the United States. Olson and A.J.R. Groom have noted that "when international relations emerged in university syllabi in the United Kingdom, it was on its own, so to speak, not as a branch of political science as was usually the case in the United States."[29] If there are numerous institutional differences separating the British and American study of international politics, then there are even greater differences in how the subject is studied in other parts of the world.[30] Thus, there are major problems involved in attempting to write a history of the field when different national approaches are presented as if they were part of a more comprehensive whole. Although the creation of a truly global discipline of international relations may, perhaps, be an aspiration, the fact of the matter is that the academic study of international relations is marked by British, and especially, American parochialism.[31]

Taken together, the interdisciplinary character of the field and differences in national settings sometimes leads to the conclusion that a discipline or field of international relations does not really exist, but despite ambiguities about disciplinary boundaries and institutional home, international relations, as an academic field of study, has a distinct professional identity and discourse.[32] As Olson and Groom have argued, "criticisms leveled against international relations as a discipline could to some degree be leveled at other subjects just as well."[33] International relations, particularly in the United States, is a distinct scholarly practice with a discernible historical career that is integrally related to the discipline of political science.

To write a history of the field of international relations, it is almost necessary to write a history of its development within the United States. In Bernard Crick's seminal study, *The American Science of Politics* (1964), he explained that political science was a distinctly American invention and scholarly enterprise, and much the same can be said about international relations. Stanley Hoffmann has noted "it was in the United States that international relations became a discipline" and "because of the American predominance, the discipline has also taken some traditional traits which are essentially American."[34] This is not to say, however, that the discourse of international relations is an exclusively American product or that there have not been major external influences. As Norman Palmer has argued, "if international relations is 'an American social science,' this is due to a large extent to the contributions of European-born and European scholars, including the author of 'An American Social Science' himself."[35] Thus, in reconstructing the conversation of international relations within the disciplinary context of political science, the contributions that Europeans and others have made to this "American science" must be included even though the institutionalized academic discussion of international relations has occurred primarily within the disciplinary matrix of American political science. Although the American conversation about international politics is not the only perspective from which an intellectual history of the field could be conducted, the American study of international relations as it emerged within the context of the discipline of political science constitutes the subject of this book.

1

THE HISTORIOGRAPHY OF ACADEMIC INTERNATIONAL RELATIONS

This chapter examines more fully some of the historiographical issues that are germane to the discipline of political science in general and international relations in particular and that inform the historical investigation in this book. The chapter begins with a brief overview of the historiography of political science. One of the salutary results of the recent attention to the history of political science is that many of the important theoretical and methodological issues concerning how the exercise of investigating the past should be conducted have been raised to the forefront of discussion. The manner in which the development of political science is recounted may be as significant as the actual history itself. In order to introduce these historiographical issues, the first section examines the intellectual exchanges among some of the leading disciplinary historians.[1]

Attention turns next to the historiography of academic international relations and to a review of existing histories of the field. There has not only been a paucity of such history, but most conventional accounts of the development of the field of international relations contain two historiographical assumptions that have led to a serious misrepresentation of the actual history of the field. One assumption is that the history of the field can be explained in terms of a classical tradition of which modern academic practitioners are the heirs. The second assumption is that events in the realm of international politics have fundamentally structured the development of international relations as an academic field of study. After discussing these historiographical problems, my alternative, the *critical internal discursive* approach to writing the history of the field, is described.

At the end of this chapter, the general substantive theme, which I have termed the political discourse of anarchy, that has constituted the internal discourse of academic international relations is discussed. Although it would not be difficult to demonstrate that today anarchy is the most important theoretical concept in the field, this book seeks to demonstrate the manner in which the development of the study of international relations has always been guided by a conception of politics without central authority. This theme of anarchy is not an external category of historical description, but an idea that has served as a connecting discursive thread throughout the field's evolution.

The Historiography of Political Science

Although post-positivist developments in the philosophy and history of science have contributed to a renewed interest on the part of political scientists in investigating their disciplinary past, both activities have been rife with controversy. Despite a consensus about the value of disciplinary history for establishing the identity of political science, there has been little agreement with respect to how the activity of historical investigation should be pursued. The historiography of international relations raises issues that are strikingly similar, but historical introspection in the field has not reached the same level of sophistication.

There are several factors that have contributed to the historiographical controversies in political science. The first is that historical accounts of the field have become closely allied with claims about disciplinary identity and legitimacy. Unlike the methodological, and essentially ahistorical, controversy associated with the behavioral revolution in the 1950s, the post-behavioral era in political science has resulted in the discipline becoming much more sympathetic to historical analysis. Disciplinary history, like references to the philosophy of science, has come to fulfill an important validation function with respect to justifying and legitimating present academic research programs. John Dryzek and Stephen Leonard, for example, have argued that "disciplinary history in political science, as in other fields, is generally used to legitimate a particular perspective while delegitimating competing approaches."[2] And John Gunnell has claimed that "existing contributions to the history of political science have not freed themselves from the partisanship associated with intellectual struggles within the field."[3] There is a tendency for these partisan struggles to raise the stakes with respect to how the past is interpreted. This has especially been the case when the issue has been one of demonstrating scientific advance. A second explanation for the historiographical disputes in political science is the increase in the number of approaches that can be used to investigate the history of the discipline, which is in part a reflection of wider controversies among intellectual historians and others who study the history of ideas.[4] There are a variety of approaches available for investigating disciplinary history, including those associated with the history of natural science;[5] contextual approaches such as those of J.

G. A. Pocock and Quentin Skinner;[6] post-structural and postmodern analyses represented in the work of Michel Foucault;[7] and, most recently, approaches linked with the new-institutionalism.[8] Finally, because political science is home to numerous approaches and research agendas, a plurality of histories and methodological positions have emerged.

In order to gain a sense of the historiographical issues involved in the study of the history of political science, it is instructive to review a symposium that included some of the leading scholars in the area.[9] The exchange was in response to an article by John Dryzek and Stephen Leonard that called for "context-sensitive" histories in political science. Following the lead of post-positivist philosophers and historians of science such as Imre Lakatos, Dryzek and Leonard argued that disciplinary history could contribute to scientific progress even if pursued for legitimating purposes. They maintained that "disciplinary history and prescription for identity are properly understood as but two moments in the same reflective enterprise."[10] Dryzek and Leonard reached this conclusion by observing how recent work by philosophers of science have utilized history to underwrite the progress of natural science.

Dryzek and Leonard claimed, however, that the methodologically pluralistic and non-paradigmatic structure of political science created unique historiographical difficulties. Unlike the case of the theoretically hegemonic character of natural science, there would always be a multiplicity of histories in political science that corresponded with the plural identities that existed at any particular time. They argued that it would be impossible to have one orthodox history so long as political science was the home of mutually competing schools of thought. They also argued that disciplinary history would inevitably be written either to legitimate or delegitimate a specific research agenda. According to Dryzek and Leonard, this was to be expected, since both challengers and defenders of the status quo always seek to write the history of the field in a manner that suggests a particular disciplinary identity.

Dryzek and Leonard did not claim, however, that one can "write a disciplinary history in any way one chooses," nor "that all disciplinary identities are created equal."[11] They argued that a contextually focused approach would both contribute to judging the degree of progress within a particular research tradition and to evaluating the utility of past methods. In addition to the contentious issue of how to gauge the progress of political science, the emphasis on a contextual approach to disciplinary history has provoked a number of different responses among disciplinary historians.[12] Dryzek and Leonard argued that disciplinary histories "should, above all else, attend to episodes of political science in context," so that "practitioners, approaches, research traditions, theories, and methods" could be "apprehended and adjudged for their success or failure according to how well they understand and resolved the problems *they* confronted."[13] They argued, for example, that the progress of the behavioral research agenda could be judged adequately only within the context of the "placid fifties." Dryzek and Leonard assigned disciplinary histories that did not adequately consider the contextual dimension of inquiry to two mutually exclusive categories: "Whigs" and "skeptics."

In Herbert Butterfield's classic study, *The Whig Interpretation of History* (1959), he described Whig history as "the tendency in many historians to write on the side of the Protestants and Whigs, to praise revolutions provided they have been successful, to emphasize certain principles of progress in the past and to produce a story which is the ratification if not the glorification of the present."[14] George Stocking, in an influential article that appeared in the first volume of the *Journal of the History of the Behavioral Sciences,* claimed that "the approach of the professional social scientist is more likely to be Whiggish or, more broadly, 'presentist,' and his motivational posture 'utilitarian.'"[15] He argued that the tendency for disciplinary histories of the social sciences to be burdened with the vices of anachronism, distortion, misinterpretation, and neglect of context stemmed from the fact that there was "a sort of implicit whiggish presentism virtually built into the history of science and by extension, into the history of the behavioral sciences."[16] Another elucidation of this historiographical principle has been provided by a recent group of intellectual historians who, nevertheless, explicitly expressed displeasure with presentist history. They claimed that the essence of Whig history

> [C]onsists in writing history backwards. The present theoretical consensus of the discipline, or possibly some polemical version of what that consensus should be, is in effect taken as definitive, and the past is then reconstituted as a teleology leading up to and fully manifested in it. Past authors are inducted into the canon of the discipline as precursors or forebears, and passed in review as though by a general distributing medals.[17]

Dryzek and Leonard were sharply critical of all histories that distorted the historical ledger by failing to take the historical contingencies of the past into account when they praised or blamed the disciplinary present. While Whigs interpret the history of the discipline as one of the triumph of present approaches over those of the past, skeptical historians, according to Dryzek and Leonard, "find little to commend in the present and still less to approve of in the modern history of the discipline." Dryzek and Leonard alleged that skeptics such as David Ricci, Raymond Seidelman, and John Gunnell "write the history of political science in terms of unremitting error."[18] They claimed that the historiographical errors of the skeptics were the obverse of the Whigs, since rather than attempting to demonstrate how the present has overcome the weaknesses of the past, the skeptic seeks to substantiate how the failures of the past have contributed to the ever "darkening skies" of the present. Dryzek and Leonard argued that skeptics had also failed to devote proper attention to past contexts.

In replying to Dryzek and Leonard, James Farr challenged the apparent exclusiveness of the poles of Whigs and skeptics and argued for the incorporation of an intervening "skeptical Whig" category that would include Dryzek and Leonard, "who want to hold on to progress but with attention to historically relative contexts."[19] By introducing a third category, Farr indicated that there is considerably more diversity in disciplinary history than Dryzek and Leonard had suggested. Farr also questioned the manner in which Dryzek and Leonard rejected the possibility of writing a "neutral" history of the discipline. Although Farr agreed that "writing a history of political science is very much a partisan activity," he was less than supportive of the idea that there can be no neutral stance from which to uncover these histories.[20] Farr acknowledged that identity in political science is largely dependent upon how we understand our history, yet he argued for an approach that is more neutral than Dryzek and Leonard deemed possible. Farr suggested that, "although neutrality is doubtless impossible with respect to how one does history at all, it seems that we can be rather *more neutral* with respect to such diverse things as the appropriation of individual figures in research traditions, the professional identity of the discipline, the actual practices of inquiry, and even contemporary ideology."[21]

Seidelman also questioned the categories of Whig and skeptic and argued that Dryzek and Leonard's approach to writing the history of the field ended up duplicating many of the same vices they sought to overcome. Seidelman claimed that although Dryzek and Leonard protested against the historical distortions that resulted from writing history backwards in defense of a present position, they, at the same time, committed many of the same errors with their own postempiricist context-sensitive approach. Seidelman argued that "while they want to reject the alleged presentism of current disciplinary histories, they only reflect presentist claims when they look at the discipline's history as simply a number of competing research traditions developed in specific political contexts."[22]

Gunnell agreed with Dryzek and Leonard's "conclusion that historical reflection is in some way constitutive of identity," but he argued that "it is considerably more contentious to claim that a less presentist historiography, eschewing the extremes of Whiggism and skepticism, can provide 'guidelines for research' and intersubjective measures of disciplinary progress."[23] Gunnell claimed that part of the difficulty with Dryzek and Leonard's position stems from the manner in which they transplanted historiographical arguments found in the philosophy and history of science to political science. He suggested that "if there is anything historians of social science might learn from approaches to the history of science, it is as likely to be problems to be avoided as it is answers about how to conduct disciplinary history."[24] Gunnell, however, has probably provided the strongest criticism against disciplinary histories that distort the past simply for the instrumental purpose of legitimating or delegitimating a partisan position in the present.

Although Gunnell acknowledged that historical inquiry is often motivated by present concerns, he argued that this should not lead directly to the conclusion that all histories will, therefore, be put in the service of validation and legitimation. He argued that "presentism is not a one-dimensional notion," and that "history may be written to explain identities without judging or seeking to transform them."[25] He maintained that there is a fundamental distinction between writing a history of an academic field in which the purpose is to shed some light on a contemporary issue, or concern, and writing a history for the primary purpose of criticizing or defending a particular disciplinary identity. It is the latter type of "presentism" that Gunnell strongly rejects, for under that scenario writing a "neutral" history of the field does indeed become inconceivable. Gunnell suggested that "it might be worthwhile, even if we believe that there are no neutral narratives, just sorting out and reporting the results of our probings of the past" for "truth is often more dramatic than fiction and carries as much rhetorical and critical force."[26]

Gunnell has advocated a distinctly internal approach for investigating elements of the history of political science and has argued that the discipline itself, rather than the wider world of politics, is often the most appropriate context. He has explained that "internal history is an attempt to provide a theoretic corrective to past research efforts, to inject a little Mendelian thinking and focus on discursive evolution."[27] To better facilitate the recovery of the history of political science from a more intrinsically derived standpoint, Gunnell has put forth an approach for doing disciplinary history that he has designated "as genealogical and methodologically archaeological, and as a study of discourse and discursive evolution."[28] The intention of this approach is to reconstruct the evolution of political science as a discursive practice.

His arguments and historiographical framework are particularly applicable to the field of international relations, but before proceeding to discuss the historiographical approach adopted in this book, which has many similarities to the approach advocated by Gunnell, it is necessary to examine the historiography of international relations, that is, the literature that recounts the history of the field and the assumptions that have informed this literature.

The Historiography of International Relations

In 1966, Martin Wight wrote a widely noted essay in which he stated that "it can be argued that international theory is marked not only by paucity but also by intellectual and moral poverty."[29] In offering an explanation for why there was such a quantitative and qualitative contrast between political theory, which he understood as speculation about the state, and international relations theory, Wight insisted that it was a manifestation of two internal factors: "the intellectual prejudice imposed by the sovereign state," and the fact that "international politics differ from domestic politics in being less susceptible of a progressivist interpretation."[30] Notwithstanding the increasingly indefensible basis of his bifurcation between political theory and theories of international relations, Wight's recognition of the importance of internal factors for explaining the condition of international theory is instructive for examining the historiography of academic international relations.

There have been few attempts by either scholars within the field or by intellectual historians to examine systematically the history of academic international relations. Earlier attempts, such as those by E. H. Carr and Kenneth Thompson, to recount the history of the ideas that have come to inform "the science of international politics" or "the main currents of an American approach to International Politics" are not really an exception to the general reluctance of international relations scholars to investigate their disciplinary past.[31] These general synoptic accounts were not intended to provide a disciplinary history, and difficulties are created when they are mistaken as historical descriptions of the development of the field. The few works that do attempt to describe the history of international relations are so readily and uncritically accepted that scholars have not deemed it necessary to investigate further either the substantive history of the field or the underlying historiographical assumptions. These assumptions entail a host of interpretive biases which raise numerous methodological issues. One difficulty is that disciplinary history in international relations, like political science, has often been written for purposes of legitimation and

[handwritten margin note: Martin Wight's essay]

critique; that is, history has been cast to support or undermine a particular interpretation of the state of the field. With the hegemony of realism seemingly cemented, the field's past, from World War I to the present, has been pervasively inscribed in these terms in college textbooks, introductory chapters to "state of the discipline" monographs, reviews of the past and present trends in the field, and obligatory footnotes. The history of the field appears to be self-evident, and this explains, in part, the dearth of disciplinary histories.

There is a prevalent notion that the history of the field can be explained in terms of a series of successive phases or, in Kuhnian terminology, paradigms. This is especially apparent in conventional disciplinary histories that depict a great divide between an earlier "idealist" and a more recent "realist" period. The successive phases of idealism and realism are presumed by many practitioners to represent the actual history of academic international relations, but they are really little more than reified intellectual constructs. Some illustrations of this common image of the field's development will be instructive before turning to the explanations that possibly can account for this erroneous conception of history. In writing about the history of the field, Hedley Bull claimed that

> [I]t is helpful to recognize three successive waves of theoretical activity: the "idealist" or progressivist doctrines that predominated in the 1920s and early 1930s, the "realist" or conservative theories that developed in reaction to them in the late 1930s and 1940s, and the "social scientific" theories of the late 1950s and 1960s, whose origin lay in dissatisfaction with the methodologies on which both the earlier kinds of theory were based.[32]

Bull, however, is merely one representative of the popular view that the history of the field can be explained in terms of successive idealist, realist, and behavioral periods. John Vasquez has alleged that "the twentieth-century history of international relations inquiry can be roughly divided into three stages: the idealist phase; the realist tradition; and the 'behavioral' revolt."[33] In one of the field's popular introductory texts, *World Politics: Trend and Transformation*, Charles Kegley and Eugene Wittkopf described the history of the field in terms of idealist, realist, and behavioral periods.[34] This sort of synoptic history of the field as evolving through a sequence of distinct phases or periods is endemic to most introductory texts.

A somewhat similar, albeit peculiar, form for writing the history of the field is in terms of a series of disciplinary "great debates." This not only reinforces the image of the field as developing through a series of successive phases but also endorses more explicitly the notion of scientific advance. C. R. Mitchel, for example, has argued that "it is possible to distinguish three very broad schools of thought within the general debate about the bases of the social sciences in general, and international relations in particular, namely, the 'classical'; the 'behavioral' (or 'scientific'); and the post-behavioral' (or paradigmatic)."[35] When approached in this manner, the history of the field becomes reduced to a series of disciplinary defining debates. Arend Lijphart has argued that two great debates mark the history of the field: "the realism-idealism debate in the 1930s and in the decade following the Second World War and the traditionalism-science debate of the 1960s."[36] The historical overview provided by Ray Maghroori exemplifies this view. He claimed that

> Since the close of World War I, two extensive debates have taken place. The first was evidenced by the clash between the realists and the idealists. The second involved the traditionalists and the behavioralists.[37]

Maghoori argued that a third disciplinary defining debate between realists and globalists recently had arisen, which encompassed the two earlier debates. This is the same framework that Michael Banks adopted in his attempt to "survey the evolution of thought in the field." He argued that "there have been three so-called 'great debates' which have arisen during the history of the discipline." In characteristic fashion, he writes:

> First, there is the realist v. idealist debate that has permeated the last four centuries. Second, there was the brief behaviouralist-traditionalist debate of the 1950s and 1960s. Third, there is the inter-paradigm debate of the recent past, the 1970s and 1980s.[38]

There is little need to extend this review of the conventional accounts of the development of the field of international relations. The chronological ordering of the history of the field in terms of idealist, realist, and behavioral periods is a story that most students of international relations have come to accept. In order to understand why there is such a ubiquitous tendency to reduce the history of international relations to a simple succession of disciplinary paradigms, it is necessary to scrutinize some more general unexamined assumptions that have informed most of the histories of the field. There are two pervasive assumptions that encumber the intellectual activity of writing the history of the field: first is the assumption that the history of the field can be explained by reference to a continuous tradition that reaches back to classical Athens and extends forward to the present; and second is the idea that the development of the field can be adequately explained by viewing it in the context of international politics.

Traditions: Analytical and Historical

A casual reading of the international relations literature in academic journals, scholarly books, and textbooks reveals numerous references to the idea that there are epic traditions of international thought that have given rise to coherent schools or paradigms such as realism and liberalism. Furthermore, and more importantly for the discussion at hand, there is a widespread conviction that these ancient traditions represent an integral part of the field's past and, therefore, are relevant for understanding the contemporary identity of the field. The idea that these epic traditions have informed the contemporary study of international relations serves as an unreflective orthodox regulative ideal for research and teaching.[39]

Nowhere does the idea of the existence of a venerable tradition of thought have more acceptance than in the field of political theory. Regardless of the particular manner in which scholars such as Leo Strauss and Sheldon Wolin have depicted the great tradition in the history of political thought, there is a pervasive idea that the academic study of political theory is the heir to a tradition that began in classical Greece and continued up to the present.[40] This belief continues to be held by many political theorists today, and is also widely accepted in the field of international relations. Wight, for example, argued that there was no mistaking the meaning of political theory, for he claimed that everyone knew that it was "the tradition of speculation and the body of writings about the state from Plato to Laski."[41] Recently, some international relations scholars such as R.B.J. Walker have argued that this dubious notion of a "great tradition" of political theory has contributed to the impoverishment of international relations theory.[42] For the past two decades the so-called great tradition of political thought has been a focal point of Gunnell's critical analysis of political theory, and it is instructive to discuss briefly the difficulties that he has identified with this idea before turning to the situation in international relations. While the idiosyncrasies of the various accounts of the tradition in theories of international relations may differ in their construction from those put forward by political theorists, they nevertheless embody many of the same inherent difficulties.

Gunnell has insisted that what is commonly taken to be "the tradition" of political theory, consisting of the conventional chronology of classic works from Plato to Marx, is nothing more than what he terms the "*myth of the tradition* or the imposition on the framework of the classic works of an elaborate story of the rise and fall of political theory and the implications of these events for the modern age."[43] He does not suggest that there is no such thing as a Western tradition of political ideas or that there are no discernible traditions of political thought, but he does insist that the grand narrative that is imposed upon the classic canon as a whole is a myth. Fundamental to the origin and construction of the myth are the very unhistorical claims that support its existence. Gunnell has argued that "the very idea of *the* tradition is an a priori concept, and its general and unexamined acceptance is a crucial aspect of the myth." He notes that there is very little, if any, attempt to demonstrate the actual historical dimension of "the tradition." The distinguishing feature of the myth of the tradition, which Gunnell has argued to be responsible for a host of interpretive and historiographical problems, is the tendency to view an *analytical* tradition as an actual *historical* one: "at its core is the reification of an analytical construct. It is the representation of what is in fact a retrospectively and externally demarcated tradition as an actual or self-constituted tradition."[44]

Since the word, tradition, is open to conflicting interpretations, it is useful to consult *The Oxford English Dictionary,* which offers the following meaning: "the action of transmitting or 'handing down,' or fact of being handed down, from one to another, or from generation to generation; transmission of statements, beliefs, rules, customs, or the like, esp. by word of mouth or by practice without writing." A historical tradition is one that closely approximates the definition given above. It is, in a fundamental sense, a preconstituted and self-constituted pattern of conventional practice through which ideas are conveyed within a recognizably established and specified discursive framework. A historical tradition can entail continuity as well as innovation within a fairly well-defined realm of discourse. Based on these criteria, Marxism is a clear example of a historical tradition. An analytical tradition, on the other hand, is an intellectual construction in which a scholar may stipulate certain ideas, themes, genres, or texts as functionally similar. It is, most essentially, a retrospectively created construct determined by present criteria and concerns. Failure to recognize the difference between a historical and analytical tradition poses significant obstacles when attempting to trace the actual historical development of an academic discipline.

Perhaps the greatest difficulty that results from viewing a retrospectively constructed analytical tradition as an actual historical tradition is that attention to the individuals and academic practices that have contributed to the development and current identity of the discipline are cast aside for a more epic rendition of the past. Gunnell has maintained that academic political theory's "built-in historical self-image" as mediated by the great tradition has obstructed efforts to investigate the real history of this scholarly practice. The pantheon of classic texts in political theory has also been accepted by many as representing the actual ancestral lineage of contemporary political science, and this, Gunnell argues, has inhibited attempts to investigate the history of the discipline. There are a number of reasons why an analytical tradition is such an appealing device for describing disciplinary history, and they are apparent in the literature that makes reference to a "great tradition" for explaining the history of the field of international relations.

The multiple references to the classic authors in political theory as representing authoritative traditions of thought in the field of international relations is in some respects an anomaly. The works customarily elevated to the classic canon have been understood as being primarily concerned with achieving the good life inside the confines of the territorial sovereign state and only, if at all, marginally interested in the external relations between states. This was recognized by Wight when he asked whether is was "more interesting that so many great minds have been drawn, at the margins of their activities, to consider basic problems of international politics, or that so few great minds have been drawn to make these problems their central interest?"[45] Mark Kauppi and Paul Viotti take this point a step further when they write that "the reason it is questionable even to conceive of international relations as a 'discipline' is the fact that even such luminaries as Machiavelli, Hobbes, and Rousseau were primarily interested in domestic politics."[46] This has not, however, prevented scholars such as Wight from referring to classic political theorists as constituent figures in the history of academic international relations.[47]

Walker has observed that "although references to a tradition of international relations theory are common enough, they are far from monolithic."[48] Notwithstanding the different typologies that have been used to classify the diverse classic traditions that supposedly exist in international relations, it is possible to discern two pervasive constructions. There is, first, the claim that the writings of political theorists such as Thucydides, Machiavelli, Hobbes, Rousseau, Kant, and Grotius reveal the essence of inter-state politics.[49] This is what allows their writings to continue to serve as the theoretical foundation for thinking about and investigating international politics. Following Wight's triad of Realist, Rationalist, and Revolutionist traditions, Bull claimed:

> Throughout the history of the modern states system there have been three competing traditions of thought: the Hobbesian or realist tradition, which views international politics as a state of war; the Kantian or universalist tradition, which sees at work in international politics a potential community of mankind; and the Grotian or internationalist tradition, which views international politics as taking place within an international society.[50]

Others have sought to build upon Wight's and Bull's classification of traditions in international relations. Ian Clark has argued that Kant's solution to the state of war in *Perpetual Peace* qualifies him for a "Kantian tradition of optimism."[51] Kant's apparent optimism is also the basis for his placement in what is commonly referred to as the liberal tradition of international relations.[52] This reading of Kant takes on added significance when it is contrasted with the tradition represented by Rousseau, which Clark and others have delegated to a "tradition of despair."[53] K. J. Holsti , for example, has claimed that "Rousseau's insights and hypothesis have formed the basis of innumerable studies of general international politics, providing the foundation of what is called the 'realist' tradition."[54]

The realist tradition is certainly regarded by an overwhelming majority of scholars to be the definitive tradition in the field of international relations. The writings of political theorists such as Thucydides, Machiavelli, Hobbes, and Rousseau are repeatedly mined for statements that purport to demonstrate realist principles. In a recent contribution to the history of the field, Jack Donnelly argued that "the tradition of political realism has a long history, going back at least to Machiavelli or Thucydides." He suggested that "tracing the fate of realism provides a partial yet still useful survey of the development of the field of international relations."[55] This statement, which portrays the disciplinary history of the field in terms of chronologically ordered luminaries cumulatively contributing to a conventional pattern of thought, provides a quintessential example of the tendency to confuse an analytical retrospective tradition for a genuine historical tradition.

A second pattern of references to the tradition, which is also evident in Donnelly's historical account, involves the idea that modern academic scholars such as E. H. Carr, Hans Morgenthau, and Kenneth Waltz have built upon the ideas of the classic political theorists and are themselves a part of this grand continuous tradition of thought. In Jacek Kugler's survey of the literature about conflict and war that appeared in the latest volume of *Political Science: The State of the Discipline* II (1993), he claimed that "the classic account of international war comes from the realist tradition in world politics." He then proceeded to argue that "this approach to the study of war has a very long tradition that can be traced from Thucydides (400 B.C.) to Machiavelli (1513), to Hobbes (1651), to Hume (1741), to von Clausewitz (1832), to Morgenthau (1948), to Organski (1958), to Waltz (1979), and to Gilpin (1981)."[56] This provides another clear example of the tendency to confound an analytical and a historical tradition.

In an essay addressed to the recent history of international relations, Robert Keohane declared that "for over 2000 years, what Hans J. Morgenthau dubbed 'Political Realism' has constituted the principal tradition for the analysis of international relations in Europe and its offshoots in the New World."[57] Keohane analyzed contemporary structural realism in terms of Imre Lakatos's work in the philosophy of science dealing with the evolution of research programs, but he began by explicating the research program of realism as extending from Thucydides' *History of the Peloponnesian War* to Morgenthau's *Politics Among Nations.* Keohane found that

> The three most fundamental Realist assumptions are evident in these books: that the most important actors in world politics are territorially organized entities (city-states or modern states); that state behavior can be explained rationally; and that states seek power and calculate their interests in terms of power, relative to the nature of the international system that they face.[58]

These three assumptions, which were allegedly derived from the work of Thucydides and Morgenthau, were defined by Keohane as "the hard core of the Classical Realist research program."[59]

With the historical foundations of realism affirmed, Keohane proceeded to his primary task of evaluating the degree to which Kenneth Waltz's structural realism and his own "modified structural realist program" conformed to the criteria that Lakatos established for scientific progress. There are many questionable meta-theoretical assumptions about the philosophy of science and its applicability to evaluating theories within international relations in Keohane's work, but it is his unsubstantiated claim about the existence of an actual "realist tradition" that is most problematic. Although Keohane insists that "Realism, as developed through a long tradition dating from Thucydides, continues to provide the basis for valuable research in international relations," there is very little, if any, attempt to demonstrate the actual historical existence of this tradition.[60] Neither Keohane nor Kugler demonstrate that academic international relations scholars have been the receivers and participants of an inherited pattern of discourse originating with the writings of a banished Athenian military officer in the fifth century

B.C. While they both provide a general definition of what constitutes a "realist tradition," the criteria are both vague and contentious.[61] Simply because Keohane and Kugler have retrospectively posited certain attributes of realism does not in any way establish a coherent tradition that can explain the genealogy of the academic field of international relations. Moreover, the real intention of Keohane's disciplinary history was to validate and legitimate his own version of realism. It is a clear example of Whig history. His purpose was clearly not one of uncovering the past to understand better the contemporary character of the field. In Keohane's presidential address to the International Studies Association in 1988, he forwent a historical argument and based his defense of the superiority of the realist approach on empirical method, but his work illustrates the legitimating function that appeals to retrospectively constructed analytical traditions serve in seeking to establish disciplinary identity.[62]

Robert Gilpin has also insisted that "the realist tradition is an old one" that predated academic scholars such as Morgenthau and Waltz. Yet when it comes to specifying the criteria for this "old" historical tradition, Gilpin simply states that "there have been three great realist writers" and that it would be difficult for anyone to "deny them inclusion in the tradition."[63] The three writers that Gilpin identifies are Thucydides, Machiavelli, and Carr. Once again, however, no attempt is made to elucidate the actual historical basis of this tradition or the manner in which writers in different centuries and intellectual contexts can be regarded as participants in an inherited pattern of thought. The very idea of the realist tradition, as articulated by Gilpin, is nebulous. This is because Gilpin is more concerned with validating contemporary neorealism than he is with understanding the history of the field of international relations. And this helps to account for the common practice of locating modern academic scholars within a much older ancient lineage without demonstrating the historicity of these claims.

This is evident in Holsti's *The Dividing Discipline* (1985), which surveyed the current trends in the field. While he may be correct in arguing that "international theory is in a state of disarray" enabling "new conceptions and images of the world" to arise, this development was understood by Holsti in terms of the breakdown of a hegemonic realist paradigm that "goes back to Hobbes and Rousseau."[64] Holsti made no attempt to demonstrate the actual historical basis of the classical tradition which, he argued, included such diverse figures as Hobbes, Rousseau, Bentham, Carr, Wight, and Morgenthau. There was also very little, if any, effort to illustrate the manner in which this tradition has been transmitted across different generations and intellectual contexts. Instead, Holsti argued that a similar *raison d'être*, focus of analysis, and image of the world united these scholars into a coherent tradition—namely, that the most fundamental issue in the subject of study concerns matters of war and peace, that nation-states are the most important actors, and these sovereign actors exist in a milieu characterized by anarchy. It was on the basis of his review of the classical works in international relations theory, along with an overview of the modern scholars who have contributed to the development of the field of international relations, that Holsti concluded: "we can legitimately claim that the main figures in the classical tradition have operated within a single paradigm, and that their modern successors have only expanded, but not altered the fundamental features, of that paradigm."[65]

The most striking implication of Holsti's uncritical acceptance of a reigning "classical tradition" is that the field is given a false sense of coherence and continuity. Yet one of the purposes behind Holsti's historical survey of international relations theory was to demonstrate that the field had a sense of continuity throughout the idealist, realist, and behavioral phases that was only now beginning to become undone with the work from a group of scholars "whose normative priorities differ fundamentally from those inhabiting the classical tradition."[66] He also wanted to defend the essential continuity of the classical tradition against the claim that the behavioral agenda and the ensuing second great debate in international relations represented, in Kuhn's terminology, a scientific revolution where one paradigm was replaced by an incommensurably different one.

Arend Lijphart has advanced the alternative thesis that the behavioral revolution in international relations did in fact represent a profound paradigm shift. Yet his account of this episode of disciplinary history was also informed by the prior belief that "traditional theory was, in fact, governed by what Kuhn called a paradigm," which revolved "around the notions of state sovereignty and its logical corollary, international anarchy."[67] According to Lijphart, the elements of the traditional paradigm first began to be systematized in the writings of Thucydides, Hobbes, and Rousseau. He argued that this paradigm was carried over when international relations was born as a discipline after World War I, and it continued to dominate "the field until at least approximately the time of World War II."[68] Lijphart maintained that the behavioralist agenda in international relations, with its emphasis on the concept of "system" and unwillingness to divorce domestic from international politics, represented a rival paradigm. He concluded that the second great debate was more significant than the previous debate between idealism and realism, and offered the promise of scientific advance.

Holsti rejected Lijphart's assessment and argued that the behavioralists accepted all the fundamental assumptions of the classical paradigm and merely sought methodological rearrangements. The more significant point, however, is that both of these accounts of the second great debate are based on the dubious notion of a reigning classical tradition. In many ways, Holsti's argument was an extension of the thesis first put forth by John Vasquez, who claimed that following the anomaly of World War II, which he argued led to the displacement of idealism and the dominance of realism, "the field has been far more coherent, systematic, and even cumulative than all of the talk about contending approaches and theories implies."[69] Vasquez also found compatibility between the "normal science" paradigm of realism—defined by the recognition that nation-states are the most important actors, a sharp distinction between domestic and international politics, and the realization that international politics is most fundamentally about the struggle for power and peace—and the behavioralists who "only attempted to bring the scientific practices of the field more in line with the practices of the physical sciences."[70] In other words, according to both Holsti and Vasquez, the second great debate was over method and not about the theoretical adequacy of the realist paradigm. This was sufficient for Holsti and Vasquez to conclude that there was an essential continuity between the realist paradigm and the behavioral project and that both flowed from an ancient tradition.

At this point, it is appropriate to ask how these accounts can contribute to an understanding of the disciplinary history of international relations when the narratives are cast in terms of a retrospective analytical tradition that obscures the individuals and academic practices that have constituted the discursive development of the field. One cannot read the work of Morgenthau or Bull and not be struck by the thoroughly damning indictment they gave to the central tenets of the behavioral project.[71] And the issue for Morgenthau and Bull was not construed as a methodological one but concerned ontological claims about the nature of social reality. That these views have been so easily misrepresented within the conventional accounts of the history of the field indicates a serious shortcoming in the historiography of international relations.

The crux of the matter is that most of the attempts to reflect on the history of the field are largely done for "presentist" purposes rather than with the intention of actually reconstructing the past. The primary concern of many disciplinary histories of international relations, like those in political science, is really to say something authoritative about the field's current character. Disciplinary histories that attempt to explain the development of the field of international relations by postulating the existence of a "historical" tradition transmitted from the ancient past to the present are legitimating mechanisms that are employed to validate present claims to knowledge. Many of the references to a presumed tradition of thought in the field of international relations are really nothing more than retrospective analytical constructs that are elicited for instrumental legitimating purposes. As Eric Hobsbawm has noted, "'traditions' which appear or claim to be old are often quite recent in origin and sometimes invented."[72] Perhaps the greatest shortcoming of this approach is the tendency to substitute a mythical epic history for the real disciplinary history of the field. Instead of a history that traces the actual lineage of scholars who self-consciously and institutionally understood themselves as participating in the academic discourse of international relations, these accounts present a version of the past in the form of a tradition stretching from ancient Athens or Renaissance Italy to the present. While such epic renderings of the field's evolution may serve a variety of rhetorical functions, they do not, in any way, contribute to an understanding of the actual disciplinary history of international relations as an institutionalized academic study, or provide a basis for a critical examination of the past and present character of the field.

A second assumption that abounds in many accounts of the history of the field is the notion that the development of international relations can be understood in light of exogenous events in the realm of international politics. The assumption is that contextual factors such as World War I or the collapse of the League of Nations can account for the particular path of disciplinary development in the field of international relations. Yet there are a number of problems that a contextual approach to disciplinary history raises. First, contextual approaches are still burdened with presentism and second, it raises historiographical issues. The next section examines the problems associated with contextualism.

Contextual Approaches to Disciplinary History

Proponents of contextualism have argued that their approach to disciplinary history, and intellectual history in general, avoids the vices of presentism by locating authors and texts in their proper historical context. A contextual approach to disciplinary history requires that consideration be given to examining the impact of the external milieu on individuals, schools of thought, and academic disciplines. There are several accounts that make an effort to explain the development of the field of international relations by reference to contextual or external factors. It is a common belief that external events in the realm of international politics have more fundamentally than any other set of factors shaped the development of the field. Yale Ferguson and Richard Mansbach, for example, have argued that "dominant schools of thought in international relations are as much a part of the *Zeitgeist* of their age as are dominant theories of art and literature."[73] However, a review of some of the contextual explanations that have been provided to account for the history of the field reveals their shortcomings for explaining the disciplinary history of international relations. Contextual accounts participate in the presentist agenda of legitimation and critique and, in one way or another, reinforce the conventional image of the field's history in terms of successive idealist, realist, and behavioral phases.

A prominent contextual explanation of the history of the field was provided by Stanley Hoffmann in his seminal essay "An American Social Science: International Relations." Although Hoffmann did claim that he was simply offering "a set of reflections on the specific accomplishments and frustrations" of the field rather than "a complete balance sheet" or a "capsule history," one of his specific aims was to explain how the field of international relations arose full-blown in the United States as a consequence of World War II.[74] While he did give recognition to the path-breaking work of Carr and Morgenthau, and dubbed the latter the "founding father" of the discipline, Hoffmann argued that the actual "development of international relations as a discipline in the United States results from the convergence of three factors: intellectual predispositions, political circumstances, and institutional opportunities."[75] The intellectual predispositions and institutional opportunities that Hoffmann identified are not unlike those that have been mentioned by a number of other intellectual historians in accounting for the tremendous growth of American social science after World War II. These factors included such things as the pervasive faith in the ability to apply the scientific method to the social realm, the transformative role of the ideas that émigré scholars transplanted to America, the tremendous increase in institutional opportunities that resulted from the expansion of the university system, and the formal interchange that developed between the academy and the United States government.

Although Hoffmann maintained that these were all important factors for explaining why the field of international relations arose as a quintessentially American one following the Second World War, he most fundamentally emphasized the external political circumstances that accompanied the rise of the United States to a position of world power. He argued that "the growth of the discipline cannot be separated from the American role in world affairs after 1945."[76] In other words, the external context of the postwar power position of the United States and its expansive political-economic role in managing the Western alliance through the Cold War with the East were argued to be decisive for understanding the internal developments within the field of international relations. Hoffmann claimed that there were two important factors in explaining the convergence of external context and internal development. First, he suggested that the customary fascination that political scientists had with power led to the growth of the field that directly studied the preponderance of international power which accrued to the United States after World War II. Second, he argued that the school of realism created by Morgenthau and other realists provided foreign policymakers with the rationale and justification they needed to promote America's new role as a global superpower. The net result for Hoffmann, and one that he greatly lamented, was that the political preeminence of the United States led to the overwhelming American dominance in the field of international relations.

Although there are obviously important relationships between the internal changes within the field of international relations and the developments in international politics, it is another thing altogether to suggest that general references to the external context can explain specific theoretical and methodological changes inside the discipline. Yet it is very common to describe the evolution of the field exclusively in contextual terms. It is often suggested that the external context provided by "real world" political events can be conceived as an independent variable that explains the character of the field at a specific historical juncture. This contextual formula is, for example, the main historiographical premise from which most accounts seek to explain the origins of academic international relations along with what is described as the field's early reformist or "idealist" approach. According to Ekkehart Krippendorf, the field of international relations "was born as a side-product of the Versailles Peace Conference in 1919."[77] This sort of contextual explanation is so pervasive that one historian recently remarked "as everyone knows it [the academic field of international relations] grew out of the liberal reaction to the First World War."[78] World War I and the Peace Treaty of Versailles are taken to be the explanatory context for the origin and early development of the American field of international relations. Fred Neal and Bruce Hamlet have commented that "international relations is an American invention dating from the time after World War I when the American intellectual community discovered the world."[79]

Steve Smith's historical analysis of how international relations has developed as a social science closely parallels the agenda set by Hoffmann. Smith's entire overview of how the field has developed was framed exclusively in contextual terms. He declared that "International Relations developed as a response to events in the real world and defined its purpose as preventing their repetition."[80] While Smith argued that World War I and its aftermath were sufficient for explaining the emergence of the "idealist" school of thought, and for conditioning "post-war thinking about the subject," he claimed that a new set of exogenous factors, which accompanied World War II, accounted for the appearance of the realist paradigm. Smith, like Hoffmann, did give recognition to the intellectual impact of Morgenthau, but insisted that it was "the political climate [that] gave Realism a much more immediate credibility."[81] In a similar manner, Robert Rothstein has argued that while realism has an ancient lineage, it "took World War II to convert Realism from a rather esoteric and private critique of the behavior of the Western democracies into a popular and fully articulated interpretation of world politics, everywhere and any time."[82] The political climate that Smith described was essentially that faced by the foreign policy interests of the United States as a superpower in the midst of the Cold War. This context was argued to have had a determinative impact upon the development of the field of international relations. Subsequent changes that the field has experienced since the 1950s are all explained in relation to external events. Smith argued, for example, that the inroads made by scholars advocating a transnationalist and globalist approach to studying international politics in the mid-1970s reached a dead end in the late 1970s and early 1980s after "a series of developments in world politics that allowed Realism to return to dominance under a new guise, Neorealism."[83]

This type of general external explanation for the internal metamorphosis of academic realism into a form of quasi-positivist, structural analysis based on a model of microeconomics, raises the issue of what the *actual* connection between external context and internal conceptual change could be. The notion that the invasion of Afghanistan by the Soviet Union or President Reagan's blatant hostility toward communism can account for the ascendance of Kenneth Waltz's theory of neorealism is, at best, nebulous. This is not to suggest that there is no relationship between the academic study of international relations and the empirical events that have periodically preoccupied international politics. Rather, the relationship between the two is often tangential and, in any case, requires demonstration. The external context is never sufficient by itself to account for what is taking place in an academic field.

This is one of the problems with the work of William C. Olson. Notwithstanding the wealth of information that he has provided about the history of academic international relations in both Great Britain and the United States, his work raises a number of historiographical issues. Olson uncritically accepted the idea that the origins of the field are to be explained in reference to the external milieu created by World War I. Olson and Nicholas Onuf claimed that "what must never be forgotten in assessing the emergence of International Relations is that it grew out of a fervent desire to understand and therefore to find ways to control world politics in order to prevent future wars."[84] According to Olson and Onuf, the external political circumstances surrounding World War I necessitated that "a new discipline was born because it had to be."[85] The subsequent growth of the field is further explained in reference to external circumstances. Olson's latest historical undertaking with A.J.R. Groom, *International Relations Then and Now* (1991), continued to place emphasis on the importance of external factors in accounting for the development of the field. They declared that their intention was to assess the disciplinary trends of the past so that we can better understand the present. Their account was marked by a dichotomy between an early consensual period of the field's history and the contemporary period marked by conflict. Olson and Groom share the common "acknowledgment of the existence of three intellectual traditions in approaches to IR" and declared that one of their tasks was "to explain how we have gone from a consensus on one approach to three salient, competing and mutually influential conceptual frameworks."[86]

This image of the history of the field is one that cannot be extrapolated easily from the general historical context, and the contextual frame of reference in the works by Hoffmann, Smith, and Olson and Groom does not escape the tendency of writing history backwards. The underlying purpose of each of these historical accounts was to make a critical claim about the contemporary identity and character of the field. For Hoffmann and Smith, the aim was to demonstrate the American dominance of the field, whereas Olson and Groom sought to illustrate the plural and eclectic identity of the field. The net result of this presentist orientation was that the historical task of reconstructing past ideas, practices, and conversations became subservient to demonstrating a thesis about the contemporary identity of the field. Moreover, the assumption that the past or present identity of the field can be explained contextually entails a host of historiographical problems. Not only are the actual connections between the external context and the internal development of the field often neglected, but the empirical details of the explanatory context are not always carefully demonstrated.

When it comes to demonstrating the connection between the field and its political context, the merits of contextualism, as it has been characteristically advanced, are suspect. One reason is that proponents of a contextual approach frequently misconstrue the relationship between external events and the internal disciplinary response manifested in conceptual, methodological, or theoretical change. This, once again, is not to suggest that there is no relationship between the field and exogenous events but rather that there is often a temporal lag between an external event and the field's reaction to the event. Furthermore, there are always instances when there is no response whatsoever to events taking place in international politics. Finally, the academic response to a significant external event can be multifarious. The various reactions on the part of international relations scholars to the collapse of the Soviet Union and the confrontational bipolar world order provides a dramatic illustration of the diverse reactions to external political events.[87] Often the issue is not so much one of a causal impact of a particular context but how the context is perceived by scholars.

This is a point that is often missed when seeking to understand the history of the field exclusively in terms of its historical context. The sweeping contextual generalizations that are offered to explain the internal character of the field do not adequately account for many of the subtle details in the field's history. Although international relations is conceived as an academic enterprise devoted to the study of international politics, this does not automatically imply that the external events that comprise the subject matter at any given point in time can explain what happens inside the field. There is often a great divide between the practice of an academic discipline and what is happening outside. The "end of ideology" argument that partly informed the behavioralist approach to politics in the late 1950s and early 1960s differed sharply from the anticolonial movements, race riots, and violent antiwar protests that characterized the external environment. If the intention is to understand the source of some of the dominant assumptions and ideas about the subject matter of international politics that are manifest in the history of the field, it is imperative to adopt a historiographical approach that will better enable us to recover the actual history of the field.

Critical Internal Discursive History

The alternative approach that I follow can be described as a critical internal discursive history. The aim of this approach is to reconstruct as accurately as possible the history of the conversation that has been constitutive of academic international relations. The intention is to reconstruct the internal developments and transformations that have occurred in the field by following and describing a relatively coherent conversation among participants in this professional field of inquiry. This approach seeks to overcome the images cast on the field's past that have been evoked and propagated by rhetorical histories. It traces the descent of the field from the point of an incipient academic discourse about international relations in the nineteenth century to the beginning of World War II. The subject matter is discourse—as embodied in scholarly journal articles, books, professional conference papers, textbooks, autobiographies, and other sources. These sources can be construed as representing the discursive artifacts of the field's past. In reconstructing the evolution of the field as a discursive practice, the goal is to provide an account of the conversations pursued by scholars who self-consciously understood themselves as participating in the formal study of international relations. This approach will not only facilitate the recovery of ideas that have long been forgotten but will also illuminate important episodes of conceptual change as well as indicate theoretical continuities. This focus on the internal discourse of the field and on its real history can be defended on both theoretical and pragmatic grounds.

Conceptual change in disciplinary practice is best understood by examining the endogenous developments in the academic field. Although the exogenous events of international politics at any given point in time may provide a relevant context for understanding the scholarly conversations, references to this context cannot explain the particular theoretical and methodological dimension of the conversation. It would be difficult, if not impossible, to explain changes in key concepts such as the state, sovereignty, anarchy, and power by reference to contextual factors. These types of conceptual changes are, most fundamentally, matters of internal academic debate. This is not to suggest, however, that exogenous events do not play a role in fostering conceptual change. Yet, no matter how great the impact of external events such as the Spanish-American War or World War I on the development of the field, they cannot by themselves account for the particular conversations and path of discursive development that they may have provoked.

In the case of the study of international relations, there are pragmatic reasons for a more internal approach. The most appropriate context for investigating the history of the field is its academic setting rather than the world at large. Developments in the field of international relations have been informed more by disciplinary trends in political science and by the character of the American university than by external events taking place in international politics. The university context from which international relations arose as a distinct field of study is the most immediate and relevant milieu for understanding its historical development.

This approach has certain affinities with Kuhn's work and his internal account of the history of natural science, in which he argued that "the textbook-derived tradition in which scientists come to sense their participation is one that, in fact, never existed."[88] Gunnell's work in political theory also reminds us that, unlike the mythical past configured of the classical canon from Plato to the present, the evolution of an academic discipline is an actual tradition about which the historian may be incorrect but which the historian can hardly be accused of creating.[89] If our concern is to understand the most immediate source of some of the central ideas and concepts that inform the study of international relations, then, unlike recent attempts to discern the modern roots of the field by reference to tangential figures such as Thucydides or Machiavelli, it would be best to attend to the works of figures such as Theodore Woolsey, Paul S. Reinsch, Philip Marshal Brown, and Pitman Potter.[90] They may not be as romantic, but they are more relevant. This is not to suggest, however, that international relations scholars have neither discussed nor been influenced by the ideas of Thucydides, Machiavelli, or any of the other figures associated with the classic canon. A central component of the discourse of international relations has involved the task of appropriating the ideas of these figures in order to validate a claim about a particular feature of international politics.

The Political Discourse of Anarchy

Nowhere is the validating function of reference to the classic texts more apparent than in what I describe as the *political discourse of anarchy* which has constituted the core conversation in the history of the field of international relations. By anarchy what is most often meant is that

> Unlike domestic politics, international politics takes place in an arena that has no central governing body. No agency exists above the individual states with authority and power to make laws and settle disputes. States can make commitments and treaties, but no sovereign power ensures compliance and punishes deviations.[91]

Anarchy is widely accepted by scholars of international relations to be the principal characteristic of modern international politics. This has especially been the case since the publication of Kenneth Waltz's *Theory of International Politics* (1979), which established the basis of the neorealist school of thought and has since become one of the leading texts in the field.

In his endeavor to develop a systemic theory of international relations, Waltz argued that the lack of a centralized governmental authority above the functionally undifferentiated units (i.e., states) wishing to survive in the international realm makes anarchy the most important structural condition in accounting for the behavior of states in the international system. Although Waltz constructed his systemic theory of realism on a model of microeconomics, this has not prevented neorealist scholars, including Waltz himself, from attempting to substantiate the significance of anarchy for understanding international politics through the insights of classic political theorists. Waltz, for example, claimed that Thucydides' history represented "an early recognition of 'the anarchic character of international politics,' which 'accounts for the striking sameness of the quality of international life throughout the millennia'."[92] In his earlier work, *Man, the State and War* (1959), Waltz focused on the writings of Rousseau to illustrate the superiority of "third image" explanations, i.e., those that emphasized the anarchical structure of the state system in understanding the cause of war. Both proponents and critics of neorealism have attempted to demonstrate the manner in which political theorists such as Thucydides, Machiavelli, Hobbes, and Rousseau recognized the importance of anarchy in comprehending international relations.[93]

With the ascendancy of neorealism to a position of disciplinary orthodoxy, it would be difficult to overstate the extent to which anarchy has become the single most discussed concept in the field of international relations. Barry Buzan and Richard Little have referred to the field's preoccupation with anarchy as an example of what they describe as "anarchophilia." By anarchophilia, Buzan and Little "mean the disposition to assume that the structure of the international system has always been anarchic, that this is natural, and (more selectively) that it is a good thing." They add that "these assumptions are strong in realism, and very strong in neorealism."[94] The focus that neorealists have placed on the anarchical structure of international politics has provided the predominant framework for analyzing a wide range of issues in the areas of international security, international organization, foreign policy, and political economy. In conceding that "neorealism has become the dominant school of thought in International Relations theory," a recent group of writers noted that "its preoccupation with anarchy as the central political condition of international relations has been widely taken up in writings about cooperation theory, game theory, regimes, and international society."[95] The concept of anarchy not only exercises a powerful hold on the field but it is sufficiently ambiguous to enable it to be reformulated and reinterpreted in countless ways.[96] Thus, at the same time that there are those who argue that anarchy is the foundational fact conditioning all international relations, there are others who maintain that patterns of interdependence and sets of legal-institutional constraints are undermining the condition of anarchy. Even for those who claim that the international system is anarchical in some sense, there is, according to David Baldwin, "disagreement as to what this means and why it matters."[97]

The disagreements that have arisen over the meaning, significance, and consequences of anarchy—especially with respect to the extent to which the absence of central authority hinders the prospects of inter-state cooperation—is at the center of the latest academic controversy between neorealism and neoliberalism.[98] Yet there has been little recognition by scholars of the extent to which the ongoing discussion about anarchy is deeply rooted in the discursive history of the field. My concern is to document the manner in which the disciplinary history of the field of international relations has, from its earliest years, been structured by a discourse about anarchy. At the most basic and fundamental level, political scientists who have been interested in the study of international relations recognized that their subject matter directly dealt with issues arising from the existence of sovereign states in the absence of a higher central authority. It is recognition of this basic fact, coupled with the multiplicity of theoretical and practical issues that it raises, which has given the field of international relations a distinct discursive identity.

Sovereignty and anarchy were the two constituent principles in terms of which the field of international relations originally took form. In focusing upon the activities of states as the central actors in international politics, political scientists recognized that the concept of sovereignty was the single most important theoretical issue. The discipline of political science gained its original identity from the study of the state, and it made the topic of sovereignty one of its paramount theoretical concerns. It was within this context that political scientists first discussed the subject matter of international relations. Students of political theory and international relations have recognized that sovereignty explicitly contains an internal and external component. Internally, sovereignty denotes absolute supreme political-legal authority over a territorially demarcated political community. When viewed externally, it entails the idea that there is no higher central authority above and beyond the individual sovereign state. In arguing that international relations is "dominated by the twin notion of the presence and the absence of sovereignty," Torbjorn Knutsen has explained that "applied to relations *within* states, this involves the belief that there is a final and absolute authority in society." Yet when "applied to relations *among* states, it expresses the antithesis of this belief, i.e. 'the principle that internationally, over and above a collection of societies, no supreme authority exists.'"[99]

It is on this basis that a discourse of anarchy has been pursued by scholars of international relations. The enigma of politics in the absence of central authority has given rise to generations of students of international relations seeking to articulate different interpretations, draw multiple conclusions, and offer alternative responses to this dilemma. In reconstructing the history of the field of international relations by following the conversation that has been pursued about anarchy a number of different interpretations and meanings that have been assigned to this concept will be revealed. The discursive history of the field indicates that there have been many episodes of conceptual change both with respect to how the concept has been understood and to the specific implications that have been drawn. In demonstrating the manner in which the history of the field of international relations can be understood through the political discourse of anarchy the importance of disciplinary history for understanding the present structure of the field will be made apparent.

2

THE THEORETICAL DISCOURSE OF THE STATE

Authors and Works Discussed

Author	1850	1860	1870	1880	1890	1900
Bluntschli				(1885)		
Burgess				(1882)	(1897)	
Lieber	(1838)	(1863)		(1880)		
Lawrence					(1895)	
Reinsch						(1900)
Smith				(1886)		
Woolsey		(1860)	(1878)			

Johann Casper Bluntschli 1808–1881
The Theory of the State [1885]

John W. Burgess 1844–1931
"The Study of the Political Sciences in Columbia College" *International Review* [1882]
"Political Science and History" *The American Historical Review* [1897]

Francis Lieber 1800–1872
Manual of Political Ethics [1838]
Instructions for Armies in the Field: General Order No. 100 [1863]
Miscellaneous Writings [1880]

Thomas J. Lawrence 1849–1919
The Principles of International Law [1895]

Paul S. Reinsch 1869–1923
World Politics At the End of the Nineteenth Century [1900]

Munroe Smith 1854–1926
"Introduction: The Domain of Political Science" *PSQ* [1886]

Theodore D. Woolsey 1801–1889
Introduction to the Study of International Law [1860]
Political Science, or the State Theoretically and Practically Considered [1878]

This chapter reconstructs the academic discourse of international relations as it emerged in the United States from the mid- to late 1800s. Although this is a much earlier date than from which most disciplinary histories of international relations originate, this "prehistory" period is important for establishing several of the early themes and issues that would constitute the young field at the turn of the century. It was, according to James Farr, during the prehistory period that political science developed *"from discourse to discipline."*[1] In other words, it was during this formative period in which the study of political science began to take on the professional characteristics and traits of a distinct academic discipline.

In the course of reconstructing the discursive transformation that political science underwent throughout the late nineteenth century, the writings of several influential scholars who helped to constitute the discipline will be examined. Particular attention will first be directed toward the pioneering work of Francis Lieber, who many have suggested was the originator of the systematic study of political science in the United States. In 1857, Lieber was named America's first professor of history and political science at Columbia College. The examination of Lieber's writings will be followed by the work of Theodore D. Woolsey and John W. Burgess. The efforts of Burgess, along with those of the other faculty members who composed the first school of political science at Columbia University, helped prepare the way for the eventual formation of the American Political Science Association in 1903.

The most important theme that structured the early study of political science can be termed the *theoretical discourse of the state,* and this is the principal focus of this chapter. Indeed, the conversation about the state that political scientists were engaging throughout the last quarter of the nineteenth century was of such paramount importance that it came to be identified as the proper domain of the discipline. The concept of the state, which has undergone countless episodes of conceptual change, fulfilled a number of vital functions that aided the enterprise of political science. It is fair to say that without the idea of the state, there may not have arisen a discipline of political science.

Of all the issues that the theoretical discourse of the state encompassed, none was more weighty than the concept of sovereignty. The significance that political scientists attached to the issue of sovereignty is extremely important for understanding the subsequent discourse of international relations. At first glance, this may appear to be no more than self-evident; after all, the textbook description of international relations has been traditionally portrayed as being preoccupied with the interactions of sovereign state actors. Yet this chapter will demonstrate the manner through which the theoretical discourse of the state, in a peculiar way, precluded the emergence of a separate and distinct conversation about international relations. The explanation lies with the fact that the early discussion of the state was not bifurcated into separate internal and external components. Political scientists, including political theorists and international lawyers, examined the issue of state sovereignty from both an internal and an external vantage point. Unlike much of the contemporary discussion that commonly divides along the lines of political theory studying the internal dimension of sovereignty and international relations studying the external dimension, the early theoretical discourse of the state encompassed both facets.

As this and the following chapters will make evident, the manner in which state sovereignty was conceptualized by political scientists exerted a major influence on how topics germane to the study of international relations, such as international organization and international law, were contemplated. Furthermore, since state sovereignty is the constitutive principle of international anarchy, the theoretical discourse of the state was also tacitly laying the groundwork for the political discourse of anarchy. This suggests that there was a close relationship between the theory of the state and the study of international relations. This was particularly the case with the discourse of international law which served as one of the earliest antecedents of the field of international relations. This chapter will focus on the writings of some of the early international lawyers to illustrate the influence that the theory of the state exercised on the discourse about international law. Finally, at the end of this chapter, the focus will turn to the work of Paul S. Reinsch, who was one of the early, seminal figures in developing a distinct discourse about international relations that centered around the phenomenon of national imperialism. It was not long before the analysis of national imperialism verged into the study of colonial administration which occupied a central place in the early history of the field.

Moral Philosophy and International Law

The early-nineteenth-century American college curriculum was not compartmentalized into clearly discernible disciplined fields of study, and much of the transmission of knowledge through college instruction was closely tied to the purpose of fostering morally responsible citizens. Moral philosophy, in the broadest sense, comprised all of the various intellectual disciplines that would eventually constitute the social sciences.[2] Anna Haddow's comprehensive analysis of the political science curriculum in American colleges makes it abundantly clear that "through moral philosophy, and with contributions from law and political economy, the elements of political science were being taught."[3] A year-long course in moral philosophy was usually offered in the senior year, and it was most often taught by the college president. The subject matter, as reflected in curriculum offerings, lecture headings, and textbooks of the time, always included topics germane to politics. In an article published in 1932, Gladys Bryson wrote, "it must be remembered that in every treatment of moral philosophy some generalized history of the origin and development of civil society and government found its place, and some consideration of the duties the citizens owes to the state." She added that "no thoroughgoing treatise was complete, moreover, which did not have, usually at the end, a large section on the law of nations, somewhat in the style of Grotius and Pufendorf."[4]

It was not uncommon for a course in moral philosophy to include the law of nations, since the latter was a logical extension of a curriculum that encompassed the study of ethics, natural liberty, economics, politics, and the laws of nature. The laws of nature were viewed as the foundation of the law of nations and the leading texts in the early 1800s continued to make reference to the law of nations (*jus gentium*), and not to international law, a term that was coined by Jeremy Bentham in *An Introduction to the Principles of Morals and Legislation* (1780). The adoption of Emmerich de Vattel's text *The Law of Nations, or the Principles of Natural Law Applied to the Conduct and to the Affairs of Nations and Sovereigns* (1758) in a number of northeastern colleges indicates the manner in which the law of nature and the law of nations closely paralleled one another.[5] Vattel claimed that ultimately, the "*Law of Nations* is in its origin merely the *Law of Nature applied to Nations*."[6] Although Vattel was beginning to recognize that the law between nations was derived from the will of nations as manifest by treaties and custom, he nevertheless continued to be influenced by the commonly accepted father of international law, Hugo Grotius (1583–1645). Grotius defended the principles that he outlined in *De Jure Belli ac Pacis* (1625) on the basis of the law of nature which he argued was derived from universal reason. In William C. Olson and A.J.R. Groom's account of the disciplinary history of international relations, they argue that *De Jure Belli ac Pacis* "must take its place in the early development of the discipline simply because international law was the context within which IR subject matter was considered by scholars of that era."[7] The discourse surrounding international law in the nineteenth and early twentieth century is the appropriate context in which to begin reconstructing the disciplinary prehistory of international relations. The writings of the international lawyers of this period are the earliest intellectual antecedents of the professional study of international politics.

Some of the most highly respected and renowned publicists in this area lived in the United States. Works by James Kent, *Commentaries on*

American Law (1826), and Henry Wheaton, *Elements of International Law with a Sketch of the History of the Science* (1836), established a lofty standard of scholarship that, according to Haddow, "helped consolidate the position of international law as a distinct body of subject matter."[8] Although both of these works continued to discuss the law of nations from the perspective of natural law, they did begin to make use of the concept of international law. Wheaton offered the following definition of the subject matter: "international law, as understood among civilized nations, may be defined as consisting of those rules of conduct which reason deduces, as consonant to justice, from the nature of the society existing among independent nations; with such definitions and modifications as may be established by general consent."[9] It was, however, the perceived instructional weaknesses of these two books for teaching "young men of liberal culture" that prompted Theodore Dwight Woolsey, of Yale, to publish a work entitled *Introduction to the Study of International Law, Designed as an Aid in Teaching, and in Historical Studies* (1860).

Woolsey had earned an undergraduate degree from Yale in 1820. After leaving Yale, he studied law and theology and, like many aspiring young intellectuals of the time, went to Europe for formal graduate instruction. He returned to his Alma Mater in 1830 as a professor of Greek and eventually became president of the college, a post he would hold until his retirement in 1871. Woolsey lectured on a wide variety of topics during his tenure at Yale. A major component of his course in political philosophy was devoted to the study of international law. By the end of his academic career, Woolsey was a recognized expert in international law and his text helped to popularize the subject matter in American colleges. But even more significantly, it was with the work of Woolsey that the relationship between the study of political science, with its theoretical focus on the state, and international law, as the appropriate context from which the external relations of states were discussed, began to take explicit form. In order to apprehend the importance of the theoretical link that was forged between the study of the state and international law, it is appropriate to begin with the work of Francis Lieber. According to Woolsey, his most influential disciple, the honor of being the originator of the American study of political science belonged to Lieber.[10]

The Discourse of the State

Lieber did more than anyone else to initiate and Americanize the discussion of *Staatswissenschaft*, or the science of the state, that would come to define the very core of political science by the end of the nineteenth century. He was the first of a long succession of European intellectuals who worked to establish and define the American science of politics. Lieber was born in Berlin on March 18, 1800.[11] He came to the United States in 1827, fleeing persecution for his republican nationalistic views that prevented him from teaching in Prussia. In Boston, with some financial security gained as a gymnasium instructor, Lieber designed a plan for the publication of an encyclopedia. His venture resulted in the publication of the *Encyclopedia Americana (1835)*, which was both a financial and intellectual success. As John G. Gunnell has noted, "it was in the *Encyclopedia Americana* that the state, as the organizing concept of political inquiry, was first introduced in the United States."[12] The theme of the state would preoccupy Lieber's intellectual and scholarly attention from his appointment to the chair of history and political economy at South Carolina College in 1835 until he resigned in 1855.

Although Lieber's personal letters and biography indicate that he regarded his residency at South Carolina College as nothing less than intellectual and cultural exile, it was during this twenty-year period that all of his principal works were written. The publication of *Manual of Political Ethics* (1838), along with *Civil Liberty and Self-Government* (1853), helped Lieber return to the North and accept his long-sought-after position as professor of history and political science at Columbia College in May 1857. It was at Columbia that the first School of Political Science in the United States would open in 1880. Some have pointed to this event as marking the birth of American political science as a learned discipline.[13] Lieber's inaugural address to the Board of Trustees at Columbia, entitled "History and Political Science: Necessary Studies in Free Countries," advanced many of the same themes that had been raised in his books, including the juristic notion of the state that he argued informed both the essence and scope of the various branches of study subsumed under his newly created chair. Lieber explained that "Political Science treats of man in his most important earthly phase; the state is the institution which has to protect or to check all his endeavors, and, in turn, reflects them."[14] One of the underlying themes of Lieber's address was the close relationship that existed between the study of history and political science—a relationship that he argued was needed in order to demonstrate the progress humankind had made in moving from degenerate forms of political association to the ideal national republican form of state.

Within this progressive account of political development, Lieber did not, however, point to emergence from a state of nature, because he flatly denied that such a condition had ever existed. Moreover, he believed that it was impossible for human beings to exist without the state. In his *Manual of Political Ethics,* which provided an extended discussion of the state as a jural society, Lieber explained that the "state is aboriginal with man; it is no voluntary association; . . . no work of contract by individuals who lived previously out of it; . . . the State is a form and faculty of mankind to lead the species toward greater perfection—it is the glory of man."[15] Lieber argued that political science represented the most comprehensive and systematic study of man, and the curriculum divisions he proposed included three branches: political ethics, the science of government, and the crowning apogee— international law. With respect to the third branch, Lieber declared:

> And now the student will be prepared to enter upon that branch which is the glory of our race in modern history, and possibly the greatest achievement of combined judgment and justice, acting under the genial light of culture and religion—on International Law, that law which, without the sword of justice, encompasses even the ocean.[16]

According to Lieber's biographer, the most important scholarly interest in his later years was the subject matter of international law.[17] Lieber's scholarly writings on international law are noteworthy in revealing the theoretical convergence that existed between the internal and external dimensions of the state. The intellectual concerns and theoretical issues that arose from the study of the state were necessarily carried over to an examination of the external relations among states and international law. The intimate connection between the internal and external character of the state was taken to be axiomatic by political scientists throughout the initial phase of the discipline's evolution, and this made it difficult to consider either sphere in isolation from the other. Lieber's writings provide a lucid illustration of the link that existed between the internal and external components of the state. Lieber's contribution to political science in defining its proper domain as the state was unparalleled during this period, and this was complemented by his prominence in international law.

Even before Lieber systematically devoted his scholarly attention to international law, his work on the science of military law, conducted upon the request of President Lincoln and General Halleck during the Civil War, was well-known.[18] In the absence of a general code of military conduct for the Northern army, Lieber, an avowed supporter of the Union, was called upon by the Secretary of War to draft a code of instructions for the government of the armies in the field.[19] The fruit of Lieber's path-breaking work was *Instructions for Armies in the Field: General Order No. 100* (1863). Johann Caspar Bluntschli claimed that *General Order No. 100* was "the first codification of International Articles of War," and that it "was a deed of great moment in the history of international law and of civilization."[20] During the Civil War period, Lieber made two additional contributions to military law: *Guerrilla Parties Considered with Reference to the Laws and Usages of War* (1862) and *Status of Rebel Prisoners of War* (1865). These three works represented some of the earliest attempts to codify international law, and they would serve as a model for future endeavors.

Johann Caspar Bluntschli had great admiration for Lieber's work on international law, and he specifically paid homage to his contributions. The writings of Bluntschli in Germany, along with those of Edward Laboulaye in France and Lieber in America, formed what the latter called a "scientific clover-leaf" of three men devoting themselves to political science.[21] Bluntschli, who was professor of International Law and Political Science, followed the general pattern of addressing the theory of the state from both an internal and external perspective. Bluntschli's *The Theory of the State* (1851) had a substantial influence on American political scientists, including Lieber, both before and after it was translated into English in 1885. Bluntschli's theoretical description of the state, including the sexist and racist overtones, was similar to that of Lieber. Bluntschli's *Staatswissenschaft* combined the historical approach, which aided in understanding the general concept (*Begriff*) of the state, with the philosophical approach, which led to the idea (*Idee*) of the state. Taken together, the state, as conceived by Bluntschli, was an organic, masculine, moral person, having both spirit and body. In adopting the conception of the state as a living organism, Bluntschli, like Lieber, regarded the idea of a social contract as absurd.

When Bluntschli turned his attention to the predicament confronting states in the international arena, he firmly denied the plausibility of states' coming together to form any type of supranational union that would require them to dissolve their own organic identity. While he admitted that a "universal state or empire (*Weltreich*) is the ideal of human progress," such a future arrangement did not entail dismantling the individual states. With respect to the ideal of a universal state, Bluntschli explained:

> To the universal empire the particular states are related, as the nations to humanity. Particular states are members of the universal empire and attain in it their completion and their full satisfaction. The purpose of the universal State is not to break up particular states and oppress nations, but better secure the peace of the former and the freedom of the latter.[22]

In contrast to world–order reforms that called for the formation of a universal state, Bluntschli proposed creating a "college of six Great

Powers" that would be used to fulfill certain legislative functions. To protect the independence of all nations, he suggested that an international code of international law be drawn up from governmental delegates comprising an international legislature and that this body be weighted in favor of the six Great Powers with respect to both voting and enforcement. This idea has often been cited as a precursor of the design behind both the League of Nations and the United Nations.[23]

Lieber shared many of the same sentiments as Bluntschli with respect to preserving the independence of the national state. Lieber described the age in which he lived as the "National Period" which was characterized by the existence of numerous independent national polities. Lieber regarded the national polity, as opposed to all other types of political arrangements, to be the only one sufficient "for the demands of advanced civilization." In offering a definition of the elusive concept of nation, Lieber emphasized that "organic intellectual and political internal unity, with proportionate strength, and a distinct and obvious demarcation from similar groups, are notable elements of the idea of a modern nation."[24] Yet at the same time that the independent national polity, with its own distinct language, literature, and common institutions, helped to differentiate the National Period from previous historical epochs, Lieber also noted that the present age was marked by the "process of internationalization." He reasoned that as a result of one alphabet; one mathematical language; one science; one division of government; one domestic economy; a united mail system; a common international law; an extending agreement in measures, weights, coinage, and signals at sea; etc., the "modern nations of our family have come to agree in much, and the agreement is growing."[25] Lieber explained that the same "law of interdependence" that made society possible also extended to the external activities of nations. While Lieber did not observe any fundamental inconsistencies between these two processes, the poles of independence and interdependence would at a later point in the field's history be viewed by many as providing two distinct analytical frameworks for describing international politics. This remains the case today as neoliberals accentuate the interdependent nature of international politics, while neorealists emphasize the independence of state actors.[26]

At no point, however, did Lieber believe that the process of internationalization represented a threat to the existence of national polities. Like Bluntschli, he was opposed to the idea of creating a world state as a way of settling the disputes that arose between sovereign bodies that found themselves in a posture of interdependence with one another. Rather, Lieber called for an improved international law among the community of nations. Interdependence, Lieber argued, aided the task of extending the reign of law to the international sphere. He wrote that "the civilized nations have come to constitute a community of nations, and are daily forming more and more of a common wealth of nations, under the restraint and protection of the law of nations, which rules *vigore divino.*"[27] It was the task of improving the law of nations to which Lieber diligently dedicated his remaining years at Columbia as Professor of Constitutional History and Public Law after the trustees abolished his chair of history and political science in 1865. Lieber focused on arbitration as the primary mechanism for settling international disputes among the family of sovereign nations. In his essay "On International Arbitration" (1865), Lieber suggested that instead of selecting a monarch as arbiter, which was the customary practice of the time, disputes should be submitted to a jurist, or law professor, so that the decisions would rest on a more solid legal foundation. He reckoned that a law faculty, "especially that of a renowned university in a minor state," would be ideally suited for such a function.[28] Lieber's suggestion for improving the process of international arbitration by appointing jurists and legal scholars of high intellectual standing from around the world, who would together serve "as an organ for the legal consciousness of the civilized world," was recognized by Bluntschli as another one of his remarkable contributions to political science and international law.

The combined efforts of Lieber and Bluntschli greatly contributed to the early development of political science in the United States during the mid-1800s. Their work represents the manner in which the study of international law and international relations were closely tied to the emerging discourse about the state—a discourse that would increasingly come to define the proper domain of political science. Before proceeding to the most formative institutional event of this period, namely, the establishment of the School of Political Science at Columbia, further attention must be directed to the work of Theodore Woolsey. Woolsey's work provides a quintessential illustration of both the early American synthesis of the study of the state and international law and the blending of the emerging theoretical discourse of the state with the earlier traditional moral philosophy curriculum.

Unlike Lieber and Bluntschli, the focus of Woolsey's first publication was the subject of international law, while his second book addressed the state. The latter he drew from the lectures in his Political Philosophy course at Yale, which were published under the title *Political Science or the State Theoretically and Practically Considered* (1878). The title of the book itself provides an indication of the close fit that existed between political science and the study of the state. Woolsey's writings on international law and the state advanced themes similar to those found in the work of Lieber. The influence of Lieber was unmistakably prevalent throughout Woolsey's career. *Civil Liberty and Self-Government* was immediately adopted in Woolsey's Political Philosophy class at Yale; and he dedicated his *Introduction to the Study of International Law* "to Francis Lieber as a token of respect for services in the field of political science." After retiring from Yale in 1872, he edited several of the later editions of Lieber's published works.

In each of Woolsey's books, the state was described as a moral person that created and protected certain fundamental rights. He defined the state as a "community of persons living within certain limits of territory, under a permanent organization, which aims to secure the prevalence of justice by self-imposed law."[29] Following from this, Woolsey identified three attributes or rights that were essential to the existence of the state: the rights of sovereignty, independence, and equality. These three attributes of the state had a significant influence on Woolsey's understanding of the nature of international law. And it was exactly this connection between the theory of the state on the one hand, and the understanding of international law on the other hand, that must be clarified. The crucial point is that issues associated with international relations were addressed within the framework provided by the theory of the state. Rather than a sharp divergence between the domestic and international realms, there was a fundamental convergence.

Woolsey's discussion of international law exemplified this convergence from the outset. Although the state, according to Woolsey, was unique in that no law was imposed on it "by an external human power," it nevertheless retained a "moral accountable nature." Woolsey argued that it was the moral accountable nature of the state, along with the corresponding view that each sovereign entity possessed rights and obligations, that contributed to the possibility of there being a law between nations in the first place. In his attempt to provide a definition of international law, Woolsey began by juxtaposing a "wide and abstract view" that embraced "those rules of intercourse between nations, which are deduced from their rights and moral claims" to a more limited view that included the system of "positive rules, by which the nations of the world regulate their intercourse with one another."[30] He then sought to achieve a synthesis between the moral and practical elements so as to foster a more scientific foundation for the study of international law. This endeavor would become one of the dominant trends in international law after the turn of the century. Yet the synthesis that Woolsey reached can only be understood within the context of his theory of the state. He concluded international law "to be the aggregate of rules, which Christian states acknowledge, as obligatory in their relation to each other, and to each other's subjects."[31] This definition conceded the voluntary nature of international law as manifest in the actual practices and agreements of states but also, according to Woolsey, preserved the character of a science by maintaining a higher foundation that could only be deduced from reason itself. He submitted that if international law "were not built on principles of right; it would be even less of a science than is the code which governs the actions of polite society."[32]

As a final note on Woolsey's contribution to the study of international law, it is appropriate to accentuate the practical dimension of his endeavor, especially since this highlights a major theme in the development of both political science and international relations. One of Woolsey's primary aims in writing his text on international law was to assist the democratic populace. He concluded his text by "hoping that it may be of some use in my native land, and to young men who may need a guide in the science of which it treats."[33] Woolsey thus pointed to the important and recurring theme of citizen training that would always be close to the surface as the emerging discipline of political science began to grapple with its purpose in the academic and public universe.

Burgess and the Columbia School

After approximately fifteen years without an institutional setting formally devoted to the study of political science, the first school of that name opened at Columbia College on October 4, 1880, under the direction of John W. Burgess.[34] Several disciplinary historians have suggested that the formation of the School of Political Science at Columbia marked the culmination of the "prehistory" period.[35] With respect to political science in general, and international relations in particular, the importance of this event does not reside in merely serving as a historical marker distinguishing one period from another. Rather, the significance of the creation of the School of Political Science was its provision of an institutional setting in which the study of politics increasingly moved from discourse to discipline and, consequently, self-consciously addressed questions of scope and domain that go along with carving out a niche in the academic cosmos.

The predominant discourse that emerged in the late 1800s was one that closely duplicated the German *Staatslehre,* or, the theory of the state. As Gunnell has demonstrated in his work on academic political theory during this period:

By the time that the major graduate programs in political science began to appear at institutions such as Columbia and Hopkins in the 1800s, the theory of the state, as advanced by Lieber,

Bluntschli, and Woolsey, constituted, both substantively and methodologically, a distinct and influential paradigm.[36]

In the process of defining the scope and domain of political science at Columbia, the niche reserved for the study of international relations would also be given a more definite form. There was little doubt among Burgess and the other original faculty members of the school at Columbia that issues concerning international relations properly belonged to the academic sphere of political science. Burgess's commitment to the study of political science was, in many ways, beholden to his personal experience on the battlefield as a Union soldier during the Civil War. On the fiftieth anniversary of the founding of the School of Political Science, Burgess recalled a pledge he made to himself during the Civil War that if his life should be spared from the carnage, he would "devote his life thereafter to the acquisition of such knowledge as might have the tendency to bring about such a change in the conduct of men and of nations."[37]

The academic career that followed Burgess's undergraduate education at Amherst College, a brief stay at Columbia Law School, and two years of graduate study in Germany, reflected the struggle that political science was itself embroiled in with respect to establishing a separate realm of discourse. Academic controversy stemming from Burgess's challenge to institutional orthodoxy followed him throughout his career. When Burgess returned to Amherst in 1873 as a professor of history and political science, opposition quickly set in when he began to introduce graduate training based on the German university model to a handful of select students. After delivering a series of guest lectures in comparative constitutional law and international law at Columbia's Law School in the Winter of 1875–1876, Burgess was offered a newly created position as Professor of History, Political Science and International Law in the School of Arts and School of Law. Shortly after accepting the position, Burgess's initial optimism was followed by disappointment over the lack of resources and the institutional inertia that existed within the School of Arts and the School of Law. His complaints were heard by some important sympathetic individuals, including the president of Columbia, Frederick A. P. Barnard, and Burgess was asked by the Trustees to draw up a plan for the formation of a separate faculty and School of Political Science. The comprehensive plan that Burgess submitted was accepted, and the Trustees "resolved, that there be established, to go into operation at the opening of the Academic year next ensuing, a school designed to prepare young men for the duties of public life, to be entitled a School of Political Science."[38] When the School opened in the Fall of 1880, the organization, content, and structure of the program became the model that many other graduate programs in political science would seek to emulate.

Burgess explained that the School of Political Science was the collective name given "to the graduate or university courses in history, philosophy, economy, public law, jurisprudence, diplomacy and sociology."[39] Students who successfully completed three years of the undergraduate program were entitled to enter the School of Political Science, where the method of instruction changed from the "gymnastic" to a pedagogy based on independent scholarly instruction. In both the undergraduate and graduate programs, the historical method was utilized to ascertain the facts surrounding the state. According to Burgess, the historical method was fundamental to the undergraduate program, because it was only "through a sound and comprehensive study of history that the foundations can be laid for a true and valuable public law and political science." History was also the key to the graduate program "but this time it is the history of *institutions,* the origin and development of the State through its several phases of *political organization* down to the modern constitutional form."[40]

The initial curricular divisions at Columbia reflected the recognition that political science was, most fundamentally, the science of the state. Consistent with Burgess's Hegelian Teutonic theory of the state, he held that the contemporary age was distinguished by the existence of "national country states." In addition to his massive two volume text, *Political Science and Comparative Constitutional Law* (1890), which established a tripartite division between political science proper, constitutional law, and public law, the most succinct articulation of the domain of political science can be found in the address that Burgess delivered to the American Historical Association. The main point of his lecture was to define the proper relationship that existed between history and political science. While Burgess conceded that there were some parts of history that were not political science, and vice versa, the more important conclusion he reached was that "the two spheres so lap over one another and interpenetrate each other that they cannot be distinctly separated." He thus insisted that "political science must be studied historically and history must be studied politically."[41]

Burgess's notion of history was thoroughly Hegelian. History embodied the progression of the human spirit, while the writing of history consisted in recording the facts and wisdom gained in the process. Political science, Burgess maintained, was the study of a class of facts present at a particular stage in history. He argued that "political science in its present meaning is, therefore, the science of the national country state, and is tending to become a science of the human world state."[42] The characteristics of the modern age required that political science be more than merely the science of government, as it might have been in the age of the classical city-states, but also a "science of liberty and the science of sovereignty." According to Burgess, the three doctrines of government, liberty, and sovereignty, which properly belonged to political science, achieved their "perfect objective realization" in constitutional law.[43] More importantly, these three doctrines also represented the constituent components of the state. Burgess was one of the foremost participants in the early discourse of the state, and his obscurity among contemporary political scientists is largely due to his unrelenting adherence to the traditional theory of the state. While Burgess assigned four specific characteristics to the state—all-comprehensive, exclusive, permanent, and sovereign—it was the last feature that most distinguished the state from other forms of political association. By sovereignty, Burgess meant "original, absolute, unlimited, universal power over the individual subject and over all associations of subjects to command and enforce obedience by punishment for disobedience."[44] Rather than being inimical to the rights and liberties of individuals, Burgess argued that it was because of the state that people could enjoy any rights at all. He was thus opposed to any formal limitations being placed on the ability of the state to exercise sovereignty.

Writers who warned of the dangers to individual liberty arising from such an image of sovereignty were, according to Burgess, confounding state and government. He drew a particularly sharp distinction between state and government; that is, between the locus of the nation and the exercise of sovereignty. While the modern Teutonic states—Germany, Great Britain, and the United States—were similar in their form of political development, they differed with respect to the manner in which sovereignty was institutionally exercised. It was on this basis that Burgess drew his various distinctions between different forms of government. He openly endorsed democratic forms of state with a meritocratic government as being the most advantageous with respect to guaranteeing the rights and liberties of individuals, and he found Germany to be a particularly good model of a modern state.[45]

Munroe Smith was another one of the original political science faculty members at Columbia who attempted to specify the domain of the new discipline. In addition to his teaching duties, Smith served as the first managing editor of the *Political Science Quarterly*, which was the official journal of the Columbia School of Political Science. The first issue of the journal appeared in 1886 and included the important lead article by Smith entitled "Introduction: The Domain of Political Science." Smith was of the opinion that the term "political science" was greatly misused, enabling the term to connote simultaneously a number of different meanings. However, instead of offering a dogmatic authoritative definition, he proposed to analyze the respective domains of the social sciences that often overlapped with those of political science.

While Smith observed a close interdependence between many of the social sciences, he maintained that political science "signifies, literally, the science of the state." By claiming that the state was the domain of political science, Smith reasoned:

> We may separate the relations of states one to another—the international relations—from the national. We may divide the national relations into questions of state organization and state action. We may distinguish between the various functions of the state. But there is no good reason for erecting these various groups of questions into distinct political sciences. The connection of each with all is too intimate.[46]

This quotation by Smith represents a paradigmatic event within the discursive formation of the field of international relations. The initial academic space reserved for the subject matter pertaining to international relations was essentially subsumed under the discourse of the state. The sharp analytical distinction that contemporary political scientists are so apt to make between the domestic and the international, the internal and external, was deemed to be an artificial and unnecessary division. One of the common arguments repeatedly made by international relations scholars to justify the bifurcation between the domestic and international functions of the state, namely, the provider of internal order and tranquillity and the external defender against continual chaos and violent aggression, was also dismissed by Smith when he wrote that "the conception of the state as a mere protective association against external force and internal disorder is antiquated," because "the state is everywhere exercising other functions than the protection of person and property."[47]

When divisions were created in the discourse of the state for purposes of instructional division of labor, it was typical for international law and diplomacy to find a place in the process that Max Weber described as academic intellectualization.[48] These divisions were not based on some theoretical or analytical schema, but rather reflected more simple pragmatic instructional needs. Examples of the curriculum divisions that were created for didactic purposes can be found in the political science course offerings compiled by Haddow. One example is that offered at Princeton University during the 1883–84 academic year. The course description reads:

a.   **The State in itself** and as related to Sociology, to ethics, the People, Government, Law, Popular Sovereignty, Diverse forms of Civil Polity, including the Federal System, particularly as shown in the State and National Governments of the United States.

b. **The Inter-relation of States.** International law, its origin and authority, as related to Nations at Peace and War, and to the obligations of Neutrals and Belligerents.[49]

In the aggregate, this particular course, while separated into two components, reflected the totality of the domain of political science; that is, the state. Before proceeding to the conversation about international law, the most fundamental and direct intellectual antecedent of international relations, attention must be focused briefly on the historical-comparative method.

The Historical-Comparative Method

The historical-comparative method stands out as one of the defining characteristics of the early study of political science. Political scientists such as Burgess claimed that the modern state, as the highest achievement of the human race, could be understood as a historical entity that had undergone fundamental transformations in the process of becoming. These transformations were believed to have both historical and political meaning in the grand development of the Teutonic state. Political scientists of this period believed that the historicity of the state could be known both synchronically and diachronically through a historical-comparative examination. This methodology was viewed as a scientific mode of investigation, similar in form to the natural sciences, that would eventually lead to the discovery of laws of political development. The orthodoxy of this shared methodological underpinning of the field has been taken by some disciplinary historians to represent a distinct period in the development of political science. Charles Merriam, for example, defined the period from 1850 to 1900 in terms of the historical-comparative method as distinguished from the a priori, deductive method that characterized the discipline from its beginnings to 1850.[50] According to Albert Lepawsky, of the five periods in the evolution of political science, the "Romantic Period" from approximately 1865–1905 was marked by an epistemology "generally designed to fit the politics of the times."[51] Lepawsky's discussion of the Romantic Period places great stress on the historical method advanced at both Johns Hopkins and Columbia University.

An influential spokesperson for the historical-comparative method, and for the explicit linkage between history and political science, was Herbert Baxter Adams. As an undergraduate student at Amherst College, Adams acquired a taste for history and after graduating in 1872, went to Germany where he heard the lectures of Wilhelm Ihne, Kuno Fischer, Ernst Curtius, and Heinrich von Treitschke. Under the direction of Bluntschli, Adams completed a course of study at the University of Heidelberg in historical and political science, and was awarded a Doctor of Philosophy on July 14, 1876. When Adams returned to America, he accepted an appointment as Fellow at Johns Hopkins, which opened in 1876 and was the first American university to be established primarily for the purpose of graduate instruction.[52]

It was to Bluntschli that Adams's understanding of the alliance between history and political science was indebted. According to Adams, like Lieber and Burgess, history and political science were so closely aligned with one another that they could not exist without each other. He adopted Edward Freeman's adage that "History is past Politics and Politics present History," along with Sir Robert Seeley's motto that "History without Political Science has no fruit; Political Science without History has no root," as defining principles throughout his scholarly career. The historical-comparative method, as an approach to discovering laws of political development, was employed in Adams's historical studies of the early colonial forms of government and local institutions in America, and in his quest to elucidate the progressive evolution of the Teutonic form of state. The intimate connection between history and political science was manifest in the Johns Hopkins Historical and Political Association that was formed in 1878, and in which Adams served as recording secretary. It would be difficult to exaggerate the significance that Adams's teaching of the historical-comparative method had on the emerging discipline of political science. Individuals such as Woodrow Wilson and Westel Woodbury Willoughby, both future Presidents of the American Political Science Association, passed through Adams's seminar room at Johns Hopkins.

One reason for drawing attention to the historical-comparative method that was being utilized by the leading political scientists of this period is to eliminate one of the persistent myths concerning the development of academic international relations. This is the myth that, in comparison to the other social science disciplines, international relations had a distinctive methodological orientation which, in turn, accounts for some of the unique features of the field today. There is a widespread belief among scholars of international relations that the field arose from the study of history, and that this disciplinary origin was different from the other social sciences. Richard Little, for example, claims that "it was on the basis of historical explanation, however, that the new discipline of international relations was established; and this tradition is very different to the philosophical foundation from which the mainstream social sciences emerged."[53] The numerous references which suggest that Thucydides, the historian of the Peloponnesian War, established the earliest foundation for the study of international relations appear, for many, to confirm the historical origins of the field.

The notion that Thucydides laid the basis for the field of international relations and was a participant in the discursive development of the field provides a quintessential example of the persistent tendency discussed in Chapter 1 to confuse an analytical with a historical tradition of thought. This is not to suggest that scholars have not derived a number of important insights from Thucydides' work, but assertions that suggest that the historical approach associated with his writings explains the subsequent path of the disciplinary development of international relations are simply incorrect.[54] It is a mistake to assume that the historical methodology underpinning the study of international relations can, in any way, account for the peculiarities of the field vis-à-vis the other social sciences. Little is incorrect when he states that the historical character of the field explains why, in direct contrast to other social sciences, "specialists in international relations felt under no compunction to search for general laws which could explain the action of states."[55]

The early study of political science, which included the subject matter of international relations and international law, was fundamentally committed to uncovering general laws of political development through the use of the historical-comparative method. The discourse of the state utilized the historical-comparative method in an attempt to understand, and ultimately explain, the peculiar evolution of the Teutonic state. Rather than being viewed as antagonistic, history and science were mutually compatible, and history was viewed as indispensable for achieving a science of politics. And just as the state provided the overarching intellectual framework for studying international relations, the historical-comparative provided the methodological underpinning. This was clearly apparent within the study of international law which served as the most direct antecedent of academic international relations. It is the conversation about international law and the close connection that it shared with the theoretical discourse of the state that must be examined.

International Law

The historical method that was an integral part of the discourse of the state also came to occupy a central role in the study of international law. Woolsey explained that "in every branch of knowledge, the history of the branch is an important auxiliary to its scientific treatment." With respect to the field of international law, he argued that "it is evident that the history of this science—both the history of opinion and of practice,—is deserving of special attention."[56] This was especially the case in the attempt to build a more "scientific" foundation for international law. Woolsey as well as several other international lawyers argued that it was only through historical inquiry that the present empirical foundation of international law could be revealed without resorting to a transcendental defense based on universal laws of nature. History was viewed as a means of narrowing the gap that existed in international law between what "ought" to be and what "is."

Thomas J. Lawrence's popular text, *The Principles of International Law* (1895), sought to place "before students of political science a clear and readable outline of one of the most important branches of their subject."[57] Lawrence stated that students of international law "are primarily inquirers into what is, not what ought to be." Therefore, he argued that "their method must of necessity be historical, since the only recognized means of discovering what rules apply to particular cases in the present takes the form of an inquiry into the history of similar cases in the past."[58] In a comparable manner, the revered text by George Grafton Wilson and George Fox Tucker argued that modern international law, in comparison to its older abstract character, now rested "largely upon historical bases."[59] Once again, the rationale behind the turn to history was to uncover the general principles and rules from which existing international law was derived. Wilson and Tucker were not, however, willing to remove completely the ethical and moral basis of their subject, which they, along with many others, believed extended back to the writings of Grotius in the early seventeenth century. Wilson and Tucker argued for a more conciliatory position between the historical and the a priori moral-ethical stance. They reasoned that "modern international law treats mainly what *is*, but what *is* in international relations is always influenced by a recognition of what *ought* to be."[60]

The discursive development of academic international relations has continually resonated with this recurring clash between the epistemological and ontological dichotomy of *ought* and *is*. New claims to authoritative knowledge about international politics have almost always been accompanied by an affirmation to better know the world. There are a number of possible explanations why the conversation of international law at the turn of the nineteenth century felt obliged to evoke the perennial dichotomy between the imaginary and the real. Most essentially, though, the contrast between "ought" and "is" in international law had its roots in the theoretical discourse of the state. Within the theoretical discourse of the state, the issue of sovereignty— its character, composition, location, and attributes—was central. The reason for this, quite simply, was that sovereignty has been understood as the distinctive characteristic of the modern entity known as the state. In F.H. Hinsley's classic study of sovereignty, he maintained that "in a word, the origin and history of the concept of sovereignty are closely linked with the nature, the origin and the history of the state."[61] And just as the issue of sovereignty was of fundamental significance to the discourse of the state, it was also of great importance to the study of international law. The main point to emphasize was the theoretical convergence that existed between the discussion of the state and international law. The particular notion of sovereignty that political scientists attributed to the state had a significant impact on the manner in which both domestic and international political issues were discussed and analyzed.

Although some exceptions can be found, most of the early international law books included a discussion of the character and nature of the state. While the bulk of an international law text was characteristically devoted to explaining the rules and procedures of the subject matter, usually divided into a section on the law of war and a section on the law of peace, it was often deemed necessary to discuss briefly the features of the sovereign state itself. Many of the same questions and issues that structured the theoretical discourse of the state were carried over to the discussion of international law. There are at least three different explanations that can be provided for why there was such a confluence of concerns. First, like political science, the domain of international law was, most fundamentally, the state—the historical form that characterized modern "civilized" nations at the end of the nineteenth century. This Eurocentric bias was important not only from an evolutionary historical-comparative perspective, but also from a legalistic point of view. It was the state in its juristic sovereign form with which international lawyers had to grapple. The particular form of state that political scientists believed was exemplified in Western nations provides a second explanation for the convergence of concerns between the discourse of the state and international law. Irrespective of whether an international law text engaged the question of where sovereignty resided within the state, it was axiomatic that the modern nation-state was distinguished by the possession of supreme authority within a specified territorial jurisdiction. This had momentous implications for the theory and practice of international law. As it was widely recognized that sovereign states, as opposed to all other types of political arrangements, were the proper subjects of international law, this necessitated that the foundations of international law would have to be derived from the voluntary actions of states, and not from the dictates of a higher sovereign authority.

Developing a new theoretical and legal foundation for international law on an empirical basis, that is, one that could be derived from the actual practices manifest in state behavior, became the central motivating activity that shaped the discourse about international law. This directly leads to the third, and perhaps most important, manner in which the concerns and issues that arose within the discourse of the state were carried over to international law. This was largely a manifestation of the reaction to the theory of jurisprudence advanced by the English jurist John Austin, who had observed that the so-called law of nations was not law at all, but rather a form of international morality. The predominant authority and influence of Austin's definition of law as "a rule laid down for the guidance of an intelligent being by an intelligent being having power over him," which was delineated in his *The Province of Jurisprudence Determined* (1832), can be attested by the large number of international law scholars who felt compelled to take issue with him.[62] The basis for challenging Austin's position was deemed to be of critical importance to a large cadre of American publicists who placed their faith in an improved international law as the primary means for reforming the international system. As long as the notion that international law was merely a form of morality, having no sanctity within legal jurisprudence, lingered in the minds of men, the optimism of American publicists appeared as nothing less than a wishful chimera. The criticism as well as the defense of the Austinian view of international law necessitated that attention be directed toward the theory of state sovereignty.

The position that Austin and the other members of the English analytical school, which included a lineage reaching to Thomas Hobbes, Jeremy Bentham, and Jean Bodin, held toward international law was a logical manifestation of their peculiar view of sovereignty. According to Austin, the power and authority to issue supreme commands coupled with the ability to ensure compliance defined the very essence of the concept of sovereignty. Sovereignty and positive law were both defined by Austin in terms of the existence of a commanding political superior that was independent from any other source of authority. This was the same conception of sovereignty held by many political scientists such as Burgess. The state, in which rested the unlimited exercise of sovereignty, possessed the ultimate power to issue and enforce laws within its own territorial jurisdiction. For Austin, although not for all of the early political scientists, state and sovereignty were completely interchangeable, though both were distinct from government. It was recognized that a power existed that could issue commands to a body of subjects and bring physical force to bear to ensure that the command was obeyed. This was, according to Austin, the essential characteristic of positive law—a command of a superior bearing the character of sovereignty. When Austin and those who adhered to the analytical school of jurisprudence focused their attention on the external relations among states, they were led to reject the claim that international law was in fact law. For it was obvious that there was no superior sovereign authority above the individual states that could issue commands to inferior subjects and enforce compliance by inflicting the ultimate sanction of force. Austin, therefore, concluded that the agreements and rules occasionally observed by sovereign states were nothing more than a form of morality. Austin declared that "since no supreme government is in a state of subjection to another, an imperative law set by a sovereign to a sovereign is not set by its author in the character of political superior." As a result, he concluded that "an imperative law set by a sovereign to a sovereign is not a positive law or a law strictly so called."[63]

The rigid and precise quality of the Austinian definition of law was widely acknowledged by political scientists and international lawyers of this period. At the same time, however, Austin's conception of law increasingly came under pointed attack. The critique of the Austinian view of law arose from a new wave of American and British publicists who would precipitate a fundamental transformation within the discourse of international law shortly after the turn of the century. The fully developed contours of this conversation will be detailed in the next chapter, but for now it is appropriate to indicate the grounds on which the Austinian position on international law would be debated. As John Bassett Moore, holder of the prestigious Hamilton Fish Chair of International Law and Diplomacy at Columbia University from 1893–1924, stated the matter, "so long as a large proportion of our law students are indoctrinated with the Austinian theory, which excludes from the sphere of law everything but a certain variety of municipal law, a refutation of that theory will not be out of place."[64]

There were several different arguments that international lawyers advanced in order to counter Austin's definition of law. One argument was that Austin took his conception of law from municipal law and misapplied it to all other realms of law, including international law. Francis Boyle has argued that this particular critique of Austin resembles the contemporary level-of-analysis problem posed by David Singer and Kenneth Waltz.[65] The reasoning behind this critique was that while municipal law was statutory and applicable to persons within the state, international law was based on custom and directed toward other sovereign states. An increasing number of international lawyers argued that since the two realms of municipal and international law were so fundamentally different, a serious analytical error was being committed on the part of Austin and his followers when the standard from one realm of law was being improperly applied to another.

In many ways, the critique of Austin was equally as damaging when attention was directed toward the historical and philological basis of his conception of law. For here, the focus turned to the internal deficiencies of Austin's understanding of law, even within the context of municipal law. Critics went so far as to suggest that Austin misconceived the true nature of law. The school of historical jurisprudence, which was inspired by the work of Sir Henry Maine, claimed to have demonstrated that the original foundation of law resided in habitual customs, not authoritative commands backed by physical force.[66] This was indeed a potentially profound discovery that buttressed the claim of those who insisted that international law was in fact a branch of law. For one of the core deficiencies that critics of international law pointed to was the lack of an external sanction that could be used to enforce compliance. In support of this claim, skeptics of international law were apt to refer to Thomas Hobbes's dictum that "where there is no common Power, there is no Law: where no Law, no injustice."[67] Therefore, if it could be shown that the fundamental attribute of law depended less on the existence of a superior authority possessing power to issue physical sanctions, and more on common convention and usage, then one of the main props used to refute the legality of international law would be undermined. The legal positivists argued that the real sanction behind both municipal and international law resided in the power of public opinion.

International relations scholars assigned an important role to public opinion for reforming the international milieu. The significance of the sanction of public opinion was that it provided a more empirical foundation on which to establish an actual science of international law. Those adhering to the international legal positivist paradigm would greatly accentuate the role of public opinion, and this will be discussed in the next chapter. For now, it is sufficient to indicate the direction that international law, once freed from the idea that it was based on a priori laws of nature, would take in the beginning of the twentieth century. The recognition that it was public opinion that bound a state to an international agreement greatly helped to establish the voluntary basis of international law which, in turn, necessitated that additional work be completed to ensure its efficacy. Perhaps the most important item on the agenda entailed clarifying the customs and norms that were believed to represent the foundation of existing international law. From the attempt to verify the customs that bound states, no matter how imperfectly, to international agreements came the impetus to codify the body of existing laws and agreements made between states. It is instructive to make reference to the contribution that Moore provided to the United States government in fulfilling this task. In 1898, Moore published his six volume *History and Digest of the International Arbitrations to Which the United States Has Been a Party* for the House Committee on Foreign Relations. By an act of the United States Congress in February 1897, a "provision was made for revising, reindexing, and otherwise completing and perfecting by the aid of such documents as may be useful, the second edition of the Digest of the International Law of the United States."[68] Moore, who was third assistant secretary in the State Department from 1886 to 1891, had assisted Francis Wharton in compiling the first edition, and was asked to undertake the writing of the second, revised edition. This undertaking, along with his other published works and public service, gained him the reputation as one of the foremost authorities on international law, and "for many years the study of international relations was synonymous with the name of John Bassett Moore."[69]

In addition to the task of codifying the corpus of existing international law, there was also a renewed interest in establishing international arbitration as the means of adjudicating international disputes. The impetus behind this undertaking was strengthened by the numerous international conferences arising across the globe and culminating with the call for a Permanent Court of Arbitration to be created at the Hague Peace Conferences in 1899 and 1907. The conferences at the Hague would provoke a strong interest among students of international relations. At a minimum, many scholars suggested that the Hague Conferences confirmed that the divide between the academic study of international relations and events occurring within the realm of world politics was narrowing.

Yet it would be wrong to conclude that the academic discourse about international relations was a monologue spoken only by international lawyers. There were others who did not submit to the idea that international law could lead to the pacification of international relations. Perhaps the most infamous was Heinrich von Treitschke. While it would be difficult to argue that Treitschke exerted as much influence on American political scientists as Lieber and Bluntschli, his ideas were, nevertheless, well known. Both Adams and Burgess studied under Treitschke during their graduate study in Germany. It was on the basis of his theoretical conception of the state that Treitschke rejected international law as a foundation for regulating the external behavior of states. The glorification of the idealized Hegelian form of state, as "the objectively revealed will of God," strong and unified in all its actions, was the image of the state that Treitschke delineated in his writings. The primary justification that Treitschke provided for the necessity of a strong and unified state emanated less from a consideration of internal domestic factors than from his view of the external factors shaping relations among states. In this respect, he differed from many of the other theorists of the state discussed in this chapter. Treitschke conceived of the international milieu as a pure Nietzschean struggle for power. He argued that "the State is power, precisely in order to assert itself as against other equally independent powers."[70] War was viewed as a contest that separated the strong from the weak. War between sovereign powers, according to Treitschke, was purposeful in that it was through war that states were created and civilization advanced.

Because Treitschke looked favorably upon the activity of sovereign states exerting their will against neighboring states, it was quite logical for him to reject the idea of a world state. When Treitschke turned his attention to international law, he found it very tenuous and certainly not a sufficient substitute for the perennial game of power politics. He recognized that all agreements between sovereigns, legal or otherwise, were of a voluntary and temporary nature. This recognition was a direct manifestation of his uncompromising view of the state as the embodiment of unlimited power and authority. According to Treitschke, it was "clear that the international agreements which limit the power of a State are not absolute, but voluntary self-restrictions," and thus "the existence of international law must always be precarious, and it cannot cease to be a *lex imperfecta,* because no power higher than the States themselves can be called upon to arbitrate."[71]

Treitschke's views are interesting for at least two reasons. First, they are not an exception to the general theme advanced in this chapter concerning the intimate connection that existed between the internal and external theoretical discussion of the state. Treitschke's ideas regarding international relations and international law only make sense when viewed within the framework of his theory of the state. Secondly, Treitschke's account of international law serves to illustrate one of the major disjunctures that existed within the study of international law, a disjuncture that provided the space for the incipient discourse of international relations. In much the same way that Treitschke delineated the limitations of international law in its application to the activities of the "Great Powers," most, if not all, of the international lawyers and theorists of the state argued that there were limitations in the domain to which the subject of international law was applicable. More specifically, the discourse reveals that international law was only applicable to the "civilized" or "Christian" states as opposed to the "barbarian" or "savage" states. While such terminology is unacceptable by today's intellectual standards, the more important issue concerns the significance of this common binary classification for the study of international relations.

National Imperialism

Maintaining that international law was only suitable to the relations among a select handful of "civilized" states that had reached a certain level of political development meant that a rather large grouping of other territories were left out of the discussion. Yet, these "other" entities did find themselves as objects of analysis in the study of national imperialism and colonialism. But here again, the discussion of national imperialism took place within the framework established by the discourse of the state. This was because one of the predominant explanations that political scientists provided for the latest wave of nineteenth-century imperialism was informed by the Teutonic theory of the state. The views that Burgess held with respect to the relationship between the Teutonic forms of state and "inferior" forms of political organization provide an interesting illustration of this sort of explanation of imperialism.

Burgess was convinced that the Teutonic form of the state represented the apogee of human history and civilization. All other forms of political organization were deemed to be of inferior character, and he insisted that the Teutonic states had an obligation to uplift the "dark places of the earth." Burgess confidently proclaimed that the "American Indians, Asiatics and Africans have no element of political civilization to contribute" and, therefore, "can only receive, learn, follow Aryan example."[72] In describing how his principal work, *Political Science and Comparative Constitutional Law,* represented "the Teutonic nations—the English, French, Lombards, Scandinavians, Germans and North Americans—as the great modern nation builders," Burgess insisted that this justified "the temporary imposition of Teutonic order on unorganized, disorganized, or savage people for the sake of their own civilization and their incorporation in the world of society."[73] In other words, the colonial system propagated by the Teutonic states was, according to Burgess, completely justifiable.

This perspective was typical of an age in which it was not uncommon for a scholar to announce his or her position as that of an imperialist when writing a journal article or reviewing a book. Subsequent to the Spanish-American War of 1898, there was a flood of literature that addressed the issue of imperialism in general and the United States policy toward the Caribbean and Far East in particular. The field of diplomatic history, which had characteristically offered a narrative counterpart to current events, focused on the new imperialistic path of

American foreign policy. However, the distinction between diplomatic history and commentary on current events was often difficult to discern. Many of the early volumes of *Political Science Quarterly* contained articles that dealt with events impinging upon American foreign policy interests. For example, prior to the war with Spain in 1898, the *Quarterly* published several articles on the Monroe Doctrine in an effort to avert hostilities with Great Britain emanating from the Venezuelan dispute.[74] Following the war with Spain, however, a distinct conversation and body of literature began to appear that dealt with the character and consequences of late-nineteenth-century imperialism and colonial administration. It was a discourse most clearly elaborated by a Wisconsin political scientist named Paul S. Reinsch.

Reinsch's course listing at the University of Wisconsin for the 1899–1900 academic year was entitled "Contemporary Politics." This was the first course dealing specifically with the subject matter of world politics to appear anywhere in the United States.[75] Similarly, Reinsch's *World Politics at the End of the Nineteenth Century, as Influenced by the Oriental Situation* (1900) was the first work to investigate directly the subject matter implied by the title "world politics." Disciplinary historians Olson and Groom note that "the first glimmerings of international relations as a discipline had appeared with the publication of Reinsch's *World Politics*."[76] Reinsch was born on June 10, 1869, in Milwaukee, Wisconsin, to parents of German descent.[77] Reinsch attended the University of Wisconsin where his education consisted of a broad liberal arts curriculum culminating in a discovery of history and the social sciences during his senior year. After graduating in 1892, and unable to fulfill his dream of graduate study in Germany due to a lack of financial resources, Reinsch decided to attend law school at Wisconsin. He graduated from law school in 1884 and was admitted to the Wisconsin bar, and began his law practice in Milwaukee.

In the interim, important institutional developments were unfolding at the University of Wisconsin that would have a momentous impact on both Reinsch and the emerging social sciences. The institutional event was the founding of the School of Economics, Political Science, and History by Richard Ely in 1892. The intellectual environment created by Ely and other renowned faculty that included Frederick Jackson Turner, along with Reinsch's disillusionment with his law career, convinced him to return to university life at Wisconsin. After being offered a position as instructor in the Department of History, in the fall of 1895, Reinsch returned to Madison and enrolled as a Ph.D. candidate in history and political science. Having already taken American History courses with Turner as an undergraduate, Reinsch selected him to be his mentor and dissertation advisor. It was from Turner that Reinsch acquired his initial interest in the events shaping international relations. And it was this interest that increasingly led Reinsch to identify with the emerging discipline of political science.

After completing his dissertation, which was entitled *English Common Law in the Early American Colonies,* and receiving his doctorate in June 1898, Reinsch embarked on his long delayed sojourn to Europe. It was during his year abroad, attending lectures in Bonn, Leipzig, Berlin, Rome, and Paris, that his manuscript on the revival of imperialism within the context of the late-nineteenth-century scramble for the Far East was written. Having produced a manuscript that Ely and the other members of the Wisconsin faculty deemed worthy of publication enabled Reinsch to secure a newly created full-time position as assistant professor of political science at Wisconsin in 1899. This marked the beginning of an illustrious career in political science, a discipline that Reinsch would do much to help establish in the United States.

Reinsch stated that his intention in writing *World Politics* was "to gather into a harmonious picture the multitude of facts and considerations that go to make up the international politics at the present time."[78] The bulk of the book was devoted to the "Chinese question," which Reinsch claimed represented "the true center of interest in present international politics." One of the reviews of *World Politics* suggested that, by dint of poor indexing and other sundry editorial problems, the book probably was published prematurely to take advantage of the interest that had arisen over the competition for the Orient.[79] While the specific focus on the activities taking place in China was evident throughout the book, Reinsch also devoted attention to German imperial politics, and provided an analysis of some of the issues confronting the United States in the wake of becoming an expansionist power following the Spanish-American War. More importantly, Reinsch began the book with a broad overview of the major economic, political, and intellectual forces that currently were influencing modern international politics. Here, it is crucial to note that the account that Reinsch provided was informed both by the theoretical discourse of the state and by an empirical assessment of the underlying forces currently shaping world politics. It was within the framework of this discussion that one of the early substantive components of the discourse of international relations can be discerned. There was for the first time, at least within the emerging discipline of political science, an autonomous discourse specifically focused on the issues and concerns arising from the political and economic interactions of states.

Reinsch, not unlike Lieber and Burgess, described the end of the nineteenth century as the age of nationalism. In fact, Reinsch believed that ever since the lingering aspiration for a universal world order had been disposed of during the Renaissance, the existence of independent nation-states striving to attain and assert their own national identities in an environment consisting of actors with similar goals had become the most prevalent characteristic of world politics. The image of international relations as a competitive power struggle in which nations strove to achieve an independent national existence was, according to Reinsch, laudable. Reinsch claimed that the power struggle among nations contributed to a dynamism in international politics that would otherwise be expunged "from the dead uniformity of a world empire."[80] The competition and rivalry that characterized politics among nations produced a vitality that Reinsch believed was beneficial to the further development of each of the separate nation-states. The content of the first chapter of *World Politics* makes it quite apparent that he had a keen awareness of the role of power in international politics. Reinsch's focus on power has led Olson and Groom to note that "his work suggests that the discipline of international relations had its real beginnings in studies of imperialism, not in world order, as has so often been suggested."[81] I draw attention to this point because one of the common myths regarding the early history of the field of international relations is that there was an absence of any recognition of the role of power.

Yet Reinsch did not exalt the Nietzschean struggle for power as the only virtuous element of international political life. He gave ample consideration to the role of international law, arbitration procedures, peace conferences, and other schemes, short of those that attempted to establish a world unity, that sought to mitigate the excesses of the power struggle in international relations. In fact, in many ways, *World Politics* aimed at drawing notice to the excessive character of the struggle for power at the end of nineteenth century. Reinsch explained that this recent phenomenon was manifest in the transition from nationalism to national imperialism—the central focus of the discussion of the Chinese question. National imperialism, according to Reinsch, represented both a qualitative and quantitative change in the development of nationalism; it signified an accelerated and exaggerated desire on the part of European states "to control as large a portion of the earth's surface as their energy and opportunities will permit." He defined the concept of national imperialism as the endeavor "to increase the resources of the national state through the absorption or exploitation of undeveloped regions and inferior races, but does not attempt to impose political control upon highly civilized nations."[82] He explained that just as Machiavelli had become the spokesman for the earlier-nineteenth-century phase of nationalism, so "Machiavellian thought and Machiavellian means" had once again become "characteristic of political action."[83]

Reinsch noted one particularly ironic consequence that could arise from the policy of national imperialism. While the policy was characterized by a heightened sense of nationalism, with countries seeking to extend their reign over the "backward" areas of the world, Reinsch argued that this unfettered competition was rekindling dreams of world empire that entailed dissolving the individual national polities. He suggested that one way to circumvent this danger was to "constantly emphasize the thought that there is sufficient work for all nations in developing and civilizing primitive regions."[84] It is important not to misconstrue the position that Reinsch held toward the practice of national imperialism that he spent much of his life studying. While he explicitly rejected national imperialism on the grounds that it greatly jeopardized world peace, unjustly established colonial rule over indigenous populations, and tended to undermine efforts at internal domestic reform by diverting attention to external crusades, he was, nevertheless, an avowed expansionist who often couched his justification in terms of "the white man's burden." To understand the manner in which Reinsch reconciled these potentially conflicting points of view, it is necessary to turn briefly to the principal motivations that he argued were behind the policy of national imperialism.

Although Reinsch gave some credence to sentimental motivations for increasing national prestige by extending the flag to distant lands, he argued that the most fundamental factor prompting states to expand was economic. Reinsch subscribed to the theory that capitalist development had reached a stage requiring that foreign outlets be found to absorb the surplus goods being produced within the more economically and politically developed nations. This explanation was, in some ways, an extension of the "frontier thesis" offered by Reinsch's mentor and noted historian Frederick Jackson Turner.[85] In Reinsch's second book, *Colonial Government* (1902), he wrote, "to-day the primary object is the search for markets, and the chief purpose of commercial expansion has come to be the desire to dispose of the surplus product of European industry."[86] This was a somewhat commonly accepted explanation, shared by both non-Marxists and Marxists alike, for the impetus behind the latest wave of imperialism. Perhaps the most famous analysis along economic lines, besides Vladimir I. Lenin's *Imperialism: The Highest Stage of Capitalism* (1917), was John Hobson's *Imperialism: A Study* (1902), which Reinsch reviewed in *Political Science Quarterly*.[87] While Hobson argued that it was primarily economic motives that were encouraging states such as Great Britain to extend political control over the tropical areas, his explicit anti-imperialist stance rested on the conviction that such behavior was based on faulty economic reasoning. Hobson argued that domestic social reform aimed at achieving a more equitable distribution of wealth would do away with the alleged necessity for capitalists to seek foreign markets, because the home market was both inherently more profitable and "capable of indefinite expansion."[88] Although Reinsch questioned "whether better social service could be obtained by distinctly improving the income of the working classes than by using the capital for the acquisition of tropical products," he concluded his review of Hobson's work by stating that "everything that the author has said should be considered in an attempt to establish a true civilizing policy of colonial administration."[89]

Before turning to the recommendations that Reinsch offered for a more enlightened policy of national commercial expansion, it is important to note a crucial difference between the theories being espoused by academic scholars such as Reinsch and the Marxist ideas that would never be able to gain a strong foothold in what Stanley Hoffmann has termed the "American science of international relations." This distinction turns on the premise, most forcefully enunciated by Lenin, that imperialism, far from being a chosen policy, represented a special stage in the development of capitalism. According to Lenin "imperialism is capitalism in that stage of development in which the dominance of monopolies and finance capital has established itself."[90] Thus, reformist-based proposals advocating ameliorative solutions to the policy of imperialism were generally regarded as less than sincere by Marxist theorists.

By contrast, according to Reinsch and Hobson, the purpose of engaging in the analysis of national imperialism was to reveal some of the negative and illogical consequences of the policy of imperialism so as to pave the way for some type of domestic-international reform. One of the reasons why Reinsch devoted specific attention to the Chinese question stemmed from his belief that the imperialist partition of China represented an unnecessary danger to world peace. Since Reinsch felt that economic expansion was necessary, he sought to find the means whereby this could be made compatible with peaceful intercourse among states. The goal, according to Reinsch, was to reduce the rivalry and tension among the expansionist powers by fostering a more rational policy whereby the riches that lay undeveloped in China, Africa, and the Caribbean could be systematically developed and enjoyed by all. For Reinsch, this included the people living in the less-developed areas, and he insisted that we "recognize that it is a serious and sad duty which the white race is performing in making way for its own further expansion."[91] He acknowledged that there often was an intimate relationship between colonialism and imperialism, but he urged that the United States and other powers be wary of establishing formal political control over the "backward regions," especially since modern expansion was primarily economic rather than political. Because Reinsch generally disapproved of colonial rule on political and moral grounds, he argued that the extension of sovereignty through outright colonial land-grabbing, or through the newest policy of creating spheres of influence, represented faulty reasoning and was a significant threat to world peace. More beneficial results could be obtained by channeling the economic competition from an exclusionary colonial format to one in which benefits accrued from open competition could be distributed in an essentially positive-sum manner. The less exclusionary and more open the competition, Reinsch believed, the more prosperous and stable the world would be.

After the American Political Science Association was formed in 1903, Reinsch continued to be concerned with the issues of national imperialism and colonial administration as well as with the further development of political science. In many ways, Reinsch must be considered one of the founding figures of the field of international relations. The study of colonial administration was an integral part of the early discourse of political science as well as the subject matter of the incipient field of international relations, and Chapter 4 examines this conversation in a more systematic fashion. This examination will leave little doubt about the importance of Reinsch to the development of international relations as an academic field of study.

Conclusion

Apart from Reinsch's work, a discrete discourse devoted exclusively to international relations did not really exist. This absence was largely the result of the fact that the theoretical discourse of the state encompassed both an internal and external examination of sovereignty. As political scientists increasingly came to identify the state as the proper domain of the discipline, discussion proceeded to address this entity in all of its various dimensions. The theoretical discourse of the state was the fundamental context in which the study of politics in the United States took shape throughout the mid- to late nineteenth century, and the discussion of international politics and international law occurred primarily within this discursive sphere.

It is necessary to take cognizance of the relationship that has been depicted in this chapter between the theory of the state and the study of international relations. The relationship between both the subject matter and the fields of political theory and international relations will be a theme that will be developed throughout this study. At this point in the narrative, I have indicated how the theory of the state structured the discourse of political science. Most of the early influential political scientists, such as Lieber, Woolsey, and Burgess, examined both the internal and external dimensions of the state. By and large, the external focus was directed to the subject matter of international law. Yet their examination of international politics in general, and international law in particular, was informed by the theory of the state. The ontology of international relations, the character of international law, the possibility of a world state, the extent to which there was international organization and cooperation among states were all determined with respect to the theory of the state. In this manner, the theory of the state that was being discussed and refined by political scientists exerted a substantial influence upon how scholars understood and analyzed international relations. The next chapter discusses this relationship in greater detail.

3

State, Sovereignty, and International Law

Authors and Works Discussed

Author	1895	1900	1905	1910	1915
Beard			(1908)		
Bryce			(1909)		
Butler				(1912)	
Gettell				(1910)(1914)	
Goodnow		(1904)			
Hill	(1896)		(1907)	(1911)	
Hull			(1908)		
Lansing			(1907)		
Leacock			(1906)		
Mahan				(1912)	
Moore	(1898)				(1915)
Oppenheim			(1908)		
Reinsch			(1907)	(1911)	
Root			(1908)		
Scott			(1907)(1909)		
Snow				(1913)	
Willoughby	(1896)	(1904)			(1918)

Charles Beard 1874–1948
"A Lecture Delivered at Columbia University" [1908]

James Bryce 1838–1922
"The Relations of Political Science To History and To Practice" *APSR* [1909]

Nicholas Murray Butler 1862–1947
The International Mind [1912]

Raymond Garfield Gettell 1881–1949
Introduction to Political Science [1910]
"Nature and Scope of Present Political Theory" *Proceedings* [1914]

Frank J. Goodnow 1859–1939
"The Work of the American Political Science Association" *Proceedings* [1904]

David Jayne Hill 1850–1932
"International Justice" *Yale Law Review* [1896]
"The Second Peace Conference at the Hague" *AJIL* [1907]
World Organization as Affected by the Nature of the Modern State [1911]

William I. Hull 1868–1939
The Two Hague Conferences and their Contributions to International Law [1908]

Robert Lansing 1864–1928
"Notes on Sovereignty in a State" *AJIL* [1907]

Stephen Leacock 1869–1944
Elements of Political Science [1906]

Alfred Thayer Mahan 1840–1914
Armaments and Arbitration [1912]

John Bassett Moore 1860–1947
History and Digest of International Arbitration [1898]
"Law and Organization" *APSR* [1915]

Lassa Francis Oppenheim 1858–1919
"The Science of International Law: Its Task and Method" *AJIL* [1908]

Paul S. Reinsch 1869–1923
"International Unions and their Administration" *AJIL* [1907]
Public International Unions Their Work and Organization [1911]

Elihu Root 1845–1937
"The Sanction of International Law" *AJIL* [1908]

James Brown Scott 1866–1943
"The Legal Nature of International Law" *AJIL* [1907]
The Hague Peace Conferences of 1899 and 1907 [1909]

Alpheus Henry Snow 1859–1920
"International Law and Political Science" *AJIL* [1913]

Westel Woodbury Willoughby 1867–1945
An Examination of the Nature of the State [1896]
"The American Political Science Association" *PSQ* [1904]
"The Juristic Conception of the State" *APSR* [1918]

The formation of the American Political Science Association on December 30, 1903, was an influential event in the history of academic international relations. With the creation of the APSA as a professional learned society, institutionally distinct from the American Historical Association (founded in 1884) and the American Economic Association (founded in 1885), the discipline that has provided the primary context of the American study of international relations officially came into existence. Westel Woodbury Willoughby, who played an active role in the movement to create the Association and later served as its ninth president, declared that "the successful establishment of this Association is undoubtedly the most important event that has occurred in the history of the scientific study of matters political in this country."[1] This chapter reconstructs the early-twentieth-century discourse of international relations as it became institutionalized in the context of the development of political science and particularly the theory of the state.

As evidenced by the address of the APSA's first president, Frank J. Goodnow, the study of political science in the early 1900s was basically synonymous with the study of the state. In this respect, there was a fundamental continuity with the preceding discourse that Lieber, Woolsey, and Burgess had initiated. This chapter reconstructs the conversation that political scientists were carrying on about the state from the time the APSA was formed until the outbreak of World War I. In reconstructing the central features of the discourse of the state, attention will be directed toward describing the influence that this conversation had on the study of international relations. The concept of sovereignty was the crucial link that joined these two discussions together. In order to illustrate the manner in which the conversation about sovereignty provided the context for discussing issues relevant to international relations, the chapter begins by explicating the orthodox juristic theory of the state. The writings of Willoughby, Raymond Garfield Gettell, and David Jayne Hill are examined to disclose the internal and external dimensions of the juristic view of sovereignty. This conception of sovereignty depicted the state as an expression of supreme authority over a territorially defined political community. When this view of sovereignty was logically extended to the international realm, the picture that emerged was one of equal, independent, and isolated states existing in an environment where there was no overarching central authority present.

In describing the international milieu as characterized by anarchy, in the sense of no supreme authority, proponents of juristic theory were pessimistic about the prospect of international law as well as a variety of other schemes of international organization to remedy the existing structure of international politics. From the perspective of juristic theory, states occupied a position similar to that of individuals living in a state of nature. It was partly upon this presumption that adherents of the juristic theory of the state denied that international law embodied the true characteristics of law. By refusing to concede legal status to international law and by rejecting all world order proposals that infringed upon the sovereignty of the state, juristic theory had profound consequences for the study of international relations.

After explicating some of these consequences, the following three sections investigate the diverse criticisms that were advanced against the juristic theory of the state and the particular interpretation of international politics that the theory informed. First, the arguments that were put forth by what other disciplinary historians have termed the political science "realists" are outlined. The critique offered by realists such as Arthur Bentley, Charles Beard, and James Bryce, which in many ways foreshadowed the scathing attack on the state that would take place after World War I, rested on their conviction that juristic theory was historically flawed and incongruous with existing political conditions. They rejected the speculative and metaphysical treatment of the state in favor of an approach based on empirical fact.

Next, a detailed account is provided of the discursive transformation that occurred with respect to the subject matter of international law, with particular emphasis placed on the group of scholars that sought to develop a legal positivist paradigm for international law. The impetus for this development was to counter the claim advanced by John Austin and propagated by his contemporary protégés that international law lacked the essential characteristics of law. Those who supported the view that international law was in fact law embraced the arguments of the realists and declared that juristic theory failed to comprehend the actual empirical attributes of both domestic and international law. In this manner, there was an overlap between the internal and external critique of the juristic theory of state sovereignty. In the effort to vouchsafe the legal character of international law, a revised ontological understanding of the international milieu began to surface. It was not so much that international lawyers dismissed the claim that the international realm was characterized by the existence of anarchy as that they rejected many of the consequences that juristic theory attributed to politics in the absence of central authority.

Finally, the last section examines some of the proposals that were made by political scientists and others for world order reform. In the course of discussing these reforms, international relations scholars put forth an alternative description of international politics that was quite different than what juristic theory depicted. The most important revision was the claim that interdependence rather than independence had become the prevailing feature of international politics. This episode of conceptual change made it possible for scholars to focus attention on what was described as a world federation or society of states and to envision ways of reforming international anarchy.

The Formation of APSA

Reinsch declared that "the purpose of the American Political Science Association is to promote the scientific study of the great problems of Political Science."[2] By the early 1900s, he had emerged as one of America's foremost political scientists, and in recognition of this fact, he was appointed as one of the fifteen members of a committee headed by Jeremiah Jenks that was assigned to canvass the degree of support for forming an independent political science association. The Jenks' Committee was created in December 30, 1902, after a plan to establish an American Society for Comparative Legislation was aborted on grounds of being too restricted in scope. Reinsch reported that "the opinion was expressed that the proposed society should not confine its efforts to the field of comparative legislation, but should include within its sphere the subjects of politics, jurisprudence, administration, diplomacy, and the other departments which properly belong to the general subject of Political Science."[3] Sufficient interest to create a political science association led the Jenks' Committee to issue an official announcement for an organizational meeting to take place on December 30, 1903, at New Orleans in conjunction with the AHA and AEA meetings.

According to the constitution that was drawn at New Orleans, the object of the APSA was "the encouragement of the scientific study of Politics, Public Law, Administration and Diplomacy." The constitution proclaimed that "the Association as such will not assume a partisan position upon any question of practical politics, nor commit its members to any position thereupon."[4] To carry out the work of the Association, seven sections, which can be considered as the equivalent to subfields, were created, and a committee headed by a chairperson was chosen for each section. The following seven sections were established: comparative legislation, comparative jurisprudence, international law and diplomacy, administration, constitutional law, political theory, and politics. With respect to the question of where the subject matter of international relations was located, the most obvious answer was in the international law and diplomacy section. Woolsey served as the first chairman of this section and J.H. Latane, John Bassett Moore, and George Grafton Wilson comprised the rest of the committee.

Less obvious, however, was the "Politics" section that was chaired by Reinsch. It appears as if this section was intended by design to be an amorphous category lacking a determinate focus. Yet by appointing Reinsch, who was one of the leading experts on colonial affairs, to serve as the chair, some direction was inevitably given to what issues the Politics section would entertain. A review of the panel topics from the early annual meetings of the APSA and the publication of many of these papers in the Association's official journal, *Proceedings of the American Political Science Association,* reveals that topics relating to the general study of colonial administration formed the nucleus of this section. The conversation concerning colonial administration is the focus of the next chapter, but at this point we can say that the issues associated with the Politics section were at the core of the early history of the field of international relations.

The formation of the APSA greatly helped to establish political science as a professionally autonomous discipline within the growing higher education system in the United States. Yet for many scholars who were not members of the APSA, and even for the original two hundred and fourteen members, the exact composition and boundaries of this new science of politics were ambiguous. The presidential address of the APSA's first president, Frank J. Goodnow, did, however, attempt to provide a description of the domain of political science. Goodnow resisted the temptation to provide an answer to the question, what is political science, by insisting that "an attempt at definition is dangerous" and not "sufficiently fruitful of practical results to justify the expenditure of thought and time necessary to secure the desired end."[5] Instead, Goodnow decided to enumerate those subjects that were not presently covered by other learned societies that "should be chosen as the field of the APSA." That subject, most fundamentally, was the study of the state. Goodnow acknowledged that other professional associations, such as the AHA and AEA, dealt with the state, but only in an indirect and incidental manner. He was confident that it could "be safely said that there was not, until the formation of the American Political Science Association, any association in this country which endeavored to assemble on a common ground those persons whose main interests were connected with the scientific study of the organization and functions of the State."[6]

Notwithstanding Goodnow's aversion to definition, he claimed that "Political Science is that science which treats of the organization known as the State." Therefore, political science, according to Goodnow, should concern itself with "the various operations necessary to the realization of the State will."[7] To carry out this aim, Goodnow closely followed the tripartite characterization of political science put forth by his teacher, John Burgess, and divided the subject of the State, and thus political science, into three distinct parts: the expression of the State will, the content of the State will as expressed, and the execution of the State will. The expression of the State will included the study of political theory and constitutional law; the content of the State will encompassed the study of comparative legislation, comparative jurisprudence, private and public law; and the execution of the State will fell under Goodnow's particular area of expertise, administration. It is interesting to note that nowhere in Goodnow's trichotomous division of political science was direct reference made to the study of international relations. This can be explained by the fact that the theoretical discourse of the state was, as noted earlier, an all-encompassing discourse. Political scientists, such as Goodnow, did not deem it necessary to make a distinction between the internal and external dimension of the state.

The Discourse of the State

Several textbooks published shortly after the creation of the APSA reveal that the state was the proper domain and subject of political science and that, both theoretically and institutionally, international relations belonged within political science. Stephen Leacock's text, *Elements of Political Science* (1906), explained that political science "deals with the state; it is, in short, as it is often termed, the 'theory of the state.'"[8] According to Leacock, the state, in the technical language of political science, embodied four physical features: territory, population, unity, and organization. These physical attributes, Leacock claimed, coincided with the state in its present national guise. The national state was viewed by many political scientists as the embodiment of a perfect form of political organization. Willoughby maintained that the focus on the state as an expression of supreme authority defined the very essence of political science. He claimed that "political science has to deal with all that directly concerns political society, that is to say, with societies of men effectively organized under a supreme authority for the maintenance of an orderly and progressive existence."[9] The significance that Willoughby and others placed on the state as representing the highest form of supreme political authority helps to explain why the issue of sovereignty engaged so much of the theoretical discourse about the state. Raymond Garfield Gettell's text, *Introduction to Political Science* (1910), acknowledged the same four physical elements of the state that Leacock's text laid out, but he argued that the "real essence of the state is found to be sovereignty; i.e., absolute authority internally and absolute independence externally."[10]

Notwithstanding the unorthodox position that Gettell advanced about political science being a subdivision of sociology, his text affirmed that political science was the science of the state. In proclaiming that political science was predominantly about the study of the state, and that sovereignty was the distinctive characteristic of the state, Gettell claimed that there were logical divisions in the subject matter. According to Gettell, the concept of sovereignty provided the logical division: "sovereignty, viewed from its internal aspect, opens up the relations of state to individual; viewed from its external aspect, it leads to a discussion of international relations and the rules of international law."[11] Leacock attempted to bring attention to the point that political science should not limit its focus to the internal organization of the state by suggesting that the discipline also take account of the external relations among states. But from a theoretical point of view, i.e., from the vantage point of sovereignty, he argued that the latter activity was a circumscribed exercise. This was because when sovereignty was examined from an external perspective, there were merely *relations* with other independent sovereign authorities. Leacock articulated the theoretical limitations of the concept of sovereignty for examining the external relations of states and, in doing so, outlined one of the main props of the political discourse of anarchy. Leacock explained that

> Viewed in a purely theoretical light, every state is an absolutely independent unit. Its sovereignty is unlimited, and it renders political obedience to no outside authority; it has no organized coercive relation with any other political body. Such theoretical isolation is the prime condition of its existence as a state, and its political independence is one of its essential attributes. This is what Hobbes meant in saying that, in regard to one another, separate states are to be viewed as in a "state of nature."[12]

The notion that the external relations of states were, in some sense, analogous to the conditions that classic political theorists had described of individuals living in a state of nature would exert a significant influence on the subsequent development of the study of international relations. This would be equally true both for those who accepted and those who rejected this particular version of the domestic analogy.[13] Leacock, for instance, claimed that while the above description was true in a "purely formal and legal sense," the actual practice of international relations was at the same time becoming characterized by increasing ties of mutual interdependence. In this manner, and unbeknownst to Leacock, he was outlining the basic terms of debate between the poles of *independence* and *interdependence* that continues to exert a powerful influence on the discourse of international relations. Leacock believed that in numerous ways, such as through trade, commerce, common interests in thought, art, and literature, the frequency of contacts among the peoples and states of the world was on the increase. He argued that interdependence had important implications for both the study and practice of international politics. For one thing, Leacock argued that growing interdependence could lead to a questioning of the durability of existing political arrangements, which might, in turn, precipitate a search for an alternative arrangement. An international form of collective governance, a world state, and a federation of states all became popularly discussed options between the end of the nineteenth century and the outbreak of World War I. The discussion of these alternative arrangements, it should be noted, was not limited to political scientists but encompassed public intellectuals, clergy, pacifists, and a wide range of other individuals. The manner in which these alternative forms of political organization were evaluated by political scientists, however, can only be understood within the context of the theoretical discourse of the state.

Gettell, in a paper that he delivered to the APSA's annual meeting in 1914, provided a lucid description of the relationship that existed between the theoretical discourse of the state and the study of international relations. The primary aim of his paper was to enunciate the nature and scope of present political theory. But in following the established orthodoxy of affirming that political theory was the theory of the state, Gettell was inevitably led to consider the "external phases of state existence and activity."[14] This was especially the case, since he believed that the modern state was expanding its functions both domestically and internationally.

Gettell suggested that political theory consisted of three fairly distinct but related elements. The first element was comprised of the traditional study of historical political theory which was concerned with the evolution of the state. The second element consisted of analytical or descriptive political theory that dealt with the present, and consisted "of philosophical concepts concerning the nature of the state, its essential attributes, and the meaning and justification of its authority." Gettell argued that descriptive political theory should not be restricted to a focus on the internal characteristics of the state but also include questions dealing with the relations between states. He claimed that although modern political theory viewed the state as "the outward organized manifestation of conscious spirit of political unity," and as a legal person that was "internally supreme and externally independent and equal," the actual operation of the state differed in some fundamental respects.[15] Gettell noted, for example, that the theory of the legal equality of states was contradicted by the existence of states that were vastly different in size, strength, and wealth. He also argued that the internal exercise of state sovereignty was often modified by a number of external political factors. The point that Gettell wanted to emphasize was that there needed to be a closer correspondence between theory and practice so that political theory could rest more securely on an empirical inductive foundation.

The final element of political theory was applied political theory, which dealt "with the immediate present and future" and consisted "of principles and ideals concerning the proper purpose and functions of the state." It was with this element that the relationship between the theoretical discourse of the state and the study of international relations was most clearly elaborated. Gettell argued that any consideration of the proper purpose or end of the state must take into account "the internal and external phases of state existence and activity." This being the case, there were "three units to be noted: the individual, the state, and the collection of states that comprise the world as a whole."[16] Gettell explained that each of these units had its own unique purpose, or end. He argued that the first purpose of the state was to provide for the welfare of the individual through securing internal order and justice, and by establishing the proper relation of individuals to each other and the community at large, which usually necessitated that the welfare of the world had to be subordinated to the needs of a states' own citizens. Yet this initial phase of establishing internal order and justice, Gettell argued, resulted in stagnation unless the state moved on to perfect its own national life. The perfection of national life was, according to Gettell, the second end of the state. This required the state to become "conscious of its own existence" and to safeguard its external independence. This was best achieved by the traditional means of securing territorial frontiers and strengthening them with fortifications and garrisons. It was within this second phase that Gettell acknowledged the relevancy of balance of power theories.

The national phase led to a third and final purpose of the state—a process that, according to Gettell, was just beginning to be discerned. The hostilities that inevitably arose as each state attempted to realize its own national consciousness vis-à-vis neighboring states was starting to be tempered by a cosmopolitan attitude that had the civilization and progress of the world as its end. Gettell claimed that evidence for this new attitude was to be found in "international understanding and sympathy, international agreements, conferences, and organizations, and the expansion of international law and adjudication." The most important conclusion that Gettell drew from this final end of the state was that the process might very well entail the dissolution of the state itself or, at a minimum, a significant loss of its external independence. He reasoned that "just as the perfection of national life demands the subordination of the individual, so the perfection of international life demands the subordination of the state."[17] While this might be a logical conclusion that a political theorist would reach, Gettell recognized that modern states had not yet arrived at the point where they would be willing to sacrifice their own national identities. He also was aware of the disagreements among political thinkers over the advantages and disadvantages of perfecting international life through the dissolution of national states.

The significance of Gettell's article was the close relationship that he depicted between the political theory of the state and international relations. He described how changes in the theoretical understanding of the internal composition of the state had a direct impact upon how the international milieu was perceived. The possibilities for international law, a world state, or some other form of international organization were largely determined in relation to the theory of the state. In order to clarify further the manner in which the discourse of the state fundamentally shaped the conversation of international relations, the writings of two representative figures of this period who espoused the juristic theory of the state will be examined. In the work of Westel Woodbury Willoughby and David Jayne Hill, the respective internal and external dimensions of the juristic theory of the state are evident.

The theoretical writings of Willoughby represented the orthodox conception of the state that most political scientists adhered to at the time the APSA was created. Willoughby played a leading role in the early development of political science, and he was often referred to as the "dean" of American political scientists.[18] He received his Ph.D. in history under Adams at Johns Hopkins in 1891, and afterwards, studied and practiced law. His true interests, however, were in the further pursuit of political science, and he returned to Hopkins in 1894 as a "reader" in political science. He became professor of political science at Hopkins in 1905 and remained there until his retirement in 1933. During the span of his career, the discipline of political science became a recognized field of study in almost every American college and university—a development to which the personal efforts of Willoughby contributed greatly.

Willoughby's first book, *An Examination of the Nature of the State* (1896) was, in part, a continuation of the theoretical discourse of the state that arose at Columbia under Lieber and Burgess. One of Willoughby's primary concerns, however, was to diminish the metaphysical basis of the theory of the state that he associated with Burgess and his German predecessors. Willoughby believed this was necessary in order to provide political theory, and thus political science, with a more solid scientific foundation. To accomplish this end, Willoughby posited a fundamental philosophical division within the discourse of the state between the state as it actually existed and the idea of what the end of the state ought to be. Willoughby explained that "a distinction is to be made between the abstract idea of the State and its empiric conception. The one is the result of abstract speculation, the other of concrete thinking."[19] It was the latter analytical conception of the state that Willoughby believed political science should base itself on, and he was of the opinion that the study of political theory was of great practical importance to the achievement of this end.

In his discussion of the essential nature of the state, Willoughby strictly adhered to the juristic conception. According to this interpretation, the state was an instrumentality for the creation and enforcement of law. Willoughby's explication of the juridical state is of crucial importance for understanding the prevailing image shared by most political scientists during the early 1900s. The juristic conception of the state provided political scientists with a hegemonic frame of reference for investigating the internal composition of the state. This largely consisted of an examination of the relationship between the state and the individual. The juristic conception of the state also provided the primary theoretical context for investigating the external relations among states, including the study of international law. What joined the internal and external components of the state together was the concept of sovereignty.

Following the orthodoxy, Willoughby insisted that an examination of sovereignty "is undoubtedly the most important topic to be discussed in political science," for "what the term 'Value' is to the science of political economy, the term 'Sovereignty' is to political science." It was only through a proper understanding of the meaning of sovereignty that the character of the modern state could be determined. Willoughby claimed that "Sovereignty is the vital principle in the life of the State. The validity of all law is dependent upon it, and all international relations are determined by it."[20] Sovereignty, in short, was the constitutive principle of the state. Willoughby defined the state as a community of individuals effectively organized under a supreme authority. In a crucial move that had tremendous consequences for the theoretical understanding of international relations, Willoughby insisted that the state, from a juristic point of view, could be regarded as a person that had a will of its own. He explained that a "politically organized group of individuals may be conceived of as constituting an essential unity, and that the entity thus created may be regarded as a person in the legal sense of the word."[21]

Consistent with the emphasis that Willoughby placed upon the analytical foundation of political theory, he approached the issue of sovereignty from a purely legal and formalistic perspective. Based on the analogy between the state and a person, Willoughby claimed that

> [T]he prime characteristic of the state is that there is posited of it a will that is legally supreme. By its express command, or by its tacit acquiescence, it is thus viewed as the ultimate source of legality for every act committed by its own agents or by any persons whomsoever over whom it claims authority. This supreme legally legitimizing will is termed sovereignty.[22]

Willoughby's conception of sovereignty connoted complete legal omnipotence which, he argued, was necessarily total and indivisible.

Willoughby, like John Austin, argued that the possession of sovereignty over a territorially defined political community granted the state the exclusive right to issue and enforce legally binding commands. This right did not merely arise from the state's possession of physical power, but from the fact that the state embodied a "supreme legally legitimizing will."

There were a number of interesting consequences that followed from Willoughby's theoretical explication of state sovereignty. For one thing, it led him to make a different type of distinction between state and government than Lieber and Burgess had drawn. Indeed, it was on the basis of the distinction that Willoughby drew between state and government that he was sharply critical of the argument that Burgess had made about the existence of perfect and imperfect forms of state. Willoughby, unlike Burgess, argued that there could be no such thing as an imperfect form of state. The presence of a supreme will exercising public authority over an organized group of people became an established fact during the natural evolution of humankind. Normative distinctions concerning how this authority was being exercised could not, for Willoughby, take away from the fact that the state represented the supreme expression of a legally binding supreme will. Willoughby claimed that the classifications that Burgess and others wanted to make about the exercise of this will were between different types of government, and not about forms of state. According to juristic theory, government did not posses sovereignty, it merely exercised it. In a passage that was directed toward Burgess, Willoughby argued that "there can be no such thing as an imperfect State, and to maintain that there can be is only to confound again the ideas of State and Government."[23]

A second implication of Willoughby's juristic conception of the state can be found in his rejection of contractarian theories to explain the origin of the state. His repudiation of social contract theory rested on the conviction that it was absurd to believe that individuals could posses rights prior to the emergence of the sovereign state. It was only through the authority structure provided by the state that the possession of rights could be secured and guaranteed. Willoughby's strict adherence to the Austinian conception of law meant that he placed little faith in the ability of natural law to regulate the affairs of human beings living outside of the state. Willoughby's conviction that so-called natural law lacked the essential characteristics of law, coupled with the belief that rights could not possibly exist in a state of nature, had a profound influence on the manner in which he conceptualized international relations. This was particularly the case because, although Willoughby rejected political theories that made reference to a state of nature and a social contract to explain the origin of the state, he nevertheless adopted this fictional imagery to describe the condition of international relations.

Willoughby claimed that apart from considering "sovereignty as expressing the supremacy of the State's will over that of all persons and public bodies within its own organization" it could also be viewed outwardly "in its international aspects." When viewed from this vantage point, Willoughby argued that "sovereignty denotes independence, or complete freedom from all external control of a legal character."[24] Based on a strict interpretation of state sovereignty as the personal expression of a supreme omnipotent will, Willoughby contended that "the term 'sovereignty' has no proper application in the field of international relations."[25] Although scholars employed the term sovereignty in their discussion of international relations, Willoughby argued that it was conceptually inappropriate to apply the idea of sovereignty in the international field, where it had a fundamentally different meaning from that which it had in the constitutional field. He suggested that the term "independency" would have been far better. Independency, Willoughby explained, "would indicate the fact that, regarded from the point of view of positive law, complete individualism prevails in the international field," where "life is atomistic, noncivic, individualistic." He added that "from this point of view nations are, as individuals, in that 'state of nature' in which Hobbes and Rousseau, and the other natural law writers placed primitive man."[26]

Willoughby's explicit reference to states occupying a position similar to that of individuals in a state of nature rested on the logical proposition that by dint of possessing absolute sovereignty internally, all states were, therefore, theoretically equal to and independent of one another. Under such a scenario, Willoughby was led to reject two of the most fundamental and basic ideas that have traditionally informed international legal theory: one, that international rights exist; and two, that international law is in fact law. The justification for rejecting these beliefs was based on the similarities that Willoughby drew between states and individuals living in state of nature. The reference to the international milieu as being analogous to a state of nature is a major component of the political discourse of anarchy. The analogy provides an analytical prop for describing a wide range of behaviors, including war, that are often associated with politics in the absence of central authority. It is ironic that Willoughby adopted this analogy to describe international relations when he completely rejected the idea of a state of nature as a basis of explaining the origin of the state.

In addition to the atomized and individualistic imagery that the state of nature provided for depicting the relations among independent sovereign states, it also, for Willoughby, accurately captured the nature of international law and rights. In exactly the same manner that Willoughby dismissed the so-called natural rights that some social contract theorists attributed to individuals living in the state of nature, he also rejected their application to states in the international realm. From a juristic perspective, international law lacked the essential characteristics of law properly understood. Willoughby, and the many others who adopted the juristic view of the state, argued that international law was not, in anyway, an authoritative command issued from a superior to an inferior. Furthermore, according to juristic theory, international law lacked a mechanism whereby force could be used to coerce and punish those who transgressed the law of nations. Willoughby insisted that, like natural law, international law only represented a moral "law" that was incapable of supplying enforceable rules of conduct. He concluded:

> The term "law," when applied to the rules and principles that prevail between independent nations, is misleading because such rules depend for their entire validity upon the forbearance and consent of the parties to whom they apply, and are not and cannot be legally enforced by any common superior. In a command there is the necessary idea of superior and inferior, while in international relations the fundamental postulate is that of the theoretical equality of the parties, however much they may differ in actual strength.[27]

The fact that Willoughby rejected the claim that international law was true law did not, however, lead him to a position of despair. At the same time that Willoughby defended the position that international law was not really law, he recognized that it was necessary to find a mechanism to reconcile the disputes that arose among independent sovereign states. He held that this was indeed a practical possibility, and placed great faith in the settlement of international disputes through the mechanism of international arbitration. The idea of creating a comprehensive system of international arbitration gained many adherents throughout the early decades of the twentieth century. Arbitration, as a means of settling international disputes, was especially favored by those, like Willoughby, who propagated the juristic conception of the state. This was because arbitration represented a judicial settlement of disputes that did not require a state to surrender its internal sovereignty.

Willoughby was opposed to any idea that called for the creation of a world state. This, once again, can be explained by reference to his theory of the state. Independence, Willoughby argued, was not diminished by the increasing ties of material interdependence that many scholars began to observe in the international realm. Regardless of the different ways that states were being drawn closer together, Willoughby maintained that the sovereign character of the state was a significant impediment to the realization of a world state. Willoughby claimed that "as time goes on the association of States will undoubtedly grow closer," and yet "a genuine World-State, or a State embracing the civilized nations of the world, will never be established." This was because such a scenario "would require the surrender of the Sovereignty and independence of the individual nations,—a surrender to which it is not conceivable they will ever submit."[28] This provides a clear example of the manner in which the theory of the state provided the framework for analyzing the external relations between sovereign states. Willoughby's theoretical description of international relations and his account of international law can be understood only in light of his theory of the state. The writings of David Jayne Hill will be examined next to highlight some of the additional implications that the juristic conception of the state had for the study of international relations. Hill, perhaps more clearly than anyone else, disclosed the possibilities, as well as the limitations, of the jusristic theory of the state for understanding international relations.

Hill began his professional career teaching at the University of Lewisburg in 1877 (Lewisburg was later re-named Bucknell University after its primary benefactor). At the age of twenty-eight, Hill became the youngest college president in the United States after his election by the trustees at Lewisburg in 1879. As president, Hill instituted large-scale reforms that were aimed at transforming everything from the curriculum to the social life. Typical of these reforms was Hill's decision to discontinue the traditional Moral Philosophy class taught by the college president in favor of a more modern course that he entitled "Psychology and Ethics." After accomplishing all that he could at Bucknell, Hill assumed the presidency of the University of Rochester in 1888. At Rochester, he attempted to implement reforms similar to those he had introduced at Bucknell University. However, his reforms were almost always met with opposition, and Hill finally resigned in March 1895.[29]

Eager for a diplomatic career, Hill became involved in the Republican party's presidential campaign for William McKinley in hopes that patronage would land him a position at a foreign embassy. After President McKinley failed to name Hill to a position within his administration, he took the advice of Andrew D. White, who was appointed to the position Hill sought as Ambassador to Berlin, and sailed to Europe to study international law and diplomacy at the *École Libre des Sciences Politiques* in Paris. Two years later, in 1898, Hill was appointed First Assistant Secretary of State, after John Bassett Moore resigned from the post. After his tenure at the State Department, Hill was first named Minister to Switzerland, then Minister to the Netherlands, where he prepared the notes for the United States delegation to the Second Hague Conference in 1907, and finally was appointed by President Roosevelt as Ambassador to Germany in 1908. Throughout his diplomatic career, Hill published extensively on topics related to international politics. The first two volumes of his multi-volume project entitled *A History of Diplomacy in the International Development of Europe* were published in 1905 and 1906 respectively. During his tenure as Ambassador to Germany, Hill was appointed to the Carpenter Foundation Lectureship at Columbia University, where he delivered a series of eight lectures on "The Political Organization of the World." These lectures were later published under the title *World Organization as Affected by the Nature of the Modern State* (1911), and taken together, provided a good illustration of the implications that the juristic conception of the state had for the discourse of international relations.

According to Hill, the juristic nature of the state was axiomatic. The modern state, Hill argued, was the embodiment of law, and its existence was tied to securing and protecting individual rights. Like Willoughby, Hill insisted that the state was not a mere mystical abstraction but rather a concrete, tangible entity. He maintained that it was the juristic character of the state that "confers upon it supreme authority over its constituents, and places its right to exist and to command above all discussion."[30] Sovereignty, in the sense of expressing absolute supreme authority, was, for Hill, the essential characteristic of the modern state. Hill was, however, careful to point out that the authority of the state no longer rested solely on its sheer physical might, as he believed it had in earlier times. He discerned an evolutionary movement through which state authority originally based on sheer might was being replaced by principles of right and justice. Hill argued that this historical transition was manifest "in the struggle between two composing conceptions of the State, and of relations between States: the Machiavellian conception, based on arbitrary power, unlimited and irresponsible; and the Althusian conception, based on inherent rights, limited powers, and organized securities."[31]

Hill thought that the theory of sovereignty developed by the German Calvinist, Johannes Althusius (1557–1638), represented a significant development in the jural consciousness of the state. Although Hill agreed with Willoughby that the original conception of sovereignty could be traced to Jean Bodin (1530–1596), he argued that Bodin's theory of state sovereignty properly belonged to the category of might. Bodin, Hill maintained, ultimately based the authority of the state on its superior force to command. By contrast, Althusius defined sovereignty as "a right indivisible, incommunicable, and imprescriptible, inherent in the whole body politic." According to Hill, Althusius's conception of sovereignty firmly belonged in the category of right, which illustrated the progressive substitution of thought for force. He argued that it was only through the rule of law that the rightful authority of the state could be exercised. In other words, the juristic nature of the state was what rendered the exercise of authority legitimate. Equally important, the juristic state made it possible for individuals to secure and enjoy the rights of life, liberty, and property. Hill believed that modern "civilized" nations, especially the United States, had reached a point of historical evolution in which the juristic basis of the state had been realized internally.[32]

The most glaring problem that remained was to extend these same juristic principles to the realm of inter-state relations. This was the task of world organization, which Hill defined as one "of so uniting governments in the support of principles of justice as to apply them not only within the limits of the State but also between States."[33] Hill submitted that the international realm continued to be plagued by archaic conceptions of right that had might and force as their only foundation. This was the conception of "right" that was behind the state's traditional claim to wage war and plunder other states. Hill argued that this notion of right resulted from the fact that "the condition of the world, from an international point of view, has long been one of polite anarchy."[34] Even if states occasionally reached limited agreements, shared certain norms of diplomatic etiquette, and recognized some principles of international ethics, he insisted that "juristically speaking, there exists a condition of anarchy."

Hill argued that the progressive substitution of law for force that characterized the history of the juristic state did not necessarily stop at the "waters edge." The fact that the modern state had entered a stage of jural consciousness meant that the external relations among sovereigns could also be reconstituted on the rightful basis of law and justice. Unlike many of the other theorists who propagated the juristic theory of the state, Hill did not encumber himself with the controversy as to whether international law was in fact law. He recognized that beginning with the work of Hugo Grotius (1583–1645), the moral element of natural law had provided the earliest foundation for the existence of a law of nations. He also acknowledged that much of the subsequent development of international law rested on the analogy that Samuel Pufendorf (1632–1694) had made between the state and a moral person. While agreeing that the state could be regarded as a moral person, in the sense of possessing rights and obligations, Hill felt that it was necessary to admit that morality was by itself insufficient to provide a binding authority over the actions of states. This represented a serious short-coming in a juristically based world order that sought to safeguard the rights of states in a manner similar to that of individuals. Since Hill insisted that there could be no deviation from established juristic principles, he, like Willoughby, embraced arbitration as the means to achieving a juristic ordering of inter-state relations.

The essential elements in Hill's proposal for achieving a system of international arbitration were outlined in a paper entitled "International Justice; With a Plan for its Permanent Organization" that he delivered before a meeting of the American Social Science Association at Saratoga Springs, New York, in 1896.[35] Hill defined the problem of realizing international justice in a manner similar to that of achieving domestic justice. He explained that in both cases, finding a method of establishing and fixing the limits of one person's or state's freedom "as restricted by the equal freedom of all, is the problem of justice." Hill pointed to three conditions that had to be fulfilled in order for a system of international justice to be rendered fully operative: first, a code of international law had to be formulated which all sovereign states would recognize as binding; second, a method of adjudicating disputes and differences had to be devised; and third, a means of enforcing the decisions reached through the process of adjudication had to be found.[36] Hill viewed the Hague Peace Conferences of 1899 and 1907 as contributing to the fulfillment of each of these three conditions. From Hill's perspective, the Hague Conferences demonstrated that states were willing to "substitute judicial procedure for military action in the settlement of international disputes."[37] He argued that with the eventual establishment of a Permanent Tribunal of Arbitration, disputes between states would be resolved in a manner similar to those between individuals living within the jural state. Hill concluded that the Hague Conferences provided concrete testimony that the governments of the world were willing "to adopt the standards of jurisprudence as the true guide in international relations, instead of asserting the right of superior force to dominate."[38]

Hill maintained that the judicial settlement of international disputes was not chimerical, but rather fit into the general evolutionary pattern whereby force was being replaced by justice. By insisting upon arbitration as the proper mechanism for limiting the scourge of war, Hill, again like Willoughby, was able to provide a logical consistency with his internal and external analysis of the juristic state. For arbitration did not infringe on a state's sovereignty—states voluntarily submitted to arbitration procedures by judges of their own choosing. In this manner, arbitration did not require recognition of any superior authority. This was different from other conflict resolution procedures that did require a state to abrogate its sovereignty. Hill's rejection of a world state as well as his feverish campaign against the League of Nations can be understood in light of his devoted support for the principles upon which the juristic state was constituted.[39]

Hill's writings displayed the theoretical bond that existed between the internal and external examination of the state. Francis Coker's review of *World Organization* recognized this convergence when he stated that "these lectures will be of interest to the student of the history of political thought; for, in indicating the relations of various theories to the progress of the idea of international justice, illuminating settings are given to familiar doctrines of theories whose preoccupation was with the internal constitution of the State."[40] It would, however, be inaccurate to imply that the juristic conception of the state was accepted without its share of critics. Although the juristic conception of the state, as enunciated by Willoughby and Hill, provided the predominant theoretical framework for understanding and explaining the internal and external dimensions of the state, criticisms began to be raised about the theoretical and practical relevancy of this view. The objections advanced against the juristic theory of the state had important consequences for the discourse of international relations.

The Political Science Realists

The critique of the orthodox juristic conception of the state has been viewed by some disciplinary historians as a phase of what has been described as the "Americanization" of political science.[41] A distinguishing characteristic of this process was the call made in behalf of a number of influential political scientists for a more "realist" treatment of political phenomena. According to this early wave of reform-oriented political scientists such as Arthur Bentley, James Bryce, A. Lawrence Lowell, and Charles Beard, it was essential that political science pay attention to the facts of political life. The archaic formalism that these and other young scholars in the discipline ascribed to the older generation of political scientists affiliated with the Columbia School was challenged as seriously antiquated. Rather than studying formal documents and ancient archives, the "realists" argued that current political events and actors should be the focus of analysis which, in turn, necessitated that new methods be introduced into the discipline. The juristic theory of the state and the historical-comparative method bore the brunt of this critique. While Willoughby had raised a number of critical issues with respect to Burgess's theory of the state, the realist critique went much further in its condemnation of all formalistic theories of the state. The desideratum to place political science on a more scientific foundation led some scholars, such as Charles Merriam, to search for a more appropriate methodology that could realize the goal of a science of politics.[42] This aspiration, which would undergo a long period of gestation, eventually culminated in the behavioral revolution of the 1950s.[43] The new scientism of the early 1900s, which was initially oriented toward the study of political attitudes, did not call for a complete rejection of the idea of the state, but did disdain the legalism associated with the juristic theory of the state.

James Bryce's presidential address to the fifth annual meeting of the APSA on January 28, 1908, made direct reference to the inadequacy of the conventional theory of the state. He asked, "what can be more windy and empty, more dry and frigid and barren than such lucubrations upon sovereignty as we find in John Austin and some still more recent writers?"[44] Bryce's address before a joint meeting of the APSA and AHA was aimed at clarifying the type of science that political science could be expected to achieve. Unlike the later and more dogmatic advocates of scientism, Bryce believed that political science could never resemble any of the exact natural sciences. Rather, he argued that political science was a historical sort of science that stood "midway between history and politics" and would provide conceptual clarification and uncover general patterns in political life that statesmen and citizens could then put to best use. According to Bryce, this meant that the gathering of historical facts was a fundamental task of political science. The generalizations to which political scientists aspired were to be induced from the historical facts they collected. In a statement that since has become famous, Bryce wrote:

> The study of facts is meant to lead up to the establishment of conclusions and the mastery of principles, and unless it does this it has no scientific value. The Fact is the first thing. Make sure of it. Get it perfectly clear. Polish it till it shines and sparkles like a gem. Then connect it with other facts. Examine it in its relation to them, for in that lies its worth and its significance.[45]

He argued that if political science was to have a practical purpose in the world, then the metaphysical and speculative inquiry that characterized the study of the state would have to be supplanted by a more factually based examination. With respect to the issue of sovereignty, Bryce suggested eschewing "artificial definitions, unreal distinctions" and "idle logomachies" for an empirical approach that required investigating where supreme legal authority was actually lodged in the state.

Bryce concluded with an example of a factually based study of political science that might provide practical relevance. He observed that the age in which he lived was characterized by the desire of each nation-state to be strong and prosperous. Yet a nationalist sentiment adhering to the belief that the greatness of one country only could be secured at the expense of another was leading states into an excessive power struggle. Bryce believed that political science could play a constructive role, since "a wide study of politics, like a wide study of literature, tends to correct the excesses of Nationalism."[46] He also suggested that historical research would raise serious doubts about the theoretical adequacy of the juristic conception of the state.

Charles Beard was another reform-minded political scientist who embraced many of the ideas articulated by Bryce. Beard received his doctorate at Columbia and wrote his dissertation, under the direction of Burgess, on the history of the justice of the peace.[47] He was hired by Columbia in 1904 as a Lecturer in History. In 1907, Beard became Adjunct Professor of Politics in the Department of Public Law, whose faculty at the time included Burgess, Munroe Smith, Frank Goodnow, and John Bassett Moore. Shortly after receiving his appointment, Beard delivered an address that revealed a number of subtle differences between himself and the older generation of political science colleagues which, in some respects, foreshadowed the disagreements that eventually would cause him to resign in 1917.

Beard echoed many of the same themes that Bryce had articulated in his presidential address before the APSA. Beard argued that the recent work of archaeologists, anthropologists, historians, and Darwinians was enabling the student of politics to amass a greater body of exact data on the origin and development of the state. Beard declared that "one of the most salutary results of this vast accumulation of data on politics has been to discredit the older speculative theorists and the utopia makers."[48] The historical data was, in short, contributing to a more accurate assessment of the true nature of the state, which Beard argued formed the first "great division" of the subject matter of political science. He stated that no apology was needed for placing the state on top of the great divisions of political science (the other divisions being government, the limits of government action, political parties, and international relations), since it was the "highest form of human association yet devised." He acknowledged that it was the principle of sovereignty that differentiated the state from earlier forms of political organization. The search for the origin of the sovereign power of the state was, Beard conceded, one of the oldest questions to have inspired political discourse and he was confident that an explanation had been finally found through the painstaking efforts of historical research. This research, Beard claimed, demonstrated that "the real origin of the state, in Western Europe at least, is to be found in conquest."[49] Beard argued that from a Darwinian perspective, the verifiable fact of human conquest illustrated that the evolution of political authority was a process through which the monopoly of political control was diffused from a single warlord to the body politic. The historical diffusion of political authority was, for Beard, the real story behind the evolution of sovereignty. He argued that this story rested "not on vacuous speculation, but upon the results of laborious research and patient winnowing on the part of innumerable historical scholars."[50] This new historical research proved, to Beard at least, that the real state could never have been a juristic state.

While Bryce and Beard were led to reject the validity of the juristic conception of the state on the basis of historical data, other political scientists began to raise serious philosophical and theoretical objections. An important source of criticism was provided by the development of philosophical pragmatism. The early origins of American pragmatism are largely attributed to the work of John Dewey at the University of Michigan, and later at the University of Chicago.[51] Although it is beyond the scope of this chapter to discuss the specific details of Dewey's pragmatism, it is instructive to note that as early as 1894, he was challenging Austin's theory of sovereignty. Dewey argued that Austin had confused the concept of "sovereignty with the organs of its exercise." In pointing to this confusion, Dewey, like many of the new generation of political scientists, was arguing for the need to differentiate government from sovereignty. He claimed that "the ultimate weakness of Austin's theory is that, in identifying sovereignty with a part only of the body politic, he gives (and allows) no reason why this limited body of persons have the authority which they possess."[52] According to Dewey, this shortcoming had serious implications for Austin's theory of law.

The critique of sovereignty that Harold J. Laski undertook at Harvard University from 1916 to 1920 was indebted to the school of pragmatism that was being developed by Dewey and William James. Before he returned to Europe, Laski would emerge as one of the foremost critics of the orthodox theory of the state. He would also be responsible for helping to introduce and popularize the idea of pluralism which had a tremendous influence on the subsequent development of American political science. Based on his extensive study of political authority, Laski concluded that the juristic doctrine of state sovereignty was a dangerous fiction. He argued that the state should be viewed as only one of many group-units that possess a corporate personality.[53] The contours of the pluralist paradigm and its influence on the discourse of international relations will be fully considered in Chapter 5. Although pluralism is most often thought of as a domestic research program, this reformulated theory of the state provided an alternative framework for analyzing international relations.

    This illustrates why it is only through an understanding of the discourse of the state within political science that we can recover the discourse of international relations. One of the difficulties of reconstructing the disciplinary history of international relations during the early 1900s is that the field did not yet have a clearly identifiable institutional setting. In a report to the APSA in 1910 addressing the question of the amount of time that colleges were devoting to the study of Political Science and Government, international relations was not even listed as a separate category.[54] The closest subject listed that dealt with issues pertaining to international affairs was American Diplomacy which finished second to last behind Municipal Government in the number of hours devoted to classroom instruction. Yet simply because international relations lacked an institutional designation as an autonomous sub-field is not to suggest that political scientists were neither interested in nor studying international politics. A casual survey of the popular "News and Notes" section in the early issues of the *American Political Science Review* reveals that events associated with international politics were an important concern for many political scientists. And there is no disputing the keen interest that political scientists placed on the study of international law which constituted the core domain of the incipient field of international relations.

The Discourse of International Law

    From 1900 until the outbreak of World War I in 1914, the subject of international law dominated the study and analysis of international relations. A 1915 APSA report on political science instruction in colleges and universities reported that international law ranked "third as to the number of institutions offering the subject." Only American Government and Comparative Government had a larger student enrollment.[55] At the turn of the century, there was a significant increase in the number of instructional textbooks on international law, and many of the older leading texts, such as those by T.J. Lawrence, George G. Wilson, and William Hall, appeared in new revised editions. It is also important to recall that the discourse of international law during this period was not strictly confined to political scientists. There was a conspicuous public movement to reform the practice of international relations on the basis of the rule of law. This movement found an important source of inspiration in the numerous international peace conferences that were taking place, especially those that occurred at The Hague in 1899 and 1907. For a great many people, these conferences demonstrated the apparent willingness of states to find a more peaceful basis for settling international disputes. The reform movement also benefited from the activities of peace societies, such as the American Peace Society and the New York Peace Society, that helped to popularize the subject of international law.

In an effort to promote those subjects that were devoted to eradicating the causes of war, Andrew Carnegie in 1910 pledged ten million dollars to the creation of an Endowment for International Peace. In a survey of the study of international relations in the United States, Edith Ware claimed that the Carnegie Endowment for International Peace "stands unique in the field of international relations and has perhaps exerted the largest single influence in the United States and throughout the world in the furtherance of better understanding between nations."[56] To fulfill the stated objective of finding a remedy for war, the trustees organized the Carnegie Endowment as an institution for research and public education. The work of the Endowment was divided into three divisions: a division of international law under the direction of James Brown Scott, who was the first Recording Secretary of the Society of International Law; a division of Economics and History under the direction of John Bates Clark of Columbia University; and a division of Intercourse and Education under the direction of Nicholas Murray Butler, president of Columbia University. Although the scholarly work of each of the respective divisions was greatly valued, many looked upon the activities of the international law division as being fundamental to realizing Carnegie's goal of world peace. Carnegie declared that once a solution to the problem of war had been found, the Endowment would then be utilized for finding solutions to other social ills plaguing humankind. In addition to the numerous conferences, scholarly studies, book publications, foreign exchanges, and funding grants, the Carnegie Endowment also published *International Conciliation*. Some historians of the field have described this as the first professional journal of international relations. Taken together, the resources supplied by the Carnegie Endowment helped to provide an institutional setting whereby academics, statespersons, and self-acclaimed "internationalists" could discuss and exchange ideas on how to achieve a more peaceful and harmonious world.

From the perspective of reconstructing the academic discourse of international relations, an event of even greater significance was the founding of the American Society of International Law in 1906 and the publication of their *American Journal of International Law* the same year (the first English-speaking journal in the world exclusively devoted to the subject of international law). The Society was initiated by several members of the Lake Mohonk Conference who were interested in forming an organization "devoted exclusively to the interests of international law as distinct from international arbitration." From 1895 through 1916, an annual Conference on International Arbitration took place at Alfred and Albert Smiley's Lake Mohonk mountain resort in New York state. An impressive array of diverse intellectuals gathered each year to advance the cause of a system of international arbitration which the members of the Mohonk Conference unanimously agreed was the best means of securing international peace. Nevertheless, there was sufficient interest among some of the members in pursuing additional measures besides arbitration to lead to the successful establishment of the American Society of International Law. According to James Brown Scott, the object of the Society was "to foster the study of international law and promote the establishment of international relations on the basis of law and justice." To achieve this objective, a constitution was drafted, officers were elected, annual meetings were held, and quarterly issues of the Society's official journal were published to "bring home to the reader the theory and practice of international law."[57]

The predominant theoretical perspective advanced in the journal was one that was directly aimed at replacing the views of Austin and those who adhered to the juristic theory of the state. Most of the contributors to the journal sought to develop a different theory based on principles of international legal positivism. Just as there was a system of positive law domestically, the international legal positivists insisted that, contrary to Austin, there also was a body of internationally recognized rules that had the status of law. They argued that a system of positive law existed internationally and that this was evident in the consent that states gave to the growing body of international rules and treaties. Boyle, in his sophisticated account of this period, has argued that the publication of the first issue of the *American Journal of International Law* was "the single most important event in the development of a distinctively legal positivist approach to international relations in the United States" that was "purposefully intended to be different from the respective approaches taken by proponents of natural law theory and political scientists."[58]

As indicated in the last chapter, the primary motivation for developing an alternative approach emanated from the refusal of those who followed Austin to acknowledge the legal status of international law. The discussion that centered on Austin's theory of law illustrates how the concept of sovereignty provided the most direct nexus between the theoretical discourse of the state and the study of international relations. In the first volume of the *American Journal of International Law*, Robert Lansing, who held a variety of appointments from the

United States government including Secretary of State under Wilson from 1915 to 1920, wrote a two-part article entitled "Notes On Sovereignty in a State" that focused on the implications that the concept of sovereignty had for the study of international law. Lansing detailed these implications from an explicitly juristic perspective which indicated the willingness of the journal's editors to confront the position they sought to supplant. He began his analysis by reciting the prevalent opinion "that the sovereignty in a state may be looked at from two points of view, namely, from *within* and from *without* the state."[59] Viewed from within the state, Lansing, in full agreement with Austin, maintained that superior physical force was the distinguishing characteristic of sovereignty. Viewed externally, sovereignty denoted a condition whereby each actor was equal to, and independent of, every other actor. Although an analytical distinction could be made between the internal and external exercise of sovereignty, Lansing admitted that both aspects really were inseparable. He explained, "there can be no *actual* independence of a state unless the real sovereignty is held within the state; and no individual or body of individuals can possess that sovereignty without being *actually* independent."[60]

Nonetheless, Lansing pointed to a discrepancy in the historical and theoretical development of the concepts of internal and external sovereignty. According to Lansing, the latter was fundamentally undeveloped in comparison to the highly determinate character of law, rights, and liberties provided through the internal exercise of sovereignty. To illustrate the different stages of development in the two aspects of sovereignty, Lansing made reference to the popular analogy between the exercise of state sovereignty in the realm of international relations and the condition of individuals living in a state of nature. Lansing wrote:

> The condition of nations in their intercourse with one another is similar to that which would exist among individuals living in an unorganized community, and unrestrained by enforced law. In such a case each person would possess absolute liberty; that is, independence, and would settle all disputes with other persons by physical combat or mutual concessions. No more rude and savage type of human society can be conceived; and yet that is the type which is today illustrated in the community of nations.[61]

This particular account of international relations resulted directly from the orthodox juristic conception of state sovereignty. Lansing's description was similar to those put forth by Leacock, Willoughby, and Hill in that they all specifically compared the international milieu to that of individuals living in a state of nature. Yet the theoretical adequacy of depicting international relations as a condition analogous to a state of nature whereby states led an isolated, brutish, nasty, and unlawful existence increasingly came to be challenged by a number of international legal scholars. A common theme that emerged was that the conventional state theory paradigm failed to depict accurately the empirical reality of international politics.

According to the international lawyers who wanted to extend legal positivism to the international realm, Austin and his contemporary protégés propagated a series of conceptual misunderstandings about the "real" nature of law when they refused to concede legal status to the body of existing international rules. In addition to challenging Austin's view of law, critics were attempting to develop what they termed a "scientific" approach to international law. In order to achieve these twin aims, it was necessary, first, to distinguish the positivist approach from the more traditional natural law roots of the field, and second, to demonstrate concretely that international law was in fact law. Many of the articles that appeared in the early issues of the *American Journal of International Law* were aimed at achieving these two goals.

The managing editor of the journal, Scott, wrote an article in the first volume entitled "The Legal Nature of International Law," which provided a brief for the legal positivists' critique of Austin. Scott had earned his undergraduate degree from Harvard in 1890. He continued at Harvard, studying international law, and then went abroad to study in Paris, Berlin, and Heidelberg. Prior to Scott's role in founding the American Society of International Law, he had served as dean of the Los Angeles Law School from 1896 to 1899, dean of the University of Illinois Law School from 1899 to 1903, and professor of international law, first at Columbia University from 1903 to 1906, and then at George Washington University from 1906 to 1911. Scott dedicated his professional life to the pursuit of reforming world politics through international law and it was not surprising that he took serious offense at the claim that international law did not properly qualify as "real" law. He submitted that the Austinian definition of positive law was "narrow, contracted, unbending," and that when tested, resulted "in an absurdity or in a mere quibble about names as such, in which the essence is sacrificed to the form."[62]

Scott, along with many other historically minded legal scholars, was convinced that Austin's theory of positive law lacked a historical basis. He found that legal historians, such as Sir Henry Maine, had convincingly demonstrated that previous political communities abided by a system of law that did not, in any way, conform to the definition of law outlined by Austin. The historical record provided compelling evidence that rules were issued and obeyed in ancient political communities without the presence of a commanding superior wielding coercive physical force. Legal historians as well as anthropologists argued that this was because the oldest basis for conformity to law rested on custom and tradition, not fear of a physical sanction. This was a very significant finding, since it demonstrated that the attribute of law could not be denied simply on the basis of whether or not a certain type of coercive sanction was present. Scott, in direct contradistinction to Austin, reasoned that "it would seem that the presence of a sanction is not essential to the quality of law, for the law as such is simply a rule of conduct, and is neither self-applying nor self-executing."[63]

As important as the critique of Austin's theory of positive law was in undermining the authority of his position, the revelation that multiple types of sanctions historically had accompanied the rule of law was even more instrumental in helping to establish the legal nature of international law. For if it could be demonstrated that the basis of law did not depend solely upon the existence of a coercive sanction, then an argument could be made that international law was law irrespective of whether its rules were always enforced. In other words, the international legal positivists argued that the criteria for either accepting or rejecting the legal nature of international law were not contingent on whether the rules were always obeyed out of fear of physical compulsion. He claimed that the intellectual exercise of determining whether a body of rules qualified as law was distinct from an investigation of the sanctions that led to its enforcement. Scott added that even if one did presume that the presence of a sanction was an essential quality of law, this still left open the question of the type of sanction. This was a topic that critics of Austin devoted considerable intellectual energy to examining. Scott declared that Austin's definition of a sanction was as narrow and restricted as his definition of a positive law. In addition to this shortcoming, he claimed that Austin seriously confounded the means and ends of a sanction. Scott explained that the ultimate end of a sanction was to ensure obedience to a given command. The means of a sanction, however, were the various mechanisms—tradition, custom, religion, physical force—utilized to ensure compliance. According to Scott, it was apparent that Austin narrowly defined a legal sanction exclusively in terms of the means of physical compulsion.

In the endeavor to refute Austin's assertion that international law lacked any credible sanctions, one of the most fruitful lines of argument that was able to be used in the defense of international law was discovered. It gradually became apparent to many legal scholars that Austin's theory of law was based exclusively on the municipal law of a state. In his presidential address to the APSA in 1915, John Basset

Moore declared "that a vast deal of time has been wasted in controversy over the question whether international law is law at all." Moore argued that "a moment's reflection suffices to show that Austin's so-called definition is at most merely a description of municipal law, and even for that purpose is not sufficiently comprehensive, since it would, for instance, exclude a large part of constitutional law, much of which, like a considerable part of international law, is not enforced by courts by means of specific penalties."[64] The insight that Austin's refusal to recognize international law as law was the result of a misapplication of the definition of law from the municipal realm to the international realm had important significance for the international legal positivists. For one thing, it demonstrated that there were two distinct realms of law of which each had its own peculiar characteristics. And this, in turn, exposed the inadequacy of using the model of municipal law as the basis of making critical judgments about the character of international law.

The task of developing an appropriate paradigm for international law was a fundamental objective of the early-twentieth-century international legal positivists. To accomplish this goal, it was necessary to devise an ontology that adequately mirrored the empirical reality of international politics. In comparison with domestic law, international law operated between states, not above them. Recognition of the descriptive fact of anarchy was taken to be an important starting point for the development of a science of public international law. By developing an appropriate ontological description of international relations that was distinct from other realms of political life, the international legal positivists concluded that the real character of international law could be discerned. With respect to the issue of sanctions, it was apparent that they operated differently in the international realm than they did within the municipal law of a state. This meant that sanctions in the former were only absent if one adopted all the definitions and characteristics of municipal law. By insisting that the features of international law were different from those of municipal law, Scott could pose the question, "may there not be a sanction for the municipal law and a different but no less binding sanction for the law of nations?"[65]

The reply that a growing number of international legal scholars gave to this query was that a system of sanctions existed internationally that bound states to an established body of international law. Many held that the most important type of sanction behind international law was that of public opinion. Conformity to the norms of an emerging international public opinion, or what Nicholas Murray Butler described as an "international mind," was argued to be a powerful sanction that constrained states from breaking international laws and put them at risk of being ostracized from the international community of nations. In an address before the second annual meeting of the American Society of International Law in 1908, Elihu Root argued that the persistent idea that international law lacked a sanction for the enforcement of rules similar to that of municipal law was more apparent than real. He claimed that the ultimate sanction behind municipal law was not the presence of physical force, but rather the force of public opinion. In this respect, the sanction for the enforcement of municipal law was actually similar to that for international law. Root argued that the "force of law is in the public opinion which prescribes it," and "in the vast majority of cases men refrain from criminal conduct because they are unwilling to incur in the community in which they live the public condemnation and obloquy which would follow a repudiation of the standard of conduct prescribed by that community for its members."[66] Demonstrating the existence and the mechanics of the sanction of public opinion was an essential part of the international legal positivists' strategy for invalidating the claim that international law was not law.

The effort to create a science of public international law did require more than simply a point by point refutation of Austin's influential theory of jurisprudence. The critique of Austin only represented an initial step in the process of differentiating existing international law, based on custom and consent, from the earlier natural law heritage. The tasks, aims, and methods of the twentieth-century international legal positivist paradigm were most eloquently delineated in a seminal article by Lassa Oppenheim entitled "The Science of International Law: Its Task and Method." Oppenheim was one of the world's foremost experts on international law, and he held the prestigious position of Whewell Professor of International Law at Cambridge University. Since Oppenheim was a European, his article was not published in the first volume of the *American Journal of International Law* which was exclusively devoted to American authors. When his article was published in 1908, the agenda for the subsequent development of the international legal positivist paradigm was established.

Oppenheim admitted that at the time he was writing, there was "no generally recognized method of the science of international law." He claimed that there was no prima facie reason for insisting upon one method over another, for just as "many roads lead to Rome, so many methods lead to good results." The criteria that Oppenheim recommended for determining the most appropriate method was that which led to the best results. The best results were defined as those that led to the proper end of the science of international law, which Oppenheim identified in a three-fold manner: "primarily, peace among the nations and the governance of their intercourse by what makes for order and is right and just; secondarily, the peaceable settlement of international disputes; lastly, the establishment of legal rules for the conduct of war and for the relations between belligerents and neutrals."[67] Based on these criteria, Oppenheim flatly rejected the methods of the Grotian school, the Naturalist school, and the followers of Austin, and insisted that there could be no other method than the positive one. He explained that "the positive method is that applied by the science of law in general, and it demands that whatever the aims and ends of a worker and researcher may be, he must start from the existing recognized rules of international law as they are to be found in the customary practice of the states or in law-making conventions."[68] This was the bedrock of the positive method, and it represented a fundamental departure from the traditional natural law roots of the field. Oppenheim declared that however useful the law of nature was to the genesis of international law, the point had been reached where it was now detrimental to its further progress. He argued that in order for international law to be authoritative, it was necessary that "no rule must be formulated which can not be proved to be the outcome of international custom or of a law-making treaty."[69]

Exposition of the existing rules of international law was, according to Oppenheim, the first task that must be undertaken in order to promote the science of international law. He was aware that the task of delineating the recognized rules of international law was made difficult by the fact that they were based largely on custom. Nevertheless, exposing the recognized rules of international law must be accomplished so that the remaining objectives on the positivist agenda could be realized. With this in mind, Oppenheim identified six additional, though closely connected, tasks that the science of international law must fulfill: "historical research, criticism of the existing law, preparation of codification, distinction between old customary and the new conventional law, fostering of arbitration, and popularization of international law."[70] All of these followed directly from the theoretical and methodological framework that informed the legal positivist paradigm. The international legal positivists were resolute in their belief that international law could no longer rest on the traditional a priori natural law basis. To acquire the authority of knowledge, the proponents of international legal positivism declared that the study of international law would have to rest strictly on an empirical foundation. They also insisted that if international law was to achieve the status of a science, there would need to be a closer correspondence between the empirical world and the theoretical description of that world.

Recognition of the fact that international law operated in an environment where there was no central authority above the individual sovereign states was a necessary, albeit preliminary, step in developing an accurate account of the international milieu. In many ways, it has been the recurring attempt to assess the legal, theoretical, and practical manifestations of international anarchy that has shaped the subsequent history of the field of international relations. It is, in part, because political scientists have drawn numerous and different conclusions about the consequences of international anarchy that we can speak of a political discourse of anarchy. While a certain consonance in depicting inter-state politics as a realm lacking a centralized authority begins to emerge in the field, little, if any, consensus surfaces about the implications that follow from international anarchy. For some, the presence of anarchy represents an insurmountable obstacle to achieving any type of lasting peaceful coexistence among sovereign independent states. Others, however, insist that either international law or international organization offer a means to a more peaceful world order. In the years leading up to World War I, there were numerous efforts to reform the existing realm of international anarchy. The next section explores some of the proposals that political scientists and others were contemplating for reforming the practice of international relations.

World Order Reform

Focusing on some of the ideas that were being put forth to reform international politics in the years leading up to World War I will demonstrate that there are many different ways of envisioning the character and manifestations of anarchy. Once freed from the constraints of the juristic theory of the state, a much wider panorama of proposals for reforming international politics became available. The intellectual history of this period offers many examples of how these proposals for reforming inter-state politics were seriously considered by the United States and other members of the international community. The extent to which self-identified international legal positivists in American universities and government positions were involved in proposing and implementing these reform proposals on a global scale has led Boyle to question the conventionally accepted isolationist posture attributed to the United States foreign policy before entering the First World War. Boyle has argued that as a group, the international legal positivists were avowed proponents of internationalism and encouraged an "activist and globalist" approach to international relations. He claims that they were "not at all naive, idealistic, or utopian," and "were not men who shrank from advocating the forceful exercise of American power around the globe, whether as teachers, scholars, and polemicists or, as many of them were, government officials, diplomats, and statesman."[71] According to Boyle, there were five common objectives that the American legal positivists sought to attain during what he terms the "classical period" from 1898 to 1917:

> (1) the creation of a general system for the obligatory arbitration of disputes between states; (2) the establishment of an international court of justice; (3) the codification of important areas of customary international law into positive treaty form; (4) arms reduction, but only after, not before, the relaxation of international tensions by means of these and other legalist techniques and institutions; and (5) the institutionalization of the practice of convoking periodic conferences of all states in the recognized international community.[72]

The objective of securing a system of compulsory arbitration was, in many ways, the central concern of those who espoused the juristic theory of the state. For the international legal positivists, however, arbitration was no longer viewed as the only possible strategy for reforming international relations, as it had been by individuals like Willoughby and Hill. Oppenheim claimed that the task of fostering arbitration was unavoidably a result of the fact that there was "no central authority above sovereign states which could compel them to comply with the rules of international law or to submit their differences to a juridical decision."[73] While it was not always stated explicitly, proponents of arbitration historically had perceived the benefits of having states voluntarily submit their disagreements to an independent judicial body. In recognizing the difficulties of achieving a judicial settlement of international disputes in a milieu characterized by anarchy, many turned their attention to developing institutional mechanisms that could facilitate a greater reliance on arbitration. The Lake Mohonk Conferences on International Arbitration that took place each spring from 1895 through 1916 were dedicated to creating the institutional measures that would lead to a compulsory system of international arbitration. The importance that the United States government placed on arbitration was revealed by the State Department's request to have Moore chronicle the international cases of arbitration involving the United States. Moore's six volume *History and Digest of International Arbitration* (1898) greatly aided the task of divulging the existing cases of international arbitration.

At the same time that international legal scholars were seeking to advance the cause of international arbitration, others charged that, as a remedy for war, arbitration was severely limited by its narrow range of application. Owing to the voluntary nature of international arbitration, critics argued that the cases that were most often submitted to this procedure did not involve questions of national honor or vital interest. These were the grounds that the American geopolitical naval strategist Alfred Thayer Mahan rejected as naive the belief that arbitration could replace armaments and the use of force as the means of maintaining peace in Europe. In his book *Armaments and Arbitration* (1912), Mahan argued that the popular motto "law in place of war" blinded proponents of arbitration and other legalistic measures to the limited number of cases that were amenable to legal redress.[74] This left a significant number of other vital, and potentially war-provoking, issues outside the limited legal purview of arbitration. These types of strategic national-interest issues, Mahan argued, must be adjusted either through diplomacy or, ultimately, force. Just as arbitration was an institution designed to ameliorate certain types of disputes, so, Mahan believed, was war. He also claimed that arbitration procedures should not encumber the ability of a state to defend vital national interests.

This was the point of view Mahan had brought to the First Hague Peace Conference in 1899 when he was chosen by President McKinley to be one of the United States' delegates. The conference itself was the result of a proposal made by Nicholas II, Tsar of Russia, to consider "a possible reduction of the excessive armaments which weigh upon all nations." This led to a meeting of twenty-six states at The Hague in 1899, and indirectly, to a second meeting in 1907. These meetings, popularly known as the Hague Peace Conferences of 1899 and 1907, were viewed by many international legal positivists as providing concrete confirmation that their own approach to the study of international affairs was leading to a reordering of international relations on the basis of law and justice. For those espousing the creed of "internationalism," the Hague Peace Conferences were evidence of an evolutionary movement leading in the direction of a true society of nations. It was these aspects of the Hague Conferences that provided a strong impetus to the theoretical critique of the individualistic state of nature characterization of international politics. While agreeing that the conferences did indeed demonstrate evolutionary progress toward an international society, the international legal positivists were more apt to accentuate the legal mechanisms created at The Hague. This was largely due to the fact that many of the institutional and legal innovations that resulted from the Hague Conferences were ones that the international legal positivists had been advocating. As a group, they also took pride in the fact that it was the United States delegation that led the way in introducing many of the most important institutional reforms.

The delegation that President McKinley appointed to represent the United States at the First Hague Peace Conference was instructed to pursue the feasibility of creating an international tribunal for obligatory arbitration.[75] Although objections were immediately raised against the idea of obligatory arbitration for all cases of dispute, the participants at the conference did agree to establish the Permanent Court of Arbitration. Even though the Permanent Court of Arbitration failed to embody all of the principles that a real court of arbitration required, it did, nevertheless, create much of the necessary institutional machinery— such as established rules of procedure, a designated meeting place, and a functioning administrative council that encouraged states to resort to arbitration for settling disputes. The general consensus that the vast literature published on the First Hague Peace Conference reached was that the creation of the Permanent Court of Arbitration was the most important institutional accomplishment.[76]

The tangible as well as symbolic success of the first meeting at The Hague provided additional inspiration for those who were investing their intellectual energy in reforming the practice of international politics. This was especially true for the members of peace societies who perceived an evolutionary movement away from the disorder and violence that historically accompanied international anarchy.[77] Some of those involved in the international peace movement in the United States, particularly Benjamin F. Trueblood and Raymond L. Bridgman, proclaimed that world sovereignty was quickly becoming an established fact. Taken together, Trueblood's *The Federation of the World* (1899) and Bridgman's *World Organization* (1905) outlined most of the central tenets concerning the composition of the incipient world federation. Although they differed in their approach, and in their enumeration of the respective legislative, judicial, and executive organs, they both shared the conviction that the federation of the world was inevitable. Bridgman, who, after graduating from Amherst College in 1871 and Yale graduate school in 1877, became a journalist in Boston, maintained that it was the claim to national sovereignty that continued to be the greatest obstacle to the development of the unity of the world. He attempted to demonstrate that the only absolute sovereign was mankind, and that world sovereignty did not pose any kind of threat to national sovereignty. Bridgman mistakenly thought that the federal structure of the United States supported his claim, and he declared that world sovereignty "does not interfere with rightful national sovereignty, any more than the sovereignty of the United States interferes with the local sovereignty of the States."[78]

Trueblood, who served as secretary of the American Peace Society during its heyday in the early 1900s, believed that with the appearance of Christianity began the whole movement for the abolition of war, ultimately culminating in the federation of the world. He argued that the essential unity and common solidarity of human beings had been foiled by the "war system," which resulted in disunity, fighting, and hatred among people of all ages. Yet beginning with the movement to create a system of arbitration, humanity had begun to confront the war system. Trueblood maintained that although arbitration was the immediate objective, it was not the highest goal humanity was capable of achieving. He argued that the real significance of arbitration was that it pointed to the higher level of cooperation that mankind was destined to achieve, namely, a federation of the world. Trueblood declared that with the creation of a world state, "the peace of the world, so far as that means the cessation of war, will be forever sealed. International chaos and anarchy, as they now deplorably exist, will have passed away."[79]

In the interim, those who continued to advocate the cause of arbitration, as well as those who sought to institutionalize the practice of convoking international conferences, encouraged President Theodore Roosevelt to issue a call for a Second Hague Conference. Roosevelt was sympathetic to the request, and after a series of diplomatic details had been worked out, a proposal on behalf of the Russian Tsar that a second conference be held at The Hague was issued. The proposal resulted in forty-four states meeting at The Hague in June 1907, with the aim of continuing the work that was begun less than eight years earlier. Many sought to build on the foundations that had been established at the first meeting, and there were high expectations that a system of obligatory arbitration could be achieved. Yet many of the optimistic expectations that were expressed at the beginning of Second Hague Conference failed to materialize into tangible results by the time that the conference concluded. The proposal to establish an obligatory arbitration treaty did not get much further than it had at the first meeting, and an agreement also could not be reached on the institutional measures that were necessary for creating a judicial court. This is not to suggest, however, that no positive outcomes resulted from the Second Hague Conference. If the creation of the Permanent Court of Arbitration was the crowning achievement of the First Hague Conference, then the creation of an International Prize Court was the great accomplishment of the Second Hague Conference. The Prize Court was intended to serve as an international court of appeal by adjudicating disputes from national courts in cases that involved the capture of merchant ships during naval warfare. An international tribunal, it was believed, would be better able to solve the disputes arising between neutrals and belligerents than the partisan decisions of national courts. In addition to the Prize Court, a number of agreements were reached concerning the rules of warfare and the rights of neutrals. And before the Conference was adjourned, a final resolution was passed that called for a third meeting to take place at a later point in time. Yet, once again, many believed that the achievements of the Second Hague Conference could not be judged simply on the basis of how many institutional mechanisms had been created. In many ways, it was the symbolic dimension of the Hague Conferences that encouraged international relations scholars to rethink the conventional ontological description of international politics.

William Hull concluded his study of the Hague Conferences by suggesting that "the indirect results of great events in the world's history are often of greater importance than are their direct and measurable ones." He argued that this was the case with the Hague Conferences, especially with respect to "their promotion of what may be called in Tennyson's phrase, 'the federation of the world.'"[80] Hull claimed that as a result of the Conferences, it was now possible to discern an international legislative, judicial, and executive branch of a world federative union. According to Hull, the Hague Conferences could be described as world legislative assemblies, the Permanent Court of Arbitration and International Prize Court could be considered judicial organs, and the rise of an international public opinion was beginning to take on the characteristics of an international executive. Although not everyone would have agreed with Hull's specification of the three branches composing the world federative union, the opinion that many did begin to share was that the character of international relations had changed. The transformation was described most generally as one in which greater interdependence and unity among states had come to replace independence and disunity.

Nicholas Murray Butler, who had been a devoted student of Burgess, was a leading advocate of the idea that the world had experienced a fundamental transition from independence to interdependence, which, in turn, made "war increasingly difficult and increasingly repulsive." During his long reign as president of Columbia University from 1901 until his retirement in 1945, Butler embodied the internationalist ethos in his scholarly writings, personal relations with world leaders, advisory roles to several United States Presidents, and the many institutional positions that he held, including the presidency of the Carnegie Endowment for International Peace from 1925 to 1945. In an address before the Lake Mohonk Conference on International Arbitration, Butler declared, "unless all signs fail, we are entering upon a period which may be described fittingly as one of internationalism."[81] He argued that the entire world had become a "brotherhood of fellow-citizens," in the sense that barriers of language had been eroded, distance in space and time had been reduced by steam and electricity, and trade between distant lands had been made as easy as trade between people living on the same street. The quintessential expression of internationalism was nowhere more apparent than in what Butler termed the "international mind." According to Butler, "the international mind is nothing else than that habit of thinking of foreign relations and business, and that habit of dealing with them, which regard the several nations of the civilized world as friendly and co-operating equals in aiding the progress of civilization, in developing commerce and industry, and in spreading enlightenment and culture throughout the world."[82]

Butler held that the international mind, or public opinion more generally, could be regarded as the international executive organ of the slowly, but steadily approaching political organization of the world. He was confident that the movement toward a world-wide international organization was "as sure as that of an Alpine glacier," and he argued that the institutional infrastructure had already become clearly visible. In addition to the international mind, Butler pointed to the Hague Conferences and the work of the Interparliamentary Union as examples of international judicial and legislative organs. In the years leading up to World War I, the argument that the constitution of inter-state politics had reached a point where it was now possible to speak of a federation of the world, or an international society, became an increasingly popular, albeit controversial, idea in both academic and public circles.

Those who supported this sentiment were expressly critical of the theory informing the atavistic view that international politics could be explained in terms analogous to the conditions found in the state of nature. The image fostered by juristic theory that every political community was autonomous and independent from every other community was held to be grossly inadequate. Some scholars began to argue that the theory of sovereignty postulating an independent and isolated existence of the life of the state was inconsistent with the fact of mutual interdependence. Philip Marshall Brown, who after holding several different governmental posts, was professor of international law and diplomacy at Harvard University, exemplified this attitude when he wrote, "as a matter of fact, the conception of states absolutely independent of each other, living as it were in a fictitious state of nature, is in antagonism with the conception of a community of nations submitting voluntarily to a common code of international law."[83] Brown acknowledged that the theory of state independence was a crucial component of the state's most basic right to exist. Yet he also maintained that the traditional right of a state to exist, which had served as one of foundations of Grotius's system of international law, was a baseless assumption that lacked any legal value. Brown argued that the existence of a state really depended on recognition from other states that it had mutual rights and obligations to the larger community of nations. Based on this criterion, the existence of a state was a formal acknowledgment of the mutual interdependence, not independence, of states.

The idea that interdependence had come to exemplify the relations among states increasingly led political scientists to conclude that the traditional ontological description of international relations as the antithesis of society was both empirically and theoretically erroneous. In an article entitled "International Law and Political Science," Alpheus Henry Snow, who was an expert on colonial affairs at George Washington University, focused attention on the conventional distinction between the law of each nation and international law. Snow claimed that the ostensible difference between these two branches of law was primarily a function of the prevalent belief that a political society existed within a nation, whereas with international law, "one finds himself expected to accept as a fundamental proposition that there is no political society which formulates, applies and enforces the law which he is told governs all nations in their external relations."[84] Snow commented on how the recent development of political science, which he described as a science that dealt with particular political societies, had augmented the difficulties of acquiring knowledge of the political and legal affairs of the world. Political science, Snow argued, shared a parochial bias similar to that which existed in the study of law. He observed that the scope of political science included the study of the "structure and working of the town, the country, the state, and the nation for the purpose of making these political societies more economical and efficient." But, he added, when it came "to apply political science to the structure and working of the whole human society, they are confronted by a prevalent idea that beyond the limits of nations, or at least beyond the limits of political organisms like the British Empire, there is political chaos."[85] This is an idea that continues to hold sway today among many participants in the political discourse of anarchy.

Snow, however, emphasized that recent events were nullifying the conventionally perceived dichotomy between community and order within, and solitariness and anarchy outside, the arbitrarily defined confines of political society. He believed that a new revolutionary philosophy had arisen that proclaimed the moral worth and dignity of all individuals. This philosophy dictated that the test of whether social arrangements were valid or not should be based on whether they corresponded to the moral worth of the individual. Snow argued that this had the practical effect of altering the outlook of people with respect to all types of economic, social, and political organizations. He insisted that this outlook was contributing to a cosmopolitan sentiment in which individuals no longer perceived themselves to be bound to any one exclusive social, economic, or political organization. Snow maintained that just "as each human being is born a citizen of his city, a citizen of his state, or a citizen of his nation, so also, it is being realized, he is born a citizen of that great inclusive society composed of all the peoples and nations of the world."[86] Snow argued that through the popular press, education, travel, and other media individuals were increasingly cognizant of the fact that their solidarity with other people extended across territorially defined political communities. This newly discovered identity among the people of the world greatly differed from the older "technical" meaning of solidarity which, Snow claimed, was embodied in the idea that nations were "the mutual guarantors of each other." It was this "technical" version of solidarity that informed the balance of power system which Snow believed represented the antithesis of political organization. The new meaning of solidarity, however, was making it possible for the people of the world to relate to other political communities in a more extensive and inclusive fashion. It was for all of these reasons that Snow argued that it was now possible to speak of the existence of a society of nations.

Snow conceded that the term "society of nations" owed itself more to popular expression than to scientific accuracy. Yet his main argument was that the society of nations be made a subject of study by political science. The fact that a society of nations was recognized by the nations and people of the world provided sufficient intellectual justification for political scientists to incorporate this inclusive political unit under its domain of study. Snow wrote:

> It requires but a moment's reflection on the part of an intelligent person to perceive that if the common sense and judgment of the world accept the society of nations as a part of present day practical politics, it can be made a subject of study by political science exactly in the same way as a town, a city, a state, a nation or an empire.[87]

Snow, like Hull and Butler, argued that when the methods and principles of political science were applied to the society of nations, it would be found that a functioning federal state, although primitive in form, was governing this all-encompassing political society. According to Snow, the constituent executive, judicial, and legislative branches of a federal state were all discernible. Although the institutions that comprised the structure of the world federal state lacked the specificity they possessed in a national federal system such as the United States, Snow argued that their existence and practical importance could not be denied.

While some political scientists debated the issue of whether or not a world federation was taking form, others began to focus their attention on the institutional mechanisms and processes fostering international organization. The focus that was placed on the study of international organization before World War I is important for understanding the discourse that would emerge during the interwar period. Evidence of this earlier conversation seriously challenges the prevalent view that the study of international organization only appeared after the League of Nations was created in 1920. Paul Reinsch was instrumental in helping to introduce and popularize the formal study of international organization in the international relations scholarly community. The publication of Reinsch's *Public International Unions Their Work and Organization* (1911) must be regarded as a foundational text in the history of the field. Unlike the late-nineteenth-century struggle for national existence, which he depicted in *World Politics*, Reinsch argued that the beginning of the twentieth century was marked by a profound sense of internationalism. Reinsch claimed to observe the occurence of internationalism in the growing ties of interdependence among nations that made it increasingly difficult for a state to achieve its national objectives without acting in concert with other nations. He argued that the underlying foundations for internationalism were to be found in the recent convergence of cultural, economic, and scientific interests that were common to all of humanity. He explained that "in our own age such bonds of union have been powerfully supplemented by the growing solidarity of economic life throughout the world, as well as by the need in experimental and applied science to utilize the experience and knowledge of all countries."[88]

Reinsch did not consider interdependence and solidarity among states to be an abstract or lofty ideal. Rather, he argued that they were the defining characteristics of international politics in the early decades of the twentieth century. Reinsch judged his age "realistic and practical," and claimed that "the idea of cosmopolitanism is no longer a castle in the air, but it has become incorporated in numerous associations and unions world-wide in their operation."[89] The crux of Reinsch's book was directed toward examining the composition, activities, and functions of the numerous public international unions that had arisen in the late 1800s and early 1900s.[90] Public international unions were defined as associations of states that had common interests in coordinating and regulating specific areas of international relations. In this sense, public international unions are very similar to what are today termed international regimes.[91] According to Reinsch, the existence of international public unions provided tangible proof of the interdependent character of international politics. The forty or more public international unions, which included the International Telegraph Union (one of the earliest examples of a public union formed in 1865), the International Labor Office, the International Institute of Agriculture, the Universal Radiotelegraph Union, were each responsible for regulating a particular segment of international civil society. Reinsch divided the existing unions into their respective areas of jurisdiction, such as communications, trade, health, and agriculture, and provided general information about their formation, organization, and operation. In each case, he attempted to demonstrate how common interests among states led to the necessity of forming international public unions. Reinsch claimed that the existence of these unions, many of which possessed executive bureaus, arbitration tribunals, and legislative assemblies, provided tangible proof that international politics was being reordered in the direction of world unity.

It was on the basis of this assumption that Reinsch concluded that the older abstract view of sovereignty was no longer applicable to the present conditions shaping international politics. He declared that

> International cooperation has become an absolute necessity to states, along all the various lines of national enterprise. National independence must not be interpreted as equivalent to national self-sufficiency, nor ought we to think of political sovereignty as enabling a nation to do exactly what it pleases without regard to others.[92]

Reinsch did not, however, believe that interdependence implied that the national state was going to be superseded by some sort of supranational organization. He maintained that the national state was still at the center of the stage in international politics. Yet he did insist that it was only by acting in conjunction with other actors through international public unions that states could achieve their individual and collective interests.

Conclusion

This last premise would undergo a significant amount of change throughout the interwar period and, indeed, continues to be a main pillar in the contemporary discourse of international relations. There is a lineage stretching from Reinsch's ideas to those associated with present-day neoliberal institutionalists.[93] Yet within the contemporary discourse on international organization there is little, if any, reference made to the writings and ideas of Reinsch. But this is to be expected, since it is a common assumption that the field of international relations did not come into existence until after World War I. The unfortunate consequence of this belief is that the period that this chapter has chronicled is not even considered. It is doubly unfortunate, because there are a number of themes and issues from this period that are extremely relevant for understanding the subsequent development of the field. For example, while the relationship between international relations and political theory would be severed as both fields increasingly became autonomous enclaves, there was originally a close fit between these academic enterprises. The juristic theory of the state, which represented the orthodoxy of the young discipline of political science, worked to forestall an analytically distinct investigation of international relations. The notion of sovereignty that informed juristic theory contributed to a specific ontological description of the international milieu. It was an ontology that logically flowed from the theory of the state.

While the juristic theory of the state would undergo a major transformation during the 1920s (Chapter 5), it is noteworthy that it was scholars working in the international field who began to question the empirical adequacy that this theory projected onto the realm of interstate relations. The image of international relations provided by the juristic theory of the state was perceived to be anomalous with respect to the practices shaping international politics in the early years of the twentieth century. Contrary to the juristic claim that states led an independent existence in their external relations with other states, critics argued that international life was characterized by mutual ties of interdependence. In this manner, it is possible to view some striking similarities between the debate among proponents and critics of juristic theory and the positions associated with neorealism and neoliberalism. Interdependence was one of the central factors that led scholars to search for an alternative theory to account for the practices taking place in international politics. In the process of seeking to formulate a more accurate representation of international politics, scholars began to put forth a different image of the international milieu than what juristic theory depicted. This reformulated ontology gave rise to the idea that a world federation or society of states had come into existence. This, in turn, led to different ways of envisioning the character and manifestations of international anarchy. Most importantly, it led some to conclude that the existing international anarchy could be reformed.

Each of these trends would be accelerated during the interwar period as political scientists and international relations scholars expunged the juristic theory of the state from their political vocabulary. Before turning to these developments, attention must be redirected toward the discourse connected with the "Politics" section that was mentioned at the outset of this chapter. This was a discourse that focused on national imperialism and colonial administration. Although scholars were beginning to embrace the idea that the sovereign states of the world were collectively forming something akin to a society or community of nations, there were definite limits to the inclusiveness of this society. Most significant was the claim that the "uncivilized" regions of the world were not members of the society of nations. Thus, while Reinsch described the influences that had led to the creation of public international unions, he also declared that it was "only the undeveloped, the out-of-the-way, half-civilized states that do not feel the pervading influence of these world-wide forces expressing themselves in international action and international law."[94] The next chapter examines the discourse that was directed toward these "out-of-the-way" regions.

4

ANARCHY WITHIN: COLONIAL ADMINISTRATION AND IMPERIALISM

Authors and Works Discussed

Author	1885	1890	1895	1900	1905	1910	1915	1920
Angell						(1911)		
Burgess			(1899)	(1900)				
Giddings			(1898)					
Goodnow				(1904)				
Hobson				(1902)	(1905)			
Ireland			(1899)		(1906)			
Kerr							(1916)	
Lippman							(1915)	
Morris					(1906)			
Reinsch				(1902)	(1905,1906)			
Snow				(1902,1906)				
Wilson	(1888)							

Norman Angell 1872–1967
The Great Illusion [1911]

John W. Burgess 1844–1931
"How May the US Govern its Extra-Continental Territory?" *PSQ* [1899]
"The Relation of the Constitution of the US to the Newly Acquired Territory" *PSQ* [1900]

Franklin Giddings 1855–1931
"Imperialism?" *PSQ* [1898]

Frank J. Goodnow 1859–1939
"The Work of the APSA" *Proceedings* [1904]

John A. Hobson 1858–1940
"The Scientific Basis of Imperialism" *PSQ* [1902]
Imperialism: A Study [1905]

Alleyne Ireland 1871–1951
Tropical Colonization [1899]
"On the Need for a Scientific Study of Colonial Administration" *Proceedings* [1906]

Philip Henry Kerr 1882–1940
"Political Relations Between Advanced and Backward Peoples" [1916]

Walter Lippman 1889–1974
The Stakes of Diplomacy [1915]

Henry C. Morris 1868–1948
"Some Effects of Outlying Dependencies Upon the People of the United States"
Proceedings [1906]

Paul S. Reinsch 1869–1923
Colonial Government [1902]
Colonial Administration [1905]
"The Problems of Colonial Administration" [1906]

Alpheus Henry Snow 1859–1920
The Administration of Dependencies [1902]
"The Question of Terminology" *Proceedings* [1906]

Woodrow Wilson 1856–1924
"The Study of Administration" *PSQ* [1888]

The last chapter concluded by arguing that the focus international relations scholars began to place on the study of world order reform in the years before World War I was largely the result of a paradigmatic change in the way the practice of international politics was conceptualized. This shift was described in terms of a transition from an ontology that emphasized the solitary nationalistic struggle for state independence to an ontology that accentuated the solidarity and interdependent character of the relationship among states. The term, internationalism, that came into popular usage indicated that nation-states as well as their respective political communities were part of a larger society of nations. The cosmopolitan element of the internationalist ontology emphasized the common interests among the individual states which comprised international society. It was the convergence of state interests in world peace, commerce, and social welfare, along with the numerous examples of state cooperation represented in The Hague Conferences and the public international unions, that encouraged scholars to construct proposals that they believed would create a worldwide political organization. International anarchy would, in short, be mitigated by an effective international organization.

Although the internationalist ethos that began to inform the study of international law and international organization occupied a large portion of the discourse within the field of international relations during this period, this was not the only discussion that political scientists were pursuing. While often ignored, or only given scant attention, the study of colonial administration within political science comprised a considerable share of the discourse about international politics. A review of the programs from the early annual meetings of the APSA reveals that there were many panels devoted to the topic of colonial administration. At the first annual meeting in Chicago, Henry C. Morris, a lawyer and author, recommended that the APSA establish a colonial section to study the problems connected with colonization and colonial policy. Morris claimed that "the government would, undoubtedly, in time, recognize the value of such an organization and those officials under whose direct supervision the administration of the colonies falls, would soon appreciate the assistance and help offered them."[1] At the third annual meeting, held in Providence, Rhode Island, in 1906, two of the eight sessions were devoted to the topic of the government of dependencies. Furthermore, the index of recently published literature in the earliest volumes of the *American Political Science Review* included a separate section entitled "colonies."

The discussion of the colonized regions of the globe, often described in language that most would today find offensive and inappropriate, fell outside the domain set by the early-twentieth-century discourse about the relations among sovereign states. Most political scientists believed that the colonized regions—the "dark" places, the "uncivilized," the "backward" or "barbaric" areas of the world—did not belong to the society of states. Rather than being viewed as constituent members of international society, the colonized regions were seen as falling outside of the society of nations and as places plagued by internal anarchy. In other words, the colonized regions of the world were not viewed as sovereign states and thus did not "fit" into the traditional discourse. A different set of discursive criteria from that used to explain the interactions of "civilized" states was formulated by political scientists to discuss the issues that pertained to these "other" regions of the world. As Martin Wight has explained, "the question of relations with barbarians was a political problem forming a bridge between international relations and colonial administrations."[2] This chapter reconstructs the discourse that was used by political scientists during the first quarter of the twentieth century to understand, elucidate, and explain the politics associated with national imperialism and colonial administration.

More specifically, the chapter begins by locating the conversation of colonialism within the larger context of the study of administration, which occupied a central position in the discipline of political science. Although it is indisputable that the acquisition of several colonial possessions by the United States following the Spanish-American War in 1898 helped to make the subject of colonial governance extremely conspicuous and relevant to American political scientists, this external event, by itself, does not explain the conversation that arose in the field of international relations. Furthermore, the specific concerns that resulted from the imperial actions of the United States were only one component of the discourse concerning colonialism. After locating this conversation in its proper context, the chapter will describe the main features of the discourse about colonial rule. This will include a reconstruction of the debate that centered on the reasons for the supposed necessity of colonial expansion and the debate over the best way to administer the dependent territories. Finally, the chapter will also reconstruct a more extensive conversation that dealt with the wider implications for world politics of the struggle between "civilized" and "uncivilized" states. This will include an examination of the conceptual change this conversation brought about in the meaning and significance of anarchy. Rather than anarchy signifying the absence of a global authority structure, the meaning of anarchy in this context was to denote internal lawlessness and chaos resulting from the lack of a domestic sovereign.

The Study of Administration and the State

From the outset, the study of administration occupied a central place within the discipline of political science. Mary Furner has suggested that it was a "common interest in comparative administration that ultimately led to the creation of a separate national association of political scientists."[3] Woodrow Wilson published his famous article, "The Study of Administration," in 1888, well before the APSA was formed. Wilson claimed that the science of administration was the most recent branch of the comprehensive science of politics, which aimed at discovering "what government can properly and successfully do," and "how it can do these things with the utmost possible efficiency and at the least possible cost either of money or of energy."[4] According to Wilson's reformist creed, it was "getting to be harder to *run* a constitution than to frame one." When the APSA was formed in 1903, administration was one of the original seven committees that were created in order to cover the whole field of political science.

Frank Goodnow, who was an original member of the committee of administration and a professor of administrative law at Columbia University, reserved a central place for the study of administration in his presidential address to the APSA. Administration, according to Goodnow, represented one of the central divisions in the study of political science. Goodnow, it will be recalled, defined political science as the science of the state that aimed at elucidating the "various operations necessary to the realization of the State will." In this respect, Goodnow considered the study of administration to be fundamental to the task of analyzing the execution of the State will once it had been expressed. The dichotomy between politics, defined as the determination of the will of the state, and administration, the execution of the will of the state, was clearly articulated in Goodnow's *Politics and Administration* (1900). Yet in this work, as in his presidential address, Goodnow was less concerned about drawing a sharp distinction between politics and administration than he was about establishing the importance of administration for the study of the state. Goodnow claimed that "a study of government which excludes the consideration of the administrative system and actual administrative methods is as liable to lead to error as the speculations of a political theorist which have no regard for the principles of public law."[5]

The request to include the study of administration within the theoretical discourse of the state was one that most political scientists generally accepted. The assumption that the state was the proper domain of political science was taken to be axiomatic. What was not self-evident, at least for Henry Jones Ford, was why political scientists restricted their study of the state exclusively to the "national, popular state of Western civilization." Ford, a professor of political science at Johns Hopkins, maintained that so long as political scientists continued to impose an unduly restrictive meaning on the term, the State, the discipline would never be able to "supply general principles for the guidance of statecraft."[6] Ford presented his argument about the parochial and subjective nature of the study of the state at the second annual meeting of the APSA, and his comments were particularly relevant with respect to the early discourse of international relations.

Ford observed that whereas the *Statesmen's Year Book* for 1905 provided data for more than 250 states in the world, political scientists restricted their scholarly attention to only a handful of them. In fact, Ford argued that according to the narrow criteria used by political scientists, many of the states listed in the *Year Book* did not even qualify as states. Ford provided several reasons why he felt this was unacceptable. First, it meant that political scientists excluded from their study many of the states that represented the "chief centers of disturbance in world politics." Second, by limiting the subject matter to only those states that had reached a certain stage of political evolution, "political science announces by its own definition that it does not pretend to be co-extensive with all forms of political authority."[7] Third, political science risked the possibility of staking its claim to the authority of knowledge on an inherently temporary and transitory form of political organization that was inevitably bound to undergo change. Finally, it illustrated that political science did not rest on an objective basis.

Those who claimed that the maxims of political science had universal validity were, according to Ford, deluding themselves. According to Ford, it was quite apparent "that when we speak of the principles of political science what we really mean is general observations based upon the race-experience of a group of peoples whose culture rests upon Greco-Roman foundations."[8] He argued that the discipline's biased approach to the study of the state was indefensible. Ford found no compelling reason why political scientists should restrict their analysis only to the activities of certain types of states, and he argued that the discipline could never consider itself properly constituted until a more objective basis was found. This meant that in addition to the traditional idea of the "civilized" state, other forms of political organization had to be included within the scope of political science.

Ford correctly recognized the highly selective criteria that were used to analyze the different forms of political communities. Although the colonized regions of the world formed an increasingly larger percentage of the total population and geographical landmass of the world, the most significant issue that this provoked within the theoretical discourse of the state concerned the question of whether it was possible for a state to extend its sovereignty to a colony. Theoretical speculation concerning the possibility of a state's granting some of its sovereignty to a colony had parallels with the discussion that centered on the question, raised by individuals such as Burgess and Dunning, of whether sovereignty was divisible. When the issue was posed in terms of the external qualities of sovereignty, it was found that, just as in the internal context, the sovereignty of a state could not be divided. This meant that it was not possible for a state to grant authority to another political body without unavoidably dissolving itself. According to the juristic theory of the state, it was, however, possible for a state to grant a large degree of political autonomy to a colonial territory and still retain sovereignty. Westel Woodbury Willoughby expressed this opinion when he wrote that "mother countries may concede to colonies the most complete autonomy of government," and "yet as long as such control exists, the Sovereignty of the mother country over its colony is not released, and such colony is to be considered as possessing only administrative autonomy, not political independence."[9] The conclusion reached by Willoughby had a number of implications for the ensuing debate over what the proper political relationship should be between the United States and the newly acquired colonial possessions.

Before turning to this debate, it is noteworthy to point out that it was not only the proponents of the juristic theory of the state who limited most of their attention to the so-called civilized states. A similar focus of analysis was also apparent among most of the international lawyers. Although there were some exceptions, the conventional view was that international law was only applicable to the existing "civilized" states. The statement in T.J. Lawrence's popular international law text that "international law may be defined as the rules which determine the conduct of the general body of civilized states in their mutual dealings" provides one indication of this perspective.[10] Many of those who were propagating the idea of a genuine society of states simply excluded the "uncivilized" nations from their purview. In an address before the American Society of International Law in 1907, Richard Olney, who had served as President Cleveland's Secretary of State from 1895 to 1897, declared that when international law makes reference to the international society of states, "savage tribes and scattered, nomadic, and casual collections of men may be disregarded." He added that "organized political communities are the units composing the society of civilized states and each is a member because it must be."[11] Although Alpheus Henry Snow had recommended that political science include the society of states as part of the subject matter, he was, at the same time, ambiguous about the exact composition of this "inclusive" society. Snow claimed that "the expression 'the society of nations,' as a term signifying the political society composed of all peoples and nations, or of all the civilized peoples and nations, is coming into common use."[12] More often than not, however, membership in the society of nations was perceived by political scientists as being confined to the few "civilized" states of European descent.

As a student of Colonial Government, Snow was interested in the different set of political relations that existed between colonial powers and their dependent territories, especially as it concerned the relations between the United States and the recently annexed insular possessions. He argued that just "as there is a recognized science of international relations and another recognized science of the internal relations of nations and states, there may yet perhaps be recognized a science of imperial relations."[13] The publication of Snow's *The Administration of Dependencies* (1902) was regarded as a major contribution to the literature devoted to the general topic of colonization. Unlike much of the existing literature, which merely provided a historical narrative of the past practices of colonial rule, Snow's work was an explicit attempt to draw lessons for the United States from the experiences of the British and French colonial systems.

The American Approach to the Administration of Dependencies

The question of how the United States should rule the colonial territories that it had acquired at the end of the Spanish-American War helped to elevate the importance of the discourse about colonial administration among political scientists. The early political science textbooks by Stephen Leacock and Raymond Gettell each included a separate chapter devoted to the topic of colonial government. Leacock acknowledged that "the recent expansion of the United States resulting from the war with Spain has rendered this portion of the study of government one of special consequence to Americans."[14] Gettell claimed that the governmental problems involved in colonial rule "are of prime importance to the student of political science."[15] Yet even before the conversation turned to the issue of the best way to administer colonial possessions, there was debate about why the United States became involved in colonialism in the first place. And while the debate over American imperialism was certainly not confined to the context of political science, political scientists did tend to accentuate certain issues.

Burgess, for example, was one of the first political scientists to raise the question of what the proper relationship between the United States Constitution and the new insular territories should be.[16] According to Burgess, Cuba and the Philippines were not fit for self-rule. Having arrived at this conclusion, attention next turned to an examination of the governing principles that should guide United States policy toward the insular regions. Burgess argued that whenever the United States placed its sovereignty over a new territory, it was expected to govern the area as if it was no longer "another country." Burgess cited several Supreme Court decisions as evidence that the Constitution applied to the United States' rule over colonial territories and he concluded that the Constitution should continue to guide colonial policy. Snow, however, maintained that the Supreme Court and the Constitution were the wrong places to seek the principles on which the United States should base its external rule. Snow argued that the Declaration of Independence provided the "fundamental principles on which all American political theory is based, and to which all American policy must conform." For Snow, this necessitated "that we ought to substitute, in our political and legal language, for the term 'colony,' the term 'free state,' for 'dependence,' 'just connection,' and for 'empire,' 'union.'"[17]

Burgess was certainly not an anti-imperialist. He believed, for example, that the acquisition of foreign colonies represented the "world-duty of carrying civilization into the dark places of the earth." According to Burgess, "the civilized states have a claim upon the uncivilized populations, as well as a duty towards them, and that claim is that they shall become civilized."[18] He was, however, strongly against the territorial expansion that followed the Spanish-American War. He maintained that the United States continued to have sufficient internal development and was thus not yet ready for external expansion. He believed that until the United States had its internal affairs in order, it should refrain from acquiring colonial possessions.[19] What induced the United States to acquire colonial territories was one of the more contentious issues that political scientists debated. For many of those who adhered to the juristic theory of the state, the acquisition of colonial possessions was a necessary stage of development. While generally rejecting the idea that material interdependence characterized the practice of inter-state relations, supporters of the juristic theory of the state were more likely to accept the idea of moral interdependence. According to this view, it was a moral duty of the "civilized" states to intervene and uplift those who inhabited the "inferior" regions of the world.

Henry Morris reacted negatively to this type of sentimentalism and, in a paper that he presented at the third annual meeting of the APSA, argued that "the original economic causes for colonization have too often been disguised under the enthusiasm of the fervent churchman or political philosopher."[20] Although Morris refrained from attributing American actions in the Caribbean and Far East solely to economic motives, he did provide empirical data that demonstrated that an expansion in trade to these regions was one of the most direct results of colonialism. Morris argued that even though an increase in American trade and commercial activity in these distant lands could have been expected to take place naturally over a ten-year span (1895–1905), it was nevertheless "doubtful if, without the stimulus inspired by the broader view of the world, gained by our military and naval experience, coupled with the acquisition of new territories, we should have accomplished any results in eastern trade comparable to those actually achieved."[21] After suggesting that the real motives behind territorial expansion were economic, Morris proceeded to discuss some of the likely effects that the administration of dependencies would have on the theory and practice of American government. He indicated that there would likely be a growing concentration of power in the executive branch of government and a manifold increase in duties toward other nations.

Reinsch, who was perhaps the leading expert on colonial affairs, was unquestionably aware of the economic motivations that Morris claimed were responsible for colonial expansion. Following the success of *World Politics* (1900), Richard Ely suggested that he write a book on colonial politics. Ely, who was the founder of the School of Economics, Political Science and History at the University of Wisconsin and the editor of the Citizen's Library of Economics, Politics, and Sociology for Macmillan Press, felt there was a need for a general textbook on colonial politics, and that no one was better qualified to produce such a work than Reinsch. Macmillan, with the urging of Ely, offered Reinsch a contract that resulted in the publication of *Colonial Government* in 1902. In the first part of the book, Reinsch surveyed the various motives and methods of colonial expansion. He viewed colonization as part of the evolutionary process through which "the more perfect forms of civiliza- tion draw into their orbit those which are less organized."[22] Of the various motives that Reinsch identified as leading to colonial expansion—movements in population, missionary work, individual exploration, adventure, commerce, and capitalistic expansion—it was the last two that he assigned to the latest wave of territorial aggrandize- ment. Reinsch observed that it had become an economic necessity for the industrialized nations to extend their commercial activities to new regions of the globe. He argued that the primary motivation behind the search for new markets was to find an outlet for the surplus goods that had been accumulated in the "advanced" states.

Yet even though Reinsch was an avowed expansionist, in the sense that he believed that it was both inevitable and legitimate to extend commerce and civilization to the far reaches of the world, he was sharply critical of the modern form of imperialism whereby one state formally possessed another. Reinsch argued that it was illogical to extend formal political rule over the "backward" regions of the world when the motivating factor behind national imperialism was economic. He had, in part, written *World Politics* as an attempt to warn of the dangers that national imperialism represented to world peace and to dissuade states from believing that economic gains could be realized through acquiring exclusive control of as large a portion of the earth's surface as possible. Reinsch recognized that it was the search by capital for outlets of profitable direct investment in foreign lands that ex- plained why "the pressure for extended political control is much stronger at present than it ever was in the days of purely commercial colonization."[23] Reinsch assumed that with large capital investments, it was only natural that investors would want to protect their assets by establishing formal political control over the dependent regions.

Yet at the same time that Reinsch believed that economic motives were the root cause of the recent wave of colonial expansion, he argued that "it was a political motive,—the desire to weaken the prestige of Spain,—that led the American government to make an attack upon Spanish dominion in the Philippine Islands, at a time when the Ameri- can nation had as yet no economic interests in the archipelago."[24] Re- insch felt that the United States had legitimate national interests in the Pacific region, and he personally supported the annexation of the Phil- ippines. He was, however, able to resolve this seemingly paradoxical position by advocating what he considered an enlightened and altruis- tic administrative policy toward the insular regions. Reinsch devoted considerable effort to devising the most appropriate institutional mechanism for reconciling the indigenous interests of those who inhabited the undeveloped regions with the need for economic expansionism on the part of the industrialized states. Reinsch supported colonial policies that granted as large a degree of autonomy to the insular regions as possible, and he was a leading critic of the United States' own attempt to assimilate the Philippines to American political ideals and values. Many of the administrative ideas that Reinsch endorsed were included in his book *Colonial Administration* (1905) which was a companion volume to *Colonial Government*. The question of how best to govern the colonial areas of the world was an important part of the discourse of political scientists, but before turning attention to this component of the conversation, it is important to consider the manner in which political scientists undertook their study of colonial administration.

The Methodology of Colonial Administration

Alleyne Ireland, a leading authority on colonial administration in both the United States and Great Britain, observed that while the subject of colonial administration increasingly was gaining the attention of both political scientists and the general public, there were few, if any, professional standards guiding research in this area. Ireland sarcastically wrote "that knowledge of calligraphy is regarded as the only qualification necessary for a writer on colonial tropics."[25] He argued that this had resulted in great damage to "the cause of a scientific study of colonial administration." Ireland traveled extensively and was the *London Times* correspondent in the Far East from 1902 to 1904. During the span of his career, Ireland served as a lecturer at Cornell University, the University of Chicago, and at the Lowell Institute. His books included *Colonial Administration in the Far East* (1907) and *Tropical Colonization* (1899). In 1906, Ireland delivered a paper at the annual meeting of the APSA in which he examined some of the fallacies that characterized the recent literature on colonization and, in the process, offered an alternative approach to the subject matter. His paper, in many ways, established the standard for future work in the field of colonial administration.

Ireland condemned the existing literature for its pervasive tendency to include issues about the morality of colonization in the analysis of the administration of dependencies. He argued that questions concerning the moral justification "for the subjection of one race under the rule of another" did not fall under the proper purview of colonial administration. Ireland also rejected assessing the morality of colonization with respect to the effects that it had on the subjected people. The morality or immorality of colonialism, Ireland maintained, was an issue that should be examined and resolved irrespective of the consequences that it might produce. When it came to articulating the method that should be followed, Ireland argued that the "method of judging by results, which is false and unscientific when applied to the moral principle of colonization, is precisely the method which must be followed when the subject under investigation is an applied science of colonial administration."[26] As with much of the administration literature, efficiency was the primary standard that was used to judge the relative merits of a specific administrative program. Ireland wrote:

> [I]t must be determined at the outset what those objects are with the attainment of which colonial administration is concerned; the examination of methods must follow, and it is only by finding out how far these methods have in practice produced the desired results that a code of administrative principles can be formulated.[27]

This, in turn, returned the conversation to the issue of the motives of colonization. Ireland argued that there was a lack of honesty on the part of many authors as to the real motives behind the effort to acquire dependencies. He agreed with Reinsch that the fundamental objective of recent imperialism was to develop and extend commerce. Ireland, along with many other political scientists, believed that this was a perfectly legitimate rationale, which, if carried out properly, would lead to positive benefits for everyone concerned. More importantly, candid recognition of the commercial objective provided a set of standards by which to evaluate the relative efficiency of the different systems of colonial administration.

Ireland identified two conflicting motives or principles from which two completely different methods of colonial administration resulted: the principle of development and the principle of exploitation. With respect to the first principle, Ireland argued that the aim of colonial administration was to provide beneficent rule. The underlying assumption behind this principle was that a prosperous and content native population would, in the long term, yield the best commercial results. Conversely, when the principle of exploitation was applied to colonial administration, the aim was to extract as many resources as possible from a country in the shortest time. He maintained that it was important to distinguish clearly between these two fundamentally different policies of colonial administration. Having established all of the preliminary foundations, Ireland proceeded to outline the details of a scientific study of colonial administration. He argued that the foremost purpose of a scientific approach to the subject was practical and it was quite apparent to Ireland that most of the existing literature was less than adequate for the task of providing practical solutions to the issues confronting the science of colonial administration. This was largely a manifestation of the fact that the purpose of the older type of research was historical rather than practical.

Ireland claimed that the study of colonial administration had, up until the present time, been "almost entirely the historic form." Albert Keller's textbook, *Colonization: A Study of the Founding of New Societies,* was typical of this genre. After an introductory chapter on definition and classification, the remainder of his work provided a chapter-by-chapter historical survey of Portuguese, Spanish, Dutch, Italian, and German colonial activities and practices. In this regard, the book was actually atypical in that Keller deliberately excluded British and French colonial experience from his analysis on the grounds that it would have "intolerably lengthened his task."[28] In any event, the main point was that most of the literature dealing with colonial administration was written strictly from a historical perspective. The aim of this research, apart from the purely antiquarian one, was to provide a comparison of the various methods that colonial powers had used to administer their dependencies.

Ireland also argued that a scientific approach to colonial administration should make use of the method of comparison, but unlike the historical element of comparison that "will be introduced into the inquiry on the basis of a broad range of time in a narrow field," the practical or scientific "comparison of phenomena will be made as far as possible within a narrow range of time and in a broad field."[29] The comparative method, Ireland argued, was the defining element of a science of colonial administration. This was largely consistent with the method that was being used in the broader field of administration within political science. In his seminal essay, Woodrow Wilson had argued that "nowhere in the whole field of politics, it would seem, can we make use of the historical, comparative method more safely than in this province of administration."[30] Wilson assured American political scientists that they had little to fear by looking at foreign systems of administration, because "so far as administrative functions are concerned, all governments have a strong structural likeness." Wilson was specifically referring to the form of efficiency that all modern governments shared. As further support for the comparative method, Wilson added that "we can never learn our own weaknesses or our own virtues by comparing ourselves with ourselves."[31]

Within the burgeoning discourse of colonial administration this last point was often met with resistance, even by those who endorsed the scientific approach that Ireland delineated. There was a prevalent belief among students of colonial administration that the principles of government embodied in the American Constitution limited the extent to which either comparisons or lessons from other states' colonial policies could be adapted by the United States. There were a number of instances in which a scholar would advocate the comparative method, while at the same time arguing for a unique American approach to colonial policy. For example, while Morris suggested that the APSA establish a colonial government sub-field, he wrote that "the need of the times in the elaboration and improvement of colonial government, administration and service seems emphatically to be an opportunity to become familiar with the experience of other nations under similar conditions."[32] Yet two years later, in a paper delivered at the third annual meeting of the APSA, he wrote that "in the organization of our colonial administration we have, naturally, followed a course peculiar to ourselves; in general, we have disregarded the methods elsewhere in force and devised our own system."[33]

The same sort of ambivalence between, on the one hand, accepting the comparative method for the study of colonial administration, and, on the other hand, advocating an unique American approach to the administration of dependencies was also apparent in the work of Reinsch. In *Colonial Government*, Reinsch explained that with the United States' unexpected possession of an extensive colonial domain, "it is the natural, and the only wise, course to turn to the experience of other nations who have had similar problems to face, and by whose failures and successes we may instruct ourselves."[34] But when he turned his attention to articulating the sort of colonial policy that the United States should follow toward the insular possessions, no one was more critical of the methods of the European powers than Reinsch. In order to understand Reinsch's ideas about what a proper and enlightened colonial policy should entail, it is necessary to consider the intellectual context in which this discourse occurred. The discussion concerning the respective merits of the different colonial policies was closely connected to the prior question of why the "uncivilized" regions had to be ruled in the first place. A consideration of this question places the discourse of colonial administration in a much wider intellectual context than the parochial concerns of the United States.

Colonial Rule

A concise inquiry into the reasons why the "uncivilized" regions of the world had to be ruled by the "civilized" powers was undertaken in both of the papers delivered at the colonial administration section of the Universal Exposition at the World's Fair in St. Louis in 1904. The main purpose of the St. Louis Exposition "was to place within reach of the investigator the objective thought of the world, so classified as to show its relations to all similar phases of human endeavor, and so arranged as to be practically available for reference and study."[35] Every important branch of scholarly endeavor was included in the Exposition. The fact that a section devoted to colonial administration was included in the Department of Politics, which itself was placed under the Division of Social Regulation, provides further support of the importance of this discourse within political science.[36]

The paper delivered by Bernard Moses, a professor of political science at the University of California who created one of the first formal courses in the subject of political theory, advanced a standard explanation of why there was no alternative to the "superior" powers controlling the "backward" regions. Moses's basic argument was that the luxury of isolated, independent, and autonomous development belonged to an earlier period. The contemporary age of interdependence, Moses explained, "made every country contiguous to every other country." The practical effect of the mutual dependence of states for the "barbaric people" was that it had become utopian to believe "that a rude people should be permitted to develop its own life without foreign interference." Moses claimed that "the spirit of contemporary civilization is intolerant of barbarian isolation."[37] He argued that this was especially apparent in light of the fact that many of the people in Africa, Latin America, and Asia failed to utilize and exploit their resources to the fullest extent possible. The interdependent character of international politics meant that the underutilization of resources in the tropics was not merely a local but a world concern. Moses argued that one of the primary justifications for external intervention into the dependent areas was to develop the resources that generally remained unused. He insisted that external interference would produce positive benefits for both the local areas and the world at large.

The paper presented by Reinsch expressed a viewpoint similar to that of Moses. Reinsch fully endorsed the idea of interdependence in the relations among states. He began his paper by declaring that "humanity is one, and the members of the brotherhood who through barbarous customs and irrational institutions are kept in a state of backwardness are to be led out into the light of freedom and reason and endowed with the multiform blessings of civilization."[38] This understanding of an affinity of all humanity and the belief in the necessity of commercial expansion were the two main pillars on which Reinsch constructed his proposal for an enlightened policy of colonial administration. Reinsch claimed that there were two points of view to consider when devising colonial policy. He held that the first point of view derived from "the needs of our own civilization." Reinsch argued that a principal feature of the "developed" states' civilization was the "mobility, concentration, and mastery over the forces of nature" which, in turn, contributed to the need for commercial expansion, in order to dispose of the surplus product in the home market, and for the investment of capital. It was particularly in the need for outlets of capital investment that Reinsch discerned a qualitative change in the relations between mother country and dependency. He maintained that the "demand for political sovereignty over extensive tracts of territory" was a direct result of capital's search for outlets of safe investment. Even though Reinsch believed that this was an erroneous path to follow, he argued that it was important to recognize the legitimate commercial motivations of the industrialized states when devising colonial policy. In addition to following Ireland's means-ends approach, Reinsch argued that the commercial end of colonial administration provided the most valid justification for extending "intensive methods to wider areas, and to introduce a productive economy into regions where at present time barbarian exploitation holds sway."[39]

The needs and interests of the inhabitants in the undeveloped regions was the second viewpoint to consider when devising colonial policy. Reinsch took this very seriously, and his book, *Colonial Administration,* was largely written from the indigenous populations' perspective. In his review of Reinsch's book, Goodnow claimed that the title was somewhat misleading, because it was "devoted to a consideration, largely from the view-point of the dependency, of the policy which should be followed by the mother country towards its colonial possessions."[40] Reinsch devoted chapters to education, colonial finance, commerce, communication, transportation, sanitation, and various other matters that a colonial policy should include. He argued that the character and needs of the indigenous people should be a crucial component of colonial administration. Reinsch claimed that when these interests were combined with the interests of civilization, the proper formula of a successful colonial administration policy was in hand: "to foster the cohesion and self-realization of native societies, while at the same time providing the economic basis for a higher form of organization,—that should be the substructure of an enlightened colonial policy."[41]

It was on the basis of Reinsch's claim that colonial policy should satisfactorily reconcile the interests of both colonizer and colonized that he was sharply critical of the policy adopted by United States toward the Philippines and the other insular regions acquired in the aftermath of the war with Spain. Reinsch argued that the United States was attempting to combine simultaneously two different and antithetical colonial policies. More specifically, he discerned a policy of assimilation, which did not take indigenous characteristics and needs into account, and a policy of autonomy, which did conform to the principles he had outlined for an enlightened colonial policy. He argued that a policy of assimilation would always lead to disastrous results because of the ethnocentric and rationalist doctrine "of the universality of human reason." Reinsch observed how the attempt to assimilate the native institutions of Philippine society into American ideas and values had been counterproductive. Yet, at the same time, he noted that colonial policy in the Philippines was aimed at fostering self-governance and autonomy. According to Reinsch, a policy of autonomy was the exact opposite of a policy of assimilation, because the aim of the former was self-determination.

Reinsch suggested that the United States move away from its two-track antagonistic policy and embrace those principles of colonial administration that fostered autonomy and which would, consequently, serve the best interests of humanity. He claimed that he had found the answer—one that granted the colonial territories the greatest amount of autonomy—in the form of the protectorate. According to Reinsch, the protectorate embraced the flexibility, insight, and imagination that was necessary for a colonial administration policy dedicated to fostering autonomy. He claimed that the international conception of the protectorate "presupposes two separate states, the weaker of which places itself, by treaty, under the protection of the stronger, retaining its internal autonomy, but permitting the protecting state to exert a guiding influence in its foreign affairs."[42] Many other students of colonial administration also began to recognize the positive attributes of a colonial policy that took the local needs and autonomy of the indigenous regions into consideration. In the discussion that followed a paper about the need for colonial autonomy in the Philippines delivered by Reinsch at the first annual meeting of APSA, Willougby responded by declaring that it was especially important within the field of colonial government to take "into account local needs, local prejudices, local habits, and, in general, the racial characteristics and political capacities of the people who are to be governed."[43]

Moses also shared Reinsch's perspective with respect to taking indigenous needs and interests into account when devising colonial policy. He stated that "to undertake to develop the wealth of a dependency peopled with semi-civilized inhabitants, without at the same time bringing about that social differentiation characteristic of a high grade of society, is simply to exploit that dependency."[44] While Moses believed that "dependence, or union with some great nation," was inevitable for the "peoples of the uncultivated races," he argued that it was also important that the advantages that accrued from union be mutually beneficial. In this regard, Moses advocated a form of colonial administration that set "a higher estimate on the dependent people than was usual when Europeans began to exercise political authority over communities composed of members of other races." And he argued that this "new policy of colonial administration, involving a people of another race, is more thoroughly carried out under the United States than elsewhere."[45]

Colonial Administration and World Politics

As indicated at the beginning of this chapter, the discourse about the relations between the "civilized" and "uncivilized" regions of the world was not simply limited to a focus on the best way to administer colonial possessions. The supposed necessity of extending political control over regions plagued by internal disorder (i.e., anarchy) helped to place the discussion of colonial administration within a much larger and extensive conversation about world politics in general. More specifically, the discourse was connected with the phenomenon on which Reinsch's first book, *World Politics At the End of the Nineteenth Century,* had focused—national imperialism. William Dunning presented a paper at the Universal Exposition that was entitled, "The Fundamental Conceptions of Nineteenth-Century Politics," in which he argued that the closing years of the century "may with a fair degree of accuracy be designated the era of imperialism."[46] Dunning wrote that the full meaning of the new wave of imperialism remained an unanswered question, especially with respect to the impact that it was having on both Aryan civilization and the uncivilized nations.

P.H. Kerr directly addressed this issue in his chapter entitled "Political Relations Between Advanced and Backward Peoples," in *An Introduction to the Study of International Relations* (1916). Kerr declared that "the problem of the relations which should exist between advanced and backward peoples has always been one of the gravest that has presented itself to mankind." He added that there was "no political question about which it is more important or more difficult to have clear ideas, for it is likely to be the crux of all the great controversies of the future."[47] In order to consider this fundamental question properly, Kerr argued, it was necessary to abandon a national perspective for a more cosmopolitan one that embraced the idea that the human race was one great family. At the same time, however, Kerr acknowledged that within this inclusive family, there existed a graduated scale of mankind "varying infinitely from the zenith of civilization to the nadir of barbarism." This great divide in the family of mankind necessitated, for Kerr, that a set of formal political relations be discovered that could produce favorable benefits for humanity at large. There was only one answer for Kerr. The states that represented superior civilization must assume responsibility for the government of the "backward" people. He argued that the civilized states could not stand aside and do nothing when the "barbaric" regions of the world continued to be plagued by injustices, chaos, and evil. The future progress of humanity, Kerr argued, was dependent on the backward races climbing the same ladder that the civilized states had successfully climbed toward law and justice. Kerr claimed that "nothing save anarchy and the disappearance of any real prospect of the internal restoration of that law and order which are the conditions of liberty and progress, can warrant any other people taking charge."[48]

It is important to emphasize that Kerr regarded this as a duty that the civilized states undertook not so much in their own interests but rather in the interests of the world at large. This, however, raised the difficult issue of deciding which of the great powers should undertake the task of intervening in the internal affairs of the "uncivilized" regions. Kerr referred to this as a problem of foreign politics. The problem was made all the more difficult by the fact that the civilized world included many great powers, and by the fact that any decision would necessarily effect the international balance of power. Kerr did not devote further attention to resolving this matter, and he concluded by suggesting that "the ruling people ought to govern the dependency as trustees for all mankind, having as their ultimate aim the raising of the inhabitants to the level which they can govern themselves and share in the greater responsibilities of the world."[49]

Other scholars, such as Franklin Giddings, the founder of academic sociology at Columbia University and a member of the original Columbia school, claimed that the different races of the world had varying capacities for progress. According to Giddings's Spencerian perspective, it was not so much that the "civilized" states should take it upon themselves to uplift the "uncivilized" tropical regions as it was a natural, biological law of selection which determined that stronger states would rule over weaker states. Giddings applied this view to an analysis of the Spanish-American War in which he also provided a spirited defense of territorial expansion in the Caribbean and Pacific. One of the primary intentions of his analysis was to debunk the arguments that had been put forth by the anti-imperialists who opposed the war. Giddings attempted to demonstrate that there were many "reasons for believing that the war with Spain was as inevitable as any event of nature and that, at this particular stage in the development of the United States, territorial expansion is as certain as the advent of spring after winter."[50]

In defense of his claim about the inevitability of territorial expansion, Giddings maintained that it was better to look at certain irrefutable scientific facts than to be "preoccupied with moral feeling." The first fact to consider was that the American population had come to represent "the most stupendous reservoir of seething energy to be found on any continent." Giddings argued that it was this same reservoir of energy that, during peacetime, "produced the American commercial spirit."[51] But with the need for foreign markets, which Giddings claimed became apparent in the United States by the late 1800s, when manufacturing and agricultural production outstripped home demand, the commercial spirit that had been held in check domestically was thrust outwardly when the opportunity arose in Cuba. Giddings considered the territorial acquisitions that followed from the war to be both justified and inevitable. Ample trade and an abundant supply of natural resources were two of the attributes shared by the great powers vying for supremacy over the weaker races. With this in mind, Giddings argued that the United States would only be able to increase its trade in the East "by maintaining our sovereignty over some territory, however small, in that quarter of the world." He acknowledged that "the task of governing from a distance the inferior races of mankind will be of great difficulty" but he argued "it is one that must be faced and overcome, if the civilized world is not to abandon all hope of continuing its economic conquest of the natural resources of the globe."[52]

In defense of this position, Giddings relied on the arguments provided by Benjamin Kidd's *The Control of the Tropics* which he regarded as one of the most significant recent contributions to political economy. Kidd was an obscure British sociologist until the publication of *Social Evolution* (1894) made him famous throughout the world. Kidd was also influenced by Herbert Spencer's ideas about social evolution which played a major role in his own attempt to create a science of human society. As a result of the financial success of *Social Evolution*, which was widely translated, Kidd was able to devote the remainder of his life to writing and travel. When he came to the United States in 1898, he wrote a series of articles for *The Times* which were later collected and published under the title *The Control of the Tropics*.

In this work, Kidd argued that an "epoch of instinctive rivalry" had accompanied the close of the nineteenth century. The rivalry, Kidd claimed, was for the control of the tropics—"the richest territories on the earth's surface." According to Kidd, there were a number of reasons why the European powers, along with America, would be locked in a struggle for the control of the tropics. First, there was the fact that these territories possessed a large amount of important natural resources that the European powers desired. Kidd argued, however, that in most cases the resources of the tropics remained undeveloped and idle. He maintained that the reason for this idleness was due to the fact that "over a considerable proportion of these regions at present we have existing a state either of anarchy, or of primitive savagery, pure and simple, in which no attempt is made or can be made to develop the natural resources lying ready to hand."[53] Kidd concluded that it was a self-evident fact that the superior races must play a direct role in surmounting the anarchy of the tropics so that the riches from these areas could be developed. Secondly, Kidd claimed that the average individual did not comprehend the full significance or importance of the trade relations between Europe and the tropics. He provided statistical data from Britain and the United States to illustrate how trade with the tropics represented a large percentage of total world trade. According to Kidd's figures, "the English-speaking world as a whole, and excluding from consideration all trade within its own borders, we found that its trade with the tropics amounted in such circumstances to some 38 percent of its total trade with all the rest of the world."[54]

Finally, Kidd pointed to the fact that the temperate regions were becoming "filled up" and were consequently looking to expand into new areas. It was because the tropics represented a lucrative and untapped reservoir of resources and, by extension, wealth, that the "civilized" powers would be willing to extend their control over these regions. Kidd wrote that "with the filling up of the temperate regions and the continued development of industrialism throughout the civilized world the rivalry and struggle for the trade of the tropics will, beyond doubt, be the permanent underlying fact in the foreign relations of the Western nations in the twentieth century."[55] Writing in 1917, Lenin reached a very similar conclusion in his pamphlet *Imperialism: The Highest Stage of Capitalism.* Although largely marginalized to a position outside the mainstream discourse of international relations, Lenin attempted to provide a defense of the view that imperialism was an iron law of capitalism at the monopoly stage. Lenin relied on the descriptions and statistical figures in John Hobson's *Imperialism: A Study* (1905). According to Lenin, one of the essential features of monopoly capitalism was that it was inevitably "*bound up* with the intensification of the struggle for the partition of the world."[56]

Rather than citing economic laws, Kidd relied on the Spencerian view that the European races had no choice but to take on the responsibility for administering the tropics. This necessity, Kidd claimed, arose from both the fact that the "civilized" powers needed the resources that were found in the tropics and the fact that the native inhabitants of the tropics, if left to themselves, would never develop the resources that they possessed. For Kidd, external intervention on behalf of the civilized states was a matter of social evolution. He claimed that the forces of social evolution no longer made it possible to tolerate "the wasting of the resources of the richest regions of the earth through the lack of the elementary qualities of social efficiency in the races possessing them." Social evolution, according to Kidd, provided but one test of superiority: "it is only the race possessing in the highest degree the qualities contributing to social efficiency that can be recognized as having any claim to superiority."[57]

Norman Angell's immensely influential work, *The Great Illusion,* disputed the type of claims that Giddings and Kidd advanced about the inevitability and necessity of imperial expansion over the "semicivilized" territories of the world. Indeed, one of the distinguishing features of Angell's thesis about the pervasive "optical illusion" which he argued affected the general public was the belief that economic benefits were gained when a state extended its territory over another region. Angell argued that, "it is a logical fallacy and an optical illusion in Europe to regard a nation as increasing in wealth when it increases its territory, because when a province or state is annexed, the population, who are the real and only owners of the wealth therein, are also annexed, and the conqueror gets nothing."[58] Originally published as a popular pamphlet in Europe, *The Great Illusion* went through several editions between 1908 and 1914. When the book was reviewed in the *American Political Science Review,* Amos Hershey wrote that "it may be doubted whether, within its entire range, the peace literature of the Anglo-Saxon world has ever produced a more fascinating or significant study."[59]

Angell defended his thesis regarding the illusionary nature of most of the fundamental axioms of statecraft on the basis that the contemporary nature of world politics was, most essentially, characterized by interdependence. This meant, for Angell, that a nation could not achieve commercial prosperity or military security through the process of conquering other nations. In fact, Angell argued that a fundamental paradox resulted from the effort to gain economic security through the employment of military might—"the more a nation's wealth is protected the less secure does it become." Angell argued that formal "ownership" of a given territory meant little when the international financial, banking, and investment activities transcended any one state. Angell went so far as to suggest that Great Britain would not suffer any material losses if she surrendered all of her colonial possessions. He concluded that Britain would be better off from trading and investing in the colonies as if they were autonomous nations rather than dependencies.

Angell argued that although the modern world had become economically interdependent, international politics continued to be dominated "by terms applicable to conditions which the process of modern life have altogether abolished." Angell viewed the current struggle for "semi-civilized" territory "as fruitful a source of conflict between the great Powers as did the scramble for the New World."[60] Besides rejecting the argument that the latest scramble for colonial possessions was a result of economic imperatives, Angell also dismissed the biological metaphors that suggested that it was somehow natural and inevitable for the "superior" states to control the "inferior" states. In the second part of the book, entitled "The Human Nature of the Case," he confronted the popular Darwinian view that the most warlike nations were the fittest to survive. Angell systematically concluded that the warlike nations do not inherit the earth; that warfare does not make for the survival of the fittest; and that the struggle between nations is no part of the evolutionary law of man's advance.

John Hobson also dismissed the biological arguments put forth by sociologists who claimed that the same laws of survival of the fittest that characterized the natural world also applied to "the physical struggle between races and types of civilization." In an article, entitled "The Scientific Basis of Imperialism," that appeared in the *Political Science Quarterly*, Hobson examined the imperialist arguments that made use of biological metaphors to defend the necessity of imperialism. Specifically, Hobson directed his analysis toward two of the popular Darwinian imperialist arguments: first, that "a constant struggle with other races or nations is demanded for the maintenance and progress of a given race or nation"; and second, that "it is desirable that the earth should be peopled, governed and developed as far as possible by the races which can do their work best, that is, by the races of the highest 'social efficiency.'"[61] This last argument was essentially the one advanced by both Giddings and Kidd for why the civilized states had the right to rule over the "uncivilized." Hobson argued that both assertions were merely rationalizations cloaked in a "natural history doctrine regarded from the standpoint of one's own nation." He believed that it was evident that domestic society had significantly ameliorated many of the elements characteristic of the struggle for survival in the animal kingdom. In fact, Hobson claimed that "social efficiency" and progress within domestic society depended more on cooperation and solidarity than it did on competition. Hobson thus queried that "if progress is served by substituting rational selection for the older physical struggle, first within small groups and then within the larger national groups, why may we not extend the same mode of progress to a federation of European states, and finally to a world federation?"[62] Within this context, Hobson stated that he was not concerned with the numerous practical difficulties of substituting international government for the existing anarchy among nations, "but with scientific theory."

According to Hobson, scientific theory demonstrated that there were no formidable obstacles to the extension of domestic solidarity and cooperation in the international realm. He argued that there already were many concrete examples of large-scale cooperation among nations and that rather than social efficiency suffering from international cooperation, it had been greatly augmented. Furthermore, he claimed that the absence of physical conflict between nations did not, in any way, hamper the progress of nations. Rather, Hobson asserted that internationalism represented both a quantitative and qualitative improvement in efficiency over nationalism. That was why, from a scientific viewpoint, he argued that the substitution of government for international anarchy represented real social progress. Hobson concluded his article with the same proposal that he would later develop in *Towards International Government*. He asserted that

> An international government is required which can furnish adequate protection to weak but valuable nationalities, and can check the insolent brutality of powerful aggressors, preserving that equality of opportunity for national self-expression which is as essential to the commonwealth of nations as to the welfare of the several nations.[63]

This was very similar to the conclusion reached by Walter Lippmann in his book *The Stakes of Diplomacy* which was written during World War I. *The Stakes of Diplomacy* was one of many works that Lippmann would write about American foreign policy during his impressive career as a journalist and public intellectual. Writing in 1915, Lippmann argued that it was the "backward" or "weak" regions of the world—the Balkans, the African sultanates, Turkey, China, and Latin America—that represented the "stakes of diplomacy." By "weak," Lippmann meant those states that were "industrially backward and at present politically incompetent"; "rich in resources and cheap labor, poor in capital, poor in political experience." He argued that "the government of these states is the supreme problem of diplomacy."[64] Not only were these states the primary stakes of diplomacy but, according to Lippmann, "the anarchy of world politics was due to the backwardness of weak states."[65] And perhaps most importantly, Lippmann did not attribute World War I to the failures of the European balance of power system but rather to the failure of diplomacy to find an adequate solution to the struggle over the backward regions. Lippmann explained that

> [T]he diplomatic struggle, the armed peace, and the war itself revolves about the exploitation of the weak territories; that the Balance of Power, the secret alliances, the desire for prestige, and the rest of the diplomatic paraphernalia are for use in the archaic and unorganized portions of the globe; that the anarchy of Europe is due to the anarchy of the Balkans, Africa and Asia.[66]

Lippmann claimed that the principal factor responsible for modern imperialism was the concurrent existence of strong and weak states. He argued that it was the presence of weak states that explained why formal political control accompanied the Great Powers' commercial expansion into these areas. Regardless of the various economic motives that Reinsch, Hobson, and Lenin attributed to commercial expansionism, the growth of foreign trade would not have resulted in imperialism, Lippmann claimed, "if countries like China or Turkey were not politically backward." It was because the regions to which the great powers were seeking to extend their foreign trade were "backward" that political imperialism accompanied commercial expansion. Lippmann defined imperialism as nothing more than the attempt "to police and pacify." The internal anarchy, in the sense of lawlessness and inept governmental authority, of these regions was the fundamental reason why external political control accompanied commercial expansion. Lippmann also insisted that contrary to Angell's "great illusion" thesis, certain individual capitalists did financially gain from their activities in the backward regions and, therefore, wished to have their investments adequately protected. In fact, Lippmann believed that financial entrepreneurs were a significant part of the formula of modern imperialism in which private economic interests were turned into "national interests."

Even though Lippmann maintained that the Great War was being fought over the backward regions, he did not believe that the outcome of the war would solve either the problem of the government of the backward regions or the complicated issue of what the proper political relationship between the great powers and the backward regions should be. The stakes of diplomacy (e.g., the problem of making the "backward" states and the world politically fit for modern commerce) would be the same as before the world went to war. Lippmann thus arrived at a resolution similar to that which many other scholars had reached by the time World War I broke out, that some sort of international organization was needed to ameliorate the excesses of international anarchy. Although Lippmann's specific recommendations for an international organization differed from many of the other proposals that were in circulation, the fact that he reached a conclusion similar to that which individuals discussed in the previous chapter had articulated is of great significance. Rather than an all inclusive world-wide international organization, such as Hobson had envisaged, Lippmann proposed that several "miniature world legislatures" be created to handle the different trouble spots in the world. Lippmann believed that this proposal was both suitable to the task at hand and feasible. He explained that

> [T]he proposal I have ventured to make provides for a series of local world governments, each charged with some one of the worlds problems. Developed out of the idea of world conferences like that about the Congo and Morocco, it would construct a number of miniature world legislatures, with the hope that they would become localized organs of a world state.[67]

Like so many other proposals for international organization, Lippmann's recommendations grew out of his perception of the anarchical character of international politics. In this regard, the distinctive features of Lippmann's proposal are less significant than the fact that he arrived at the same conclusion that many other scholars had reached before the outbreak of World War I.

Conclusion

In addition to reconstructing the main contours of the discussion about colonial administration that represented a significant component of the formative discourse of international relations, this chapter provided a different account of the anarchy thematic. Rather than anarchy denoting the lack of a centralized world authority, the discourse reconstructed in this chapter accentuated the internal chaos and disorder that international relations scholars attributed to those regions that had not yet become members of the so-called society of states. This particular account of anarchy displaced attention away from the issues resulting from the absence of a centralized authority in the international realm and toward the problems that resulted from the internal disorder within "non-civilized states." While the focus on the problems confronting a world of sovereign states without a common superior power was suspended, the concept of anarchy nevertheless continued to provide a common point of departure for discussion in the field of interna-

tional relations. Instead of a conversation emanating from the dichotomy between domestic order and international disorder, the discussion centered on the implications that internal disorder within certain
regions had for world politics. This is one reason why both Hobson's
and Lippmann's recommendation that an international or supra-
national organization be created to address the problems stemming
from the disorder of the "backward" regions is of significant importance. Even though the focus of the anarchy problem shifted, the solution stayed the same. In addition to the central importance of the idea of
anarchy, no matter how it has been constructed, in the disciplinary
history of international relations, it is significant that some scholars
recognized that an international organization was needed to govern the
relations among states.

Contrary to conventional orthodoxy, the field of international relations does not owe its origin or birth to the outbreak of World War I. The
notion that the field did not come into existence until after the war is
one of the dominant myths that informs most conventional accounts of
the history of the field. The study of international organization would
be a major preoccupation among international relations scholars after
the war, but this in many respects had less to do with the external
context and events such as the Treaty of Versailles and the creation of
the League of Nations than with the fact that for the previous twenty
years scholars had discussed the merits of creating some type of organizational structure that could mitigate international anarchy. The next
chapter examines the discourse that followed the First World War.

5

INTERNATIONAL ANARCHY AND THE CRITIQUE OF SOVEREIGNTY

Authors and Works Discussed

Author	1910	1915	1920	1925	1930	1935
Borchard				(1924)		
Brown		(1918)				
Bryce			(1922)			
Dickinson		(1916)	(1920)	(1926)		
Dunning			(1923)			
Fenwick			(1924)			
Follett		(1918)				
Garner				(1925)		
Gettell			(1924)			
Laski			(1921)	(1927)		
Pound			(1923)			
Reeves		(1916)				
Root		(1916)				
Russell						(1936)
Seligman		(1915)				
Willoughby		(1915)(1918)				
Wilson		(1915)		(1925)		
Wright					(1930)	

Edwin M. Borchard 1884–1951
"Political Theory and International Law" [1924]

Philip Marshall Brown 1875–1966
"War and Law" *AJIL* [1918]

James Bryce 1838–1922
International Relations [1922]

Goldsworthy Lowes Dickinson 1862–1932
The European Anarchy [1916]
Causes of International War [1920]
International Anarchy, 1904–1914 [1926]

William A. Dunning 1857–1922
"Liberty and Equality in International Relations" *APSR* [1923]

Charles G. Fenwick 1880–1973
International Law [1924]

Mary Parker Follett 1868–1938
The New State: Group Organization the Solution of Popular Sovereignty [1918]

James Garner 1871–1938
"Limitations on National Sovereignty in International Relations" *APSR* [1925]

Raymond Garfield Gettell 1881–1949
History of Political Thought [1924]

Harold J. Laski 1893–1950
The Foundations of Sovereignty and Other Essays [1921]
"International Government and National Sovereignty" [1927]

Roscoe Pound 1870–1964
"Philosophical Theory and International Law" [1923]

Jesse S. Reeves 1872–1942
"The Justicability of International Disputes" *APSR* [1916]

Elihu Root 1845–1937
"Outlook for International Law" *AJIL* [1916]

Frank M. Russell 1895–1972
Theories of International Relations [1936]

Edwin R.A. Seligman 1861–1939
"An Economic Interpretation of the War" [1915]

Westel Woodbury Willoughby 1867–1945
"Relation of the Individual to the State" [1915]
"The Prussian Theory of the State" *AJIL* [1918]

George G. Wilson 1863–1951
"The War and International Law" [1915]
"The Modernization of International Law" *APSR* [1925]

Quincy Wright 1890–1970
Research in International Law Since the War [1930]

This chapter, as well as the next, reconstructs the interwar discourse of international relations. Students of international relations have considered this to be a crucial phase in the development of the field, and there are at least two reasons for this judgment. The first is that the interwar period has been given the dubious distinction of representing the emergence of the idealist side of the idealist–realist dichotomy in the history of the field. The dichotomy between idealism and realism is rooted in the field's first "great debate," which occurred after World War II and which continues to structure discussion in the field today. Writing at the end of the interwar period and, of even greater significance, at the beginning of what many regard as the "realist" phase of international relations theory, E.H. Carr, who along with Hans Morgenthau is credited with reorienting the field toward realism, proclaimed that during the preceding twenty years, "the science of international politics has been markedly and frankly utopian."[1] More pointedly, Carr maintained that the utopian or idealist character of the field was the result of the strong desire among the interwar scholars to find a remedy whereby the scourge of war finally could be eliminated from human experience. There is no more pervasive assumption about this period of disciplinary history than that it was characterized by idealism.

A second reason for the importance attributed to this period is that many believe that World War I marked the official birth of the academic field of international relations. The historical synopsis that Carr provided in his seminal text, *The Twenty Years' Crisis, 1919–1939*, has helped to ingrain the popular belief that the emergence of the field of international relations was a direct manifestation of World War I. Carr based his explanation of the correspondence between the World War and the beginnings of a science of international politics on Karl Mannheim's sociology of knowledge. Carr argued that "the wish is father to the thought" and that just as it was once the desire to turn common metals into gold that precipitated the science of chemistry, so the science of international politics "took its rise from a great and disastrous war; and the overwhelming purpose which dominated and inspired the pioneers of the new science was to obviate a recurrence of this disease of the international body politic."[2]

Partly as a consequence of the importance that has been attached to this period, it has been the subject of a large number of broad generalizations that have made it very difficult to understand the actual conversation that was taking place among political scientists who were studying international relations. Many of the accounts that seek to explain this period of disciplinary history confuse an analytical tradition with a historical tradition of thought and, as was argued in Chapter 1, they have inhibited understanding the actual features of the conversation that was taking place. This chapter continues to reconstruct the main contours of the academic conversation of international relations in the same manner as the preceding chapters. Emphasis will thus be placed on the internal discursive development of the field and the works of scholars who self-consciously understood themselves as participants. Important continuities, as well as innovations that produced discontinuities in the development of the field, will be highlighted through an examination of the work of a number of notable, albeit often forgotten, voices in the field.

The most important continuity was the further refinement of the theoretical discourse of the state. Yet the theory of the state within political science and its role in theoretically explaining international politics underwent a significant change during the interwar period. This chapter examines the theory of pluralism that arose as a challenge to the orthodox conception of state sovereignty and provides another example of the manner in which a change in the theoretical understanding of the state significantly impacted the discourse of international relations. A number of different explanations have been offered to account for the critique of the traditional conception of the state during the early decades of the twentieth century. One explanation that particularly stands out, and which will be closely examined, suggests that the critique of the state, and especially the influential German theory of the state, was a reaction to the events of World War I. Whatever its cause, there is no disputing the fact that many political scientists in the 1920s became deeply skeptical of the older juristic theory of the state. Fundamental to the critique of the state was an assault on the theory of sovereignty, and since sovereignty explicitly embodies an internal and external component, this had significant implications for the study of international relations. This chapter is primarily devoted to elucidating the nature of the pluralist critique and demonstrating the consequences that this had for the study of international relations, but several other interrelated topics and themes will also be discussed.

After describing the institutional growth that the field experienced subsequent to the war, attention will be directed toward some of the explanations that political scientists offered to account for the cause of the First World War. The discussion that was devoted to understanding the cause of the Great War provides an appropriate context for investigating the changes that occurred within the theoretical discourse of the state, especially with respect to the pluralist critique of state sovereignty. The repercussions of this critique with respect to the theoretical understanding of the external relations among states will be made apparent through an examination of a number of different mediums. One of the more important areas to be examined is the impact that this critique had on the traditional discourse of international law. Just as the critique of sovereignty had important implications for understanding the external relations among states, it also had implications for the theoretical understanding of both domestic and international law. While the early years of the twentieth century could be considered the "golden years" of international law, the period that followed the First

World War was one in which proponents of international law were very much on the defensive.

Institutional Growth

A common assumption about the history of the field of international relations is that its institutional origins emanated directly from World War I. Many have pointed to the creation of the first academic Chair of International Politics at the University College of Wales at Aberystwyth in 1919 as evidence that the genesis of the field was World War I.[3] The Chair was established by David Davies, along with his sisters, Gwendoline and Margaret Davies, "as a memorial to the students of the college who had fallen in the war."[4] The endowment establishing the Chair defined "International Politics" as "political science in its application to international relations, with special reference to the best means of promoting peace between nations," and was intended "for the study of those related problems of law and politics, of ethics and economics, which are raised by the prospect of a League of Nations and for the truer understanding of civilizations other than our own."[5] In 1922, the Chair was named the "Woodrow Wilson Chair," in honor of Wilson's advocacy of the League of Nations.

In the United States, however, the field of international relations did not suddenly arise full-blown at the war's end. The volume of academic literature and course offerings in international relations that appeared in the 1920s and 1930s would not have been possible without the foundations that had been provided by the earlier generation of international relations scholars. What the war did, from the standpoint of the disciplinary development of international relations, was to popularize the subject. In the introduction to Farrell Symons's *Courses On International Affairs in American Colleges, 1930–31,* James T. Shotwell, eminent professor of history and political science at Columbia University and director of the Carnegie Endowment's division of Economics and History as well as its president after World War II, wrote that "the World War first threw open the doors of American education to a world view of politics and history."[6] He argued that based on the results of Symons's work, it was obvious that the World War had a most pronounced effect on the study of international affairs. Symons's comprehensive survey of undergraduate instruction in international affairs at 465 American colleges and universities was sponsored by the World Peace Foundation—an endowment that was created in 1910 by the philanthropist Edwin Ginn.

Symons acknowledged that the task of surveying the college catalogs in search of course offerings in international affairs was made arduous by the fact that "opinions as to what is germane to instruction on international affairs are by no means at one." Symons added that "study of the catalogs of the colleges afforded no clue to any underlying general conceptions which could serve as a guide either to selection or arrangement; and this was true both from the point of view of logic and of philosophy."[7] There was also a fair amount of ambiguity at Aberystwyth concerning the proper scope of the "new" field of international relations. Alfred Zimmern, who was the first to occupy the Woodrow Wilson Chair, claimed that "the study of International Relations extends from the natural sciences at one end to moral philosophy," and added that "from the academic point of view, International Relations is clearly not a subject of the ordinary sense of the word."[8] Charles K. Webster, Zimmern's successor, argued that "the study of International Relations must obviously include many different branches of academic learning, so many and so different, indeed, that one individual cannot hope to have more than a nodding acquaintance with the greater portions of the field of inquiry."[9]

In order to fulfill his stated objective of "throwing some light on the extent to which courses bearing on international affairs are being offered, and of furnishing some sort of basis for estimating the significance of the role they play in the colleges of the United States at the present time," Symons classified the various branches of instruction in international affairs into fifteen different categories. These categories included International Law, International Organization, defined as "courses dealing with the practice and organs of international intercourse, with particular reference to the League of Nations, the International Labor Office, the World Court and other international bodies," and International Relations and Politics, which included "all courses dealing with the fundamental factors and problems of international relations and world politics."[10] According to the survey of 465 colleges and universities, there were approximately 204 courses on international relations, 196 on international law, and 67 on international organization.[11]

In a similar type of endeavor, the Institute of International Education, which operated in New York and was committed to "the development of international good-will by means of educational agencies," commissioned the publication of a syllabus and bibliography on international relations. Stephen Duggan, who was the director of the Institute, argued that there were too few courses offered by American colleges "to enable students to understand the difficult problems that confront men today in their international relations." He wrote that it was "in the hope that such a need might be partially supplied" that the Institute "determined, if possible, to publish a syllabus and bibliography on international relations which because of its adequacy, accuracy and objectivity, would command the approval not only of college teachers but of the public in general."[12] In 1925, a group of scholars at Columbia University under the direction of Parker T. Moon proceeded to assemble an exhaustive bibliography consisting of more than 1200 citations relating to the subject of international relations.

Institutional growth in the field was evidenced by the appearance of new introductory textbooks. These included works by David P. Heatley, *Diplomacy and the Study of International Relations* (1919); C. Delisle Burns, *International Politics* (1920); Steven H. Allen, *International Relations* (1920); and James Bryce, *International Relations* (1922).[13] Some of the earliest scholarly journals in the field of international relations began to be published during the interwar period. In Britain, the Royal Institute of International Affairs at Chatham House published the first issue of *International Affairs* in 1922, and in the United States the Council on Foreign Relations began publishing the quarterly journal *Foreign Affairs* in 1922. Finally, the first of the specialized schools of international relations were instituted during this period. In 1930, the Walter Hines Page School was opened at Johns Hopkins University, and in 1935, the Yale Institute of International Studies was formed.

Causes of the War

The First World War prevented the APSA from holding its annual meeting in 1918, but served as a focal point of discussion among political scientists. This was especially the case with respect to investigating the causes of the war. The explanations put forth were very diverse and encompassed the entire domain of political science. In a review of the war literature in the "News and Notes" section of the *American Political Science Review*, Edward Raymond Turner stated that "as was to be expected, the war of the nations has already produced an extensive literature, which is increasing rapidly, and bids fair in a little while to become enormous."[14] Edwin R.A. Seligman, who was a renowned economist at Columbia University and a member of the inner circle of political scientists at the Columbia School, commented that "there have been almost as many explanations of the great war as there have been writers."[15] Seligman's own contribution to the discussion appeared in an edited volume entitled *Problems of Readjustment After the War* (1915), which included essays by Willoughby, Franklin Giddings, and George Grafton Wilson. Seligman titled his chapter, "An Economic Interpretation of the War," after his seminal book *The Economic Interpretation of History* (1902), and argued that it was nationalism, particularly in its economic aspects, that was the root cause of the war. His argument was in many ways similar to the analysis Lippmann had developed in *The Stakes of Diplomacy*. This was evident, for example, when Seligman explained that the present struggle was rooted in the fact that only a few nations had reached the "third stage" of economic nationalism, that is, one where the export of capital rather than of goods had become predominant, and had resulted in the exploitation of the countries that continued to be in the initial stages of national development. According to Seligman, the character of this evolutionary struggle suggested that no individual country was responsible for the war, because all countries were "simply following the same law which is found in all life from the beginnings of the individual cell—the law of expansion or of self-preservation."[16]

Seligman did, however, point to a peculiar paradox that was manifest in the outbreak of the war. He argued that "modern capitalism, which on the one hand works toward real internationalism, peace and public morality and which will ultimately be able to accomplish its beneficial results, is at the same time responsible for the weakening of international law and the revival of a more conspicuous and determined nationalism."[17] This statement indicates that the thematic issues of nationalism and internationalism continued to guide inquiry into international politics. Seligman's liberal and progressive view of society convinced him that with the inevitable spread of industrialism, the pacific and internationalist aspects of capitalism would eventually hold sway over the world. This was, of course, different from the conclusion that Lippmann had reached as well as from that which Charles Beard would later develop in his book *The Devil Theory of War*. The influence that Seligman had on Beard while they were colleagues at Columbia was apparent when Beard's *An Economic Interpretation of the Constitution of the United States* was published in 1913.

It was during the midst of the First World War that Beard severed his institutional ties with Columbia University. He resigned in 1917 over opposition to the trustees' decision to dismiss one of his colleagues, J. McKeen Cattell, on grounds that "he had been lecturing about international peace under Carnegie auspices."[18] After his resignation, Shotwell, who was one of Beard's close friends at Columbia, wrote in his autobiography that "Beard and I later differed very much in outlook. He became an isolationist and I went into the field of international relations."[19] This did not, however, prevent Beard from writing a series of important articles and books on topics germane to international relations. In almost all of his work, including the *Devil Theory of War* (1936) and *The Idea of the National Interest* (1934), Beard's aim was to demonstrate the manner through which identifiable groups having specific economic interests influenced and, at times, determined the foreign policy of the United States. With respect to the motivations behind America's entrance into the First World War, Beard pointed to the conduct of powerful leaders in banking and politics who worked to extend commercial and financial credit to Britain and the allies which, in turn, "facilitated the slide toward the war abyss."[20]

Like so many other political scientists of this period, James Bryce redirected his attention to international relations and, in doing so, produced one of the early foundational texts of the field. Two themes that had characterized much of Bryce's earlier work—the importance of history for understanding the present and the need to ascertain correctly the "facts"—were both evident in his book, which he simply titled *International Relations* and which consisted of a series of lectures and round-table discussions that he had given in the summer of 1921 to inaugurate the Williams College Institute of Politics. In his characteristic fashion, Bryce declared that his aim was "to lay before you a statement, clear and impartial, so far as I can make it so, of Facts." In this respect, he wrote that "history is the best—indeed the only—guide to a comprehension of the facts as they stand, and to a sound judgment of the various means suggested for replacing suspicions and enmities by the cooperation of States in many things and by their good will in all."[21]

One feature that was particularly conspicuous in Bryce's analysis of the cause of the war was his explicit reference to the notion that the political relations among states were analogous to the relations that once existed among men living in a state of nature. As with other references to this analogy, the inference was that the realm of international relations was, most essentially, characterized by the condition of anarchy. Although examples of this analogy have been noted in earlier chapters, it becomes utilized more frequently after World War I to describe the basic condition as well as the dilemmas of inter-state politics. Bryce explained that the significance of the state of nature for the study of international relations was that

[A]lthough in civilized countries every individual man is now under law and not in a State of Nature towards his fellow men, every political community, whatever its form, be it republican or monarchical, is in a State of Nature towards every other community; that is to say, an independent community stands quite outside law, each community owning no control but its own, recognizing no legal rights to other communities and owing to them no legal duties. An independent community is, in fact, in that very condition in which savage men were before they were gathered together into communities legally organized.[22]

The proposition "that every independent political community is, by virtue of its independence, in a State of Nature towards other communities" was the fundamental starting point of Bryce's inquiry into the "relations of states to states."[23] With respect to his explanation for the cause of the Great War, Bryce provided a broad analysis that entertained such influences as religion, racial sentiment, and nationality. His analysis of the forces and influences making for either war or peace did, however, include what he called "a third intermediate category of relations, viz., that which includes cases where outward peace and a diplomatic intercourse apparently normal coexist with, and scarcely conceal, an attitude of suspicion which leads States to watch its neighbors distrustfully, expecting and preparing for hostilities with one or more of them."[24] This statement provides a clear example of what scholars since John Herz have described as the "security dilemma"—a dilemma intimately associated with the logic of international anarchy.[25]

There was perhaps no better elaboration of the meaning and significance of international anarchy during the interwar years than that which G. Lowes Dickinson provided in his numerous writings. Even more than in the case of Bryce, Dickinson felt compelled to respond to the calamities of World War I. Before the war, Dickinson served as a don at King's College in Cambridge.[26] He lectured and wrote on morals and religion and was particularly interested in the relative values of Greek, Chinese, and Western civilizations. Yet less than two weeks after the outbreak of the war, Dickinson completely changed intellectual directions and embraced the study of international relations. He is generally credited with being the first person in Great Britain to formulate both the idea and the phrase "League of Nations."[27] Although it is difficult to explain the intellectual metamorphosis that Dickinson underwent, there is little doubt that he was an important figure in the field of international relations during the interwar period.

As the founder of the Bryce Group, whose members included Bryce and John Hobson, Dickinson worked on developing his design for a League of Nations. Like other intellectuals who were studying the problem of international organization, debate amongst the members of the Bryce Group centered on the dual problems of reconciling national sovereignty with supra-national authority and finding a mechanism whereby coercive sanctions could be applied to non-compliant states. The Bryce Report was the result of the Group's studies, and it proved to be extremely influential when the League of Nations was instituted at the Paris Peace Conference. In 1915, Dickinson joined the League of Nations Society, which was a group of individuals who worked to build public support for the adoption of such an international organization.

It is necessary to keep these activities in mind when surveying Dickinson's writings, for behind the painstaking analysis of the causes of the war was his sincere belief that the future of humanity hinged on the successful introduction of an international organization devoted to preserving peace among states. Furthermore, Dickinson's work reveals the conviction that international anarchy could be reformed. In *Causes of International War* (1920), he wrote that "a comprehension of the causes is important only because it is a condition of the cure."[28] Perhaps Dickinson's commitment to finding a cure for war is why contemporary scholars have completely overlooked the significant contributions that he made to the political discourse of anarchy. *Causes of International War* provided a broad analysis of the different factors such as general militarism, secret diplomacy, a belligerent press, and various economic motives that contributed to international conflict. Dickinson did not view any one of these factors to be sufficient for explaining the origin of war, and he was also careful not to blame human nature. Dickinson provided two reasons for his dismissal of human nature as the cause of war. First, he explained that war referred specifically to war between sovereign states and not to general competition among individual men. Second, he argued that war was "not a fatal product of human nature" but rather was "an effect of that nature when put under certain conditions."[29] In the process of describing these conditions, Dickinson articulated the structural factors associated with anarchy that he believed accounted for the occurrence of war.

In *The European Anarchy,* Dickinson claimed that "in the great and tragic history of Europe there is a turning point that marks the defeat of the ideal of a world-order and the definite acceptance of international anarchy. That turning-point is the emergence of the sovereign State at the end of the fifteenth century."[30] He argued, in much the same way as neorealists, that the existence of independent sovereign states recognizing no higher authority other than themselves was the single most important cause of war. He maintained that as long as "anarchy continues the struggle between States will tend to assume a certain stereotyped form."[31] This struggle was characterized by a relentless quest for national security that on the one hand was manifest in the striving for empire and on the other by an attempt to prevent it through the mechanism of the balance of power. Dickinson argued that it was the mutual suspicions of other states' actions and intentions, which inevitably arose in international anarchy, that characterized the behavior of states from the time of Machiavelli to the outbreak of World War I. Dickinson's main thesis that "whenever and wherever the anarchy of armed states exists, war does become inevitable" was most clearly developed in his seminal work *The International Anarchy, 1904–1914* (1926). This book was a culmination of the themes that Dickinson had been developing, and it represented another attempt to analyze the causes of the Great War as well as to find a remedy for its recurrence. When the book was reviewed in the *American Political Science Review,* James Garner, who was a professor of political science at the University of Illinois and the nineteenth president of APSA, wrote that "on the whole no keener, more profound, or more dispassionate analysis of the international situation which caused the war—which in fact rendered it inevitable—has been made."[32]

Dickinson began his analysis by making an important distinction between the immediate and underlying causes of war. He argued that behind all of the particular circumstances that had contributed to the war, such as the assassination of the Archduke Franz Ferdinand, "lies a general situation which makes it certain that war will come," and "it is this general situation which is the real theme of this book."[33] The general situation that Dickinson was referring to was the existence of international anarchy, which he explained resulted "from the juxtaposition of a number of States, independent and armed." Under these circumstances, such as characterized ancient Greece, Renaissance Italy, and now modern Europe, war has been, and always will be, a logical result. He maintained that "international war, in our own age as in the others referred to, is a clash between sovereign and armed States," and that "it arises in consequence of the international anarchy."[34] According to Dickinson, it was the condition of international anarchy that provided the fundamental explanation for the cause of World War I.

Although this was the central focus of Dickinson's analysis, it was not his only concern. Unlike much of the scholarship in the field of international relations today, Dickinson stated that his objective in writing the book was "consciously and deliberately, to point a moral." He believed that although war may have been prevalent throughout much of world history, "modern war, with all the resources of science at its disposal, has become incompatible with the continuance of civilization."[35] He argued that the ubiquitous attitude of skepticism, which was reflected in the common belief that war was simply an inevitable fact of history, could no longer persist if civilization was to survive. Dickinson's analysis of the international anarchy was not only meant to indicate the cause of war but also to point humanity toward the direction of peace. Dickinson concluded that "the way to salvation is the development of the League of Nations into a true international organ to control the interests of peace."[36] This was a logical and realistic conclusion that was entirely consistent with Dickinson's analysis of the underlying conditions conducive to war.

The Theory of the State Revisited

There were, however, other explanations for the cause of World War I that were less concerned about the formal existence of anarchy than with certain theories of state sovereignty which was considered to be the constitutive element of international anarchy. This was especially the case with respect to the German theory of the state that many political scientists concluded helped to facilitate the outbreak of war across Europe. The general nature of the argument was that the metaphysical theory of the state espoused by political theorists such as Hegel, Fichte, and Treitschke contributed to the irresponsibility and unrestraint of the German state both before and during the war. Even Willoughby, who had done much to define the state as the proper domain of political science, claimed that the World War would not have occurred "had there not existed in Germany a controlling political philosophy which marked her off from other States and made her a menace to the rest of humanity."[37] He argued that the German philosophy was one that endowed the state with a divine and mystical character. This peculiar conception of the state as an abstract and metaphysical entity had two important corollaries which Willoughby claimed linked the German theory of the state to the outbreak of the war. First, it was a theory that set no limits whatsoever on the authority of the state. Second, the theory fostered the idea that the state had interests and ends that were separate and distinct from its subjects. Willoughby argued that the net result of this theory was "the laudation of war as an instrument or means divinely intended, whereby the relative worth of States, standing in essential opposition and antagonism to one another, may be demonstrated."[38]

Not everyone, however, accepted the argument that the German theory of the state was responsible for the hostilities associated with the war. This was especially true of the older generation of political scientists who had largely founded American political science on the *Staatswissenschaft* they had imported from Germany. Burgess, for example, felt obliged to undertake a defense of Germany's actions in his *The European War of 1914: Its Causes, Purposes, and Probable Results* (1915). Burgess argued against the idea that either the German theory of the state or form of government was in any way responsible for the war, and he asserted that history would eventually demonstrate the superiority of the German system of governance. Yet Burgess's traditional ideas about the state were becoming obsolete as new ideas began to circulate that were directly aimed at discrediting the older concept of the state. In his classic 1924 survey of the discipline of political science, Charles Merriam claimed that the generation of scholars writing in the aftermath of the war were "characterized by a remarkable development of 'anti-stateism,' converging from many points in an attack upon the validity of the state."[39] Responses to World War I brought about a profound change in the traditional theory of the state, but in order to understand the conceptual change that the theory of the state underwent throughout this period, it is necessary to examine the internal discursive developments within political science. As Willoughby noted, "to the political philosopher that which gives extraordinary significance to the great struggle taking place in Europe is that, critically viewed, it exhibits a contest between divergent and, in the main, contradictory conceptions of the nature of the state, of its ends, and of the relation which exists between it and the individuals subject to its authority."[40] Notwithstanding the subtle critique that he had directed against Burgess's metaphysical organic theory of the state at the turn of the century, Willoughby's orthodox juristic theory of the state was also subject to sharp criticism in the years after the war. The juristic or monistic theory of the state was challenged by a new group of political scientists who collectively put forth the theory of pluralism which fundamentally transformed the discourse of political science.[41]

Once again, the proper theoretical, and increasingly empirical, explication of sovereignty was at the center of controversy about the state. Although there were many distinguishing features of the pluralist critique of the state, Francis Coker captured its essence when he wrote that "pluralistic theories of the state are theories which assail the traditional doctrine of state sovereignty."[42] In a similar manner, Ellen Deborah Ellis, who was one of the first political scientists to provide a comprehensive summation of the controversy over the state, claimed that "the pluralist begins his attack on the monistic doctrine by denying what the monist states as the underlying facts of political organization, and especially the essential unity and absoluteness of the state and sovereignty."[43] And Raymond Garfield Gettell, who was now professor of political science at the University of California, concluded that pluralism was a "critical political theory" that stood in opposition to the "conservative political theory of state monism."[44]

The leading pluralists included Harold Laski (who taught at Harvard University from 1916 to 1920, and afterwards returned to England to teach at the London School of Economics), Roscoe Pound (who was Carter Professor of Jurisprudence at Harvard University), Leon Duguit (professor of constitutional law at the University of Bordeaux), Hugo Krabbe (professor of public law at the University of Leyden), Ernest Barker, Graham Wallas, and J. Neville Figgis (all English scholars and publicists).[45] They traced the descent of the modern monistic theory of the state back to the writings of Bodin, Hobbes, and Austin. It was in the work of these theorists, especially Bodin, that the doctrine "of the state as an essential institution of society, supplying, in its capacity as an exclusive agency of law, an indispensable means whereby men having common and competing interests can live together rationally; with the corollary that the state is legally supreme and unlimited" first arose.[46] George Sabine, who early in his career at the University of Missouri was sympathetic to the pluralist critique, maintained that this theory was "practically identical with what is otherwise called the juristic theory of the state."[47]

It was in many ways the critique of sovereignty that Laski had been pursuing while he was at Harvard that helped to generate the debate about the orthodox conception of the state within political science. Pluralism, for Laski, was not merely an alternative conception of the state but also a normative theory of politics. Laski thought that the modern monistic state, which he argued had its origins in the philosophical and legal response to the crisis caused by the decline of the medieval idea of a unified Christendom, was a threat to individual liberty. Consequently, Laski aimed to challenge the idea of the monistic state with the thesis of a decentralized polity that was more consistent with current political, economic, and sociological conditions. He declared that "the monistic state is an hierarchical structure in which power is collected at a single center," and that "advocates of pluralism are convinced that this is both administratively incomplete and ethically inadequate."[48] Pluralists argued that the state was not, in any meaningful or legitimate sense, superior or prior to the various groups and associations present in society. The state, according to Laski and the other adherents of the pluralist paradigm, was only one of many forms of human association to which the individual belonged. Moreover, the pluralists insisted that the different associations found in modern society, such as trade unions, civic associations, and religious groups, each, in its own distinct way, possessed sovereignty on a parity with the state. Each of these associations, the pluralists maintained, represented a distinct "group-life" and manifested a specific "will." By a logical inference, this meant that the state could not be the sole possessor of sovereignty. In short, Laski argued that state sovereignty was neither indivisible nor supreme.

Once the idea that the state was indivisibly supreme over all other institutions and associations was rejected, which Laski maintained was never anything more than a legal fiction, the accompanying ethical premise that the state had an a priori moral right to the allegiance of all individuals was also dismissed. The pluralists argued that there was no transcendental basis for bestowing moral significance on the acts of the state. Laski argued that the appropriate test that should be used to determine the moral righteousness of a given command was pragmatic rather than a priori and transcendental. He claimed that individuals were not ethically obligated to obey commands that directly interfered with their capacity to be productive and moral citizens. To suggest that there should be unconditional allegiance to an order issued from only one specific source of sovereign authority was, for Laski, "a contradiction of all that is worth most in the ethical precepts of 2,000 years."[49]

In a similar manner, pluralists also rejected the ethical doctrine that asserted that moral limitations could not be placed on the acts of the state. This doctrine, which many associated with the German idealism of Hegel and Treitschke, was held by the pluralist writers to have contributed to the "irresponsibility" of the state. The actions that were undertaken during the Great War, particularly by Germany, were considered a prime instance of the irresponsibility of the state. Without moral or legal limitations, the state was free to act in an irresponsible manner both internally, in relation to the individual and other groups, and externally, in relation to other sovereign states. In a lecture that Laski delivered in 1926 at the Geneva Institute of International Relations, he argued that

> The state is irresponsible. It owes no obligation save that which is made by itself to any other community or group of communities. In the hinterland between states man is to his neighbour what Hobbes says was true of him in the state of nature—nasty, mean, brutish.[50]

Gettell argued that the recommendation that moral limitations be placed on the state was one of the most valuable contributions that the pluralists had made to political thought. He explained that it was "a desirable reaction against the idealization of the state, and the doctrine that the state is an end in itself, free from all moral restraint."[51]

The freeing of the state from the realm of moral abstraction also had implications for the normative discourse of international ethics. In an article in the *American Political Science Review* that dealt with the issue of state morality in international relations, Bruce Williams argued that "the reaction against the philosophy which considered all state action as moral and which posited the realization of national aims as a paramount ethical end, has been followed by an increasing emphasis on the ethical liability of the state to interests in addition to its own."[52] In this respect, Williams acknowledged that there were a number of ways in which pluralist theory aided the discussion of international morality. First, it helped to dismantle the metaphor whereby a state was assumed to be an individual possessing an abstract moral and legal personality.

Second, if the state was merely a collection of differentiated groups, as pluralists suggested, then, according to Williams, "the conduct of the state, in its external relations, represents the attitude of one group of individuals in their collective dealings with another group of similar or related characteristics, and by its acts contributes to the standards which will govern these relations."[53]

Before proceeding to examine other areas where pluralism facilitated a transformation in the discursive evolution of international relations, it is necessary to focus more fully on the pluralist theory of politics. What Laski was able to accomplish through his critique of sovereignty was to bring together the work of a number of different scholars into a unified and coherent thesis about the functioning of pluralist society. In this regard, the theory of pluralism represented not only a reformulation of the theory of the state but increasingly a normative theory of how politics should operate in the modern world. And as Laski's account of pluralism as both an empirical and normative theory of politics gained increasing acceptance among political scientists, the cogency of the critique of the monistic theory of sovereignty became more intense.

Pluralist Theory and International Politics

Pluralists identified groups, along with the individuals who collectively belonged to them, as the essence of political life. The normative significance that was attached to the autonomous functioning of the various groups in society led pluralists to reject the idea that the state was an organic collective community that underlay government. Increasingly, the conventional distinction between state and government disintegrated as pluralists subsumed the functions of the state in government. Pluralist theory, following the insights provided by Arthur Bentley in his *The Process of Government* (1908) and the work of various sociological theorists, maintained that because society was fundamentally disaggregated into numerous groups, governmental authority, the organ of political power, should also be disaggregated into its many constituent parts. The centralization of political power in the hands of the state, and exercised through the machinery of government, was held by the pluralists to be not only empirically anomalous with respect to contemporary conditions but also a threat to the functioning of democratic society. Drawing upon the middle ages and contemporary America as a model, Laski argued that the type of polity that could best achieve Aristotle's form of democratic citizenship was one in which the "structure is not hierarchical but coordinate" and in which "sovereignty is partitioned upon some basis of function." He reasoned that "the

division of power makes men more apt to responsibility than its accumulation." Laski argued that since society was fractionalized, government should be partitioned into its component parts, and he claimed
that "administratively we need decentralization" so as "to revivify the
conception of federalism which is the greatest contribution of America
to political science."[54]

Mary Parker Follett's book, *The New State* (1918), also contributed
to discrediting the idea of the centralized administrative state, even
while attempting to reconstitute the state and democracy on the basis of
the group principle, which she argued was the cornerstone of political
life. Although Follett's version of pluralism incorporated some unique
features, and while she may not have been the central voice in the
conversation about pluralism, her work is instructive for illustrating the
profound consequences that pluralist theory had for the study of international relations. At the outset of her work, Follett proclaimed that
"group organization is to be the new method in politics, the basis of our
future industrial system, the foundation of international order."[55] Follett insisted that the importance of the group arose from the fact that it
enabled the individual, which she argued was the basic unit of politics,
to be heard above the crowd. Furthermore, she argued that it was only
through the group that individuals could realize their full potential and
gain true freedom.

Although the group was to serve as the basis for refounding
democracy and restoring political primacy to the individual, Follett was
equally concerned about the anomie associated with modern diver-
sified society. It was on this point that Follett voiced her opposition to
certain trends within pluralist thought. She argued that although
writers such as Laski and Barker had helped to destroy the legal fiction
of "a single unitary state with a single sovereignty," pluralists did not
always offer an adequate alternative to fill the void created by their
critique. More specifically, Follett declared that many of the pluralists
failed to appreciate the relevance of the new group psychology and
consequently to "lose the individual in the group" or "abandon the
group for the state." Follett's response to this lacuna within pluralist
thought was to recommend a new type of unity in the state that could
be achieved by building on the collective diversity of the individuals
and groups present in society. Her work provided a response to some of
the critics of pluralism, such as William Yandell Elliott, an assistant
professor at the University of California, who argued that with the
destruction of state authority, social chaos and disunity would ultimately result.[56] Follett argued that a more comprehensive whole could
be constituted through the integration of the various localized group
parts. An appropriate balance between the parts and the whole was

necessary in order to preserve both diversity and unity within the state. The individual and society, according to this view, were one and the same, and both were inseparable from one another.

With respect to the issue of sovereignty, it was, once again, the group principle that provided the proper frame of reference for understanding its true nature. Follett judged that the juristic theory of sovereignty, which granted complete omnipotence to the state, was entirely inconsistent with modern conditions. In what amounted to a major revision in the orthodox understanding of sovereignty, Follett argued that both the individual and the state were sovereign, because "sovereignty is the power engendered by a complete interdependence becoming conscious of itself." She explained:

> The individual is sovereign over himself as far as he unifies the heterogeneous elements of his nature. Two people are sovereign over themselves as far as they are capable of creating one out of two. A group is sovereign over itself as far as it is capable of creating one out of several or many. A state is sovereign only as it has the power of creating one in which all are.[57]

This represented a significant change in the theoretical understanding of sovereignty—a change that had profound consequences for the theoretical discourse of the state, and which, inevitably, affected the discourse of international relations.

At the domestic level, Follett, like Laski, endorsed the principle of federalism, which she argued was the only type of political arrangement that could embody the twin principles of interpenetration and multiplism. The conjoining and integration of neighborhood groups with each other as well as to a larger whole was only possible under a federal type of state similar to the form toward which the United States had been evolving since acquiring independence from Britain. The principle of federalism, Follett argued, was what enabled the new conception of sovereignty to emerge. She argued that the health of American democracy ultimately hinged on the formation of a true federal state that could embody the diversity present in American society. At the international level, Follett believed that it was imperative to extend her analysis of group psychology to an analysis of the interactions among states. She claimed that just as the group process at the domestic level revealed that isolated individualism was no longer feasible and, consequently, had to be transcended through integration with other individuals and groups, nation-states also had to move beyond their narrowly defined self-interests and play a role in the creation of a larger whole. If successful, the further development of the group principle at the international level would result in the emergence of the "true" world state. Yet, and this was the essence of the problem for international politics, the whole had to be one in which identity and difference could be reconciled. She argued that "there is no way out of the hell of our present European situation until we find a method of compounding difference" and that "war can never cease until we see the value of differences."[58] Follett had specific ideas about how the integration process in international relations should proceed if a lasting peace was to be found.

Follett argued that interdependence had become "the keynote of the relations of nations" as it had "of the relations of individuals within a nation," and she maintained that economic interests were one of the primary factors bringing nations closer together into a larger interdependent union.[59] Yet she was adamant in insisting that the process of international integration should not be committed to making all nations alike through the espousal of a universal interest or ethic. It was important, Follett claimed, not to confuse cosmopolitanism and internationalism: "the aim of cosmopolitanism is for all to be alike; the aim of internationalism is a rich content of widely varying characteristic and experience."[60] The group principle demonstrated that it was only by the reconciliation of, and respect for, difference that a larger world community could be built on the foundation provided by federal states.

Follett did not perceive any fundamental antagonism between the dual forces of nationalism and internationalism. On the contrary, she argued that meaningful nationalism, that is, one that resulted from the integration of groups within a particular nation state, "looks out as well as in." From this integration came a new definition of patriotism that was capable of embodying a loyalty to a larger and more comprehensive whole. The lesson of the group principle proved that loyalty to a larger community beyond one's own immediate local community was not a substitute for the patriotism that one feels toward his or her own nation but rather was a qualitative addition to it. She explained that the prospect for a lasting peace "depends upon whether we have advanced far enough to be capable of loyalty to a higher unit, not as a substitute for our old patriotism to our country, but in addition to it."[61]

It was thus quite apparent to Follett that the orthodox theory of sovereignty, which conferred on the state complete external independence from all other states, was a formidable obstacle to reconstituting international relations on the basis of the group principle. She claimed that "the idea of 'sovereign' nations must go as completely as is disappearing the idea of sovereign individuals." Yet although the traditional notion of sovereignty had to be expunged, Follett argued that "with our present definition of sovereignty we may keep all the real sovereignty we have and then unite to evolve together a larger sovereignty."[62] According to Follett, this revised meaning of "sovereign" nations was consistent with the spirit and institutional form taken by the newly created League of Nations. In fact, the League of Nations was in many ways a logical result of the extension of the group process to the international level. She argued that more practical experiments in integration were needed so that a world state could finally be realized. In conclusion, Follett explained that "the group process thus shows us that a genuine community of nations means the correlation of interests, the development of an international ethics, the creation of an international will, the self-evolving of a higher loyalty, and above all and including all, the full responsibility of every nation for the welfare of every other."[63] This was a theoretical exposition that could not have been mounted on the basis of the monistic theory of state sovereignty.

The Theory of External Sovereignty

There were other scholars who recognized that the external implications of monistic theory represented a significant obstacle to reconceptualizing international politics. Laski acknowledged this when he wrote that "only by the abrogation of the idea of sovereignty in international affairs is there any real prospect of the working of international ideas being placed upon a basis at once successful and sound."[64] Pluralism, as a whole, provided a critical perspective on the juristic view of external sovereignty. Pluralist theory was, after all, opposed to the idea that the state represented a sovereign legal person that was omnipotent, unaccountable, and immune from any other authority. The political and legal omnipotence that monistic theory granted to the state meant that the independence and equality of all states were taken to be axiomatic facts of international life, but pluralists challenged each of these external attributes of sovereignty. Thus, it is entirely understandable that insofar as pluralism represented a "critical theory," it was also, as Gettell claimed, "no accident that pluralism is closely associated with internationalism."[65] He stated that "the internationalist would shackle Leviathan with chains, while the pluralists would perform necessary operations on his interior."[66] Just as the pluralists maintained that the state was not supreme over all the constituent groups present in society, those espousing the idea of internationalism claimed that the state was not completely sovereign with respect to every other actor in international society. Many scholars concluded that the conception of external sovereignty that followed from juristic theory was no longer consistent with the reality that it was attempting to explain.

Sabine understood pluralism to be an alternative point of view to monism, and he argued that it was the complexity of modern political

conditions that posed the greatest challenge to the naive idea of a unified sovereign authority presiding over the affairs of the state. He explained that the pluralist "finds that accepted juristic relations are too
narrow and rigid to fit at all accurately the great variety of relations
actually in force between states and between the parts or organs of
states."[67] To illustrate the divergence between juristic theory and contemporary practice, Sabine made direct reference to examples in international politics. With respect to the numerous international treaties
into which states were increasingly entering, Sabine noted how the
political monist logically insisted that these "agreements" were nothing
more than moral promises that lacked legal validity. The political monist, Sabine argued, had no choice but to insist on the non-legal nature
of the agreements reached between states in order to "leave the will of
the state unimpaired." Yet Sabine held that any theory that had to
pervert existing facts and conditions merely to fit them in with old
juristic categories was grossly inadequate. He claimed, for example,
that the League of Nations was transforming the character of inter-state
relations to the point where it was no longer possible to deny the legally
binding nature of the agreements reached between states. Sabine argued that against the simplicity of the monist, the pluralist insisted that
political relations between states "are in fact various, that beyond a
certain point they cannot be simplified and generalized, and that there
are always growing edges where political relations depend more upon
agreement and good will than upon authority."[68] He determined that
the pluralist point of view was helpful in bridging the gap left between
monistic theory and the current practice of international politics.

James Garner was another political scientist who recognized the
wide gulf between the traditional conception of external sovereignty
and the reality of international politics. Garner devoted his 1924 APSA
presidential address to the topic of national sovereignty in international
relations. This was the second presidential address in three years that
dealt with the issue of external sovereignty. Garner began his speech by
chronicling the fading historical relevancy of the traditional notion of
absolute sovereignty defined by Bodin in the sixteenth century. He
explained that

> The old theory of absolute sovereignty *vis à vis* other states fitted
> in very well with the actual conditions of international society at
> the time it was formulated by the jurists. Today the situation is
> totally different. In the place of an "anarchy of sovereignties" we
> have a society of interdependent states, bound by law and pos-
> sessing a highly-developed solidarity of interests.[69]

On the basis of this assessment, Garner argued that it was no longer credible, either theoretically or empirically, to maintain that international relations existed in a condition of anarchy populated by states possessing unlimited power and "subject to no control except that which is self-imposed." He provided examples from international law, treaties, and diplomacy to indicate that states did not have an absolute right to act in any manner they chose. The existence of a genuine society of states, which Garner argued predated the establishment of the League of Nations, meant that there were a variety of instances in which states owed specific obligations to the larger community of nations and were prohibited from exercising rights that would be contrary to the interests of international society. According to Garner, this was a fact of international life and not merely an idealistic proposition.

The crux of Garner's message to the APSA was that it was necessary for political scientists to relinquish the axiom that the prerogative of sovereignty gave a state an exclusive right to act in any manner it deemed expedient. Like Follett, he attempted to demonstrate that this archaic notion of international "right" was not only empirically false but, in fact, contrary to the real interests of a state. For if a state should "conform its conduct to the theory of absolute sovereignty and refuse to assume any obligations which involved restrictions upon the exercise of sovereignty," then, Garner argued, "the condition of international society would, indeed, be that which Hobbes in his day conceived it to be."[70] In a statement that was directed at the United States for refusing to surrender the small degree of sovereignty that was necessary in order to join the League of Nations, Garner argued that "limitations upon liberty is the price which must be paid for all social progress, whether it be local, national, or international," and he concluded that the security and welfare of a state "could be better promoted by surrendering their sovereignty and uniting in federal unions rather than by remaining independent."[71]

Implicit in Garner's critique of external sovereignty was an attack on the doctrine of the equality of states—one of the main pillars of international law. The claim that every state is equal to, and independent of, other states was a logical inference derived from the theory of absolute sovereignty. In the same manner that juristic theory posited that the state was a legally supreme person, it judged that each of these sovereign persons had an equal capacity for rights. In both instances, the theoretical justification for these doctrines was drawn from the analogy between the state and a person. In Edwin Dewitt Dickinson's historical study of the principle of the equality of states, which was originally written as a doctoral dissertation at Harvard under the direction of George Grafton Wilson, he argued that its inception was to be found in four important sources: "(a) the law of nature, (b) the idea of natural equality, (c) the conception of the state of nature, and (d) the analogy between natural persons and separate states in the international society." Of the four, Dickinson argued that "the last was one of the major premises upon which the law of nations was founded in the sixteenth and seventeenth centuries."[72] It is on the basis of this analogy that many had argued that international politics is an anarchy composed of equal and independent states.

In his presidential address to the APSA, William Dunning undertook "some consideration of the manifestation and influence of the conceptions of liberty and equality in the field of international relations." The fact that Dunning concluded his eminent career as one of America's foremost political scientists and political theorists with a critical examination of the doctrine of the equality of states indicates the prominence that this issue had achieved. Dunning died in August 1922, before the annual meeting of APSA was held, and his presidential address was read by Jesse S. Reeves, the vice-president of the Association. Dunning argued that the "question of liberty and equality" was at the "very root of all political science," and he declared that the purpose of his address was twofold: first, to consider the history and manifestations of these two doctrines in the external affairs of states; and two, to assess whether they had been beneficial or destructive to the study of international relations.

He began by noting that "the principle of political science on which the equality of states was at last firmly fixed and on which it rests today is the principle of sovereignty" and that Jean Bodin was the philosopher who first formulated "this principle as the basis of the state."[73] Dunning argued that as a consequence of Bodin's definition of sovereignty as "supreme power over citizens and subjects, unrestrained by the laws," one reached the "conclusion that all states are equal!"[74] Despite Bodin's own preference for monarchies, sovereignty entailed unqualified supremacy over the affairs of the state. In the eyes of political science, it did not matter whether a state was an aristocracy, monarchy, or democracy, for as long as a state exhibited sovereign power, it was considered equal to all other states. Bodin was, according to Dunning, "philosophizing in the air, out of touch with terrestrial realities," since there were glaring disparities between the various powers in Europe. But the doctrine of the equality of states "was adopted by the whole line of thinkers who in the seventeenth century created the science of international law." A key analytical prop for this doctrine, as well for international law more generally, was the law of nature, which Dunning argued had exerted a major influence in political theory with respect to the idea that all individuals were, in principle, free and equal. He argued that the dictum of the Roman jurists "that all men are by nature free and equal" proved to be a major stimulus to the development of the idea of popular sovereignty which was used to challenge the theory of monarchy. Dunning maintained that the doctrine of the equality of states within international law rested on "the same law of nature that the Roman jurist found asserting that all men are equal."[75]

Dunning was, however, skeptical of some of the manifestations of the idea of equality in the affairs of both individuals and states. Internally, Dunning claimed that the demand for equality and liberty was the catalyst for the civil war in France that, paradoxically, resulted in the absolutism of the Bourbons "in which neither liberty nor equality had any place whatever." In England, the consequence was "two revolutions in the seventeenth century; the loss of the American colonies in the eighteenth; intense economic and social struggles throughout the nineteenth." Dunning alleged that the historical record of international politics was equally grim. The Protestant revolt against the unity of Christian Europe culminated in the Thirty Years' War, which Dunning argued reproduced in Europe the anarchical "condition of the Hellenic world two thousand years before." The Peace Treaty of Westphalia not only ended the war but formally sanctioned the principle of equal rights for sovereigns, which, according to Dunning, provided the opportunity for "equal" states to seek domination over others. He claimed that the subsequent one hundred years of international relations was a period of almost continuous warfare in which the mechanism of the balance of power, the basis of which was equality, "obviously did not avail to preserve peace and order in Europe."[76]

Dunning concluded, on the basis of his historical survey, that "theories of political science and the practice of international relations are hopelessly at variance." He attributed the discrepancy more to an error in theory than in practice, maintaining that such theoretical ideals of liberty and equality were hard "to detect in the sordid record" of international relations and that, moreover, their importance had "been greatly exaggerated in modern political science." Dunning argued that social existence becomes impossible when equality is taken as the characteristic attribute of liberty. International relations, according to Dunning, provided ample proof of the correctness of this assertion. He claimed that what was most needed to make social existence possible was authority. Dunning maintained that authority was "as indispensable to a society of peoples as it is to a society of individuals."[77] Recent political science, however, had lost sight of this fact by concentrating on groups rather than political society as a whole.

Before turning to the discussion of the study of international law, where the critique of sovereignty had direct applicability, it is appropriate to consider a work that was published toward the end of the interwar period and that indicates the growth in the body of thought associated with theories of international relations. The publication of Frank M. Russell's *Theories of International Relations* in 1936 was a landmark contribution. Russell, who was professor of political science at the University of California, claimed that although the literature on international relations had expanded significantly, there still was "no book in any language that attempts to present from the earliest times, and in light of environmental influences, the more significant ideas, whatever their character or implications may be, that men have entertained concerning international relations."[78] The only possible exception was F. Melian Stawell's book, *The Growth of International Thought,* in which an attempt was made to substantiate the author's conviction "that a sane nationalism, when it understands itself, points the way to internationalism as its completion."[79] Russell's book represented what he claimed as a new and different approach: it was "designed to do for the field of international relations what historical surveys of political theory have done for the entire field of political thought."[80]

Russell argued that, until recently, political theorists and philosophers, with a few notable exceptions, had dealt with the subject of international relations only incidentally. Yet, according to Russell, international political thought was "as old as the existence of separate independent political communities." This meant that it was possible to chronicle the history of international political thought in a manner similar to that which political theorists such as Gettell, Dunning, and Sabine had employed in the field of political theory. Russell devoted his study to "the reflections, speculations, ideas, and conclusions of men concerning the interrelations of the national states composing the modern international community."[81] His book consisted of more than 600 pages of text which began with a survey of primitive man and inter-group relationships, continued with discussions of ancient Greece, medieval Europe, seventeenth-, eighteenth- and nineteenth-century international thought, and concluded with an examination of the modern phenomena of interdependence culminating in international organization. In the last chapter, which was entitled "Laissez-Faire vs. Organization," Russell argued that the interdependent world of the twentieth century was at great odds with the "theory of sovereignty developed in its absolute form in the sixteenth century" and he concluded that

If peace and justice are measurably to be realized in the international sphere, and the requisite conditions for men and women to live the good life within states attained, it would seem that states must abandon the notion that the ultimate in political authority is and must continue to be the national state, and that they must accept a much greater degree of international government than they have as yet been willing to tolerate.[82]

The Discourse of International Law

The revisions in the older juristic theory of the state that political scientists were making had a direct bearing on the subject of international law. It was, after all, the juristic conception of state sovereignty that proved to be the most formidable obstacle to establishing the legal basis of international law. Many of the leading figures involved in developing the theory of pluralism were legal scholars who rejected the Austinian dictum that law was simply a command issued from an omnipotent sovereign authority. Consequently, the critique of the juristic state had profound implications for the study of international law. As Walter Sandelius, professor at the University of Kansas, noted, "the relation of international law, as of law in general, to the state depends upon what the state is conceived to be."[83] In this respect, there was an intimate connection between the critique of the state that was occurring within political science and the ongoing attempt by international legal scholars to provide a theoretical defense of their subject matter.

Edwin M. Borchard, professor of law at Yale University, undertook a detailed examination of the relationship between the subject matter of political theory and international law in his contribution to the edited volume of *A History of Political Theories: Recent Times*—a work that was dedicated to the scholarly achievements of Dunning. Although Borchard appreciated the fact that political theory had exerted a substantial influence upon the development of international legal theory, he argued that with respect to the theory of sovereignty, the influence had been largely detrimental and harmful. He wrote:

> The present anarchical state of international relations, with no present hope of any improvement, is the most tangible evidence of the destructiveness of the theory of state sovereignty in international relations, and for its long survival the political theorists of the nineteenth century and the analytical school of jurists are largely to blame.[84]

Like other modern writers, such as Garner and Dunning, Borchard concluded that the theory of sovereignty, as propounded by Hobbes, Bodin, and Austin, was essentially invalid when it was applied to the external relations among states. He maintained that there was a fundamental inconsistency between the internal and external components of sovereignty that resulted from the premise that the state was an omnipotent entity unfettered by any type of internal and, by logical extension, external conditions. This meant, quite simply, that if limitations could not be placed upon the external exercise of sovereignty, then there could be no effective international law to regulate the behavior of states. He admitted that the followers of Austin avoided this inconsistency by refusing to concede legal status to international law. But while Austinians avoided this particular discrepancy, Borchard argued that their peculiar conception of law was grossly inadequate. He claimed that the underlying problem with Austin and the entire analytical school was the pervasive tendency to transplant the internal attributes of state sovereignty to external relations. The result of this practice for the science of international relations was, according to Borchard, nothing less than disastrous.

Borchard was equally resolute in attempting to demonstrate the destructive influence that the political theory of natural law had exerted on the development of international law. As Dickinson and Dunning had claimed, it was the theory of natural law that had most fundamentally established the basis of the doctrine of the equality of states and, more generally, the perception of international law itself. Borchard admitted that "few notions of political theory have played a more important part in the conceptual development of international law than the equality of states." He maintained that it was the alleged rights and duties existing in the state of nature, which were "deduced from considerations of human reason and natural justice," that promoted the idea that sovereign states possessed an equality of rights similar to that of individuals. Borchard suggested that "the equality of states became axiomatic and was naturally applied to states when sovereignty became impersonal." Yet he argued "that the notion of equality is incidental to sovereignty and, when used logically by the proponents of the theory of absolute sovereignty of the state, leads to conclusions incompatible with the existence of international law."[85]

One dimension of this incompatibility was that the theory of equality, like that of absolute sovereignty, no longer corresponded with existing conditions. This was best evidenced by the vastly different degrees of political power that states possessed. To expect that states would yield to the demand of equality of representation in the face of glaring inequality was, according to Borchard, further evidence of an outworn doctrine of political theory causing havoc in the science of international law. Borchard joined with the international legal positivists in asserting that the modern basis of states' rights was derived more from custom and practice than from reference to archaic natural law. Furthermore, Borchard also maintained that adherence to the doctrine of the equality of states was a handicap in ameliorating the anarchy of international relations. The net result of the attempt to reconcile the demand for the equality of states with the glaring inequalities of power was the inability of international organizations to function at all.

Borchard, however, did not consider the situation hopeless. He argued that to improve international law it was necessary to relinquish the theory of absolute sovereignty and its corollary, the equality of states. He applauded the revised theory of sovereignty and the corresponding reconceptualization of law that was being put forth by the pluralists. He made direct reference to the work of Krabbe, who argued that "authority in the modern state is itself the creature of law, that is, that in a legal state the law and not arbitrary will is sovereign."[86] Krabbe resisted the juristic fiction that the state represented a unified and omnipotent will and maintained that there were a variety of wills present in a political community. According to Krabbe, the basis of law could not, therefore, rest on the alleged superiority of one particular will present in society. Rather, he argued, "the essential quality of a rule of law is its generation by the sense of right of the majority of the community constituting the state." In this sense, law was less a product of an authoritative state than the state was a result of law determined by a political community's sense of right. The consequence of Krabbe's pluralistic account of law was that international law occupied the same position as municipal law. Borchard explained that both were "the product not of the will of any particular state or states or, naturally, of any authority above the states, but of man's 'sense of right,' which operates equally to create law in the state community as a regulative agency for the delimitation of individual interests as it does in the international field."[87]

Krabbe's account of law, and the inferences that he drew with respect to international law, were similar to the claims of other pluralist writers. Laski, for example, completely rejected the dubious proposition that law originated from the command of an omnipotent sovereign. Laski, like Krabbe, believed that law was "in reality something sociologically generated from the 'opinion' of individuals and instances of their consent or 'fused good-will.'"[88] Laski, in turn, found inspiration in the idea of sociological jurisprudence, which he drew from the work of Roscoe Pound while they were colleagues at Harvard. In a lecture delivered at the University of Leiden, Pound reiterated the popular theme of the divergence between the theory and practice of international law. He argued that "all juristic, if not indeed all philosophical thinking goes on analogies, and the nearer the analogy is to the phenomena of life to which the juristic theory is to be applied, the more effective that theory will be as a guide to juristic activity."[89] This, for Pound, explained why the international law of the remote past was more effective in action than that of the present. Pound argued that the analogies on which the jurisprudence of international law were originally based had become outdated. He insisted that the need for revision was great, because as "the facts from the condition for which the theory of international law was devised" changed, there "was no corresponding revision in the theory of international law nor attempt to set up newer and closer analogies."[90] According to Pound, this was apparent in the continued reliance of international lawyers on natural law, and by the comparison of a "politically organized people or group of peoples to the individual man." The recent revival of philosophical thinking, which Pound argued had been eclipsed by historical and analytical methods in the nineteenth century, was to be applauded for its attempt to bring about a closer correspondence between the theory and facts of international law. He noted that the new sociological jurisprudence had been making great strides in reconceptualizing international law, and he was hopeful that "it will yield a creative juristic theory and may well enable jurists of the next generation to do as much for the ordering of international relations as Grotius and his successors did in their day by a creative theory founded on the philosophy of that time."[91]

Several other authors acknowledged the impact of sociology on the attempt to fit legal theory to contemporary practice. Sandelius, for example, argued that "in order to maintain its function," law "must of necessity feed upon fresh materials of change." He argued that "so evident has become the reality of the international community on the one hand, and that of occupational groups on the other, that sociology, which is more concerned with social tendencies than with formal doctrine of any kind, has largely discarded the idea of the sovereign nation-state."[92] Harry Elmer Barnes, who was professor of historical sociology at Smith College, claimed that "what modern sociology has done for political science is put the lawyers of the metaphysical and mechanical schools to rout." He was convinced that "one cannot well escape from the conviction of the triumph of the 'sociological movement,' for there was certainly nothing in Austin or Dumount which would lead directly to Roscoe Pound and Leon Duguit."[93]

Duguit's contributions to legal theory aided the attempt to provide a theoretical foundation for international law. Duguit, like Krabbe, argued that law preceded the origin of the state and this was what allowed him to reject the idea that international law was not true law. According to Duguit, the state was not sovereign, because it was subject to limitations imposed by law, both internally and externally. He argued that laws were the rules of conduct that made social existence possible.

Laws, therefore, were not binding simply because they were decreed by an authoritative command. Rather, Duguit argued that laws were obligatory, because they made social existence possible. And in this respect, the rules of international law were as necessary and valid as were the rules regulating the internal affairs of a political community.

As important as the conversation generated by the pluralist writers was in helping to provide a theoretical defense of international law, there was another urgent task that confronted the international law community once the warfare in Europe had ended. That task, most simply stated, was to quell the critics who charged that World War I had demonstrated the bankruptcy of international law. The period that preceded the war was often considered to be the "golden years" of international law. Yet the international gatherings that took place at The Hague, the establishment of the Permanent Court of Arbitration and the International Prize Court, the improvements made in arbitration procedures, and the progress made in codifying the body of existing international law did not appear to be as impressive after the world witnessed some of the most blatant breaches of acceptable state conduct in recorded history. Reviving international law and convincing skeptics that the outbreak of World War I did not necessarily mean that international law was dead became major undertakings of the international law community.

Some of the most important figures in international law attempted to provide a defense of their subject matter. George G. Wilson, for example, declared that "international law is not dead," and that in fact "far from being dead, the subject is receiving a recognition which is a striking tribute to its vitality." Wilson claimed that one example of the vitality of international law was to be found in "the attempts of states at war to put themselves right in the eyes of the world and to cite precedents in international law in support of their acts."[94] Besides seeking legal justification for taking up arms, Wilson observed that from the beginning of the war there was "a respect for conventional forms which shows in a marked degree the influence of the work of the Hague Conferences and for legal purposes gives a definiteness to the relations consequent upon the state of war which has existed in few of the wars of modern times."[95] The fact that specific rules of conduct regarding belligerency were adhered to during the war demonstrated, for Wilson at least, that international law was far from moribund. He argued that if the obituaries of international law were correct, the last thing to have been expected was for states to observe international law during a time of war.

Philip Marshall Brown, who was professor of International Law at Princeton University, claimed that the critics of international law, whether the disciples of the Austinian school of jurisprudence or the latest scoffers "who naturally ask: 'What is the use of a law which cannot prevent war or regulate its methods once it has begun?'" failed to recognize the "fundamental distinctions between the law of peace and the law of war."[96] The real function of international law, Brown argued, was "not to regulate war, but to regulate the *peaceful* relations of states." According to Brown, the arrival of war brings with it the maxim *inter arma silent leges* along with a return to measures of self-help. War, in short, was the negation of law, and in this respect, Brown argued that the laws defining the rights and obligations of neutral states also lose their strength once they are challenged by an outlaw state such as Germany. When viewed in this context, Brown maintained that there was "no evidence of what some cynics have chosen to regard as the breakdown either of civilization, of Christianity, or of international law." Instead, Brown insisted, much as Wilson did, that it was "truly a war in defense of law." He concluded that "the union of twenty or more nations against one outlaw nation with its dupes and accomplices is striking evidence of the vigor of law and of the respect with which it is held."[97] Since the war was, in Brown's opinion, essentially in defense of international law and order, the imperative of securing justice among states was as compelling now as it had been before the war.

George Finch, an expert in international law who served as assistant secretary of the American Society of International Law from 1909 to 1924, also attempted to counter the common view that the war in Europe "demonstrated the ineffectiveness of international law, both conventional and customary, to bind nations in their mutual intercourse in peace and to restrict and control their actions in war." He argued that "the recurrence of war affords no more reason for losing faith in international law than the recurrence of private crime would be a justification for abolishing domestic law and substituting a reign of internal anarchy."[98] Finch drew attention to the fact that it was against the backdrop of the Thirty Years' War that Grotius had formulated the legal principles that should regulate the relations among states. According to Finch, it was from the desire to regulate war that a sense of justice had first entered into the relations of states, and that from the regulation of war, "that system of jurisprudence which we call the law of nations has largely sprung." He maintained that arguments that rejected the efficacy of international law simply on the basis of the outbreak of the latest European war were unfounded.

One of the weaknesses in arguments that attempted to establish a causal link between the outbreak of the war and the futility of international law was, Finch claimed, a lack of historical perspective. He argued that not only was such a perspective lacking on the part of those who failed to grasp the context in which the law of nations developed, but it was also apparent in the failure to recognize that the abrogation of warfare was not "the work of a single lifetime or of a single generation." He maintained that the most that could be hoped for was to detect incremental progress in the development of the science of international law, which Finch believed was in fact taking place. He concurred with Wilson, claiming that it was significant that in a time of war the leading European powers had felt compelled to justify their actions to the larger international community of nations. Finch claimed that such an appeal demonstrated that the "public opinion of mankind—which is the great, indeed the only, practicable sanction for international law—is at last recognized, even by monarchs not supposed to be responsible to popular approval for their actions."[99] This was not to suggest, however, that substantial work in improving the existing system of international law did not lie ahead.

Quincy Wright, who was a member of the influential Chicago school of political science, undertook an analysis of the postwar research in international law for the Carnegie Endowment for International Peace. Wright earned his doctorate from the University of Illinois, where he studied public law under Garner. Although Wright is best known for his monumental work *A Study of War* (1942), his early work at the University of Pennsylvania, Harvard, Minnesota, and even at Chicago when he first arrived in 1923, was primarily devoted to the subject of international law. Wright claimed that international law was a "method, a philosophy, and a process." He explained that as a method, international law "seeks to formulate current international relations as precisely as possible, as a philosophy it seeks to formulate them as usefully as possible, as a process it seeks to eliminate occurrences contrary to the most precise and useful formulation it can make."[100] In assessing the present tendencies in international law research, six core themes were enumerated. Wright commented that

(1) the tone of international writing has on the whole been optimistic and confident, (2) the elimination of war has come to be a generally accepted objective, and as a result, detailed discussion of the rules of war and neutrality have received little attention, but on the other hand (3) international organization, the procedure of pacific settlement, codification and international legislation have had a dominating importance. As a result of this, (4) there has been a bold effort to study the world as it is revealed by the social sciences and contemporary politics, and to mold the law more effectively to serve its needs. (5) For this task old methods of juristic formulation have been reinvestigated and new ones sug-

gested. (6) Perhaps the outstanding characteristic of the literature, however, has been its practical character.[101]

This account of the interwar tendencies in international law research clearly reveals the practical and realistic orientation that scholars adopted toward their subject matter. This attitude was manifest in the efforts of international lawyers to modernize international law so as to contribute to the practical reform of international politics.

In his 1916 presidential address to the American Society of International Law, Elihu Root continued to embrace the idea that public opinion was the ultimate sanction of international law, but he noted that there were circumstances when public opinion was inadequate by itself to ensure compliance. Root admitted that "occasionally there is an act the character of which is so clear that mankind forms a judgment upon it readily and promptly, but in most cases it is easy for the wrongdoer to becloud the issue by assertion and argument and to raise a complicated and obscure controversy which confuses the judgment of the world."[102] Root's discovery of the possibility that public opinion might be misguided, and thus at times prove to be an ineffective sanction, was similar to the findings that some political scientists were reaching about the irrationality of public opinion in pluralist society.[103]

There were several measures apart from improving the rationality of public opinion that Root suggested for making the laws regulating inter-state affairs binding. For one thing, he advocated the establishment of a court of international justice that would be in a position to decide authoritatively what the law required or prohibited in specific cases. Yet he realized that, since there was no international legislature to make laws or a "body of judicial decisions having the effect of precedent to declare what international laws are," international law was, in many respects, imperfect and uncertain. This, he argued, would continue to handicap the operation of an international court of justice unless there were clearly enunciated laws for the court to administer. Thus, in addition to establishing an international court, Root advocated that additional work be undertaken in an effort to codify existing international law. Lastly, he argued that international law had to change the customary practice whereby breaches of conduct were simply treated "as if they concerned nobody except the particular nation upon which the injury was inflicted and the nation inflicting it." This practice, he argued, followed from the traditional view of states as sovereign independent actors. Yet in the contemporary age of interdependence, an injury to one state represented an injury to the other members of international society. He concluded that "there must be a change in theory, and violations of the law of such a character as to threaten the peace and order of the community of nations must be deemed to be a violation of the right of every civilized nation to have the law maintained and a legal injury to every nation."[104]

George Grafton Wilson also proclaimed that "the adaptation of international law to modern conditions" was required. Wilson argued that "many of the old doctrines, regarded as fundamental to the concepts of international law, such as equality, independence, rights of property, have been subjected to careful scrutiny and redefinition has been found necessary."[105] He claimed that redefinition was needed because of recent developments in the composition of the society of nations. He argued that conditions had drastically changed "since the old days when 'strange air made men unfree,'" and when Machiavelli's dictum that "whoever is the occasion of another's advancement is the cause of his own diminution" reigned supreme. Wilson concluded that these conditions no longer held true and, consequently, that new principles which better suited present conditions were necessary.

The theme of modernizing international law to fit present conditions was the topic of a paper that Jesse S. Reeves, professor of political science at the University of Michigan and the twenty-third president of the APSA, delivered at the twelfth annual meeting of the APSA. Reeves asserted that the events exhibited by the war ought to make those "interested in international law extremely modest," because "professing that we expound international law as it is, we have been deluding ourselves and really setting forth international law as we believed that it ought to be."[106] He argued that future attempts to reconstruct international law must not look at international society as a static condition of mankind, as it had been in the past, but as "one in which there are dynamic factors too vast and intricate for any decisive plan adequately to include and reckon with all the circumstances." The dynamic factors that Reeves had in mind not only included the relations of states with each other but also "the larger relations of groups to groups both within and without states, of individuals to individuals, of world movements of population, of earth-hunger and its appeasement, and of the strivings of international commercial competition."[107] This vision represented a substantial expansion in the scope of international law which traditionally had been restricted to the activities of sovereign states.

One dimension of international law that needed to be reformulated, Reeves argued, was the traditional conception of states' rights. He claimed that a science of international law built upon the principle of the absolute rights of states immediately connects it "with the absolutist theory of the state, makes world-society simply the sum of the relationships between primordial units, and has little to do with what lies back of and within such units."[108] Reeves declared that it was not so much that the idea of the rights of states had to be eliminated as that it had to be reformulated to suit the dynamic factors present in international society. He argued that the dynamic conditions present in international society meant that the rights of states could no longer be understood simply in state-centric terms but had to be restated "in terms of humanity and of a world-society." Reeves recognized that in order for this alternative conception of states' rights to have any validity, it was necessary to reconstruct the twin doctrines of the independence and equality of states in terms of current social dynamics. He asserted that "the theoretical position of sovereignty within the state must be attacked anew," and argued that if international law was to be a valid law among states, then it could not depend upon the "idealistic portrayal of the philosophic jurist or the policy adopted by the bureaucrat." Reeves concluded by arguing that

> It may be that the state is but a passing phenomenon. It must be that the theory of the state as a juristic person must be re-examined in terms of humanity. Until this is done the prospects of the future in the way of the settlement by legal methods of all or even the more important international disputes cannot be predicted with anything like confidence.[109]

Charles Fenwick, a political scientist who was an expert on international law, agreed with Reeves's assessment that the traditional principle of the sovereignty of the state must be attacked anew if international law was to shed its quixotic character. Fenwick articulated the essence of the discourse about international relations when he asserted that "of all the outworn conceptions of international law sovereignty is the most illogical," for "a world of literally sovereign nations is a world of anarchy."[110] He claimed in this context that the critique of sovereignty had to include "a new statement of the rights and duties of nations in their normal pacific relations."[111] Fenwick argued that it was neither acceptable nor suitable for scholars of international law to adhere to the abstract notion that states had an a priori right of self-preservation, independence, and legal equality. These archaic principles, which originated from the writings of the naturalists and the followers of Grotius, were irrelevant in light of present conditions and a handicap to any further improvement in establishing a legal basis for the settlement of international disputes. This argument was consistent with the positive approach to international law that Fenwick adopted in his text *International Law* (1924). In the Preface to this work, Fenwick explained that his task was "to present international law as a positive system, and to distinguish as sharply as is feasible between such rules as have legal validity, in the sense that they are generally accepted, and such other rules as individual governments or writers, guided by altruistic or by selfish motives, have asserted are or should be the law."[112]

Conclusion

This chapter as well as previous chapters has focused on the manner in which the discourse on international law established an influential medium for understanding and interpreting the subject matter of international politics, and the connection between the discourse on international law and the study of international organization is one of the themes to be explored in the next chapter. It is essential to have an adequate sense of the discussions of international law that were taking place among political scientists throughout the early decades of the twentieth century, since various "realist" scholars from the late 1930s and 1940s to the present have charged that they were a fundamental indication of the idealistic orientation of the field. The discursive history reconstructed in this chapter suggests, on the contrary, that scholars in the field were not addressing the subject matter of international relations based on a conception of how things ought to be or how they wished them to be. The situation was actually quite the reverse.

The distinguishing feature of international relations scholarship discussed in this chapter was the attempt to reconcile the theories and concepts of the field with the empirical reality of inter-state politics. This was especially evident in the conviction expressed by a number of political scientists that the constitutive elements of the theoretical discourse of the state were no longer consistent with the reality it sought to explain. According to a great many political theorists, international lawyers, and scholars of international relations, this discrepancy was nowhere more apparent than in the theory and practice of external sovereignty. This in turn helps to account for the close relationship that existed between the fields of political theory and international relations. The critique of the juristic theory of state sovereignty that was being pursued by political theorists was of direct significance to political scientists in the international field. The theory of pluralism offered an account of sovereignty and law that not only was deemed more consistent with the political experiences being observed by political scientists but allowed new possibilities to be considered that juristic theory had prohibited. The development of the theory of pluralism within political science and the manner through which it impacted on the theory of international relations indicates the artificiality of the common contemporary dichotomy that has been drawn between political theory and international relations theory.

6

INTERNATIONAL ORGANIZATION AND INTERNATIONAL POLITICS

Authors and Works Discussed

Author	1920	1925	1930	1935	1940	1945
Brown	(1923)					
Carr				(1939)		
Dunn				(1937)		(1948)
Hicks	(1920)					
Kirk					(1944)	(1947)
Lasswell			(1933)	(1935)		
Lawrence	(1919)					
Morgenthau					(1946)	(1948a,b)
Potter	(1923)	(1925)	(1929)(1933)			
Schuman			(1933)			
Wilson	(1918)					
Wright						(1952)
Zimmern				(1936)		

Philip Marshall Brown 1875–1966
International Society: Its Nature and Interests [1923]

E.H. Carr 1892–1982
The Twenty Years' Crisis, 1919–1939 [1939]

Frederick Sherwood Dunn 1893–1962
Peaceful Change: A Study of International Procedures [1937]
"The Scope of International Relations" *World Politics* [1948]

Frederick Charles Hicks 1875–1956
The New World Order [1920]

Grayson Kirk 1903–
and Walter R. Sharp, *Contemporary International Politics* [1944]
The Study of International Relations in American Colleges and Universities [1947]

Harold D. Lasswell 1902–1978
"The Problem of World-Unity: In Quest of a Myth" *International Journal of Ethics* [1933]

World Politics and Personal Insecurity [1935]

Thomas J. Lawrence 1849–1919
The Society of Nations: Its Past, Present, and Possible Future [1919]

Hans J. Morgenthau 1904–1980
Scientific Man Versus Power Politics [1946]
"The Political Science of E.H. Carr" *World Politics* [1948a]
Politics Among Nations: The Struggle for Power and Peace [1948b]

Pitman B. Potter 1892–1981
"Political Science in the International Field" *APSR* [1923]
An Introduction to the Study of International Organization [1925]
This World of Nations: Foundations, Institutions, Practices [1929]
"International Organization" [1933]

Frederick L. Schuman 1904–1981
International Politics: An Introduction to the Western State System [1933]

Woodrow Wilson 1856–1924
"Fourteen Points" [1918]

Quincy Wright 1890–1970
"Realism and Idealism in International Politics" *World Politics* [1952]

Sir Alfred Zimmern 1879–1957
The League of Nations and the Rule of Law [1936]

This chapter continues to reconstruct the interwar discourse of international relations. More specifically, two of the central motifs of this period are carefully examined—motifs that continue to structure much of the contemporary discourse of international relations. The first revolves around the institutionalization of the study of international organization. Students of international relations often interpret this period of disciplinary history as both a direct response to the creation of the League of Nations and as one in which "international organization was viewed not so much as a subfield [but] as practically the core of the discipline."[1] Although the existence of the League of Nations did provide a focal point of discussion about the character of international organization, the internal dynamics of this conversation must be reconstructed. The contemporary significance and relevance of the interwar discourse of international organization for international relations scholars is readily apparent in the field's preoccupation with the study of international regimes and inter-state cooperation.[2] Yet in the recent literature there are few, if any, references to many of the scholars who virtually were the founders of the study of international organization. This chapter focuses on the work of Pitman Potter who was one of the seminal, albeit forgotten, figures in the interwar study of international organization.

The focus that international relations scholars of the interwar period placed on the study of international organization can be construed as representing a distinctive development in the political discourse of anarchy. Yet, contrary to conventional accounts of the history of the field in which international relations scholars of the interwar period are characterized as "idealists," the distinctiveness of their contribution lies not in their idealism but in their explicit attempt to mitigate the international anarchy that many political scientists recognized as one of the fundamental causes of World War I. Although the interwar scholars may have been optimists, in that they believed something could be done about the existing international situation, they were not idealistic in the sense that they failed to face the real character of international politics. This attempt to reform the international anarchy does not, by itself, automatically imply that the interwar discourse was "idealistic," since the criterion of this judgment lies in the manner in which they understood and confronted the situation they faced.

This last point is closely related to the second major theme of this chapter, which considers the arguments that were advanced toward the end of the interwar period by the self-identified "realists" who declared that international politics should replace international organization and law as the core of the field. This turn of events has been conventionally understood as marking the beginning of the realist phase of the field's history. There is no more commonly accepted assumption about the history of academic international relations than that the field experienced an intellectual controversy in the late 1930s and early 1940s that pitted the scholars of the interwar period and their predecessors against a distinctively new group of scholars who were conspicuous by their advocacy of a "realist" approach to studying international politics. The controversy between the "idealists" and the "realists" has been accepted as marking the field's first "great debate."

This chapter considers the arguments that were advanced by some of the early realists, such as E.H. Carr, Hans Morgenthau, Frederick Schuman, Grayson Kirk, and Frederick Sherwood Dunn. While there is no denying the distinctive elements that the realists introduced into the field of international relations, there was also a continuity with the earlier approaches and concerns of the field. Although many of the realists rejected both the focus on, and the concern with, mitigating anarchy, they nevertheless in many cases shared the same analytical and conceptual scheme that earlier scholars in the field had developed. And while a focus on power and war was at the forefront of the realist research agenda, there was often lurking beneath the surface a concern with how to achieve peace in an international environment in which there was no central authority. The great divide that has been depicted between the interwar scholars and the first generation of realist scholars cannot withstand much critical scrutiny when the actual discourse of this period is carefully reconstructed.

A Society of Nations

The last chapter revealed that the interwar discourse of international relations was largely committed to reconciling the theory of external sovereignty with the empirical practice of international politics. The older ontology of inter-state politics as a realm characterized by isolated, independent, and equal entities free of external authority was judged to be inconsistent with contemporary conditions. A revised ontology that accentuated the interdependent character of the relations between states and the mutual interconnections that existed among people, states, and international organizations became the more common basis for viewing the international milieu. This alternative image, in turn, helped give rise to the judgment that a genuine society or community of nations had come into existence. This opinion was exemplified in the numerous texts published after the war that adopted titles such as *International Society* or *The Society of Nations*.[3] But here again, the idea of an international society, and the discussion it engendered, was not a novel development. Snow, for example, had encouraged political scientists in 1913 to make the society of nations a subject of study (Chapter 3), and his recommendation gained increasing acceptance throughout the interwar period. Yet the precise meaning of the concept of a society of nations continued to be a contentious issue.

This was in part because the idea of a society of nations was often part of a normative claim that was immune from strict empirical verification. Philip Marshall Brown recognized this in his study of international society when he stated that "I do not cherish the illusion that everybody will see the facts of international society as they are here presented, or draw the same conclusions."[4] According to Brown, however, it was incontrovertible that a society of nations did in fact exist. This view was shared by another prominent international lawyer, T. J. Lawrence, who was Reader of International Law at the University of Bristol. In the autumn of 1917, Lawrence gave six lectures on the society of nations in which he attempted to demonstrate that "there is a real Society of Nations, that it grew up by a gradual process of evolution that can be followed historically, and that it was at the point of developing certain much needed judicial and legislative organs when the present war brought about a crisis in its life."[5]

Brown and Lawrence both agreed that the political structure of the society of nations was built on the foundation of the sovereign state, and they did not cherish any illusion that this was going to give way to some form of supra-national authority. They argued that, properly speaking, the society of nations should be termed a "society of states." Lawrence articulated three conditions that had to be fulfilled in order for a society of states to exist. First, there must be a plurality of members, for if the "world were one great state, there could not be a Society of States." Second, "it is necessary that among the members of a society there should be some community of thought and aspiration." Finally, states must be "regarded as possessors of a definite portion of the earth's surface," and, "the conception of territorial sovereignty is essential."[6] This reveals how the principle of state sovereignty continued to structure the discourse of international relations. Brown considered nationalism to be the single most important factor shaping inter-state politics. He argued that nationalism must "be accepted as the basic fact of international society," and he claimed that for the foreseeable future, it was "idealistic" to believe that international politics would be based on any other principle. Consequently, he concluded that

> The supreme problem of international society is to find unity out of the divergences and differences of nations; to discover a greatest common denominator that will enable men to interpret their varying interests and aims, that will enable them to come together on a plane of genuine brotherhood.[7]

This passage indicates that conflict rather than concord among nations was the basic assumption of those studying international society. In his endeavor to diminish the differences present in international society, Brown declared that the only method available was "the laboratory method—the practical, hard, objective test of analysis." Brown adopted this method in his analysis of the various procedures of international society, which included international law, diplomacy, international politics, the balance of power, international organization, and the League of Nations. He explained that each of these procedures represented a different mechanism through which the disagreements that arose in international society were adjusted. From Brown's perspective, the inauguration of the League of Nations did not represent a qualitatively new phase in the relations between states but rather a further attempt to reconcile differences among members of the society of nations. He did not expect the League of Nations to rid international politics of all the problems associated with nationalism. This was because the League of Nations was, most essentially, a mechanism of conciliation and not an international sovereign. Yet even without the formation of a world sovereign, Brown believed that the society of nations was ameliorating many of the worst features associated with the absence of centralized authority. He attributed this development to the fact that while the sovereign state continued to be the fundamental actor in international politics, the modern state no longer embodied the characteristics of an independent isolated unit possessing a freedom of will to do as it pleased. Brown argued that the contemporary practice of international law had rendered this image of the state obsolete. He maintained that international law was evidence for the existence of a society of nations. The formation of the League of Nations provided additional confirmation to those who adhered to the idea of a society of nations.

The League of Nations

In retrospect, it is entirely understandable why the establishment of the League of Nations would occupy the attention of those in political science who identified with the study of international relations. The Treaty of Versailles provided for a formal organization to be established whose purpose was to prevent any future armed hostilities between states. The League of Nations, in turn, provided political scientists with the opportunity to study the form and function of such an organization with respect to fulfilling the stated objective of securing a lasting peace. There were some who expected the international anarchy, which G. Lowes Dickinson and others argued was responsible for World War I, to be quelled through the effective functioning of the League and that its formation represented a stage in the evolution of international politics toward a more harmonious world order. It also is understandable why Woodrow Wilson has been so often identified as the exemplar of this period of disciplinary history, since it was, after all, Wilson's fourteenth point of his famed postwar peace program that proposed that "a general association of nations must be formed under specific covenants for the purpose of affording mutual guarantees of political independence and territorial integrity to great and small states alike."[8] Before being elected President of the United States, Wilson enjoyed an illustrious academic life: eminent political scientist at Hopkins and Princeton, author of several important texts, sixth president of the APSA, and university president.[9] Yet by the time that he arrived at the White House in 1913, he was far removed intellectually from political science. It is wrong to assume a special link between Woodrow Wilson and the birth and growth of academic international relations.

By the onset of World War I, Wilson was only one of many public intellectuals and academic scholars who were involved in the movement to create an institutional structure to secure peace.[10] Regardless of the fact that the war had disrupted progress toward peace, many of the same individuals and societies that had been working to achieve peace prior to the war continued their work to reform inter-state politics. There were, however, several new advocacy groups that arose in response to the outbreak of the war and that, in turn, directly helped to build the foundation for the establishment of the League of Nations. The first of these was the Bryce-Dickinson group, referred to earlier (Chapter 5), which grew to become the League of Nations Society in the spring of 1915. The society was located in England, and was based on the ideas that Dickinson and Bryce had drafted in their "Proposals for the Avoidance of War." The membership of the League of Nations Society became one of the leading voices in Europe advocating a post-war international organization that would have sufficient power to impose coercive sanctions on any outlaw state. John Hobson was a member of the League of Nations Society, and many of the ideas that the Society advocated were included in his book *Towards International Government* (1916). After the war, Hobson turned his attention away from the study of imperialism and toward the study of international organization. He argued that "if a really efficacious scheme for the establishment of peaceable relations is to be secured, it must assign to some duly accredited international body legislative, judicial, and executive powers."[11] Hobson was especially attracted to the idea of creating a strong international executive that would have sufficient power, including the use of armed force, to compel states to fulfill their obligations. Hobson realized that international public opinion did not always satisfy the requirements of an international executive and he argued that an executive organization that lacked the necessary power to compel its members was doomed to obsolescence.

Across the Atlantic in New York City, there arose the League to Enforce Peace that had close contact with the members of the League of Nations Society. The League to Enforce Peace was composed of a group of American internationalists who, as members of the New York Peace Society, began to discuss formally the idea of establishing an international union of states. The four initial meetings were held at the Century Club in New York City on January 25 and 31, March 30, and April 19, 1915, to discuss the specific details of a postwar international organization. Although there were many differences of opinion expressed by those who attended these founding meetings, especially on the subject of whether the proposed organization should possess the ability to apply coercive sanctions, agreement was reached to support the platform of the League to Enforce Peace.[12] In their effort to popularize the need to establish an international union of states, the League to Enforce Peace enlisted a number of prominent figures to speak on its behalf.

This included President Wilson, who agreed to address the first annual meeting in Washington, D.C. on May 27, 1916.

Although the significance of Wilson's speech for the cause of the League to Enforce Peace was indeed great, there were, nevertheless, difficulties with what he proposed. Wilson began his address by re-iterating the common theme of interdependence, asserting that "we are participants in the life of the world," and that "what affects mankind is inevitably our affair as well as the affair of the nations of Europe and of Asia."[13] Wilson reckoned that this required a "new and more whole-some diplomacy." He proclaimed that

> [T]he principle of public right must henceforth take precedence over the individual interests of particular nations, and that the nations of the world must in some way band themselves together to see that that [sic] right prevails as against any sort of selfish aggression; that henceforth alliance must not be set up against alliance, understanding against understanding, but that there must be a common agreement for a common objective, and that at the heart of that common object must lie the inviolable rights of people and of mankind.[14]

Yet while rejecting the older principles of diplomacy, Wilson at the same time endorsed the traditional principle of sovereignty that would also figure prominently in his Fourteen Points. He declared, "that every people has a right to choose the sovereignty under which they shall live," and, "that the small states of the world have a right to enjoy the same respect for their sovereignty and for their territorial integrity that great and powerful nations expect and insist upon."[15]

Although Wilson was influenced by a number of prominent inter-nationalists, it would appear that he did not heed his former political science colleagues. Many of these scholars, it will be recalled, had con-cluded that the greatest obstacle to achieving an effective international organization resulted from fifty or more states each claiming to possess equal and absolute sovereign rights. In short, many international rela-tions scholars already had determined that the establishment of an effective international organization hinged on certain conditions being fulfilled: namely, that states relinquish a certain degree of their sov-ereignty; that strong and weak states not be treated as equals; that the rights of states not be regarded as absolute; and that coercive sanctions be imposed on states that did not abide by the dictates of the organiza-tion. Some of the critics of the League of Nations plan, such as Butler and Hill, based their opposition to the United States' joining the League upon what they perceived as an infringement on the traditional concep-tion of state sovereignty.

In addition to refusing to become a member of the League to Enforce Peace, Butler wrote a series of letters to the *New York Times,* under the pseudonym Cosmos, that were sharply critical of its platform. These letters were later published in book form under the auspices of the Carnegie Endowment for International peace.[16] Butler continued to place his faith in the further development of the "international mind" which he argued would eventually result in greater international understanding. When this proved to be insufficient, Butler advocated the judicial approach to peace as exemplified in the first two meetings at The Hague. He completely rejected any plan for postwar peace that required the United States to depart from its traditional path of foreign policy as set forth in Washington's Farewell Address and the Monroe Doctrine. Similarly, although Hill recognized "that any effective form of international government implies the renunciation, to some extent at least, of absolute sovereignty," he was unwilling to concede the degree of sovereignty that the League to Enforce Peace was advocating, especially with respect to the idea that the League of Nations should utilize military sanctions against aggressor states.[17] Hill, like Butler, continued to champion the judicial approach to peace and argued for a third meeting of The Hague (a meeting that the outbreak of the war had prevented). He asserted that without the rule of law, there was no hope for a lasting peace. Hill viewed the existing plan to establish a League of Nations as neither possible nor desirable and advocated perfecting international law through discussion and decision in international conferences, codification procedures, and by the creation of a real judicial world court.

In any event, the implementation of the League of Nations proceeded, although ironically and disappointingly without the participation of the United States after the Senate refused to endorse American membership in the League. The establishment of the League prompted a large body of literature devoted to explaining its form and function. One work of prominence was Stephen Duggan's edited book *The League of Nations: The Principle and the Practice* (1919), which included contributions from John Bassett Moore, A. Lawrence Lowell, Frederic Ogg, Harry Barnes, Edwin Borchard, Raymond Gettell, and several other well-known political scientists. In the Preface, Duggan wrote that it was "undeniable that the great mass of intelligent people of Europe and America have come to the belief, as a result of the catastrophe that befell the civilized world in 1914, that a different international organization from the one existing at that time was essential to the peaceful development of humanity."[18] He argued that this conviction had resulted in the demand for some sort of League of Nations that would be able to preserve future peace. Yet while a certain degree of consensus had been reached on the need for a League of Nations, Duggan claimed that many of the specific questions concerning the organization, function, purpose, and America's relation to the League remained unanswered. It was for the purpose of providing answers to these questions for both intelligent laymen and students in need of a textbook on the subject that the volume was "written in simple and untechnical language" with the aim of providing clarification of the numerous issues surrounding the League. Part One of the book dealt with the history, philosophy, and organization of the League; Part Two discussed international cooperation as applied to concrete problems; and Part Three addressed the place of the United States in the League of Nations. An appendix was provided which included the peace plans of the Abbé Saint-Pierre, Kant, the texts of the Holy Alliance, and the provisions of the Hague Conventions in order to lend "a more detailed study of the subject." One of the underlying concerns in each of the chapters was the manner in which national sovereignty could be reconciled with the operation of the League of Nations. This was the most significant theoretical issue that the literature dealing with the League addressed, and it was deeply rooted in the discourse of earlier years.

Another early contribution to the literature that focused on the League of Nations, and which also dealt with the relationship between national sovereignty and international organization, was Frederick Hicks's *The New World Order* (1920). The book was the result of a series of lectures that Hicks delivered at Columbia University on the subject of international organization and cooperation. The League of Nations, as well as its general relation to international organization, international law, and international cooperation, was the basic focus of the book. Hicks did not conceal his support for the principles of the League nor his conviction that it should be adopted by the United States. He argued that the League of Nations should be supported, because it emphasized "the necessity for cooperation between sovereign states" and represented "an end in itself, the benefits of which are felt directly by the people of all participating states."[19] Hicks claimed that the design of the League of Nations would provide a more determinate organizational structure than that of the preexisting society of nations. He deemed it essential to differentiate the older society of nations from the more recent attempt to create an international organization, and argued that the term "League of Nations" should not be confused with, or used in place of, the "society of nations." He argued that the society of nations predated the First World War and believed that it would continue to exist regardless of the particular fortunes of the League. Like Brown, he argued that evidence of its existence was best revealed by the body of international law that imposed obligations and duties on all members.

Hicks also recognized that the underlying constitutive principle of the society of nations was sovereignty. He argued that it was the principle of sovereignty that explained why international society was most successful at regulating inter-state relations during peace and was fatally weak in time of war. Hicks explained that this weakness was a result of the "fact that nothing but self-interest can, under the theory of absolute sovereignty, restrain a powerful state from declaring war." He added that it was quite apparent that there was "something wanting in an international system which can be maintained only by four years of war."[20] Nevertheless, Hicks argued that it was better to understand the principles and features of the older society of nations than to ignore them. Like other previous attempts to institute an international organization, Hicks considered the League to be simply the latest effort "to give more definite organization to the existing Society of Nations upon which it is based and out of which it has grown."[21] Thus, it was necessary to understand that regardless of the intellectual energy that was being devoted to renouncing the claim of absolute sovereignty, the principle was not going to disappear any time soon.

Sir Alfred Zimmern, on the other hand, judged the efforts to establish a League of Nations as representing a radical break with the past. Zimmern is generally considered to be one of the leading interwar scholars of international relations. In addition to being the first person to hold the Wilson Chair of International Politics at Aberystwyth, Zimmern also held appointments at Cornell University, Trinity College, and Oxford University where he was Montague Burton professor of international relations. He was a dedicated advocate of the League of Nations and, before the Armistice, served on the League of Nations Union research committee. He was also responsible for helping to found the Institute of International Affairs in London, and after World War II, he played an active role in UNESCO.[22] In his most popular text, *The League of Nations and the Rule of Law* (1936), Zimmern argued that the League of Nations

> [P]resupposes a transformation of Power-politics into Responsibility-politics, or, at the very least, a sincere and consistent effort on the part of the Great Powers to begin to face the innumerable tasks of adjustment which such a transformation would carry with it. It involves the inauguration of a real Society of States in place of the anti-social traditions and policies of the pre-war era.[23]

Although Zimmern claimed that the inauguration of the League of Nations represented a major transformation in the basic character of international politics, he did not consider the organizational structure of the League itself to be all that revolutionary. He maintained that the League of Nations accepted the world of states as it then existed and essentially sought "to provide a more satisfactory means for carrying on some of the business which these states transact between one another."[24] On the basis of his analysis of the pre-1914 system of international politics, which comprised the first third of his book, Zimmern concluded that a new system was needed if the kind of cataclysm associated with the First World War was to be avoided in the future.

The League of Nations, Zimmern argued, was the cornerstone of the new system that was being put into place. At its core, the League represented an experimental method that was "being attempted at a particular moment of history when there are certain principal Powers with clearly marked characteristics and policies." In this regard, Zimmern believed that the League did not so much "supercede the older methods" of world politics as supplement them.[25] He argued that the success of the new international system in maintaining concord among nations would depend less on the institutional features of the League itself than on "politics and psychology." The League of Nations, according to Zimmern, was simply the machinery of the new system, and its effectiveness would be determined by the way states and, more specifically, people made use of it. He argued that the Covenant of the League *"assumes* a new spirit in the whole field of international politics," which entailed replacing the older "anti-social traditions and policies of the pre-war era." In a statement that foreshadowed the future, Zimmern concluded that "failing the adoption of such a new attitude, the new machinery not only cannot by itself bring about the passing of Power-politics, but may even provide a new and more sensational and even dangerous arena for its exercise."[26]

When Zimmern directed his attention to the task of explaining the exact configuration of the League of Nations, he claimed that it was difficult, if not impossible, to define, because "we were living through an interregnum in political science" from which "the old books are out of date and the new cannot yet be written."[27] Much of the literature concerning the League of Nations sought to provide a definitive account of its institutional form. There were almost as many explanations of the form of the League as there were books and articles written on the subject. Zimmern thought that the structure of the League stood somewhere between the two extremes of a Super-state and a multilateral alliance. Since neither of these two descriptions adequately reflected the character of the League, Zimmern preferred to define it as a "Co-operative Society of States." Others, however, insisted that the League was much more than simply a society of states. Here, the descriptions of the League ranged from a world federal state or international government, on the one hand, to a weak alliance of sovereign states on the other hand.[28] At the root of the controversy over the proper definition of the League was the issue of sovereignty. The different descriptions of the League were largely a function of the manner in which scholars reconciled national sovereignty with the structure of the League. Those who maintained that sovereignty was compatible with the new form of international organization created at Versailles were inclined to believe that the League represented a federal structure of government, while those who perceived an opposition between the two principles argued that the League was merely a voluntary association or alliance of independent states.

In order to understand properly the nature of this dispute, it is necessary to locate the discourse of the League of Nations within its proper academic context. That context was the study of international organization which represented the core of the field of international relations throughout much of the interwar period. When examined from this viewpoint, the discussion of the League was only one component of a much larger discourse concerned with the study of international organization. Although a change would take place at the end of this period, when the study of international organization was rejected in favor of an approach described as international politics, it is absolutely essential to first gain a sense of what the discourse of international organization entailed. Most fundamentally, it cannot be construed as "idealist" in the sense that the term was later understood.

International Organization

In addition to the debate about the League of Nations with respect to its form, function, and significance for reforming the international anarchy, the calamities of the First World War helped to elevate the status of the formal study of international organization within the discipline of political science in general and in the field of international relations in particular. Apart from Reinsch, the person most responsible for giving definite form to the study of international organization in the United States was Pitman Benjamin Potter. After earning his doctorate from Harvard University in 1918, Potter held a brief position at the University of Illinois before joining the department of political science at the University of Wisconsin in 1920. At Wisconsin, Potter assumed the role that Reinsch had occupied earlier as the preeminent scholar of international relations. The study of international organization throughout the interwar period was essentially synonymous with the work of Potter, who, like Reinsch, is one of the forgotten figures from the past.

In an article that appeared in the *American Political Science Review*, Potter chastised his colleagues for not devoting sufficient attention to the problem of international organization which he regarded as the most important problem in political science. Potter claimed that a direct result of political scientists' neglect of the subject matter of international organization in the years leading up to the war "has been suffering and death for millions of human beings, wasting and destruction of billions of dollars of property, and the present grievous sickness in the world society."[29] The various plans of international organization that were in circulation before the war were, according to Potter, devised "chiefly by the advocates of peace and not by persons trained in formal political science." It was Potter's intention to explain the factors responsible for the reluctance on the part of political scientists before the war to study the problem of international organization. Potter claimed that one of the explanations was that methodological changes were underway in the discipline. He was specifically referring to the tendency on the part of political scientists to adopt the more "scientific" inductive method in place of the older deductive method. Potter maintained that as a result of this change in methodological orientation, political science was "concerned primarily with the description of facts, the formulation of principles of interpretation and explanation to fit those facts in retrospect, not with the declaration of rules of action to be followed in the future."[30] Potter insisted that as a result of this misplaced methodology, the study of international organization was neglected, since political scientists "did not feel called on to study what did not appear to exist."

Potter argued that a second explanation for indifference toward studying the problems of international organization was the secrecy that shrouded the diplomatic process. He argued that students of international government actually condoned the practice of secret diplomacy by "assuming the ridiculous position that certain vital political processes must in their entirety forever remain a *terra incognita* to political science."[31] Potter felt this was inexcusable, and claimed that if political scientists were to make an attempt to study these various diplomatic practices, they would find that the excuse of secrecy was entirely unfounded. The last factor that Potter argued was responsible for neglecting the study of international organization was one that directly related to the political discourse of anarchy; that is, the problem of sovereignty. He explained that "acceptability" was one of the fundamental criteria that political scientists used to judge the feasibility of the various plans for international organization. Acceptability referred to the extent to which a typical state reasonably could be expected to endorse the principles of the proposed organization. Potter claimed that most plans of international organization were declared unacceptable by political scientists on the basis of the principle of sovereignty. He declared that the absurdity of this position was made apparent by the fact that it was political scientists who invented the doctrine of state sovereignty, developed it to extreme proportions, and set it "loose in the world in a day when we [political scientists] were leaders of public thought, and left by our abdication of the task of leadership in these later days unsupported by any complementary doctrine of international solidarity." He added that political scientists "taught an extreme doctrine hostile to international organization to begin with," and "remained hostile or at least indifferent to the latter movement throughout its formative years."[32]

Potter argued that to make up for their past neglect, political scientists must accept intellectual and moral responsibility for assisting the study of international organization. As further evidence of continuing neglect, Potter pointed to the fact that as of 1910, only six institutions of higher learning in the United States gave courses in subjects akin to, or part of, the field of international organization. By comparison, he found that there were more than 150 universities and colleges giving academic instruction in international law. He concluded that political science had not awaked to the urgent and important task of studying international organization. This was a theme that Potter would continually reiterate throughout his numerous writings. In *This World of Nations* (1929), for example, he again claimed that "as astounding and as scandalous as it may seem—and as it should seem to the professional political scientists in the international field—the dawn of the twentieth century saw in existence no scientific works of importance on the serious problems of international organization and intergovernmental cooperation."[33] He rejected the contention that since international organization was a new political phenomenon, it would take time to learn the subject before it could be taught. Echoing Snow's earlier complaint about political scientists' resistance to studying the larger society of nations because of its supposed lack of determinateness, Potter argued that many of the activities and practices associated with international organization had been in existence for centuries. He found that, in many ways, the principles of international organization were similar to those of inter-state federation in general—a "problem thousands of years old." Potter claimed that the inattention had less to do with the existence or non-existence of international organization than with the basic fact that political science simply overlooked this realm of political activity. In any event, even assuming that the practice of international organization was new, an assumption he entirely rejected, Potter asked: "would it not be the duty of political scientists to lead the way in that direction, by pointing out the need for international organization to remedy the existing international anarchy by the adaptation of known political practices to the international sphere?"[34] This was a duty that Potter felt compelled to fulfill throughout his academic career. He was convinced that political scientists in the international field had missed their opportunity to make a contribution to the study of international organization before the war, and he declared that "all we can do is to attempt to repay the world for our indifference and neglect by increased efforts now." What this required, at least initially, was "the training of greater numbers of students and teachers in the field of international organization."[35] Concomitant with this requirement was the need to distinguish clearly the sub-field of international organization from the larger disciplinary matrix of what Potter referred to as political science of the international field. And here lies another one of the notable contributions that Potter made to the study of international relations.

Before turning to Potter's explication of the international field of political science, it is necessary to mention that the term "international organization" carried both an academic and a "real world" meaning. Just as the term "international relations" is used to refer to an academic field and an identifiable realm of political activity, the phrase "international organization" was intended to signify a realm of political activity as well as a branch of academic study. This is not merely a semantic issue, for it was the empirical practice of international organization that gave the field of international organization its object of inquiry. Potter attempted to clarify this issue through his discussion of the term "international organization" in the 1933 edition of the *Encyclopaedia of the Social Sciences*. He claimed that international organization was "a phase of the relations among the nation states of the world." It was a phase that, according to Potter, was marked by the need on the part of states to cooperate mutually with other states in order to realize their own particular national objectives. Potter claimed that when instances such as these arose, "nations need a system of institutions and procedures whereby national policies may be communicated by one nation to another, socially synthesized (internationalized) and executed." He explained that "this body of institutions and procedures is referred to by the now fairly familiar phrase international organization."[36] In this regard, Potter argued that international organization was to be contrasted strongly with international politics. The latter, Potter argued, was characterized by the absence of any process of international harmonization or coordination. He claimed that in fact it was the types of interactions characteristic of international politics that constituted "one of the principal reasons for the establishment of machinery and methods for synthesizing national policies." Potter identified three principal motivations that were behind the historical development of international organization: first, the desire for "satisfactions obtainable only from beyond national boundaries, which gives rise to the whole body of international intercourse"; second, the desire of state officials and citizens "for effective international cooperation in the regulation of this intercourse"; and third, a "desire to avoid international friction and violence."[37]

Potter argued that a change in motives alone, however, would not result in international organization. The first prerequisite, and one that clearly differentiated international organization from other world order projects, such as the creation of a world state, was the need for a plurality of states. He argued that the existence of a multiplicity of states was indispensable for international organization, because without it, there would be no need to harmonize national policies. Second, Potter argued that a degree of homogeneity and equality among the various states was needed in order for them to enter into cooperative arrangements. He reasoned that vast discrepancies in either material resources or interests could result in an unwillingness of certain states to cooperate with the other members of international society. These first two prerequisites clearly established the state as the basic unit upon which international organization was to be built and discussed. Potter, moreover, not only defined international organization in terms of the state-centric assumption but perceived international cooperation as being based on motives of self-interest rather than altruism. Finally, Potter deduced that a third prerequisite was needed, namely, "there must exist a science of international organization if these facts and potential causes and consequences are to be adequately realized, interpreted and acted upon."[38] This referred to his earlier criticism of political scientists' neglect of the study of international organization.

Potter took it upon himself to delineate the domain of the subfield of international organization. He explained that "the political science of the international field may be divided into two major parts, namely, international law and international government, the latter called more frequently international organization."[39] With respect to the first component, Potter alleged that international law was of minimal use to the study of international organization. He concluded that despite the vast amount of intellectual energy that had been devoted to the topic, the literature had contributed little to achieving either world peace or international cooperation. In a particularly poignant passage, Potter criticized the traditional study of international law as well as the field of diplomatic history, claiming that they had "come perilously near to ruining the whole study of international relations." He added that "they have scared people away from the study of the field which is of fascinating interest, of primary importance to human welfare, and no more difficult of understanding than human affairs on any level." Lastly, and most damning, he maintained that they had "amounted to little or nothing as aids to the solution of the problem of peace, order, and progress, and they have set up absurd pretensions to their own importance and their own scientific soundness and have insisted on frightening the common layman away from the study of international affairs."[40]

International organization, as the second sub-field of the larger international field of political science, was, according to Potter, divisible into two major parts: international institutions and international practices. He explained that international institutions encompassed the study of the structure and function of international courts, commissions, conferences, and federations, while international practice was devoted to the general study of international politics. In light of the later realist critique, it is significant that Potter viewed the study of international politics as being an integral part of the sub-field of international organization. Potter's choice of the term "international organization" to define the field was deliberate, since he was determined to differentiate international organization as a field of study from the more amorphous but popular subject of international government, which was closely tied to the study of the League of Nations. Potter was not so much opposed to the term "international government" on principle as concerned to classify with scientific rigor the various branches of study that constituted the sub-field of international organization. Potter considered international organization to be a more comprehensive term than international government which he claimed "consists essentially of control exercised over one or more nations by one or more other nations."[41] On the basis of this definition, Potter concluded that international government was pervasive in the present international system, and he even suggested that a world state was "conceivable, and even imminent, to a certain degree; indeed it is an actual fact in certain very limited terms."[42] This did not, however, imply that international governance entailed the dissolution of the sovereign state.

The thread that tied each of these claims together was international organization. Potter wrote that the "distinguishing characteristic of official international organizations, and their fundamental purpose, lies in their functioning as institutions for international government, for the exercise of control by one or more states over one another."[43] When viewed in this context, international organization was conceptualized as a procedure of facilitating international harmonization and coordination between states and one that eventually might lead to a truly functioning international government. Potter's *An Introduction to the Study of*

International Organization (1925) was devoted to elucidating the different elements of this procedure, which included treaty-making, international law, international arbitration, international administration, international conferences and congresses, and the League of Nations. Along with describing the particular form and function of each of these activities, Potter attempted to demonstrate the manner through which these procedures of international organization were providing the foundation for an effective form of world governance. With respect to the composition of the emerging world government, Potter argued that the only form possible was an international federation of states. He claimed that "at whatever point the problem of international government is opened for examination, the indications all point in one direction, toward the creation of a permanent world-wide federation of states for the performance of the minimum services of definition, adjudication, and enforcement of national rights in international relations." He added that "in no other way can law and order, peace and justice, be secured."[44] Potter viewed joining together the six procedures of international organization—diplomacy, international administration, treaty negotiation, international law, arbitration, and international conferences—into one federal system as the final step in creating international government. Potter recognized, however, that this final step "brings us in touch with the most difficult problem in international organization, namely, the reconciliation of international organization with national sovereignty."[45] And this statement is, in turn, a way of summarizing the major problematic that the political discourse of anarchy attempted to solve throughout the interwar period.

Potter did not consider the task of reconciling national sovereignty with international government as either impossible or actually all that difficult. He wrote that "it does not appear to be at all impossible to reconcile the concepts of international federation, international federal government, world government, world state, super-state—making the concept as strong as possible—with the concept of state sovereignty, as long as we keep scrupulously in mind the exact steps in the process of creating such an international federation or world state."[46] Reconciliation was made possible, he contended, by the "doctrine of the original agreement." He argued that the principle of sovereignty did not preclude a state from voluntarily making agreements that resulted in self-imposed restraints on its external exercise of sovereignty. Potter emphatically insisted that these agreements, such as those resulting from treaties, arbitration hearings, administrative unions, and international conferences, did not result in a loss of sovereignty. On the contrary, Potter argued that one of the positive prerogatives of sovereignty was the freedom to make and enter agreements that were deemed to be in the best interests of a state. In fact, Potter took the extreme position of arguing that the doctrine of original consent meant that a state might voluntarily agree to surrender its "entire sovereignty without violating the doctrine of sovereignty." By original agreement, Potter argued, a state could self-impose any type of obligation or duty upon itself without necessarily abrogating its sovereignty.

Potter reasoned that if there was no loss of sovereignty from the more conventional practices of international organization such as treaties, international law, and conferences, then there was "no obstacle in national sovereignty to the creation of an international federation with legislative, executive and judicial functions, for that result would be obtained by merely gathering together into one system the various organs or institutions of international government already existing on independent foundations."[47] From Potter's perspective, a federal form of international government simply represented a quantitative expansion of the practices of international organization that already were in place. Once again, Potter claimed that there was no loss of sovereignty to a state when abiding by the rules and decisions of the international federal government so long as the state had originally consented to its establishment. In abiding by the decisions of the international government, a state was not surrendering its sovereignty to an external or alien source of authority. Rather, through the conditions established in the original agreement, a state was merely conceding to the general will of the federation of states of which it was a lasting member. Potter explained that he had belabored the issue of sovereignty in his text because it was the supporters of the traditional doctrine of national sovereignty who most forcefully opposed the procedure of international organization. According to the champions of national sovereignty, international government was antithetical to sovereignty. What Potter attempted to do through his detailed explication of international organization was to demonstrate that this was both theoretically and empirically incorrect. In the same manner that he attempted to debunk the arguments of those who maintained that the principles of sovereignty and international organization were irreconcilable, he scorned those who proclaimed that only a true world state could put an end to the present international anarchy. Although the argument that a world government would solve the problem of international anarchy was logically consistent, Potter claimed that it helped make the process of realizing international organization appear to be a mere phantasm. Potter wrote that "to scorn international federation and cry after a unified state is to deny support to an attainable improvement over the present anarchy, and waste it upon an unattainable ideal."[48]

As evidenced by Potter's work, as well as by the work of many of those who have been discussed in the last two chapters, the perception that the international anarchy of states was susceptible to a certain degree of progressive reform served as an axiomatic assumption of those studying international relations. Yet the more important point that deserves to be emphasized is that in most cases the discussion directed toward international organization, international governance, and even international society was firmly lodged within the political discourse of anarchy. In other words, the discussion about reforming the international milieu operated within the established parameters whereby it was presumed that states were the major actors, central authority was absent, and conflicts of interest rather than natural harmony prevailed. The noteworthy contribution that interwar scholars such as Potter made to the political discourse of anarchy was in both advancing and defending the claim that modification in the relations of states was possible even in the absence of a global sovereign. Their recommendations were in most cases logically consistent with the empirical conditions conveyed through the analytical framework of anarchy. In this sense, the interwar scholars were realists. However, as the League of Nations was seemingly unable to cope with a number of international crises in the early 1930s, which ultimately culminated in the onset of World War II, some scholars began to focus attention away from solutions and toward the enduring and intractable problems associated with international anarchy. This conceptual shift was reflected in the argument, beginning in the late 1930s, that the study of international politics should replace international organization as the central focus of the field.

International Politics

By the early 1940s, it was apparent that the field was undergoing a transition. This sequence of events has been conventionally understood as marking a fundamental turning point in the development of international relations, and is most often described in terms of a "great debate" pitting the interwar scholars, who stereotypically were caricatured as naive "idealists," against a new generation of "realists." Disciplinary historians Olson and Groom write that "conventional wisdom contended that idealist internationalist assumptions, having dominated early postwar thinking about world politics, were gradually replaced by realism as the League inexorably demonstrated its inability to cope with aggression." They note, however, that "neither paradigm was very often expressed in unadulterated form."[49] Although there are numerous misconceptions that surround this period, there is no denying that a new set of writers, which included E.H. Carr, Hans J. Morgenthau, Frederick Sherwood Dunn, Frederick L. Schuman, Grayson Kirk, Georg Schwarzenberger, Nicholas J. Spykman, and John Herz, entered the field. They were conspicuous by their advocacy of what they termed a "realist" approach to the study of international politics, and they precipitated a transformation in the discourse of international relations.[50] Several of the most influential members of this original group of realists were German émigrés who brought with them to America a profound sense of pessimism akin to Oswald Spengler's *Decline of the West.*[51] Most fundamentally, these self-ascribed realists sought to direct attention away from the study of international law and international organization and toward international politics, in which the enduring and endless quest for power and survival was central. The realists reacted negatively to the mode of inquiry that they associated with the interwar period and argued that in light of the failure of the League of Nations to prevent the outbreak of World War II, an entirely new approach rooted in an analysis of power politics was needed.

This point of view was symptomatic of many of the new texts that began to enter the field in the late 1930s and early 1940s. In *Contemporary World Politics* (1939), for example, the editors, Francis James Brown, Charles Hodges, and Joseph Slabey Roucek, announced that their "book utilizes the new approach to the field of international politics." In representative fashion, they explained that

> The post-War years were under the spell of the legalistic approach, owing to the emphasis laid on the newly introduced techniques in world affairs emphasizing the legalistic aspects of world problems—such as the League of Nations, the World Court, and other institutions. Hence many studies were concerned primarily with this approach to international relations. Today, however, international anarchy has broken the backbone of—although it has not given a *coup de grace* to—these highly desirable devices, and the institutions of international law, of international order, are violated with impunity and scorn by many aggressive states. Consequently, the major emphasis is on the policy of "Blood and Iron," on the "Realpolitik," on the pragmatic aspects of international relations rather than on the legal aspects.[52]

This statement provided a concise description of the realist challenge to the interwar discourse and outlined the basic terms and positions of the so-called first great debate. The "debate" was one in which the new scholars who embraced the tenets of realism questioned and challenged the essential assumptions, commitments, and approach of their predecessors. But while the first great debate has most often been depicted as representing a dispute pitting "idealists," which was the name that the challengers retrospectively imposed on the interwar scholars, against "realists," and resulting in a profound paradigm change, there is an important sense in which there was an essential continuity between the pre- and post–World War II periods. There is also a sense in which it was less a case of an intellectual exchange or debate between the interwar scholars and the realists than of the latter imposing their own views and legitimating their own account of recent developments in the field.

The theoretical innovations that the realists brought to the field meshed in many ways with the earlier political discourse of anarchy. Although there is no disputing the distinct emphasis that the realists placed on making international politics rather than international organization or international law the central focus of study, and while realists argued that the role of power was paramount in understanding the dynamics of inter-state relations, their analysis emphasized that international politics was a realm demarcated by sovereign state actors. Although realists argued that the study of international politics should serve as the nucleus of the field, political scientists writing before World War II had not ignored politics. And while the disorder that commonly is equated with anarchy often replaced the focus on order, the older commitments to peace, international organization, and even, in some cases, international law, were not entirely expunged from the discourse of international relations. An examination of the writings of some of the early realists reveals that there was much more continuity between the pre- and post–World War II discourse of academic international relations than many have assumed.

One of the most popular texts that appeared toward the end of the interwar period, and which was a harbinger of the new realism, was Frederick Schuman's *International Politics* (1933). Schuman began his academic career in 1927 at the University of Chicago, which was where he had earned his doctorate. In 1936, he took a position as professor of political science at Williams College where he remained until retiring in 1968. During this period, Schuman held a number of visiting appointments at Harvard, Cornell, Columbia, and Stanford. The title of Schuman's widely adopted text, which has been published in seven revised editions, provided an indication of the new direction in the field, and in the Preface, he stated that "an effort has been made to escape from the limitations of the traditional approaches and to deal with the subject from the point of view of the new Political Science." One of Schuman's primary intentions in writing *International Politics* was to differentiate what he termed the "new approach" of political science from the "older approach." He declared that "the political scientists of the old school who have dealt broadly with international relations have either wandered up the blind alley of legalism or have contented themselves with elaborate fact gathering on a variety of scattered topics which they are unable to put together into any unified scheme of interpretation." He argued that this had resulted in the clarification of some of the basic concepts and principles of international law and organization, but it did not in any way generate a coherent image "of the inner nature and significance of the established patterns of behavior in the relations between States." Schuman argued that the new approach, by contrast, "assumes that Political Science, as one of the social sciences, is concerned with the description and analysis of relations of power in society—i.e., with those patterns of social contacts which are suggested by such words as rulers and ruled, command and obedience, domination and subordination, authority and allegiance."[53]

The manner in which Schuman articulated the new approach of political science revealed the influence of his graduate training at the University of Chicago. Throughout the 1920s and 1930s, the Chicago school of political science, whose members included Charles Merriam, Harold Lasswell, and Quincy Wright, was at the forefront of developing what they claimed was a scientific approach to the study of politics. What this endeavor most fundamentally entailed was a conscious and deliberate effort to develop an appropriate methodology for realizing the aspiration of creating a genuine science of politics.[54] Merriam was the leading champion of this vision. In his presidential address to the APSA in 1925, he argued that it was necessary that "social science and natural science come together in a common effort and unite their forces in the greatest task that humanity has yet faced—the intelligent understanding and control of human behavior."[55] While Merriam's principal work, *New Aspects of Politics* (1925), put forth some general ideas about how a science of politics could be achieved, which involved extensive scholarly borrowing from related fields, particularly psychology, his major role in the scientific movement was in securing external funding and providing an institutional infrastructure for like-minded scholars. In this capacity, Merriam served on the APSA Committee on Political Research, participated in three National Conferences on the Science of Politics, and played a leading role in the creation of the Social Science Research Council.

Lasswell was a student of Merriam's, and upon completing his degree in 1926, he became one of the most prominent figures in the Chicago school.[56] He was both a prolific and eclectic writer who played a major role in elaborating the scientific approach in the discipline of political science in general, including the field of international relations. Lasswell was greatly attracted to psychology, especially to psychoanalysis and Freud, and he envisioned a scientific study of politics as leading to what he called a "therapeutic policy science." His most significant work was *World Politics and Personal Insecurity* (1935), which represented an attempt to apply to world politics the framework of configurative analysis that he had been developing. He explained that "political analysis is the study of changes in the shape and composition of the value patterns of society," and that "the analysis of world politics therefore implies the consideration of the value pattern of mankind as a whole."[57] Lasswell argued that the role of power was fundamental to the analysis of value. He wrote:

> Since a few members of any community at a given time have the most of each value, a diagram of the pattern of distribution of any value resembles a pyramid. The few who get the most of any value are the *élite;* the rest are the rank and file. An elite preserves its ascendancy by manipulating symbols, controlling supplies, and applying violence. Less formally expressed, politics is the study of *who gets what, when, and how.*[58]

In Schuman's attempt to apply certain aspects of the scientific approach to the field of international relations, he stated that the aim was to envisage the phenomena of international politics "as aspects of the whole pattern of political behavior and power relations which has developed in western civilization." He designated this pattern as the "Western State System" and declared that the purpose of his work was to describe this system "realistically and objectively in terms of its cultural origins, its institutionalized forms, its dynamic forces, and its apparent prospects." Schuman argued that in this manner a more comprehensive and holistic framework for understanding international politics would be provided and that this represented a significant improvement over the "fragmented, particularistic, partial views inherent in narrow traditional concepts and approaches."[59] Yet when it came to describing the attributes of the Western State System, Schuman advanced many of the same ideas that scholars in the field had been discussing for decades. According to Schuman, "the concept of State sovereignty, the principles of international law, and the politics of the balance of power may be regarded as the three cornerstones upon which the Western State System has come to rest."[60] The "older" school of political scientists directly accepted at least two of these three cornerstones, but although there was a basic agreement about certain elements of the state system, there were some important differences between the older school and Schuman with respect to the basic processes of international relations.

Perhaps the greatest difference between the two groups of scholars was that the realists deliberately sought to accentuate the disordering effects associated with the struggle for power and prestige in the international system. Schuman argued that the older approaches in the field had fatefully discounted the competitive and power-driven aspect of inter-state politics. He claimed that the interwar scholars had been too concerned with discovering the means to reconcile the differences that arose among states and that this had resulted in insufficient emphasis on understanding the factors that led to conflict. The net result, Schuman argued, was that many of the interwar scholars had come to assume that "the forces making for international cooperation and world unity are more significant than those making for international differences and conflict." More than anything else, Schuman, and the realists more generally, aimed to rid the field of this assumption which they perceived to be both idealistic and erroneous. Schuman argued that his conception of international politics was "based upon the opposite assumption—so much so that the treatment of forces will be largely limited to those values, attitudes, behavior patterns, and policies leading to tensions and rivalries between States."[61]

Rather than emphasizing the role of international law or international organization, Schuman accentuated the divisive forces in international politics. The most important of these was power itself which the realists argued was the main determinant of international politics. Schuman maintained, much as Hans J. Morgenthau later would, that "all politics is a struggle for power, but while power is sought in domestic politics as a means toward other ends, power is sought as an end in itself in international politics."[62] He argued that it was this feature of international politics that accounted for the regularly repeated patterns of behavior including the widespread use of violence in the Western state system, and he concluded that the interwar scholars were idealistic to believe that the violence and competition that characterized the political relations between independent sovereign states could be surmounted. Yet this raises an interesting question about the extent to which Schuman correctly perceived the interwar period as well as the most recent developments that were underway in the field. For if the label "idealism" can be applied to any group of scholars with a modicum of validity, it would be to some of his colleagues at Chicago who intended to use the scientific methods of political science to foster progressive change in the realm of world politics. Merriam, for example, wrote that

> It is not to be presumed that in the near future any system of political science can prevent war, revolution and imperfect adjust-

ment, but the shock of these conflicts may gradually be minimized. Probably war can be prevented, revolutions reduced to remote possibilities, and maladjustments vastly reduced in number and intensity.[63]

Based on his extensive study of psychology and propaganda, Lasswell was committed to the possibility of transmitting knowledge to elites who would be able to manipulate signs and symbols in such a manner as to foster the "myth of world unity." Lasswell explained that "the formal requirements of stable order in the world are for a universal body of symbols and practices sustaining an elite which propagates itself by peaceful methods and wields a monopoly of coercion which it is rarely necessary to apply to the uttermost."[64]

The general assumption, however, was that the emphasis that scholars such as Schuman, Morgenthau, and Carr attached to the analysis of power in international politics was what distinguished the new "realist" literature in the field. This assumption was propagated in a number of surveys of the field that appeared shortly after World War II which helped to entrench the dichotomy between idealists and realists. In an article written in 1949 and originally prepared for the Committee on International Relations Research of the Social Science Research Council, William T.R. Fox, another product of the Chicago school, who earned his doctorate in 1940 and was one of the founding members of the Institute of International Studies at Yale, argued:

> What is today in the United States conventionally known as international relations is a subject different in content and emphasis from its counterpart of even two decades ago. Much of what seemed important in 1929 seems irrelevant, and some of it even trivial, in 1949.[65]

Fox claimed that one of the main differences between 1929 and 1949 was that whereas the older "analytical model used for investigative purposes was a world commonwealth characterized by permanent peace," the present situation is one in which "international politics is moved to the focus and other subjects are related to it."[66] In *The Study of International Relations in American Colleges and Universities* (1947), sponsored by the Council on Foreign Relations, Grayson Kirk, who came to Columbia from the University of Wisconsin in 1940 and went on to become president of the University in 1953, proclaimed that "international politics constitutes the nucleus of the modern study of international relations." International politics, Kirk declared, "deals with those forces which mold the foreign policies of national states, the manner in which they are exercised, and the influences which limit their effectiveness."[67] He argued that as a result of the disproportionate amount of emphasis that scholars such as Potter had attached to the study of international organization, these forces had been ignored throughout the interwar period. According to Kirk's account,

> [A]n emphasis upon what has been variously called "sentimentalism," "idealism," and "Utopianism," dominated the teaching in the new field, and a wholly disproportionate amount of time and energy was given to discussing "international cooperation," while analyses of the forces of conflict in society, and of the institution of war, were subordinated and tainted with the stigma of moral reproach.[68]

The task that Kirk and others who shared this new conflict perspective set for themselves was to remedy this alleged defect in the field. Kirk claimed that the approach of the interwar scholars had been nothing less than disastrous to the development of a science of international relations. First, he argued that it had "caused a generation of American college students to underestimate the strength of the divisive forces of international society." This was, according to Kirk, a consequence of their complete neglect of the study of international politics. Second, he claimed that the "unfortunate result of the concentration upon Utopianism was to cast a shadow of academic disrepute over the new field." Kirk concluded that "after a quarter-century of activity, the study of international relations is still in a condition of considerable confusion."[69] Kirk was convinced that by making international politics the nucleus of the field the shortcomings of the past could be overcome and international relations would acquire a degree of scholarly repute. Yet at the same time, Kirk acknowledged that this would be a difficult undertaking, because international politics was an immensely complex subject that encompassed much of what other established disciplines, such as geography, economics, and sociology, studied. Thus, in order to differentiate the field of international relations from these other related disciplines, he claimed that it was necessary to develop a "special method and approach." He argued that the unique character of international relations emanated from the types of questions with which it was concerned and by the mode of analysis that was used to answer these questions. The question of power and the analysis of the effects of power on national foreign policies was, according to Kirk, what defined the field of international relations.

In a textbook that Kirk wrote with Walter R. Sharp entitled *Contemporary International Politics* (1940), the authors explained that the paramount role of power in international politics was a consequence of the fact that, unlike domestic politics, there was "no effective *supra*national agency either to secure observance of existing international agreements or to assure their *orderly* revision against the stubborn insistence of one or more nations that the *status quo* must remain undisturbed—long after it has begun to breed trouble." Therefore, they argued, "lacking the will to establish, let alone maintain, an effective political organization on a world scale, the vital points of conflict in the world community are, in the last resort, still resolved by *power politics.*"[70] Once again, however, it must be noted that the "new" nucleus of the field, international politics, despite its emphasis on the centrality of power, did not conflict with the theoretical core of the pre-established political discourse of anarchy. The ontological description of international politics as a realm defined by the existence of sovereign states in the absence of central authority continued to be the framework for studying international relations.

The continuity in conceptualizing the subject matter of international relations as arising from a condition of anarchy was clearly recognizable in Frederick S. Dunn's landmark article "The Scope of International Relations" (1948), which appeared in the first issue of *World Politics.* Dunn was one of the original members of the Yale Institute of International Studies that was formed in 1935 and which published the quarterly journal *World Politics.*[71] Dunn's training as a graduate student at Johns Hopkins had been in international law and organization, but when he arrived at Yale his interests turned to the study of international politics. Yet Dunn never relinquished his original concern with discovering the best means of reconciling conflict between states, and when he described the scope of the field in 1948, there were elements of both innovation and continuity. The purpose of Dunn's essay was "to state certain propositions about the nature and scope of IR which seem to represent the present views of some mature scholars in the field."[72] He argued that although international relations was "still in an early stage of development," it was nevertheless possible to advance certain statements about the scope of the field.

Like Kirk, Dunn argued that the "distinguishing characteristic of IR as a separate branch of learning is found in the nature of the questions with which it deals." Dunn claimed (proposition three) that "IR is concerned with the questions that arise in the relations between autonomous political groups in a world system in which power is not centered at one point." This proposition implied that while international relations shared a basic affinity with the discipline of political science and the general study of power, it was also unique in that the wider sphere of political relations that the field studied was fundamentally different from the social relations found inside a national community. The distinct quality of the field was captured in proposition five which stated that "international politics is concerned with the special kind of power relationships that exist in a community lacking an overriding authority."[73] As evidenced by these two propositions, the anarchy framework continued to be the core element of the discourse of international relations. Another indication of continuity was revealed in proposition four which stated "an IR analyst is one who purports to have some skill in dealing with the questions that arise out of the relations of nations," and whose core "interest lies in the conflict, adjustment and agreement of national policies."[74] This point was amplified in proposition six, where Dunn argued that international relations was a "policy science." According to Dunn, international relations was "concerned primarily with knowledge that is relevant to the control and improvement of a particular set of social conditions," and "its goal is not merely knowledge for its own sake but knowledge for the purpose of molding practical events in desired directions."[75] Dunn stated that foremost among these desired ends was "a deep interest in how wars may be avoided." Yet while it would appear, on the basis of this statement, that there was an essential continuity with the past, it was exactly on this point that Dunn and several of the other realists attempted to construct a sharp contrast between the interwar scholars and themselves. Dunn argued that "early students of IR tended to conceive of ideal social systems in which wars did not exist and then to evaluate existing practices in the light of these ideal conceptions," whereas "the present tendency among scholars is to give primary attention to the ascertainable facts of international life and the forces and conditions that influence the behavior among nations."[76] In light of the actual character of the earlier discourse, it would be difficult, if not impossible, to defend Dunn's characterization of interwar scholarship.

The tendency on the part of the realists to dichotomize the development of the field was manifest in two of the texts that provided the early theoretical foundation for realism: E.H. Carr's *The Twenty Years' Crisis, 1919–1939: An Introduction to the Study of International Relations* (1939), and Hans J. Morgenthau's *Politics Among Nations: The Struggle for Power and Peace* (1948). Many accounts of the history of the field maintain that the debate between idealism and realism ended with the publication of these two books. Olson, for example, argues

It was Edward Hallett Carr's brilliant realist critique of utopianism, published as it was on the eve of the Second World War, which both focused and ended the debate. Or rather it should have, because Morgenthau felt obliged to end it again in the immediate post-war years, when *Politics Among Nations* and the Cold War together ushered in a new era in the history of international relations. The realist-idealist debate had, for all practical purposes, ended.[77]

Even a superficial understanding of the contributions of Carr and Morgenthau to the discourse of international relations reveals that their work has been reduced to a caricature that misrepresents its significance.

Carr, perhaps more than anyone else, is generally credited with being responsible for creating the image of the interwar discourse of international relations as idealist or utopian in character.[78] Carr worked at the British Foreign Office and then as a journalist for *The Times* before being appointed in 1936 to the Woodrow Wilson Chair at Aberystwyth. Although Carr was not formally a political scientist by training, international relations specialists embraced the argument that he laid out in *The Twenty Years' Crisis.* Published on the eve of World War II, Carr remarked that the science of international politics was "markedly and frankly utopian," and "in the initial stage in which wishing prevails over thinking, generalisation over observation, and in which little attempt is made at a critical analysis of existing facts or available means."[79] Carr took it upon himself to diagnose the utopian shortcomings and to direct the field toward realism, which he argued was desperately needed in light of the current tumultuous situation in international politics. He began by depicting a fundamental contrast between utopia and reality as represented in the dichotomies between free will and determinism, theory and practice, intellectual and bureaucrat, left and right, and ethics and politics.[80] Yet Carr's purpose in drawing attention to the contrast between utopia and reality was not to dichotomize the history of the field. Rather he sought to establish the fact that utopia and reality are "the two facets of political science" and that "sound political thought and sound political life will be found only where both have their place."[81]

In describing the main characteristics of the interwar scholarship, Carr argued that "nearly all popular theories of international politics between the two world wars were reflexions, seen in an American mirror, of nineteenth-century liberal thought."[82] This was, according to Carr, evident in the universal belief in the harmony of interest doctrine, which he claimed nearly all of the interwar scholars had adopted in their writings. Some of the other features of the liberal view included a pervasive faith in reason and rationalism, a belief in the infallibility of public opinion, the view that war was irrational, and that the best way to end conflict was through education, international law, world government, and the League of Nations. Carr concluded that it was the adoption of these liberal postulates during the interwar period, especially the doctrine of the harmony of interests, that led to the complete breakdown of the international system in the nineteen-thirties.

Having exposed what he termed the "bankruptcy of the idealist approach," Carr next turned his attention to explicating realism. Beginning with the work of Machiavelli, who Carr claimed was "the first important realist," he identified realism as synonymous with the "hard ruthless analysis of reality." According to Carr, "realism tends to emphasise the irresistible strength of existing forces and the inevitable character of existing tendencies, and to insist that the highest wisdom lies in accepting, and adopting oneself to, these forces and these tendencies."[83] Like Schuman, Kirk, and the other realists of this period, Carr argued that it was the ubiquity of power that most essentially characterized international politics. Carr alleged that it was the interwar scholar's total neglect of the role of power in international politics that doomed all of their efforts to reform international anarchy. Carr argued that international politics, like politics in general, was always power politics. He denied the possibility that this could ever change, since power in the international milieu was both omnipresent and inescapable. He claimed that the popular idea, expressed during the interwar period, that power politics was somehow sinister revealed a complete misunderstanding of the basic character of international relations. Carr explained that the issues that arose between separate political communities were almost always political and thus necessarily involved power. He argued that in international politics, power was both a means and an end, and, although indivisible, could for analytical purposes be divided into three component parts: military power, economic power, and power over opinion. Carr's discussion of each of these three aspects of power was intended to demonstrate that although often masked by the image of a universal harmony of interest, power politics, even during the time of the League of Nations, was the essence of international affairs. Carr maintained that "the exposure of the real basis of the professedly abstract principles commonly invoked in international politics is the most damning and most convincing part of the realist indictment of utopianism."[84]

For those like Georg Schwarzenberger, who continued to conceptualize international politics in terms of a society of nations, Carr's focus on the role of power represented only a partial analysis. Schwarzenberger, although generally considered to be one of the first generation of realists, was an international lawyer and professor of international law and relations at the London Institute of World Affairs. In 1941, Schwarzenberger published *Power Politics* which, as the title implied, reflected the field's new concentration. Schwarzenberger argued, however, that "international relations was a special branch of sociology which is concerned with those phenomena which essentially affect international society."[85] While he concurred with some features of Carr's analysis, Schwarzenberger claimed that an exclusive focus on power was insufficient for understanding the dynamics of international society, and he concluded that the traditional focus on international law and organization was still needed.

Although often disregarded in the numerous commentaries on *The Twenty Years' Crisis,* Carr never suggested that either realism or power were sufficient by themselves for understanding the complexities of world politics. While his work is usually read as the classic indictment of the errors of the idealists, and the classic statement of realism, Carr actually argued:

> [T]hat any sound political thought must be based on elements of both utopia and reality. Where utopianism has become a hollow and intolerable sham, which serves merely as a disguise for the interests of the privileged, the realist performs an indispensable service in unmasking it. But pure realism can offer nothing but a naked struggle for power which makes any kind of international society impossible. Having demolished the current utopia with the weapons of realism, we still need to build a new utopia of our own.[86]

Although Carr was troubled by what he took to be the previous generation's complete disregard of power in the international field, he was equally concerned with finding a satisfactory synthesis of the poles of utopianism and realism. Discovering an appropriate compromise between power and morality was the crux of the problem of peaceful change in international politics which Carr considered to be the central predicament of his age. Indeed, Carr's foremost concern was to discover the means to foster peaceful change.

The two books that Carr wrote during World War II, *Conditions of Peace* (1942) and *Nationalism and After* (1945), were both devoted to discovering the appropriate steps for peaceful change. This concern was also apparent in the work of other realists such as Dunn, who published *Peaceful Change: A Study of International Procedures* in 1937. The term "peaceful change," Dunn explained, referred "to the alteration of the status quo by peaceful international procedures rather than by force."[87] Similarly, Carr defined the problem of peaceful change as how, in national politics, "to effect necessary and desirable changes without revolution and, in international politics, how to effect such changes without war." Carr claimed that the answer to the problem of peaceful change could "only be achieved through a compromise between the utopian conception of a common feeling of right and the realist conception of a mechanical adjustment to a changed equilibrium of forces."[88] In his attempt to work out a synthesis and provide a historical example of a successful compromise between morality and power, which in the domestic realm he argued was exemplified by the bargain reached between labor and capital, Carr found that "the negotiations which led up to the Munich Agreement of September 29, 1938, were the nearest approach in recent years to the settlement of a major international issue by a procedure of peaceful change."[89] Incidentally, but significantly, this was one of the few passages that was omitted from the second edition of Carr's classic text.

While Carr is most often credited with destroying the utopian edifice of the interwar scholars, and although he has been immortalized by the dichotomy that he drew between idealism and realism, *The Twenty Years' Crisis* in many ways built upon the discursive foundation of the earlier generation of international relations scholars. Carr did not so much reject, in principle, the traditional study of international law, international cooperation, and international organization, as attempt to incorporate and view these as elements in the broader process of international politics. He argued that power was always present in international politics and, therefore, had to be taken into account whenever students of international relations studied a particular facet of interstate relations. This does not imply, however, that Carr glorified power politics for its own sake or dismissed as utopian attempts to reform international anarchy. Thus, rather than judging the historical significance of Carr's work on the basis of his rejection of idealism and his espousal of realism, it should instead be evaluated on the merits of the solution that he proposed for bridging utopia and reality.

This was the basis, however, on which Morgenthau deemed Carr's work a failure. Morgenthau argued that while Carr had made a considerable contribution to exposing "the essential defects of Western political thought," the proffered synthesis of realism and utopianism was untenable, since it was based on "a relativistic, instrumentalist conception of morality." Relativism, Morgenthau claimed, left Carr "philosophically ill-equipped" and with "no transcendent point of view from which to survey the political scene and to appraise the phenomenon of power."[90] Although it is undeniable that Morgenthau's emigration in 1937 to the United States and his subsequent teaching appointments at Brooklyn College (1937–1939), the University of Kansas City (1939–1943), the University of Chicago (1943–1971), and the New School of Social Research in New York (1975–1981) had a major influence on the development of the field, his work and the historical context in which he was writing have been greatly misunderstood. While it is beyond the scope of this chapter to deal with the intricacies of Morgenthau's work, it is necessary to clarify some elements that are pertinent to understanding the subsequent history of the field.

In 1923, Morgenthau entered the University of Frankfurt where he took up the study of philosophy and literature. Unhappy with the type of philosophy he encountered and discouraged by his father from pursuing the study of literature, Morgenthau transferred in 1924 to the University of Munich and embarked on the study of law. After passing his law examination in Munich, Morgenthau returned to Frankfurt to earn his doctorate and wrote a dissertation entitled "The International Judicial Function and the Concept of Politics," which combined his interests in law and political philosophy. By his own admission, he had come to the realization that the weakness of international law stemmed "from the intrusion of international politics." Morgenthau noted "from that discovery there was but one step to the conclusion that what really mattered in relations among nations was not international law but international politics."[91] Both of Morgenthau's first two principal works, *Scientific Man Versus Power Politics* (1946) and *Politics Among Nations* (1948), aimed at revealing that "international politics, like all politics, is a struggle for power."[92] The theoretical underpinning of Morgenthau's realism was the tenet "that politics, like society in general, is governed by objective laws that have their roots in human nature." As Morgenthau explained, the theory of realism took its name from a "theoretical concern with human nature as it actually is, and with the historic processes as they actually take place."[93]

Morgenthau's work, like that of Carr, was distinguished by its analysis of the role of power in international politics. Morgenthau defined power as "man's control over the minds and actions of other men," and claimed that domestic and international politics were "but two manifestations of the same phenomenon: the struggle for power." Yet he argued that the struggle for power operated differently in the domestic and international realms primarily because "in the international sphere, no sovereign power exists."[94] Unlike his behavioral adversaries, such as Morton Kaplan, who challenged the scientific pretensions of realism in the course of the second great debate, Morgenthau insisted on the necessity of maintaining an analytical distinction between domestic and international politics, and this was of great significance for his discussion of ethics and power.[95] Morgenthau maintained that the struggle for power in the international realm took three typical forms: keeping power (policy of status quo), increasing power (policy of imperialism), and demonstrating power (policy of prestige). In his analysis of each of these three aspects of the struggle for power in international politics, Morgenthau attempted to demonstrate that despite claims to the contrary, "the struggle for power is universal in time and space and is an undeniable fact of experience."[96] But, also like Carr, Morgenthau argued that international politics could not be understood by considerations of power alone. Morgenthau's theory of realism was at once a theory of power and a theory of morality. He explained that "if the motivations behind the struggle for power and the mechanics through which it operates were all that was needed to be known about international politics, the international scene would indeed resemble the state of nature described by Hobbes."[97] This was an image that Morgenthau thoroughly rejected. Although Morgenthau did begin *Politics Among Nations* with a description of the six principles of political realism, in the second half of the book he undertook a discussion of subjects such as international law, sovereignty, international morality, world public opinion, international government, and the general problem of achieving lasting peace. In this regard, it is important to point out that Morgenthau concluded his text with a discussion of the nine rules of diplomacy that were needed to establish the preconditions of permanent peace.

A careful reading of Morgenthau's work reveals many examples of how he was greatly indebted to the discourse of international relations that had evolved during the previous fifty years. Morgenthau did not reject the interwar discourse as idealist in the sense that these scholars completely failed to address the reality of inter-state politics. In fact, Morgenthau directed his scathing criticism toward the proponents of a scientific approach to politics. Scientism was, according to Morgenthau, another indication of the decay of Western political thought. He wrote that "this decay is represented most typically by the belief in the power of science to solve all problems and, more particularly, all political problems which confront man in the modern age."[98] His arrival in Chicago most certainly initiated an episode of disciplinary change but what Morgenthau did was to direct attention to the realities of international politics that he perceived as characteristic of his own age. With the dawn of the nuclear era and the destruction of Europe facilitated by the emergence of total war, international politics was bound to be interpreted differently than before, but this does not in any way mean that earlier scholars did not also address the realities of their own age or that they can be dismissed as idealists.

The dubious nature of the dichotomy between idealism and realism was recognized early on but somehow forgotten. Writing in 1952, Quincy Wright, who was at Chicago when Morgenthau joined the department, argued that "the distinction between 'realism' and 'idealism' is of doubtful value in either political analysis or political philosophy."[99] He added that

> "[R]ealism" and "idealism" have functioned as propaganda terms according to which everyone sought to commend whatever policy he favored by calling it "realistic." The terms do not, in other words, throw light on the policies, institutions, personalities, or theories which they are used to qualify but only on the attitude toward them of the speaker and, it is hoped, of the listener. From this usage we learn that in the past two decades political propagandists have regarded "realism" as a plus term and "idealism" as a minus term.[100]

Even earlier, in 1940, Leonard Woolf reviewed E.H. Carr's *Twenty Years' Crisis* and, like Morgenthau, deemed the book a failure. Woolf argued that the

> [B]ook fails in its purpose. It does not give us the beginnings of a science of international relations, because its method is unscientific. It attempts to interpret the events of the last twenty years by means of a distinction between what is utopia and what is real in policy. But, although the whole of his argument depends upon the difference between "utopia" and "realism," he never makes clear the distinction between them either to himself or to his reader.[101]

It is necessary to assess some of the consequences of continuing to view the discursive history of the field in terms of the dichotomy between idealism and realism.

7

CONCLUSION

It is difficult to overstate the extent to which the contemporary discourse of international relations remains embedded in the dichotomy between idealism and realism. What makes the so-called great debate between idealists and realists more than simply a matter of antiquarian interest is the manner in which the terms of this controversy have continued to structure fundamentally much of the ensuing discourse of international relations. Not only do students of international relations continue to recount the history of the field in terms of the founding myth whereby "realism" replaced "idealism," but the latest developments in the field are often understood against the backdrop of this earlier debate. Michael Banks has argued that of the three great debates that characterize the history of the field "the realist-idealist debate is the most significant because it gave us structures and institutions which still operate," and it "endowed us with a durable vocabulary."[1]

A recent example of this "durable vocabulary" can be found in the endeavor of some scholars to resurrect the ideas that have been typically associated with idealism. This particular undertaking was conspicuous in Charles Kegley's 1993 presidential address to the International Studies Association, where he asked whether "the emergent conditions in this 'defining moment' transcend the *realpolitik* that has dominated discussion of international affairs for the past five decades and invite a reconstructed paradigm, perhaps one inspired by the idealist ideas associated with the Wilsonian vision."[2] Another indication that the field has come full circle is manifest in the attempt of those espousing the theory of the democratic peace to vindicate the ideas of Kant and Wilson with respect to their vision of a lasting peace among democratic states.[3] It is noteworthy that Bruce Russett, who is Dean Acheson Professor of International Relations and Political Science at Yale University, suggested that if the "Kantian perspective is correct," then it "may be possible in part to supersede the 'realist' principles (anarchy, the security dilemma of states) that have dominated practice to the exclusion of 'liberal' or 'idealist' ones."[4]

Although realism has been resistant to the various challenges that have been mounted by critics during the past forty years, the end of the Cold War has witnessed further attempts to contest the realist hegemony. The latest dissatisfaction with the central assumptions of realism is at the forefront of the controversy between those identifying themselves as neoliberals and neorealists.[5] Kegley maintained that "the hottest topic in international relations theory today [is] the challenge to the dominant realist paradigm that is currently being mounted from diverse perspectives grounded in the liberal—or its subset, the so-called 'idealist'—theoretical orientation."[6] Kegley claimed that to understand the controversy between neoliberalism and neorealism, it is necessary to view the debate as part of a much older theoretical debate that was rooted in the history of the field, yet in Kegley's endeavor to provide a historical basis for the current debate, he proceeded to summarize the "divergent realist and liberal traditions" and, in doing so, confounded a mythical history of the field with its real history. While David Baldwin acknowledged that the debate between neorealism and neoliberalism is rooted in an older debate, he also suggested that "perhaps the closest counterpart of the modern debate between realism and neoliberalism is found in the works of the *philosophes* at the end of the eighteenth century."[7] As long as political scientists continue to substitute a mythical account of the history of the field for the actual history, these sorts of descriptions will do little more than further entrench the erroneous interpretations that most students already hold about how international relations developed as an academic field of study. This is, however, profoundly unfortunate, since the early discourse of the field has direct relevance for the present-day study of international relations, including the debate between neoliberalism and neorealism.

The aim of this final chapter is twofold: first, to recapitulate the themes that have been recovered from the early history of the field; and second, to explore the implications of the findings of this study for the contemporary discourse of international relations. My intention is to highlight once more the core assumption on which this book was premised, namely, that the actual history of the field of international relations is fundamentally different from the dominant image that has been portrayed most often by academic practitioners. The conclusion accentuates the critical function and liberating potential of disciplinary history in fostering critical insights and opening theoretical space within which to think about world politics. Some of the deep discursive continuities between the earlier-twentieth-century discourse of international relations and the contemporary discourse will be brought to light. The main point, however, is not simply to demonstrate that international relations scholars continually reinvent the wheel—even though there are many striking instances of this practice, which lends support to the adage that those who do not know their history are doomed to repeat it. The more fundamental point is that by continuing to either neglect or distort the history of the field, international relations scholars cut themselves off from a wealth of potentially useful insights about international politics and fail to recognize the degree to which the contemporary discourse of the field is deeply rooted in the past. In this respect, the history of political science is unlike the history of natural science. Many of the ideas that have been recovered from reconstructing the history of the field continue to have direct relevance for the present-day study of international politics. This is in part what makes it absolutely essential to recover the formative history of the field. On the basis of the last chapter, which briefly offered a different account of the significance of Carr, Morgenthau, and some of the other early "realists," it should be apparent that the post–World War II phase of the field's development has also been greatly misrepresented. This points to a need for more work on the history of the field, and some of the avenues of future research are indicated in this chapter.

Reconsidering the First Great Debate

One of the consequences of viewing the development of the field within the analytical framework of three successive great debates is that many historically specific controversies such as that which took place between the proponents and critics of the juristic theory of the state are expunged from our collective memory. This is the case especially with respect to the first debate, since it most often serves as a convenient frame of reference for denoting the birth of the field. Discussion of earlier developments are generally limited to the period after World War I and are referred to primarily for illustrating the alleged utopian character of the interwar years. Yet, as the previous chapters demons-trate, the descent of the field can be traced from the mid-nineteenth century, and it is difficult to construe the early discourse as idealistic in the sense that international relations scholars failed to engage the em-pirical realities of international politics or imagined possibilities that had no grounding in reality.

The attempt to establish a link between the institutional origins of the field and the formation of the League of Nations has made it appear that the initial discourse of the field was basically idealistic. This contex-tual myth not only serves as one of the informing assumptions about the early history of the field but, at the same time, functions as a crucial prop in explaining the rise of the realist school in late 1930s and early 1940s. Conventional accounts of the history of the field have made it appear as if the ill fortunes of the League of Nations explain the fall of the interwar "idealists" and the rise of the postwar "realists." Yet there are a number of fundamental difficulties with this story that are revealed by a critical internal approach to the history of the field. There never was a coherent group of scholars writing during the interwar period who adhered to something akin to an idealist paradigm. This is simply one of the field's most pervasive myths which has prevented students from understanding how the field actually developed. This myth has also precluded scholars from acknowledging, let alone utilizing, the insights that earlier generations of international relations scholars offered about international politics. There are indications, however, that this myth is beginning to lose its traditional appeal and that disciplinary history can be a vehicle for fostering critical insights about both the past and the present study of international relations.

In a recent essay, Miles Kahler argued that there is "evidence that the interwar 'idealists' have been misunderstood and their arguments misrepresented."[8] In a similar manner, Ken Booth commented recently that the field of international relations in general, and the Department of Politics at the University of Wales, Aberystwyth, in particular, "has both flourished and laboured under powerful foundational myths." Booth explained that one element of this myth was "made up of the belief that Carr's 'realism' triumphed in every sense over [David] Davies' 'idealism', and that this represented a definite advance in the academic development of the subject."[9] In a slightly different context, David Baldwin began his review of recent work in the area of strategic studies with an acknowledgment, contrary to conventional wisdom, that the sub-field of strategic studies did not suddenly arise with the onset of the Cold War. Baldwin argued that "if security studies is defined as the study of the nature, causes, effects, and prevention of war, the period between the First and Second World Wars was not the intellectual vacuum it is often thought to be."[10] The common theme in each of these essays was that the interwar period of the field's history has been systematically misrepresented.

In order to gain a more accurate sense of the interwar discourse, it was necessary, first, to separate developments in the field from the external context of the League of Nations and, second, to trace the descent of the field prior to World War I. With respect to first point, it is difficult to gauge with any degree of certitude the influence that exogenous events have had on the discourse of the field, but if the purpose is to understand the discursive history of the field, then the issue of how to assess the impact of external events is, in many respects, the wrong issue. The more important issue is that of how the field has comprehended external events rather than how external events have impacted the development of the field. With respect to the second point, the interwar period cannot be understood properly without taking into account the academic context within which political scientists were operating.

Whether the period before World War I is considered the field's "prehistory" or not is less important than recognizing that the history of this preceding period is absolutely essential for understanding the interwar discourse of international relations. It was this earlier conversation that provided the most important discursive framework for those who were studying international relations after World War I, and what links these periods is what I have described as the political discourse of anarchy. The idea that the subject matter of the study of international relations was most fundamentally a world defined by the existence of sovereign political communities without a common superior authority was endemic to the discursive history of the field. From an early point in the history of academic international relations, scholars embraced the view that the topics of central concern to the field—topics that included the study of the factors leading to war and peace, international law, international organization, colonial administration, and the means of achieving world order reform—were grounded in an ontology of anarchy. The idea that international relations was characterized both by the presence and the absence of sovereignty has provided the intellectual paradigm within which the academic discourse of international relations has taken place. In the process of reconstructing the political discourse of anarchy, which has served as the core constituent conversation of the field, a number of themes have been recovered that continue to have a bearing on current issues in the field.

Constructing Anarchy

While the concept of anarchy provided discursive continuity in the development of the field, there have been, at the same time, episodes of conceptual change within this discourse that have periodically reconstituted the basic character of the conversation. Although students of international relations are repeatedly taught that the international milieu has for the past several centuries formally existed in a condition of anarchy, scholars have debated almost continuously the meaning, as well as the implications, of this highly contested concept. This strongly suggests that the concept of anarchy is more a function of internal disciplinary debate than a self-referential empirical fact of the external world. The discourse of international relations constructs its own image of the world of international politics. A similar point is reflected in the recent argument that scholars such as Alexander Wendt and other constructivists have been making with respect to the social construction of state interests under anarchy.[11] Wendt claims that "anarchy is what states make of it," and the disciplinary history of international relations reveals that anarchy is also largely what political scientists have made of it.

Proponents of the juristic theory of the state constructed their own peculiar account of the international milieu. The analytical description of the external relations of states that individuals such as Willoughby provided was deeply rooted in the juristic theory of the state which constituted the original disciplinary identity of political science. Lieber, Bluntschili, and Burgess conceived of political science as *Staatswissenschaft,* and their account of international politics was connected so intimately to the organic theory of the state that they found it impossible to bifurcate its internal and external dimensions. Although almost never acknowledged by neorealists who continue to trace their genealogy through tangential figures such as Thucydides and Rousseau, there are a number of themes in the work of Bluntschili and Burgess that have been characteristically identified with realism. In discussing the realist conception of the state, Ronen P. Palan and Brook M. Blair have argued that the realist theory of international relations only emerged "after the advent of the organic theory of the state," in which "the state as a sovereign entity was endowed with an autonomous will, only marginally subject to the individual will of the citizens of the state."[12] This was the exact same conception of the state that most of the early American political scientists embraced.

According to the orthodox juristic theory of sovereignty, the international realm was one where states led an independent and isolated existence. By dint of their equal possession of absolute and unlimited sovereignty, states were assumed, in principle, to have complete freedom from all sources of external authority. States, according to this view, did not have obligations to any other entity but themselves, and compliance with external rules was deemed to be strictly voluntary. Although rejecting the idea of a social contract to explain the origins of the state, adherents of the juristic theory of sovereignty nevertheless evoked the pre-contractual image of individuals living in a state of nature. In depicting states as existing in an international state of nature, proponents of the juristic theory of the state outlined the essential characteristics that contributed to the notion that the international realm was plagued by anarchy. In their effort to describe the structure of international anarchy, juristic theorists often employed the insights of classic political theorists such as Hobbes. There is nothing wrong with surveying the history of political thought in search of insights into the patterns of behavior that characterize the political relations of separate political communities or to explore the manner in which the atomized existence of these communities can be transcended. This is exactly the type of exercise that is needed to counter the common assumption that the study of international relations theory is impoverished. Yet, simply because political scientists made reference to the work of classic thinkers to elucidate a specific feature of international politics does not mean that individuals such as Machiavelli and Hobbes can be construed as belonging to the genealogy of the academic field of international relations.

The sense of pessimism among adherents of the juristic theory of sovereignty who studied the external relations of states was not limited solely to the belief that the anarchical arrangement of states was unalterable. It also affected their view of international law and the prospects for international collaboration. The less than favorable prospects for international reform and the dubious value that was attached to international law were deeply rooted in the particular ontology of anarchy that juristic theory attributed to the international realm. As long as states were regarded as sovereign actors, and unwilling to acknowledge any superior power, proponents of juristic theory argued that anarchy would always be a significant impediment to a harmonious international life. The reformist and prescriptive component of the political discourse of anarchy, however, represents a major discursive thread in the history of the field. The concept of anarchy was shared by pessimists who believed its consequences, particularly war, were uncontrollable and by optimists who were convinced that the international realm was susceptible to a certain measure of progressive reform. States were perceived as existing in what today is described as a security dilemma, and problems such as how to have order without an orderer, how to ensure that self-interested actors comply with agreements when reciprocity could not be guaranteed, and how to enforce rules and laws without a centralized authority were matters of concern. There was also a recognition that the problem of insecurity and war was, as G. Lowes Dickinson and others explained, an inevitable result "whenever and wherever the anarchy of armed states exist."[13] This insight, which has served as one of the core premises of contemporary realism, predates by some thirty to forty years John Herz's classic articulation of what he termed the "security dilemma."

Writing in 1950, Herz, a German émigré and a member of the original realist school, argued that the "plight in which a bipolarized and atom bomb-blessed world finds itself today is but the extreme manifestation of a dilemma with which human societies have had to grapple since the dawn of history." According to Herz, the dilemma of never being able to achieve a sense of security despite a vast accumulation of power stemmed "from a fundamental social constellation, one where a plurality of otherwise interconnected groups constitute ultimate units of political life, that is, where groups live alongside each other without being organized into a higher unity."[14] The main point of Herz's article, however, was not simply to draw attention to the plight of the security dilemma. He also contributed to the historical bifurcation of interwar idealism and the post–World War II realism that was well underway in the field. Idealism and realism were, according to Herz, two analytical categories that could be used to describe the manner in which an individual dealt with the security dilemma. He explained that "realist thought is determined by an insight into the overpowering impact of the security factor and the ensuing power-political, oligarchic, authoritarian, and similar trends and tendencies in society and politics, whatever its ultimate conclusion and advocacy." Conversely, he claimed that idealist thought "tends to concentrate on conditions and solutions which are supposed to overcome the egoistic instincts and attitudes of individuals and groups in favor of considerations beyond mere security and self-interest."[15] On the basis of this distinction, Herz argued that it was tempting "to sum up the history of the great modern social and political movements as the story of the credos of Political Idealism and their successive failures in the face of the facts observed and acclaimed by Political Realism."[16] The implication was that this dichotomy could also be used to describe the history of the field of international relations. It is important to note that Herz, like Carr, sought a synthesis of political idealism and political realism and suggested an approach that he termed "realist liberalism," but this component of his work has received much less attention than the emphasis on the difference between idealism and realism.[17]

There is a great need to sort out the arguments of Herz and the "realist phase" of the field's history in much more careful detail. There was much more ambiguity in the writings and positions of the original realists such as Carr, Morgenthau, and Herz than has been acknowledged in conventional accounts of this period. Just as the early period of the field's history is generally unknown, the same can be said about some of its more recent history, but whatever the merit of Herz's conceptualization of idealism and realism with respect to clarifying the range of positions that one may take toward the security dilemma, most of the scholars writing before World War II do not qualify as idealists in Herz's sense of that concept. Proponents of the juristic theory of the state did not focus on how egoistic sovereign actors might surrender their self-interests in order to realize a harmony of interests whereby the scourge of war would be eliminated. In fact, the early discourse of international relations was limited by its renunciation of any international procedure that infringed on the sovereignty of the state. Additionally, by accepting Austin's dictum that law was an authoritative command issuing from a political superior to an inferior, the juristic theory of the state denied the possibility of an effectual international law.

Not surprisingly, one of the earliest and most sustained discourses to arise about international politics was directed toward the activity of imperialism and colonial administration. By focusing on these activities, attention was directed toward entities that were construed as representing something "other" than sovereign states. In the ensuing discussion about the relationship between the "civilized" and "barbaric" territories, a newly constructed concept of anarchy arose. Rather than anarchy denoting the lack of a centralized world government, anarchy in this context evoked the image of chaos, disorder, and lawlessness resulting from the lack of a domestic sovereign authority in the "barbaric" regions of the globe. This particular reference to anarchy gave rise to a discussion about the best way to administer regions plagued by internal lawlessness and disorder. This episode of disciplinary history reveals the highly mutable character of the concept of anarchy and indicates that the meaning of anarchy does not constitute a single unchanging form. It also parallels some of the criticisms that have been raised against the neorealist conception of anarchy.[18]

The discourse of this period reveals how the field of international relations, and the discipline of political science more generally, has constructed and dealt with the category of the "other." For postmodern scholars and other critics of the mainstream, the politics through which certain identities are privileged and perceived as relevant is an integral component of the study of international relations.[19] The discourse dealing with colonial administration provides ample opportunity to condemn specific features of the field's earlier history, and this may explain in part the reluctance of scholars to investigate their disciplinary origins. Yet, in a more instructive manner, the discourse about imperialism and colonialism provides an opening to investigate the way in which identities are constructed in the field of international relations and how particular subjects are either included or excluded from its purview. This earlier discourse also provides an opportunity to explore the manner in which constructed identities change over time and to take cognizance of the degree to which the field of international relations today remains more or less exclusionary with respect to its scope of inquiry.

No matter how much the disorder in the tropical regions captured the attention of political scientists, the tensions in the European state system remained the central focus of the field of international relations. The upheavals that loomed large in international politics were understood to be a consequence of the fact that states existed in an environment in which there was no central authority. The difficulties with instruments of conflict resolution such as international law and various modes of international organization were attributed to the anarchical structure of inter-state politics. However, during the earlier periods of the field's history, it was less the anarchical character of international politics than the problem of state sovereignty that was identified as the most pressing theoretical issue. It was assumed that the condition of international anarchy arose from the fact of state sovereignty. This relationship between anarchy and sovereignty is of crucial significance for understanding the discourse of international relations from the interwar period to the present.

The Primacy of Sovereignty

Unlike the most recent discourse about anarchy in which the concept of sovereignty is either ignored or taken for granted and states are conceptualized as unitary rational actors, the interwar scholars recognized that it was the principle of state sovereignty that gave rise to international anarchy. Although the structural condition of anarchy was held responsible for the onset of World War I, there was an understanding among international relations scholars that the condition itself was a consequence of numerous independent sovereign states that refused to recognize any higher power than themselves. This was one of the principle bases on which the interwar scholars launched their critique of the orthodox juristic theory of state sovereignty. The foundation of their theoretical attack was not simply that juristic theory fostered an inimical image of inter-state relations that was adverse to genuine reform but, more fundamentally, that the theory of sovereignty which informed the juristic conceptualization of international anarchy was inconsistent with the empirical reality of international politics. Beginning with Lieber and Burgess, the conversation about the state was central to both political science and international relations, and the significant episode of conceptual change that occurred after World War I revolved around the adequacy of the traditional conception of sovereignty. Although the discourse of international relations has been state-centric, the concept of sovereignty originally served as the focal point of the discussion about the state.

When political scientists began to challenge the traditional doctrine of state sovereignty in the early 1920s, their aim of discrediting the state was not conceived as an idealistic or wishful aspiration. Rather, the argument put forth by individuals such as Harold Laski, Mary Parker Follett, George Sabine, and James Garner was that existing political conditions were different from those that the juristic theory of state sovereignty posited. Certain scholars of international relations and international law argued that the inconsistencies between juristic theory and empirical fact were conspicuous in the realm of international politics. Although juristic theory presented an image of autonomous states exercising unrestricted rights equally and independent of external impediments, many argued that this contradicted the actual observable practice of world politics. The claim that international law lacked the essential characteristics of law was increasingly considered by the interwar scholars to be not only theoretically erroneous but contrary to the concrete practices shaping international affairs. The positivist approach to the subject attempted to prove that even without a centralized world authority, international law was, nevertheless, law and, moreover, able to regulate effectively the external affairs of states. The legal scholars of this period based their aspiration to establish the rule of law internationally on what they argued was a realistic understanding of international politics, yet they have been understood as idealists or utopians. With the ascendancy of realism after World War II, the study of international law has been greatly neglected, but the early history of the field reveals that the study of international law was one of the most influential contributions to the development of international relations. And the discourse that it precipitated was devoted to reconciling legal theory with international practice.

A radically different view of the interwar period emerges once it is established that the discourse was informed by the theory of pluralism rather than idealism. This period of the field's history offers a wealth of insights into the contemporary study of international relations. There are deep discursive continuities between the interwar pluralists and the various schools of thought such as transnationalism, functionalism, and complex interdependence, which are often placed under the broad rubric of pluralism.[20] The debate between the interwar pluralists and the proponents of the juristic theory of the state adumbrated the many challenges that have been mounted against the theory of realism since the late 1950s, including the current controversy between neoliberalism and neorealism. Like these more recent controversies, the debate of the 1920s centered on whether it was analytically and theoretically appropriate to conceptualize international politics as a global state of nature populated by independent autonomous state actors who operated on the basis of self-help and pursued their own self-interests without regard for the interests of international society as a whole.

In rejecting the archaic ontology that depicted international relations as a global state of nature, the interwar scholars benefited from the theoretical critique of sovereignty that the pluralists were pursuing.

This particular instance of symmetry between the study of domestic politics and international politics illustrates the more general tendency of the earlier generation of political scientists to refuse to divorce domestic and international affairs, and it offers an example for scholars who have begun to rethink the contemporary conventional division between domestic politics and international politics.[21] The theory of pluralism fostered a substantial modification in the way political scientists comprehended sovereignty, which in turn promoted an alternative conceptualization of the state. Pluralists argued that the state was but one of the many different forms of group association to which individuals belonged. The theoretical claim that the state had unlimited and supreme sovereignty was more of a metaphysical fiction than an empirical fact. While international politics continued to be conceived as a realm that lacked an overarching central government, the pluralist account of sovereignty enabled scholars to conceptualize the manner in which individuals, groups, organizations, and states were integrated in a myriad of ways. The pluralist image of a dense arrangement of disaggregated state and non-state actors interacting in a highly interdependent environment provided an alternative ontology of the international milieu that permitted students of international relations to appreciate the degree to which inter-state cooperation, international law, and different forms of international governance characterized the actual practice of international politics.

The manner in which the pluralist account of sovereignty facilitated an amended ontology of international politics suggests a number of lessons for the political discourse of anarchy. Most importantly, this episode of disciplinary history reveals that the meaning and implications of anarchy were contingent upon a particular theoretical understanding of sovereignty. The interwar scholars as well as their predecessors found it impossible to understand the meaning of anarchy without seriously engaging the concept of sovereignty. This finding has direct relevance for a variety of conversations that have arisen recently about sovereignty and its relationship to the concept of anarchy. Unlike the attempt made by neorealists such as Kenneth Waltz to convey the structural characteristics of anarchy without ever carefully addressing the issue of sovereignty, the scholars of the interwar period took the exact opposite approach and focused their attention on assessing the validity of competing conceptions of sovereignty and indicating the implications for the concept of anarchy. The idea advanced in Waltz's *Theory of International Politics,* that states can be considered "like-units" in the sense "that each state is like all other states in being an autonomous political unit" and thus analogous to firms in a market, would have been considered very unrealistic by many of the scholars discussed in this study.[22] Similarly, the manner in which the present-day conversation about international cooperation has been pursued by envisioning states as autonomous rational utility-maximizing actors seeking to achieve favorable outcomes in Prisoner Dilemma–type games also would have appeared to the interwar scholars' to be an unrealistic extrapolation of the actual international setting.[23] Finally, the interwar scholars' adoption of the pluralist account of sovereignty is what gave added significance to the claim that international politics had experienced a transition from independence to interdependence.

<h2 style="text-align:center">Independence and Interdependence</h2>

As much as the challenge to the ontology depicting international politics as a global state of nature rested on the theory of pluralism, it also was based on what was considered to be a realistic assessment of the empirical conditions shaping the practice of world politics. This is what made the phenomenon of interdependence extremely pertinent to the debate between proponents and critics of the juristic theory of the state. Interdependence, which was defined by the fact that states were highly integrated with, and mutually dependent on, one another, was of significant importance, since it demonstrated that the image depicted by juristic theory of independent and autonomous state actors was inadequate. Interwar scholars argued that the fact of interdependence pointed to a major discrepancy between juristic theory and the practice of international politics. The image of independent and isolated states was rendered historically obsolete with the increasing frequency of interaction between citizens of different states and by the large number of international conferences and international agreements into which states were entering. This image was also contradicted by the presence of numerous international public unions that were effectively regulating the affairs of states. As the discourse reconstructed in Chapters 5 and 6 reveals, international relations scholars were fundamentally devoted to reconciling the gap that had been created between the older theories for comprehending international politics and the new realities of interdependence and international organization.

Yet, just as Robert Keohane and Joseph Nye's pronouncement in 1977 that "we live in an era of interdependence" was not in any way novel, neither was the interwar scholars' discovery of the phenomenon of interdependence.[24] Lieber had made reference to a law of interdependence among modern nations in the late 1800s, and the discursive history of the field reveals the existence of a continuous line of conversation about interdependence and, more generally, different forms of international solidarity. The poles of independence and interdependence, and the discussions and debates that students of international relations have generated about these two analytical categories, are deeply rooted in the discursive history of the field. The discussion about whether the concept of independence or interdependence best characterizes international politics represents one of the significant components of the political discourse of anarchy. Just as disagreement existed in the past with respect to the theoretical meaning of these concepts as well as the degree to which either independence or interdependence typified the practice of international politics, the same basic scenario continues to exist in the field today. The earlier history of this conversation does, however, offer two important lessons.

First, simply endorsing the attribute of interdependence by itself does not, in any way, imply a theoretical position of idealism. Certainly this was not the case when Keohane and Nye made their argument for complex interdependence, despite the fact that their characterization of this "ideal type" of politics bears a striking resemblance to the account offered by the interwar pluralists. By wrongly construing the interwar discourse as idealist, the antecedents of not only complex interdependence but functionalism, integration theory, and regime theory are lost and replaced with what has been termed a "liberal" or "Grotian tradition." The writings of the interwar scholars contained a keen recognition that the autonomy of state actors was diminished by transnational forces and actors, and that the very process of interdependence was fostering integration that could possibly lead to a higher form of global governance. Moreover, there were very few interwar scholars who believed that the phenomenon of interdependence rendered obsolete all of the difficulties of achieving international organization or global governance in an environment where the principal actors continued to retain the attribute of sovereignty. As evidenced by the work of Pitman Potter, who virtually was the founder of the study of international organization within the field of international relations, anarchy continued to guide the discussion of inter–state cooperation throughout the interwar period.

This leads to the second lesson, namely, it is impossible to gauge either the theoretical content or practical effect of interdependence without addressing the concept of sovereignty. Once again, the significance of interdependence was that it lent legitimacy to the pluralist conception of the state and its corresponding account of international politics. In a similar manner, the practical significance that proponents of the juristic theory of the state attributed to independence can only be understood in light of their theory of sovereignty. The recent attention that scholars have begun to direct toward the elusive concept of sovereignty is an indication of the fundamental importance that this principle continues to have for the study of international relations.[25] The disciplinary history of international relations clearly reveals that the discourse about sovereignty was really what animated the political discourse of anarchy.

Unless or until states renounce their exclusive claim to sovereignty, the study of international relations will continue to be guided by a discourse of anarchy. This discourse is deeply rooted in the history of the field, and there have been numerous conceptual shifts in the manner in which political scientists have understood the meaning of anarchy as well as in what they believed could be done about the situation. The contemporary discourse of international relations continues to revolve around the dangers and opportunities of politics in the absence of central authority, and an investigation of the history of the field can contribute to understanding one of the central predicaments of our age. This understanding, however, depends on dispelling the misconceptions that have been cast upon the disciplinary history of international relations.

NOTES

Introduction

1. Miles Kahler, "Inventing International Relations: International Relations Theory After 1945," in Michael W. Doyle and G. John Ikenberry, eds., *New Directions in International Relations Theory* (Boulder, Colo.: Westview Press, forthcoming).

2. Examples of the recent plethora of works addressing the disciplinary history of political science include John G. Gunnell, *The Descent of Political Theory: The Genealogy of an American Vocation* (Chicago: University of Chicago Press, 1993); David Easton, John G. Gunnell, and Luigi Graziano, eds., *The Development of Political Science: A Comparative Study* (London: Routledge, 1991); David Easton, Michael Stein, and John G. Gunnell, eds., *Regime and Discipline: Democracy and the Development of Political Science* (Ann Arbor: University of Michigan Press, 1995); James Farr and Raymond Seidelman, eds., *Discipline and History: Political Science in the United States* (Ann Arbor: University of Michigan Press, 1993); James Farr, John S. Dryzek, and Stephen T. Leonard, eds., *Political Science in History: Research Programs and Political Traditions* (Cambridge: Cambridge University Press, 1995); and Michael A. Baer, Malcolm E. Jewell, and Lee Seligman, eds., *Political Science in America: Oral Histories of a Discipline* (Lexington: University Press of Kentucky, 1991).

3. I owe this phrase to Sanford F. Schram. See his insightful *Words of Welfare: The Poverty of Social Science and the Social Science of Poverty* (Minneapolis: University of Minnesota Press, 1995).

4. John G. Gunnell, "The Historiography of American Political Science," in David Easton, John G. Gunnell, and Luigi Graziano, eds., *The Development of Political Science,* p. 16.

5. John G. Gunnell, *Philosophy, Science and Political Inquiry* (Morristown, N.J.: General Learning Press, 1975), p. ix. Gunnell has also examined this influence in "Political Theory: The Evolution of a Sub-Field," in Ada W. Finifter, ed., *Political Science: The State of the Discipline* (Washington, D.C.: APSA, 1983); *Between Philosophy and Politics: The Alienation of Political Theory* (Amherst: University of Massachusetts Press, 1986), pp. 43–90; and "Realizing Theory: The Philosophy of Science Revisited," *The Journal of Politics* (Vol. 57, No. 4, 1995).

6. Thomas S. Kuhn, *The Structure of Scientific Revolutions,* 2nd ed., (Chicago: University of Chicago Press, 1970), p. 92.

7. Terence Ball, "Is There Progress in Political Science?" in Terence Ball, ed., *Idioms of Inquiry: Critique and Renewal in Political Science* (Albany: State University of New York Press, 1987), p. 20.

8. For a general overview of the "voices of dissent" in international relations, see the special issue of *International Studies Quarterly*—Speaking the Language of Exile: Dissident Thought in International Studies (Vol. 34, No. 3, 1990); James Der Derian and Michael J. Shapiro, eds., *International/Intertextual Relations: Postmodern Readings of World Politics* (Lexington, Mass.: Lexington Books, 1989); Jim George, *Discourses of Global Politics: A Critical (Re)Introduction to International Relations* (Boulder: Lynne Rienner Publishers, 1994); Christine Sylvester, *Feminist Theory and International Relations in a Postmodern Era* (Cambridge: Cambridge University Press, 1994); and Pauline Rosenau, "Once Again Into the Fray: International Relations Confronts the Humanities," *Millennium: Journal of International Studies* (Vol. 19, No. 1, 1990).

9. For an elucidation of the third debate, see Yosef Lapid, "The Third Debate: On the Prospects of International Theory in a Post-Postivist Era," *International Studies Quarterly* (Vol. 33, No. 3, 1989); Jim George, "International Relations and the Search for Thinking Space: Another View of the Third Debate," *International Studies Quarterly* (Vol. 33, No. 3, 1989); Ray Maghroori and Bennett Ramberg, *Globalism Versus Realism: International Relations' Third Debate* (Boulder: Westview Press, 1982); John A. Vasquez, "The Post-Positivist Debate: Reconstructing Scientific Enquiry and International Relations Theory After Enlightenment's Fall," in Ken Booth and Steve Smith, eds., *International Relations Theory Today* (University Park: Pennsylvania State University Press, 1995).

10. Yosef Lapid, "Quo Vadis International Relations? Further Reflections on the 'Next Stage' of International Theory," *Millennium: Journal of International Studies* (Vol. 18, No. 1, 1989): p. 77.

11. Lapid, "The Third Debate: On the Prospects of International Theory in a Post-Positivist Era," pp. 235–238.

12. George, "International Relations and the Search for Thinking Space," p. 272.

13. Yale H. Ferguson and Richard W. Mansbach, "Between Celebration and Despair: Constructive Suggestions for Future International Theory," *International Studies Quarterly* (Vol. 35, No. 4, 1991): p. 364.

14. V. Spike Peterson, "Transgressing Boundaries: Theories of Knowledge, Gender and International Relations," *Millennium: Journal of International Studies* (Vol. 21, No. 2, 1992): pp. 186–187.

15. George, "International Relations and the Search for Thinking Space," p. 273.

16. Richard K. Ashley and R. B. J. Walker, "Speaking the Language of Exile: Dissident Thought in International Studies," *International Studies Quarterly* (Vol. 34, No. 3, 1990): p. 265.

17. An excellent theoretical discussion of the binary construction of international relations theory is provided by R. B. J. Walker, *Inside/Outside: International Relations as Political Theory* (Cambridge: Cambridge University Press,

1993). Other very good theoretical explanations are provided by Bradley S. Klein, *Strategic Studies and World Order: The Global Politics of Deterrence* (Cambridge: Cambridge University Press, 1994); J. Ann Tickner, *Gender in International Relations: Feminist Perspectives on Achieving Global Security* (New York: Columbia University Press, 1992); V. Spike Peterson, ed., *Gendered States: Feminist (Re)Visions of International Relations Theory* (Boulder: Lynne Rienner, 1992); James Der Derian and Michael J. Shapiro, eds., *International/Intertextual Relations;* and Jim George, *Discourses of Global Politics.*

18. K. J. Holsti, "Mirror, Mirror on the Wall, Which Are the Fairest Theories of All?" *International Studies Quarterly* (Vol. 33, No. 2, 1989): p. 256.

19. Mark Hoffman, "Critical Theory and the Inter-Paradigm Debate," *Millennium: Journal of International Studies* (Vol. 16, No. 2, 1987): p. 231.

20. For those who have discussed the third debate in terms of an inter-paradigm debate, see Ray Maghroori and Bennett Ramberg, *Globalism Versus Realism;* Michael Banks, "The Inter-Paradigm Debate," in Margot Light and A. J. R. Groom, eds., *International Relations a Handbook of Current Theory* (London: Francis Pinter Publishers, 1985); Mark Hoffman, "Critical Theory and the Inter-Paradigm Debate"; Sandra Whitworth, "Gender in the Inter-Paradigm Debate," *Millennium: Journal of International Studies* (Vol. 18, No. 2, 1989); and Steve Smith, "The Self-Images of a Discipline: A Genealogy of International Relations Theory," in Ken Booth and Steve Smith, eds., *International Relations Theory Today.*

21. For example, see V. Spike Peterson, "Transgressing Boundaries: Theories of Knowledge, Gender, and International Relations" and Steve Smith, "The Forty Years' Detour: The Resurgence of Normative Theory in International Relations," *Millennium: Journal of International Studies* (Vol. 21, No. 3, 1992).

22. Jean-Francois Lyotard, *The Postmodern Condition: A Report on Knowledge* (Minneapolis: University of Minnesota Press, 1989), p. xxiv.

23. I have deliberately chosen to use the term "field" rather than "discipline" to indicate that I am examining the history of international relations as an officially recognized sub-field or section of the discipline of political science.

24. Quincy Wright, *The Study of International Relations* (New York: Appleton-Century-Crofts, 1955), pp. 23–60. The eight root disciplines that Wright identified were international law, diplomatic history, military science, international politics, international organization, international trade, colonial government, and the conduct of foreign relations. The disciplines with a world point of view included world geography, world history, psychology, sociology, language, and biology.

25. See Stanley H. Bailey, *International Studies in Modern Education* (London: Oxford University Press, 1938); Grayson Kirk, *The Study of International Relations in American Colleges and Universities* (New York: Council on Foreign Relations, 1947); William C. Olson, "The Growth of a Discipline," in Brian Porter, ed., *The Aberystwyth Papers: International Politics 1919–1969* (London:

Oxford University Press, 1972); and Harry Howe Ransom, "International Relations," *The Journal of Politics* (Vol. 30, No. 2, 1968).

26. Olson, "The Growth of a Discipline," p. 17.

27. There are several works that have dealt with this issue, including K. J. Holsti, *The Dividing Discipline: Hegemony and Diversity in International Theory* (Boston: Allen & Unwin, 1985); Hayward R. Alker Jr. and Thomas J. Biersteker, "The Dialectics of World Order: Notes for a Future Archeologist of International Savoir Faire," *International Studies Quarterly* (Vol. 28, No. 2, 1984); David J. Dunn, "On Perspectives and Approaches: British, American and Others," *Review of International Studies* (Vol. 13, No. 1, 1987); and Steve Smith, ed., *International Relations: British and American Perspectives* (Oxford: Basil Blackwell, 1985).

28. For a discussion of some of the issues involved in a comparative analysis of the development of political science, see David Easton, John G. Gunnell, and Luigi Graziano, eds., *The Development of Political Science.*

29. William C. Olson and A.J.R. Groom, *International Relations Then and Now: Origins and Trends in Interpretation* (London: Harper-Collins, 1991), p. 62.

30. Although the manner in which the subject is studied in other parts of the world has not received much attention, this has recently begun to change. See the review essays by A.J.R. Groom, "The World Beyond: the European Dimension," and Stephen Chan, "Beyond the North-West: Africa and the East," both in A.J.R. Groom and Margot Light, eds., *Contemporary International Relations: A Guide to Theory* (London: Pinter Publishers, 1994).

31. Several works have commented on the American dominance of the field of international relations. For example, see Stanley Hoffmann, "An American Social Science: International Relations," *Daedalus* (Vol. 106, 1977); Miles Kahler, "International Relations: Still an American Social Science?" in Linda B. Miller and Michael Joseph Smith, eds., *Ideas and Ideals: Essays on Politics in Honor of Stanley Hoffmann* (Boulder: Westview Press, 1993); K.J. Holsti, *The Dividing Discipline,* pp. 102–128; and Hayward R. Alker Jr. and Thomas J. Biersteker, "The Dialectics of World Order: Notes for a Future Archeologist of International Savoir Faire."

32. For those who have questioned the existence of international relations as a discipline, see Quincy Wright, *The Study of International Relations;* Harry Howe Ransom, "International Relations"; Morton A. Kaplan, "Is International Relations a Discipline?" *The Journal of Politics* (Vol. 23, 1961); Waldemar Gurian, "On the Study of International Relations," *The Review of Politics* (Vol. 8, No. 3, 1946); and Norman D. Palmer, "The Study of International Relations in the United States," *International Studies Quarterly* (Vol. 24, No. 3, 1980).

33. Olson and Groom, *International Relations Then and Now,* p. 115.

34. Hoffmann, "An American Social Science: International Relations," p. 43.

35. Palmer, "The Study of International Relations in the United States," p. 347.

The Historiography of Academic International Relations

1. The disciplinary historians that I am referring to include John Dryzek, James Farr, John G. Gunnell, Stephen Leonard, and Raymond Seidelman.

2. John S. Dryzek and Stephen T. Leonard, "History and Discipline in Political Science," *American Political Science Review* (Vol. 82, No. 4, 1988): p. 1247.

3. John G. Gunnell, "The Historiography of American Political Science," in David Easton, John G. Gunnell, and Luigi Graziano, eds., *The Development of Political Science: A Comparative Survey* (London: Routledge, 1991), p. 15.

4. For examples of work by intellectual historians who address the history of political science, see Dorothy Ross, *The Origins of American Social Science* (Cambridge: Cambridge University Press, 1991); Mary O. Furner, *Advocacy and Objectivity: A Crisis in the Professionalization of American Social Science, 1865–1905* (Lexington: University Press of Kentucky, 1975); and Thomas Haskel, *The Emergence of Professional Social Science: The American Social Science Association and the Nineteenth Century Crisis of Authority* (Urbana: University of Illinois Press, 1977).

5. Examples include Thomas S. Kuhn, *The Structure of Scientific Revolutions,* 2nd ed. (Chicago: University of Chicago Press, 1970); Marry Hesse, *Revolutions and Reconstructions in the Philosophy of Science* (Bloomington: Indiana University Press, 1980); Imre Lakatos and Alan Musgrave, eds., *Criticism and the Growth of Knowledge* (Cambridge: Cambridge University Press, 1970); and Larry Laudan, *Progress and Its Problems: Towards a Theory of Scientific Growth* (Berkeley: University of California Press, 1977).

6. Examples of a contextual approach can be found in Quentin Skinner, "Meaning and Understanding in the History of Ideas," *History and Theory* (Vol. 8, 1969); J. G. A. Pocock, *Politics, Language, and Time* (London: Methuen, 1972); James Tully, ed., *Meaning and Context: Quentin Skinner and His Critics* (Princeton: Princeton University Press, 1988); and Quentin Skinner, "Language and Political Change," in Terence Ball, James Farr, and Russell L. Hanson, eds., *Political Innovation and Conceptual Change* (Cambridge: Cambridge University Press, 1989).

7. Works by Michel Foucault include: *The Order of Things: An Archaeology of the Human Sciences,* trans. Alan Sheridan-Smith (New York: Vintage Books, 1975); *The Archaeology of Knowledge,* trans. Alan Sheridan-Smith (London: Tavistock, 1972); and *Discipline and Punish: The Birth of the Prison,* trans. Alan Sheridan (New York: Vintage Books, 1979).

8. See, for example, Karen Orren and Stephen Skowronek, "Order and Time in Institutional Study: A Brief for the Historical Approach," in James Farr, John S. Dryzek, and Stephen T. Leonard, eds., *Political Science in History: Research Programs and Political Traditions* (Cambridge: Cambridge University Press, 1995), and David Brian Robertson, "The Return to History and the New Institu-

tionalism in American Political Science," *Social Science History* (Vol. 17, No. 1, 1993).

9. See James Farr *et al.*, "Can Political Science History Be Neutral?" *American Political Science Review* (Vol. 84, No. 2, 1990).

10. Dryzek and Leonard, "History and Discipline in Political Science," p. 1249.

11. *Ibid.*, p. 1252.

12. On the issue of progress, see Terence Ball, "Is There Progress in Political Science?" in Terence Ball, ed., *Idioms of Inquiry: Critique and Renewal in Political Science* (Albany: SUNY Press, 1987). A discussion of internal and external history can be found in Gunnell, "The Historiography of American Political Science."

13. Dryzek and Leonard, "History and Discipline in Political Science," p. 1257.

14. Herbert Butterfield, *The Whig Interpretation of History* (London: G. Bell and Sons, 1959), p. v.

15. George W. Stocking, Jr., "On the Limits of 'Presentism' and 'Historicism' in the Historiography of the Behavioral Sciences," *Journal of the History of the Behavioral Sciences* (Vol. 1, No. 3, 1965): p. 213.

16. *Ibid.*, p. 213.

17. Stefan Collini, Donald Winch, and John Burrow, *That Noble Science of Politics: A Study in Nineteenth-Century Intellectual History* (Cambridge: Cambridge University Press, 1983), p. 4.

18. Dryzek and Leonard, "History and Discipline in Political Science," p. 1254.

19. Farr *et al.*, "Can Political Science History Be Neutral?" p. 589.

20. James Farr, "The History of Political Science," *American Journal of Political Science* (Vol. 32, No. 4, 1988): p. 1177.

21. Farr *et al.*, "Can Political Science History Be Neutral?" p. 589. Emphasis in the original.

22. *Ibid.*, p. 597.

23. *Ibid.*, p. 591.

24. John G. Gunnell, "Disciplinary History: The Case of Political Science," *Strategies: A Journal of Theory, Culture and Politics* (Vol. 4/5, 1991): p. 190.

25. Farr *et al.*, "Can Political Science History Be Neutral?" p. 595.

26. Gunnell, "Disciplinary History: The Case of Political Science," p. 218.

27. John G. Gunnell, *The Descent of Political Theory: The Genealogy of an American Vocation* (Chicago: University of Chicago Press, 1993), p. 11.

28. *Ibid.,* p. 8.

29. Martin Wight, "Why is There No International Theory?" in Herbert Butterfield and Martin Wight, eds., *Diplomatic Investigations: Essays in the Theory of International Politics* (London: George Allen & Unwin, 1966), p. 20.

30. *Ibid.,* pp. 20, 26.

31. See E.H. Carr, *The Twenty Years' Crisis, 1919–1939: An Introduction to the Study of International Relations,* 2nd ed. (New York: Harper & Row, 1964), and Kenneth W. Thompson, *Political Realism and the Crisis of World Politics* (Princeton: Princeton University Press, 1960).

32. Hedley Bull, "The Theory of International Politics, 1919–1969," in Brian Porter, ed., *The Aberystwyth Papers: International Politics 1919–1969* (London: Oxford University Press, 1972), p. 33.

33. John A. Vasquez, *The Power of Power Politics: A Critique* (New Brunswick, N.J.: Rutgers University Press, 1983), p. 13.

34. See Charles W. Kegley, Jr. and Eugene R. Wittkopf, *World Politics: Trend and Transformation,* 3rd ed. (New York: St. Martin's Press, 1989), pp. 12–21.

35. C. R. Mitchell, "Analysing the 'Great Debates': Teaching Methodology in a Decade of Change," in R.C. Kent and G.P. Nielsson, eds., *The Study and Teaching of International Relations* (London: Frances Pinter Publishers, 1980), p. 28.

36. Arend Lijphart, "International Relations Theory: Great Debates and Lesser Debates," *International Social Science Journal* (Vol. 26, No. 1, 1974): p. 11.

37. Ray Maghroori, "Introduction: Major Debates in International Relations," in Ray Maghroori and Bennett Ramberg, eds., *Globalism Versus Realism: International Relations' Third Debate* (Boulder: Westview Press, 1982), p. 9.

38. Michael Banks, "The International Relations Discipline: Asset or Liability for Conflict Resolution?" in Edward E. Azar and John W. Burton, eds., *International Conflict Resolution: Theory and Practice* (Boulder: Lynne Rienner Publishers, 1986), p. 9.

39. This idea recently has received critical attention. See, for example, James Der Derian, "Introducing Philosophical Traditions," *Millennium: Journal of International Studies* (Vol. 17, No. 2, 1988); R.B.J. Walker, "History and Structure in the Theory of International Relations," *Millennium: Journal of International Studies* (Vol. 18, No. 2, 1989); and Timothy Dunne, "Mythology or Methodology? Traditions in International Thought," *Review of International Studies* (Vol. 19, No. 3, 1993).

40. See, for example, Leo Strauss, *What is Political Philosophy?* (Glencoe, Ill.: Free Press, 1959), and Sheldon S. Wolin, "Political Theory as a Vocation," *American Political Science Review* (Vol. 63, No. 4, 1969).

41. Wight, "Why is There No International Theory?" p. 17.

42. See R.B.J. Walker, *Inside/Outside: International Relations As Political Theory* (Cambridge: Cambridge University Press, 1993).

43. John G. Gunnell, *Political Theory: Tradition and Interpretation* (New York: University Press of America, 1979), p. xx. Emphasis in the original.

44. John G. Gunnell, *Between Philosophy and Politics: The Alienation of Political Theory* (Amherst: University of Massachusetts Press, 1986), p. 95.

45. Wight, "Why is There No International Theory?" p. 20.

46. Mark V. Kauppi and Paul R. Viotti, *The Global Philosophers: World Politics in Western Thought* (New York: Lexington Books, 1992), p. 3.

47. See Martin Wight, "An Anatomy of International Thought," *Review of International Studies* (Vol. 13, No. 3, 1987); Martin Wight, "Western Values in International Relations," in Herbert Butterfield and Martin Wight, eds., *Diplomatic Investigations;* and Martin Wight, *International Theory: The Three Traditions,* ed. Gabriele Wight and Brian Porter (New York: Holmes & Meir, 1992).

48. Walker, *Inside/Outside: International Relations As Political Theory,* p. 31.

49. The following articles provide a critical account of this practice: Michael C. Williams, "Rousseau, Realism and *Realpolitik," Millennium: Journal of International Studies* (Vol. 18, No. 2, 1988); Michael C. Williams, "Reason and Realpolitik: Kant's 'Critique of International Politics,'" *Canadian Journal of Political Science* (Vol. 25, No. 1, 1992); Michael W. Doyle, "Thucydidean Realism," *Review of International Studies* (Vol. 16, No. 3, 1990); Andrew Hurrell, "Kant and the Kantian Paradigm in International Relations," *Review of International Studies* (Vol. 16, No. 3, 1990); R. John Vincent, "The Hobbesian Tradition in Twentieth Century International Thought," *Millennium: Journal of International Studies* (Vol. 10, No. 2, 1981); A. Claire Cutler, "The 'Grotian Tradition' in International Relations," *Review of International Studies* (Vol. 17, No. 1, 1991); and R.B.J. Walker, "The Prince and the 'Pauper': Tradition, Modernity, and Practice in the Theory of International Relations," in James Der Derian and Michael Shapiro, eds., *International/Intertextual Relations* (Lexington: Lexington Books, 1989).

50. Hedley Bull, *The Anarchical Society: A Study of Order in World Politics* (New York: Columbia University Press, 1977), p. 24.

51. See Ian Clark, *The Hierarchy of States: Reform and Resistance in the International Order* (Cambridge: Cambridge University Press, 1989).

52. See, for example, Nicholas G. Onuf and Thomas J. Johnson, "Peace in the Liberal World: Does Democracy Matter?" in Charles W. Kegley, Jr., ed., *Controversies in International Relations Theory* (New York: St. Martin's Press, 1995), and Michael W. Doyle, "Liberalism and World Politics," *American Political Science Review* (Vol. 80, No. 4, 1986).

53. See Clark, *The Hierarchy of States,* especially Ch. 4, and Stanley Hoffmann, *The State of War: Essays in the Theory and Practice of International Politics* (New York: Frederick A. Praeger, 1965).

54. K. J. Holsti, *The Dividing Discipline: Hegemony and Diversity in International Theory* (Boston: Allen & Unwin, 1985), p. 19.

55. Jack Donnelly, "Realism and the Academic Study of International Relations," in James Farr, John S. Dryzek, and Stephen T. Leonard, eds., *Political Science in History,* p. 175.

56. Jacek Kugler, "Political Conflict, War, and Peace," in Ada W. Finifter, ed., *Political Science: The State of the Discipline II* (Washington, D.C.: The American Political Science Association, 1993), pp. 483–484.

57. Robert O. Keohane, "Theory of World Politics: Structural Realism and Beyond," in Ada A. Finifter, ed., *Political Science: The State of the Discipline* (Washington, D.C.: The American Political Science Association, 1983), p. 503.

58. *Ibid.,* p. 507.

59. *Ibid.,* p. 508.

60. *Ibid.,* p. 520.

61. On the ambiguous nature of realism, see Kjell Goldman, "The Concept of 'Realism' as a Source of Confusion," *Cooperation and Conflict* (Vol. 23, 1988), and Martin Griffiths, "Order and International Society: The Real Realism," *Review of International Studies* (Vol. 18, No. 3, 1992).

62. See Robert O. Keohane, "International Institutions: Two Approaches," *International Studies Quarterly* (Vol. 32, No. 4, 1988).

63. Robert G. Gilpin, "The Richness of the Tradition of Political Realism," in Robert Keohane, ed., *Neorealism and its Critics* (New York: Columbia Univerisity Press, 1986), p. 306.

64. Holsti, *The Dividing Discipline,* p. 1.

65. *Ibid.,* p. 11.

66. *Ibid.,* p. 39.

67. Arend Lijphart, "The Structure of the Theoretical Revolution in International Relations," *International Studies Quarterly* (Vol. 18, No. 1, 1974): pp. 42–43.

68. *Ibid.,* p. 49.

69. Vasquez, *The Power of Power Politics,* p. 22.

70. *Ibid.,* p. 23.

71. See Hans J. Morgenthau, *Scientific Man Versus Power Politics* (Chicago: University of Chicago Press, 1946), and Hedley Bull, "International Theory: The Case of the Classical Approach," in Klaus Knorr and James N. Rosenau, eds., *Contending Approaches to International Politics* (Princeton: Princeton University Press, 1969).

72. Eric Hobsbawm, "Introduction: Inventing Traditons," in Eric Hobsbawm and Terence Ranger, eds., *The Invention of Tradition* (Cambridge: Cambridge University Press, 1983), p. 1.

73. Yale A. Ferguson and Richard W. Mansbach, *The Elusive Quest: Theory and International Politics* (Columbia, S.C.: University of South Carolina Press, 1988), p. 36.

74. Stanley Hoffmann, "An American Social Science: International Relations," *Daedalus* (Vol. 106, 1977): p. 41.

75. *Ibid.,* p. 45.

76. *Ibid.,* p. 47.

77. Ekkehart Krippendorf, "The Dominance of American Approaches in International Relations," *Millennium: Journal of International Studies* (Vol. 16, No. 2, 1987): p. 211.

78. Alan Sked, "The Study of International Relations: A Historian's View," in Hugh C. Dyer and Leon Mangasarian, eds., *The Study of International Relations: The State of the Art* (New York: St. Martin's Press, 1989), p. 90.

79. Fred Warner Neal and Bruce D. Hamlet, "The Never-Never Land of International Relations," *International Studies Quarterly* (Vol. 13, No. 3, 1969): p. 283.

80. Steve Smith, "Paradigm Dominance in International Relations: The Development of International Relations as a Social Science," *Millennium: Journal of International Studies* (Vol. 16, No. 2, 1987): p. 192.

81. *Ibid.,* p. 194.

82. Robert L. Rothstein, "On the Costs of Realism," *Political Science Quarterly* (Vol. 87, No. 3, 1972): p. 349.

83. Smith, "Paradigm Dominance in International Relations," p. 196.

84. William C. Olson and Nicholas Onuf, "The Growth of a Discipline: Reviewed," in Steve Smith, ed., *International Relations: British and American Perspectives* (Oxford: Basil Blackwell, 1985), p. 12.

85. *Ibid.,* p. 2.

86. William C. Olson and A.J.R. Groom, *International Relations Then and Now: Origins and Trends in Interpretation* (London: HarperCollins, 1991), p. 137.

87. A sampling of these reactions is provided in Richard Ned Lebow and Thomas Risse-Kappen, eds., *International Relations Theory and the End of the Cold War* (New York: Columbia University Press, 1995).

88. Kuhn, *The Structure of Scientific Revolutions,* p. 138.

89. See Gunnell, *The Descent of Political Theory,* pp. 1–13.

90. For one recent example of the former tendency, see Haward R. Alker Jr., "The Humanistic Moment in International Studies: Reflections on Machiavelli and las Casas," *International Studies Quarterly* (Vol. 36, No. 4, 1992).

91. Robert J. Art and Robert Jervis, eds., *International Politics: Anarchy, Force, Political Economy, and Decision-Making,* 2nd. ed. (Boston: Little, Brown and Co., 1985), p. 2.

92. Waltz, as cited in Daniel Garst, "Thucydides and Neorealism," *International Studies Quarterly* (Vol. 33, No. 1, 1989) p. 3.

93. See, for example, Steve Forbe, "International Realism and the Science of Politics: Thucydides, Machiavelli, and Neorealism," *International Studies Quarterly* (Vol. 39, No. 2, 1995), and Michael C. Williams, "Hobbes and International Relations," *International Organization* (Vol. 50, N0. 2, 1996).

94. Barry Buzan and Richard Little, "The Idea of 'International System': Theory Meets History," *International Political Science Review* (Vol. 15, No. 3, 1994): p. 236

95. Barry Buzan, Charles Jones, and Richard Little, *The Logic of Anarchy: Neorealism to Structural Realism* (New York: Columbia University Press, 1993), pp. 1–15.

96. A good illustration of this is provided by Helen Milner, "The Assumption of Anarchy in International Relations Theory: A Critique," *Review of International Studies* (Vol. 17, No. 1, 1991), and Alexander Went, "Anarchy is What States Make of it: The Social Construction of Power Politics," *International Organization* (Vol. 46, No. 2, 1992).

97. David A. Baldwin, "Neoliberalism, Neorealism, and World Politics," in David A. Baldwin, ed., *Neorealism and Neoliberalism: The Contemporary Debate* (New York: Columbia University Press, 1993), p. 4.

98. For a good introduction to the debate between neorealism and neoliberalism, see Charles W. Kegley Jr., ed., *Controversies in International Relations Theory: Realism and the Neoliberal Challenge* (New York: St. Martin's Press, 1995), and David A. Baldwin, ed., *Neorealism and Neoliberalism: The Contemporary Debate*.

99. Torbjorn L. Knutsen, *A History of International Relations Theory: An Introduction* (Manchester: Manchester University Press, 1992), p. 3.

The Theoretical Discourse of the State

1. For an explanation of this idea, see James Farr, "Francis Lieber and the Interpretation of American Political Science," *Journal of Politics* (Vol. 52, No. 4, 1990).

2. General information concerning the relationship between moral philosophy and the origins of the social sciences is provided by Gladys Bryson, "The Emergence of the Social Sciences from Moral Philosophy," *The International Journal of Ethics* (Vol. XLII, No. 3, 1932), and Dorothy Ross, *The Origins of American Social Science* (Cambridge: Cambridge University Press, 1991).

3. Anna Haddow, *Political Science in American Colleges and Universities, 1636–1900* (New York: Octagon Books, 1969), p. 113.

4. Bryson, "The Emergence of the Social Sciences from Moral Philosophy," p. 317.

5. Some of the eastern colleges that adopted Vattel's text included the College of William and Mary, Brown University, and Yale University. See Haddow, *Political Science in American Colleges and Universities*, pp. 43–63, 74–76.

6. Emmerich de Vattel, *The Law of Nations or the Principles of Natural Law*, in M.G. Forsyth, ed., *The Theory of International Relations: Selected Texts from Gentili to Treitschke* (New York: Atherton Press, 1970), p. 104.

7. William C. Olson and A.J.R. Groom, *International Relations Then and Now: Origins and Trends in Interpretation* (London: HarperCollins, 1991), p. 6.

8. Haddow, *Political Science in American Colleges and Universities*, p. 149.

9. Henry Wheaton, *Elements of International Law*, in George Grafton Wilson, ed., *The Classics of International Law* (Oxford: Claredon Press, 1936), p. 20.

10. Many disciplinary historians of political science have acknowledged Francis Lieber as being the founder of American political science. For example, see Haddow, *Political Science in American Colleges and Universities*; Farr, "Francis Lieber and the Interpretation of American Political Science"; John G. Gunnell, *The Descent of Political Theory: The Genealogy of an American Vocation* (Chicago: University of Chicago Press, 1993); and Albert Lepawsky, "The Politics of Epistemology," *The Western Political Quarterly* (Vol. 17, 1964).

11. For biographical information on the life and thought of Francis Lieber, see Lewis R. Harley, *Francis Lieber: His Life and Political Philosophy* (New York: Columbia University Press, 1899).

12. John G. Gunnell, "In Search of the State: Political Science as an Emerging Discipline in the U.S.," in Peter Wagner, Bjorn Wittrock, and Richard Whitley, eds., *Discourses on Society: The Shaping of the Social Science Disciplines* (Boston: Kluwer Academic, 1990), p. 132.

13. For example, see Albert Somit and Joseph Tanenhaus, *The Development of American Political Science: From Burgess to Behavioralism* (New York: Irvington Publishers, 1982).

14. Francis Lieber, *Miscellaneous Writings* (Philadelphia: J.B. Lippincott & Co., 1880), Vol. I, p. 367.

15. Francis Lieber, *Manual of Political Ethics*, 2nd ed. (Philadelphia: J.B. Lippincott & Co., 1885), Vol. I, p. 162.

16. Lieber, *Miscellaneous Writings*, Vol. I, p. 367.

17. See Harley, *Francis Lieber: His Life and Political Philosophy*, especially pp. 141–155.

18. For example, see George B. Davis, "Doctor Francis Lieber's Instructions for the Government of Armies in the Field," *The American Journal of International Law* (Vol. I, No. 1, 1907), and Elihu Root, "Francis Lieber," *The American Journal of International Law* (Vol. 7, No. 3, 1913).

19. See Harley, *Francis Lieber: His Life and Political Philosophy,* pp. 148–154.

20. Johann Caspar Bluntschli, "Lieber's Service to Political Science and International Law," in Francis Lieber, *Miscellaneous Writings,* Vol. II, p. 12.

21. Bluntschli writes: "From 1860 to 1870, Francis Lieber in New York, Edward Laboulaye in Paris and I in Heidelberg, formed what Lieber used to call a 'scientific clover-leaf,' in which three men, devoting themselves especially to political science, and at the same time uniting the historical and philosophical methods, combining theory with practical politics, and belonging to three different nationalities, to three states, and to three peoples, found themselves growing together by ties of common sympathy, and thus figuratively speaking, representing also the community of Anglo-American, French, and German culture and science," see *Ibid.,* p. 13.

22. Johann Caspar Bluntschli, *The Theory of the State,* 3rd ed. (Oxford: Claredon Press, 1921; first edition 1885), p. 32.

23. See F.H. Hinsley, *Power and the Pursuit of Peace* (Cambridge: Cambridge University Press, 1963), pp. 134–137, and Hidemi Suganami, *The Domestic Analogy and World Order Proposals* (Cambridge: Cambridge University Press, 1989), pp. 54–61.

24. Lieber, *Miscellaneous Writings,* Vol. II, p. 228.

25. *Ibid.,* p. 241.

26. A classic case for interdependence is provided by Robert O. Keohane and Joseph S. Nye, *Power and Interdependence,* 2nd. ed. (Boston: Scott, Foresman and Co., 1989), while the neorealist case for independence is most forcefully enunciated by Kenneth N. Waltz, *Theory of International Politics* (New York: Random House, 1979).

27. Lieber, *Miscellaneous Writings,* Vol. II, p. 223.

28. *Ibid.,* pp. 322–329.

29. Theodore D. Woolsey, *Introduction to the Study of International Law Designed As An Aid in Teaching and in Historical Studies,* 4th ed. (Littleton, Colo.: Fred B. Rothman and Co., 1981; first edition, 1860), p. 49.

30. *Ibid.,* pp. 18–19.

31. *Ibid.,* p. 19.

32. *Ibid.,* p. 29.

33. *Ibid.,* p. 356.

34. For general information on the founding of the School of Political Science, see Ralph Gordon Hoxie, ed., *A History of the Faculty of Political Science, Columbia University* (New York: Columbia University Press, 1950); Haddow, *Political Science in American Colleges and Universities,* pp. 178–182; Somit and

Tanenhaus, *The Development of American Political Science,* pp. 16–21; and Ross, *The Origins of American Social Science,* pp. 68–77.

35. Although disciplinary historians of political science such as Somit and Tanenhaus, Farr, and others make the claim that the formation of the School represented the culmination of the "prehistory" period, this is an especially contentious claim with respect to the field of international relations.

36. Gunnell, *The Descent of Political Theory,* p. 36.

37. John W. Burgess, "The Founding of the School of Political Science," *Columbia University Quarterly* (Vol. 22, No. 4, 1930): p. 352.

38. Hoxie, *A History of the Faculty of Political Science Columbia University,* p. 15.

39. John W. Burgess, "The Study of the Political Sciences in Columbia College," *The International Review* (Vol. 12, 1882): p. 348.

40. *Ibid.,* pp. 347–348.

41. John W. Burgess, "Political Science and History," *The American Historical Review* (Vol. 2, No. 3, 1897): p. 408.

42. *Ibid.,* p. 404.

43. *Ibid.,* p. 404.

44. John W. Burgess, *The Foundations of Political Science* (New York: Columbia University Press, 1933), p. 56.

45. For an interesting account of Burgess's view of the state, and particularly the German state, see Ido Oren, "The Subjectivity of the 'Democratic' Peace: Changing U.S. Perceptions of Imperial Germany," *International Security* (Vol. 20, No. 2, 1995).

46. Munroe Smith, "Introduction: The Domain of Political Science," *Political Science Quarterly* (Vol. 1, No. 1, 1886) pp. 2–3.

47. *Ibid.,* p. 8.

48. See Max Weber, "Science As a Vocation," in H.H. Gerth and C. Wright Mills, *From Max Weber: Essays in Sociology* (New York: Oxford University Press, 1948).

49. Haddow, *Political Science in American Colleges and Universities,* p. 183.

50. See Charles E. Merriam, "Recent Advances in Political Methods," *American Political Science Review* (Vol. 17, No. 2, 1923).

51. Lepawsky, "The Politics of Epistemology," p. 22.

52. Biographical information on Herbert Baxter Adams is provided by John Martin Vincent, "Herbert B. Adams," in Howard W. Odum, ed., *American Masters of Social Science* (Port Washington, N.Y.: Kennikat Press, 1965).

53. Richard Little, "The Evolution of International Relations as a Social Science," in R.C. Kent and G.P. Nielsson, eds., *The Study and Teaching of International Relations* (London: Frances Pinter, 1980), p. 9.

54. Recent discussions of Thucydides include Michael W. Doyle, "Thucydidean Realism," *Review of International Studies* (Vol. 16, No. 3, 1990), and Daniel Garst, "Thucydides and Neorealism," *International Studies Quarterly* (Vol. 33, No.1, 1989).

55. Little, "The Evolution of International Relations as a Social Science," p. 9.

56. Woolsey, *Introduction to the Study of International Law Designed As An Aid in Teaching and in Historical Studies,* p. 47.

57. T.J. Lawrence, *The Principles of International Law,* 7th edition (Boston: D.C. Heath & Co., 1923; first edition, 1895), p. vi.

58. *Ibid.,* p. 11.

59. See George Grafton Wilson, *International Law,* 9th edition (New York: Silver, Burdett and Company, 1935; editions 1901–1917, with George Fox Tucker).

60. *Ibid.,* p. 9. Emphasis in the original.

61. F.H. Hinsley, *Sovereignty,* 2nd edition (Cambridge: Cambridge University Press, 1986), p. 2.

62. John Austin, *The Province of Jurisprudence Determined and the Uses of the Study of Jurisprudence* (New York: The Noonday Press, 1954), p. 78.

63. *Ibid.,* p. 139.

64. John Bassett Moore, review of *The Science of International Law,* by Thomas Alfred Walker, in *Political Science Quarterly* (Vol. 8, No. 2, 1893): p. 369.

65. See Francis Anthony Boyle, *World Politics and International Law* (Durham: Duke University Press, 1985), p. 20. For a discussion of the level-of-analysis problem, see J. David Singer, "The Level-of-Analysis Problem in International Relations," in James N. Rosenau, ed., *International Politics and Foreign Policy* (New York: Free Press, 1969), and Kenneth N. Waltz, *Man, the State and War: A Theoretical Analysis* (New York: Columbia University Press, 1959).

66. See Henry Sumner Maine, *Ancient Law, Its Connection with Early History and Its Relation to Modern Ideas,* 4th edition (London: Murray, 1930).

67. Thomas Hobbes, *Leviathon,* edit. with an introduction by C.B. Macpherson (New York: Penguin Books, 1985), p. 188.

68. See John Bassett Moore, *History and Digest of International Arbitrations to Which the United States Has Been a Party,* 6 vols. (Washington, D.C.: Government Printing Office, 1898).

69. Hoxie, *A History of the Faculty of Political Science, Columbia University,* p. 264.

70. Heinrich von Treitschke, *Politics,* in M.G. Forsyth, ed., *The Theory of International Relations,* p. 326.

71. *Ibid.*, pp. 328, 335.

72. John W. Burgess, "The Ideal of the American Commonwealth," *Political Science Quarterly* (Vol. 10, No. 3, 1895) p. 406.

73. John W. Burgess, *Reminiscences of an American Scholar* (New York: Columbia University Press, 1934), pp. 254–255.

74. The following articles appeared in *Political Science Quarterly* (Vol. 11, No. 1, 1896): John Bassett Moore, "The Monroe Doctrine"; Frederic Bancroff, "The French in Mexico and the Monroe Doctrine"; and John W. Burgess, "The Recent Pseudo-Monroeism."

75. Additional evidence in support of this claim can be found in Haddow, *Political Science in American Colleges*, p. 211; *Goals for Political Science* (New York: William Sloane Assoc., Inc., 1951), p. 46; Merle Curti and Vernon Carstensen, *The University of Wisconsin: A History, 1848–1925*, Vol. I (Madison: University of Wisconsin Press, 1949), pp. 630–638.

76. Olson and Groom, *International Relations Then and Now*, p. 47.

77. Biographical information is provided by Noel H. Pugach, *Paul S. Reinsch: Open Door Diplomat in Action* (Millwood, N.Y.: KTO Press, 1979).

78. Paul S. Reinsch, *World Politics At the End of the Nineteenth Century, As Influenced by the Oriental Situation* (New York: Macmillan Company, 1900), p. v.

79. See Pugach, *Paul S. Reinsch: Open Door Diplomat*, pp. 11–12, and William R. Shepherd, review of *World Politics At the End of the Nineteenth Century*, in *Political Science Quarterly* (Vol. 15, No. 3, 1900): pp. 719–722.

80. Reinsch, *World Politics At the End of the Nineteenth Century*, p. 6.

81. Olson and Groom, *International Relations Then and Now*, p. 47.

82. Reinsch, *World Politics At the End of the Nineteenth Century*, p. 14.

83. *Ibid.*, p. 16.

84. *Ibid.*, p. 69.

85. See Frederick Jackson Turner, "The Significance of the Frontier in American History," American Historical Association, *Annual Report for the Year 1893* (Washington, 1894).

86. Paul S. Reinsch, *Colonial Government: An Introduction to the Study of Colonial Institutions* (New York: Macmillan Co., 1902), p. 60.

87. See Paul S. Reinsch, review of *Imperialism: A Study*, by John A. Hobson, in *Political Science Quarterly* (Vol. 18, No. 3, 1903): pp. 531–533.

88. John A. Hobson, *Imperialism: A Study* (Ann Arbor: The University of Michigan Press, 1965; original edition, 1902), p. 88.

89. Reinsch, review of *Imperialism: A Study*, pp. 532–533.

90. V.I. Lenin, *Imperialism: The Highest Stage of Capitalism* (New York: International Publishers, 1939), p. 89.

91. Reinsch, *World Politics At the End of the Nineteenth Century,* p. 43.

State, Sovereignty, and International Law

1. Westel Woodbury Willoughby, "Political Science As A University Study," *Sewanee Review* (Vol. XIV, No. 3, 1906): p. 258.

2. Paul S. Reinsch, "The American Political Science Association," *The Iowa Journal of History and Politics* (Vol. 2, 1904): p. 156.

3. *Ibid.,* p. 155.

4. "Constitution of the American Political Science Association," *Proceedings of the American Political Science Association* (Vol. 1, 1904): p. 16.

5. Frank J. Goodnow, "The Work of the American Political Science Association," *Proceedings of the American Political Science Association* (Vol. 1, 1904): p. 35.

6. *Ibid.,* p. 36.

7. *Ibid.,* p. 37.

8. Stephen Leacock, *Elements of Political Science* (Boston: Houghton, Mifflin and Company, 1906), p. 12.

9. Westel Woodbury Willoughby, "The American Political Science Association," *Political Science Quarterly* (Vol. 19, No. 1, 1904): p. 108.

10. Raymond Garfield Gettell, *Introduction to Political Science* (Boston: Ginn and Company, 1910), pp. 12–13.

11. *Ibid.,* p. 14.

12. Leacock, *Elements of Political Science,* p. 89.

13. I should be clear what I mean by the *domestic analogy.* Most fundamentally, the domestic analogy conveys the idea that the condition of sovereign states in the international arena can be likened to the condition that social contract thinkers such as Locke, Rousseau, and especially Hobbes, described of individuals living in a state a nature, which is explained as a hypothetical tract of time before the emergence of political society. According to the analogy, one of the crucial similarities between state of nature amongst states and amongst individuals is the absence of central authority. For a similar explanation as well as a critique of the domestic analogy, see Hedley Bull, *The Anarchical Society: A Study of Order in World Politics* (New York: Columbia University Press, 1977), pp. 46–51.

14. Raymond Garfield Gettell, "Nature and Scope of Present Political Theory," *Proceedings of the American Political Science Association* (Vol. 10, 1914): p. 55.

15. *Ibid.,* p. 52.

16. *Ibid.,* pp. 54–55.

17. *Ibid.,* pp. 58–59.

18. Willoughby's contribution to political science is chronicled by James W. Garner, "Westel Woodbury Willoughby: An Evaluation of His Contributions to Political Science," in John Mamby Mathews and James Hart, eds., *Essays in Political Science in Honor of Westel Woodbury Willoughby* (Freeport, N.Y.: Books for Libraries Press, 1937).

19 Westel Woodbury Willoughby, *An Examination of the Nature of the State* (New York: Macmillan and Co., 1896), p. 14.

20. *Ibid.,* p. 185.

21 Westel Woodbury Willoughby, "The Juristic Conception of the State," *American Political Science Review* (Vol. 12, No. 2, 1918): p. 194.

22. *Ibid.,* p. 194.

23. Willoughby, *An Examination of the Nature of the State,* p. 17.

24. *Ibid.,* p. 196.

25. Willoughby, "The Juristic Conception of the State," p. 202.

26. *Ibid.,* p. 207.

27. Willoughby, *An Examination of the Nature of the State,* p. 200.

28. *Ibid.,* p. 409.

29. Biographical information on David Jayne Hill is provided by Aubrey Parkman, *David Jayne Hill and the Problem of World Peace* (Lewisburg, Pa.: Bucknell University Press, 1975).

30. David Jayne Hill, *World Organization As Affected by the Nature of the Modern State* (New York: Columbia University Press, 1911), p. 54.

31. *Ibid.,* p. 24.

32. See David Jayne Hill, *The People's Government* (New York: D. Appleton and Company, 1915).

33. Hill, *World Organization,* p. 1.

34. *Ibid.,* p. 15.

35. This paper was published in the *Yale Law Journal* under the title "International Justice" (Vol. 6, No. 1, 1896).

36. *Ibid.,* pp. 3–5.

37. David Jayne Hill, "The Second Peace Conference at the Hague," *American Journal of International Law* (Vol. 1, No. 3, 1907): p. 690.

38. *Ibid.,* p. 679.

39. See David Jayne Hill, *Present Problems in Foreign Policy* (New York: D. Appleton and Co., 1919), and *The Rebuilding of Europe,* A Survey of Forces and Conditions (New York: Century and Co., 1917).

40. Francis W. Cocker, review of *World Organization As Affected by the Nature of the Modern State,* by David Jayne Hill, in *American Political Science Review* (Vol. 7, No. 2, 1912).

41. For additional information concerning the Americanization of political science, see Albert Somit and Joseph Tanenhaus, *The Development of American Political Science* (New York: Irvington Publishers, 1982), and Dwight Waldo, "Political Science: Tradition, Discipline, Profession, Science, Enterprise," in Fred I. Greenstein and Nelson W. Polsby, eds., *Handbook of Political Science,* Vol. I (Reading, Mass.: Addison-Wesley Publishing Co., 1975).

42. For example, see Charles Merriam, *New Aspects of Politics* (Chicago: University of Chicago Press, 1925), and "The Present State of the Study of Politics," *American Political Science Review* (Vol. 15, No. 2, 1921).

43. See the historical account provided by James Farr, "Remembering the Revolution: Behavioralism in American Political Science," in James Farr, John S. Dryzek, and Stephen T. Leonard, eds., *Political Science in History: Research Programs and Political Traditions* (Cambridge: Cambridge University Press, 1995).

44. James Bryce, "The Relations of Political Science To History and To Practice," *American Political Science Review* (Vol. 3, No. 1, 1909): p. 9.

45. *Ibid.,* p. 10.

46. *Ibid.,* p. 16.

47. For an informative biography, see Ellen Nore, *Charles A. Beard: An Intellectual Biography* (Carbondale: Southern Illinois University Press, 1983).

48. Charles A. Beard, "Politics," in James Farr and Raymond Seidelman, eds., *Discipline and History* (Ann Arbor: University of Michigan Press, 1993), p. 115. This is a shortened version of "A Lecture Delivered at Columbia University in the Series on Science, Philosophy, and Art, February 12, 1908." (New York: Columbia University Press, 1908).

49. *Ibid.,* pp. 117–118.

50. *Ibid.,* p. 119.

51. For information on John Dewey, see Dorothy Ross, *The Origins of American Social Science* (Cambridge: Cambridge University Press, 1991), pp. 162–171, and George Dykhuizen, *The Life and Mind of John Dewey* (Carbondale: Southern Illinois University Press, 1973).

52. John Dewey, "Austin's Theory of Sovereignty," *Political Science Quarterly* (Vol. 9, No. 1, 1894): p. 41.

53. See Harold J. Laski, *Authority in the Modern State* (New Haven: Yale University Press, 1919), and *Studies in the Problem of Sovereignty* (New Haven: Yale University Press, 1917).

54. See Charles G. Haines, "Is Suffient Time Devoted to the Study of Government in Our Colleges?" *Proceedings of the American Political Science Association* (Vol. 7, 1910).

55. See "Report of Committee of Seven on Instruction in Colleges and Universities," *American Political Science Review* (Vol. 9, No. 2, 1915).

56. Edith Ware, *The Study of International Relations in the United States; Survey for 1937* (New York: Columbia University Press, 1938), p. 26.

57. James Brown Scott, "Editorial Comment," *American Journal of International Law* (Vol. 1, No. 1, 1907): p. 133.

58. Francis Anthony Boyle, *World Politics and International Law* (Durham: Duke University Press, 1985), p. 23.

59. Robert Lansing, "Notes On Sovereignty in a State," *American Journal of International Law* (Vol. 1, No. 2, 1907): p. 298. Emphasis in the original.

60. *Ibid.,* p. 305.

61. *Ibid.,* p. 300.

62. James Brown Scott, "The Legal Nature of International Law," *American Journal of International Law* (Vol. 1, No. 4, 1907) p. 838.

63. *Ibid.,* p. 839.

64. John Bassett Moore, "Law and Organization," *American Political Science Review* (Vol. 9, No. 1, 1915): p. 4.

65. Scott, "The Legal Nature of International Law," p. 845.

66. Elihu Root, "The Sanction of International Law," *American Journal of International Law* (Vol. 2, No. 3, 1908): pp. 452–453.

67. Lassa Oppenheim, "The Science of International Law: Its Task and Method," *American Journal of International Law* (Vol. 2, No. 2, 1908): p. 314.

68. *Ibid.,* p. 333.

69. *Ibid.,* p. 334.

70. *Ibid.,* p. 314.

71. Boyle, *World Politics and International Law,* p. 22.

72. *Ibid.,* p. 28.

73. Oppenheim, "The Science of International Law," p. 322.

74. See Alfred Thayer Mahan, *Armaments and Arbitration, or the Place of Force in the International Relations of States* (New York: Harper and Brothers, 1912).

75. The formal details of the Hague Conferences are chronicled by James Brown Scott, *The Hague Peace Conferences of 1899 and 1907,* 2 vols. (Baltimore: Johns Hopkins University Press, 1909).

76. For example, see *Ibid.*, and William I. Hull, *The Two Hague Conferences and their Contributions to International Law* (Boston: Gin & Co., 1908).

77. For an excellent intellectual history of the early-twentieth-century American peace movement, see Warren F. Kuehl, *Seeking World Order: The United States and International Organization to 1920* (Nashville: Vanderbuilt University Press, 1969).

78. Raymond L. Bridgman, "World-Sovereignty Already a Fact," *The Advocate of Peace* (Vol. LXIX, April 1907): p. 84.

79. Benjamin F. Trueblood, *The Federation of the World* (Boston: Houghton, Mifflin, and Company, 1899), p. 145.

80. Hull, *The Two Hague Conferences*, p. 497.

81. Nicholas Murray Butler, *The International Mind* (New York: Charles Scribner's Sons, 1912), p. 4.

82. *Ibid.*, p. 102.

83. Philip Marshall Brown, "The Theory of the Independence and Equality of States," *American Journal of International Law* (Vol. 9, No. 2, 1915): p. 324.

84. Alpheus Henry Snow, "International Law and Political Science," *American Journal of International Law* (Vol. 7, No. 2, 1913): p. 315.

85. *Ibid.*, pp. 315–316.

86. *Ibid.*, p. 318.

87. *Ibid.*, p. 319.

88. Paul S. Reinsch, "International Unions and their Administration," *American Journal of International Law* (Vol. 1, No. 3, 1907): p. 579.

89. Paul S. Reinsch, *Public International Unions Their Work and Organization: A Study in International Administrative Law* (Boston: Ginn and Company, 1911), pp. 2–4.

90. See Craig N. Murphy, *International Organization and Industrial Change: Global Governance Since 1850* (Oxford: Oxford University Press, 1994).

91. See Stephen D. Krasner, ed., *International Regimes* (Ithaca: Cornell University Press, 1983).

92. Reinsch, *Public Intenational Unions*, p. 5.

93. See Murphy, *International Organization and Industrial Change*, p. 17.

94. Reinsch, *Public International Unions*, p. 10.

Anarchy Within: Colonial Administration and Imperialism

1. Henry C. Morris, "Discussion," *Proceedings of the American Political Science Association* (Vol. 1, 1904): p. 140.

2. Martin Wight, *International Theory: The Three Traditions,* Gabriel Wight and Brian Porter, eds. (New York: Holmes and Meier, 1992), p. 50.

3. Mary O. Furner, *Advocacy and Objectivity: A Crisis in the Professionalization of American Social Science, 1865–1905* (Lexington: The University Press of Kentucky, 1975), p. 287.

4. Woodrow Wilson, "The Study of Administration," *Political Science Quarterly* (Vol. 2, No. 2, 1888): p. 197.

5. Frank J. Goodnow, "The Work of the American Political Science Association," *Proceedings of the American Political Science Association* (Vol. I, 1904): p. 42.

6. Henry Jones Ford, "The Scope of Political Science," *Proceedings of the American Political Science Association* (Vol. II, 1905): p. 198.

7. *Ibid.,* p. 200.

8. *Ibid.,* p. 203.

9. Westel Woodbury Willoughby, *An Examination of the Nature of the State* (New York: Macmillan and Co., 1896), p. 196.

10. T.J. Lawrence, *The Principles of International Law,* Seventh Edition (Boston: D.C. Heath and Co., 1923), p. 1.

11. Richard Olney, "The Development of International Law," *American Journal of International Law* (Vol. 1, No. 2, 1907): p. 421.

12. Alpheus Henry Snow, "The Law of Nations," *American Journal of International Law* (Vol. 6, No. 4, 1912): p. 894.

13. Alpheus Henry Snow, "Neutralization Versus Imperialism," *American Journal of International Law* (Vol. 2, No. 3, 1908): p. 590.

14. Stephen Leacock, *Elements of Political Science* (Boston: Houghton, Mifflin and Company, 1906), p. 259.

15. Raymond Garfield Gettell, *Introduction to Political Science* (Boston: Ginn and Company, 1910), p. 348.

16. See John Burgess, "The Relation of the Constitution of the US to the Newly Acquired Territory," *Political Science Quarterly* (Vol. 15, No. 1, 1900).

17. Alpheus Henry Snow, "The Question of Terminology," *Proceedings of the American Political Science Association* (Vol. 3, 1906): p. 226.

18. John W. Burgess, *The Foundations of Political Science* (New York: Columbia University Press, 1933), p. 47.

19. See John W. Burgess, "How May the US Govern its Extra-Continental Territory?" *Political Science Quarterly* (Vol. 14, No. 1, 1899).

20. Henry C. Morris, "Some Effects of Outlying Dependencies Upon the People of the United States," *Proceedings of the American Political Science Association* (Vol. 3, 1906): p. 195.

21. *Ibid.,* p. 198.

22. Paul S. Reinsch, *Colonial Government* (New York: Macmillan Company, 1902), p. 15.

23. *Ibid.,* p. 86.

24. Paul S. Reinsch, "Colonial Autonomy, With Special Reference to the Government of the Philippine Islands," *Proceedings of the American Political Science Association* (Vol. 1, 1904): p. 116.

25. Alleyne Ireland, "On the Need for a Scientific Study of Colonial Administration," *Proceedings of the American Political Science Association* (Vol. 3, 1906): p. 210.

26. *Ibid.,* p. 214.

27. *Ibid.,* p. 214.

28. See Henry C. Morris, review of *Colonization: A Study of the Founding of New Societies,* by Albert Galloway Keller, in *American Political Science Review* (Vol. 3, No. 3, 1909): p. 472.

29. Ireland, "On the Need for a Scientific Study of Colonial Administration," p. 217.

30. Wilson, "The Study of Administration," p. 45.

31. *Ibid.,* p. 45.

32. Morris, "Discussion," p. 140.

33. Morris, "Some Effects of Outlying Dependencies Upon the People of the United States," p. 206.

34. Reinsch, *Colonial Government,* p. 13.

35. Howard J. Rodgers, ed., *Congress of Arts and Science,* Vol. I (Boston: Houghton, Mifflin and Co., 1906), p. 3.

36. The Department of Politics division included: Political Theory and National Administration, Diplomacy, Colonial Administration, and Municipal Administration.

37. Bernard Moses, "The Control of Dependencies Inhabited by the Less Developed Races," in Rodgers, ed., *Congress of Arts and Science,* Vol. 7, p. 388.

38. Paul S. Reinsch, "The Problems of Colonial Administration," in Rodgers, ed., *Congress of Arts and Sciences,* Vol. 7, p. 399.

39. *Ibid.,* p. 403.

40. Frank J. Goodnow, review of *Colonial Administration,* by Paul S. Reinsch, in *Political Science Quarterly* (Vol. 21, No. 1, 1906): p. 135.

41. Reinsch, "The Problems of Colonial Administration," p. 412.

42. Reinsch, *Colonial Government*, p. 109.

43. Westel Woodbury Willoughby, "Discussion," *Proceedings of the American Political Science Association* (Vol. 1, 1904): p. 142.

44. Moses, "The Control of Dependencies Inhabited by the Less Developed Races," p. 393.

45. *Ibid.*, pp. 394–395.

46. William A. Dunning, "The Fundamental Conceptions of Nineteenth-Century Politics," in Rodgers, ed., *Congress of Arts and Science*, p. 290.

47. P.H. Kerr, "Political Relations Between Advanced and Backward Peoples," in *An Introduction to the Study of International Relations* (London: Macmillan and Co., 1916), pp. 141–143.

48. *Ibid.*, p. 165.

49. *Ibid.*, p. 179.

50. Franklin H. Giddings, "Imperialism?" *Political Science Quarterly* (Vol. 13, No. 4, 1898): p. 586.

51. *Ibid.*, pp. 590–591.

52. Ibid., p. 600.

53. Benjamin Kidd, *The Control of the Tropics* (New York: Macmillan Co., 1898), p. 15.

54. *Ibid.*, p. 18.

55. *Ibid.*, p. 46.

56. V.I. Lenin, *Imperialism: The Highest Stage of Capitalism* (New York: International Publishers, 1939), p. 78.

57. *Ibid.*, p. 98

58. Norman Angell, *The Great Illusion*, 3rd edition (New York: G.P. Putnam's Sons, 1911), p. 36.

59. Amos S. Hershey, review of *The Great Illusion*, by Norman Angell, in *American Political Science Review* (Vol. 5, No. 2, 1911): p. 312.

60. Angell, *The Great Illusion*, pp. 50, 129.

61. John A. Hobson, "The Scientific Basis of Imperialism," *Political Science Quarterly* (Vol. 17, No. 3, 1902): p. 461.

62. *Ibid.*, p. 469.

63. *Ibid.*, p. 487.

64. Walter Lippmann, *The Stakes of Diplomacy* (New York: Henry Holt and Company, 1915), pp. 87–88.

65. *Ibid.,* p. 127.

66. *Ibid.,* p. 113.

67. *Ibid.,* p. 144.

International Anarchy and the Critique of Sovereignty

1. E.H. Carr, *The Twenty Years' Crisis, 1919–1939: An Introduction to the Study of International Politics,* 2nd ed. (New York: Harper & Row Publishers, 1964), p. 1.

2. *Ibid.,* p. 8.

3. Information about the Chair that was established at Aberystwyth can be found in Ieuan John, Moorhead Wright, and John Garnett, "International Politics at Aberystwyth, 1919–1969," in Brian Porter, ed., *The Aberystwyth Papers: International Politics 1919–1969* (London: Oxford University Press, 1972).

4. Brian Porter, "David Davies: A Hunter After Peace," *Review of International Studies* (Vol. 15, No. 1, 1989): p. 27.

5. Ieuan John, Moorhead Wright, and John Garnett, "International Politics at Aberystwyth, 1919–1969," p. 87.

6. James T. Shotwell, "Introduction," in Farrell Symons, *Courses On International Affairs in American Colleges, 1930–31* (Boston: World Peace Foundation, 1931), p. xii.

7. Farrell Symons, *Courses On International Affairs in American Colleges, 1930–31,* p. xv.

8. Sir Alfred Zimmern, *University Teaching of International Relations* (Paris: International Institute of Intellectual Co-operation, 1939), pp. 7–9.

9. Charles K. Webster, *The Study of International Politics* (Cardiff: The University of Wales Press Board, 1923), p. 6.

10. Symons, *Courses On International Affairs in American Colleges,* pp. xv–xvi. The other twelve categories included: Asia and Africa, British Empire, Contemporary History, Europe, Far East, Foreign Relations of the United States, International Economics, Latin America, National Governments and Problems, Near East, World War and After, and Miscellaneous.

11. These are the numbers that I derived from Symons's work. Other references to his work provide different numbers. Grayson Kirk, for example, writes that Symons's "survey of 465 colleges and universities indicated that some 264 courses on international relations, 234 on international law, and 75 on international organization were available for American College Students." See Grayson Kirk, *The Study of International Relations in American Colleges and Universities* (New York: Council on Foreign Relations, 1947), p. 6.

12. Parker T. Moon, *Syllabus On International Relations* (New York: Macmillan Co., 1925), p. v.

13. For additional information on some of the early texts in the field, including a model table of contents, see William C. Olson and A.J.R. Groom, *International Relations Then and Now: Origins and Trends in Interpretation* (London: HarperCollins, 1991), pp. 68–70, 130.

14. Edward Raymond Turner, "War Literature," *American Political Science Review* (Vol. 9, No. 1, 1915): p. 142. Also, see Edward Raymond Turner, "The Causes of the Great War," *American Political Science Review* (Vol. 9, No. 1, 1915).

15. Edwin R.A. Seligman, "An Economic Interpretation of the War," in *Problems of Readjustment After the War* (New York: D. Appleton and Co., 1915), p. 37.

16. *Ibid.*, p. 52.

17. *Ibid.*, p. 62.

18. See Ralph Gordon Hoxie, ed., *A History of the Faculty of Political Science, Columbia University* (New York: Columbia University Press, 1955), p. 266.

19. James T. Shotwell, *The Autobiography of James T. Shotwell* (Indianapolis: Bobbs-Merrill Co., 1961), p. 43.

20. See Charles A. Beard, *The Devil Theory of War: An Inquiry into the Nature of History and the Possibility of Keeping Out of War* (New York: Vanguard Press, 1936).

21. James Bryce, *International Relations* (Port Washington, N.Y.: Kennikat Press, Inc., 1922), pp. iv–2.

22. *Ibid.*, p. 3.

23. *Ibid.*, pp. 5–6.

24. *Ibid.*, p. 112.

25. The classic elucidation of the security dilemma is often attributed to John Herz, "Idealist Internationalism and the Security Dilemma," *World Politics* (Vol. 2, No. 2, 1950).

26. Biographical information about G. Lowes Dickinson is provided by Catherine Ann Cline in the "Introduction," to G. Lowes Dickinson, *Causes of International War* (New York: Garland Publishing, Inc., 1920; reprint, 1972).

27. *Ibid.*, p. 21.

28. Dickinson, *Causes of International War*, p. 90.

29. *Ibid.*, p. 16.

30. G. Lowes Dickinson, *The European Anarchy* (New York: Macmillan Company, 1916), p. 13.

31. *Ibid.,* p. 14.

32. James W. Garner, review of *International Anarchy, 1904–1914,* by G. Lowes Dickinson, in *American Political Science Review* (Vol. 20, No. 4, 1926): p. 887.

33. G. Lowes Dickinson, *International Anarchy, 1904–1914* (New York: Century Co., 1926), p. 3.

34. *Ibid.,* p. v.

35. *Ibid.,* p. v.

36. *Ibid.,* p. 478.

37. Westel Woodbury Willoughby, "The Prussian Theory of the State," *American Journal of International Law* (Vol. 12, No. 2, 1918): p. 251.

38. *Ibid.,* p. 257.

39. Charles Merriam, "Recent Tendencies in Political Thought," in Charles Merriam and Harry Elmer Barnes, eds., *A History of Political Theories: Recent Times* (New York: Macmillan Company, 1924), p. 24.

40. Westel Woodbury Willoughby, "Relation of the Individual to the State," in *Problems of Readjustment After the War,* p. 98.

41. The impact that the theory of pluralism had on political science is discussed by John G. Gunnell in "The Genealogy of American Pluralism: From Madison to Behavioralism," *International Political Science Review* (Vol. 17, No. 3, 1996), and "The Declination of the 'State' and the Origins of American Pluralism," in James Farr, John S. Dryzek, and Stephen T. Leonard, eds., *Political Science in History: Research Programs and Political Traditions* (Cambridge: Cambridge University Press, 1995).

42. Francis W. Coker, "Pluralistic Theories and the Attack Upon State Sovereignty," in Merriam and Barnes, eds., *A History of Political Theories,* p. 80.

43. Ellen Deborah Ellis, "The Pluralistic State," *American Political Science Review* (Vol. 14, No. 3, 1920): p. 399.

44. Raymond Garfield Gettell, *History of Political Thought* (New York: Century Co., 1924), p. 470.

45. The ideas of some of these figures are discussed in David Nicholls, *The Pluralist State: The Political Ideas of J.N. Figgis and his Contemporaries,* 2nd ed. (New York: St. Martin's Press, 1994).

46. Coker, "Pluralistic Theories and the Attack Upon State Sovereignty," p. 83.

47. George Sabine, "Pluralism: A Point of View," *American Political Science Review* (Vol. 17, No. 1, 1923): p. 34.

48. Harold J. Laski, *The Foundations of Sovereignty and Other Essays* (New York: Harcourt, Brace and Co., 1921), p. 240.

49. Harold J. Laski, "International Government and National Soveriegnty," in *The Problems of Peace* (London: Oxford University Press, 1927), p. 292.

50. *Ibid.*, p. 292

51. Gettell, *History of Political Thought*, p. 468.

52. Bruce Williams, "State Morality in International Relations," *American Political Science Review* (Vol. 17, No. 1, 1923): p. 17.

53. *Ibid.*, p. 22.

54. Laski, *The Foundations of Sovereignty and Other Essays*, pp. 241–242.

55. Mary Parker Follett, *The New State: Group Organization the Solution of Popular Sovereignty* (London: Longmans, Green and Co., 1934; first edition, 1918), p. 3.

56. See William Yandell Elliott, "The Pragmatic Politics of Mr. H. J. Laski," *American Political Science Review* (Vol. 18, 1924), and "Sovereign State or Sovereign Group?" *American Political Science Review* (Vol. 19, 1925).

57. Follett, *The New State*, p. 271.

58. *Ibid.*, p. 344.

59. *Ibid.*, p. 351.

60. *Ibid.*, p. 345.

61. *Ibid.*, p. 348.

62. *Ibid.*, pp. 351–352.

63. *Ibid.*, p. 354.

64. Laski, "International Government and National Sovereignty," p. 290.

65. Gettell, *History of Political Thought*, p. 470.

66. *Ibid.*, p. 466.

67. Sabine, "Pluralism: A Point of View," p. 43.

68. *Ibid.*, pp. 43, 49.

69. James W. Garner, "Limitations on National Sovereignty in International Relations," *American Political Science Review* (Vol. 19, No. 1, 1925): p. 18.

70. *Ibid.*, pp. 23–24.

71. *Ibid.*, pp. 22–25.

72. Edwin DeWitt Dickinson, *The Equality of States in International Law* (Cambridge: Harvard University Press, 1920), p. 6.

73. William A. Dunning, "Liberty and Equality in International Relations," *American Political Science Review* (Vol. 17, No. 1, 1923): p. 5.

74. *Ibid.,* p. 6.

75. *Ibid.,* pp. 7–8.

76. *Ibid.,* pp. 10–11.

77. *Ibid.,* p. 15.

78. Frank M. Russell, *Theories of International Relations* (New York: Appleton-Century-Crofts, Inc., 1936), p. vi.

79. F. Melian Stawell, *The Growth of International Thought* (New York: Henry Holt and Co., 1930), p. 7.

80. Russell, *Theories of International Relations,* p. v.

81. *Ibid.,* p. 4.

82. *Ibid.,* p. 544.

83. Walter Sandelius, "National Sovereignty Versus the Rule of Law," *American Political Science Review* (Vol. 25, No. 1, 1931): p. 8.

84. Edwin M. Borchard, "Political Theory and International Law," in Merriam and Barnes, eds., *A History of Political Theories,* p. 122.

85. *Ibid.,* p. 136.

86. See Hugo Krabbe, *The Modern Idea of the State* (New York: D. Appleton and Co., 1922).

87. Borchard, "Political Theory and International Law," p. 130.

88. See Harold J. Laski, *Studies in the Problem of Sovereignty* (New Haven: Yale University Press, 1917).

89. Roscoe Pound, "Philosophical Theory and International Law," in *Bibliotheca Visseriana,* Vol. I (Leyden, 1923), p. 76.

90. *Ibid.,* p. 78.

91. *Ibid.,* p. 89.

92. Sandelius, "National Sovereignty Versus the Rule of Law," p. 1.

93. Harry Elmer Barnes, "Some Contributions of Sociology to Modern Political Theory," *American Political Science Review* (Vol. 15, No. 4, 1921): pp. 532–533.

94. George Grafton Wilson, "The War and International Law," in *Problems of Readjustment After the War,* p. 129.

95. *Ibid.,* p. 134.

96. Philip Marshall Brown, "War and Law," *American Journal of International Law* (Vol. 12, No. 1, 1918): pp. 162–163.

97. *Ibid.,* p. 164.

98. George A. Finch, "The Effect of the War on International Law," *American Journal of International Law* (Vol. 9, No. 2, 1915): p. 475.

99. *Ibid.*, p. 477.

100. Quincy Wright, *Research in International Law Since the War* (Washington: Carnegie Endowment for International Peace, 1930), p. 23.

101. *Ibid.*, p. 24.

102. Elihu Root, "The Outlook for International Law," *American Journal of International Law* (Vol. 10, No. 1, 1916): p. 5.

103. For example, see Walter Lippmann, *The Phantom Public* (New York: Harcourt Brace, 1925); William Bennett Munro, *Invisible Government* (New York: Macmillan, 1928); and John Dewey, *The Public and its Problems* (Boston: Holt, 1927).

104. Root, "The Outlook for International Law," p. 9.

105. George Grafton Wilson, "The Modernization of International Law," *American Political Science Review* (Vol. 19, No. 2, 1925): p. 270.

106. Jesse S. Reeves, "The Justicability of International Disputes," *American Political Science Review* (Vol. 10, No. 1, 1916): p. 70.

107. *Ibid.*, pp. 70–71.

108. *Ibid.*, p. 72.

109. *Ibid.*, p. 79.

110. Charles G. Fenwick, "Notes on International Affairs," *American Political Science Review* (Vol. 14, No. 3, 1920): pp. 483–484.

111. Charles G. Fenwick, "Notes on International Affairs," *American Political Science Review* (Vol. 12, No. 2, 1918): p. 303.

112. Charles G. Fenwick, *International Law,* 2nd ed. (New York: D. Appleton-Century Company, 1934; first edition, 1924), p. ix.

International Organization and International Politics

1. J. Martin Rochester, "The Rise and Fall of International Organization as a Field of Study," *International Organization* (Vol. 40, No. 4, 1986): p. 690.

2. The literature on the subject of international organization is enormous. For a general introduction, see Stephen D. Krasner, ed., *International Regimes* (Ithaca: Cornell University Press, 1983); Friedrich Kratochwil and John Gerard Ruggie, "International Organization: A State of the Art on an Art of the State," *International Organization* (Vol. 40, No. 4, 1986); and Friedrich Kratochwil and Edward D. Mansfield, eds., *International Organization: A Reader* (New York: HarperCollins, 1994).

3. For example, see Philip Marshall Brown, *International Society: Its Nature and Interests* (New York: Macmillan Co., 1923); T.J. Lawrence, *The Society of Nations: Its Past, Present, and Possible Future* (New York: Oxford University Press, 1919); S.H. Bailey, *The Framework of International Society* (New York: Longmans, Green and Co., 1932); and Felix Morely, *The Society of Nations: Its Organization and Constitutional Development* (Washington, D.C.: The Brookings Institution, 1932).

4. Brown, *International Society*, p. ix.

5. Lawrence, *The Society of Nations*, p. vi.

6. *Ibid.*, pp. 5–8.

7. Brown, *International Society*, p. 165.

8. Woodrow Wilson, "The Fourteen Points," in John A. Vasquez, ed., *Classics of International Relations* (Englewood Cliffs, N.J.: Prentice-Hall, 1986), p. 19.

9. For background information on Woodrow Wilson's life and work, see Niels Aage Thorsen, *The Political Thought of Woodrow Wilson* (Princeton: Princeton University Press, 1988), and David Steigerwald, *Wilsonian Idealism in America* (Ithaca: Cornell University Press, 1994).

10. For an excellent account of the individuals and issues that shaped the peace movement of this period, see Warren F. Kuehl, *Seeking World Order: The United States and International Organization to 1920* (Nashville: Vanderbilt University Press, 1969).

11. John A. Hobson, *Towards International Government* (New York: Macmillan Co., 1916), p. 117.

12. The platform that was adopted by the League to Enforce Peace contained four resolutions: one, that it is the opinion of those present that it is desirable for the United States to form a League of all the great nations in which all justiciable questions between them would be submitted to a judicial tribunal; two, that members of the league shall jointly use their military force to prevent any one of their number from going to war or committing acts of hostility against any member before the question at issue has been submitted to the tribunal; three, that nations shall be compelled to submit non-justiciable questions to a Council of Conciliation before going to war, under the same penalty as provided above; four, that conferences between the parties to this agreement shall be held from time to time to formulate and to codify rules of international law which, unless some nation shall signify its dissent within a stated period, shall thereafter govern in the decision of the aforementioned tribunal. See Kuehl, *Seeking World Order*, p. 190 and pp. 184–192, 214–240.

13. *Enforced Peace: Proceedings of the First Annual National Assemblage of the League to Enforce Peace*, Washington, May 26–27, 1916, (New York: League to Enforce Peace, 1916) p. 160.

14. *Ibid.*, pp. 161–162.

15. *Ibid.*, p. 162.

16. See Nicholas Murray Butler, *The Basis of Durable Peace* (New York: Charles Scribner's Sons, 1917).

17. See David Jayne Hill, *The Rebuilding of Europe: A Survey of Forces and Conditions* (New York: The Century Co., 1917).

18. Stephen Pierce Duggan, ed., *The League of Nations: The Principle and the Practice* (Boston: The Atlantic Monthly Press, 1919), p. v.

19. Frederick Charles Hicks, *The New World Order: International Organization, International Law, International Cooperation* (New York: Doubleday, Page & Co., 1920), p. vi.

20. *Ibid.*, pp. 7–13.

21. *Ibid.*, p. 14.

22. A good biographical retrospective on the life and work of Sir Alfred Zimmern is provided by D.J. Markwell, "Sir Alfred Zimmern: Fifty Years On," *Review of International Studies* (Vol. 12, No. 4, 1986).

23. Alfred Zimmern, *The League of Nations and the Rule of Law* (London: Macmillan and Co., 1936), p. 285.

24. *Ibid.*, p. 4.

25. *Ibid.*, pp. 5–6.

26. *Ibid.*, p. 285.

27. *Ibid.*, p. 278.

28. For examples of some of these descriptions, see Felix Morley, *The Society of Nations;* Stephen Pierce Duggan, ed., *The League of Nations;* William E. Rappard, *The Geneva Experiment* (Oxford: Oxford University Press, 1931); Herbert Brown Ames, "What is the League of Nations?" *American Political Science Review* (Vol. 22, No. 3, 1928); and Charles K. Webster, *The League of Nations in Theory and Practice* (London: Allen and Unwin, 1933).

29. Pitman B. Potter, "Political Science in the International Field," *American Political Science Review* (Vol. 27, No. 3, 1923): p. 383.

30. *Ibid.*, p. 382.

31. *Ibid.*, p. 384.

32. *Ibid.*, p. 385.

33. Pitman B. Potter, *This World of Nations: Foundations, Institutions, Practices* (New York: The Macmillan Co., 1929), p. 13.

34. *Ibid.*, p. 388.

35. *Ibid.*, pp. 388–389.

36. Pitman B. Potter, "International Organization," in *Encyclopaedia of the Social Sciences, Vol. 7* (New York: Macmillan Co., 1933), p. 177.

37. *Ibid.*, p. 179.

38. *Ibid.*, p. 179.

39. Potter, "Political Science in the International Field," p. 389.

40. Potter, *This World of Nations*, p. 11.

41. Potter, "International Organization," p. 178.

42. Pitman B. Potter, "News and Notes," *American Political Science Review* (Vol. 25, No. 3, 1931): p. 714.

43. Pitman B. Potter, "The Classification of International Organizations, II," *American Political Science Review* (Vol. 29, No. 3, 1935): p. 403.

44. Pitman B. Potter, *An Introduction to the Study of International Organization* (New York: The Century Co., 1925), p. 369.

45. *Ibid.*, p. 380.

46. *Ibid.*, p. 381.

47. *Ibid.*, p. 389.

48. *Ibid.*, p. 441.

49. William C. Olson and A.J.R. Groom, *International Relations Then and Now: Origins and Trends in Interpretation* (London: HarperCollins, 1991), p. 79.

50. There is an enormous literature that provides a survey of the central figures of the realist school. See, for example, Joel H. Rosenthal, *Righteous Realists: Political Realism, Responsible Power, and American Culture in the Nuclear Age* (Baton Rouge: Louisiana State University Press, 1991); Michael Joseph Smith, *Realist Thought from Weber to Kissinger* (Baton Rouge: Louisiana State University Press, 1986); and Kenneth W. Thompson, *Masters of International Thought: Major Twentieth Century Theorists and the World Crisis* (Baton Rouge: Louisiana State University Press, 1980).

51. The impact that the German émigrés had on political science as well as most branches of learning was great and there is an extensive literature on this topic. See John G. Gunnell, *The Descent of Political Theory* (Chicago: University of Chicago Press, 1993), pp. 175–198; Lewis A. Coser, *Refugee Scholars in America* (New Haven: Yale University Press, 1984); and Robert Boyers, ed., *The Legacy of the German Refugee Intellectuals* (New York: Schocken, 1972).

52. Francis James Brown, Charles Hodges, and Joseph Slabey Roucek, eds., *Contemporary World Politics: An Introduction to the Problems of International Relations* (New York: John Wiley & Sons, Inc., 1939), pp. vii–viii.

53. Frederick L. Schuman, *International Politics: An Introduction to the Western State System*, 2nd ed. (New York: McGraw-Hill Book Co., 1937), p. xii.

54. The Chicago school's quest as well as the more general attempt on the part of American political scientists to achieve a science of politics is a major theme in the history of the discipline. This theme is discussed by Bernard Crick, *The American Science of Politics* (Berkeley: University of California Press, 1959); David M. Ricci, *The Tragedy of Political Science* (New Haven: Yale University Press, 1984); Raymond Seidelman, *Disenchanted Realists: Political Science and the American Crisis, 1884–1984* (Albany: State University of New York Press, 1985); Albert Somit and Joseph Tanenhaus, *The Development of American Political Science* (Boston: Allyn and Bacon, 1967); Gunnell, *The Descent of Political Theory;* and Derek McDougall, *Harold D. Lasswell and the Study of International Relations* (Lanham: University Press of America, 1984).

55. Charles E. Merriam, "Progress in Political Research," *American Political Science Review* (Vol. 20, No. 1, 1926): p. 12.

56. For a comprehensive account of Lasswell's work, see McDougall, *Harold D. Lasswell and the Study of International Relations.*

57. Harold D. Lasswell, *World Politics and Personal Insecurity* (New York: McGraw-Hill, 1935), p. 3.

58. *Ibid.,* p. 3. Emphasis in the original.

59. Schuman, *International Politics,* pp. xii–xiii.

60. *Ibid.,* p. 37.

61. *Ibid.,* p. 218.

62. *Ibid.,* p. 491.

63. Charles E. Merriam, *New Aspects of Politics* (Chicago: University of Chicago Press, 1925), pp. viii–ix.

64. Harold D. Lasswell, "The Problem of World-Unity: In Quest of a Myth," *International Journal of Ethics* (Vol. 44, 1933): p. 68.

65. William T.R. Fox, *The American Study of International Relations* (Columbia: Institute of International Studies, University of South Carolina, 1967), p. 1.

66. *Ibid.,* pp. 10–12.

67. Grayson Kirk, *The Study of International Relations in American Colleges and Universities* (New York: Council on Foreign Relations, 1947), p. 10.

68. *Ibid.,* p. 4.

69. *Ibid.,* pp. 4–7.

70. Walter R. Sharp and Grayson Kirk, *Contemporary International Politics* (New York: Rinehart & Co., 1944), p. 7. Emphasis in the original.

71. For information on Frederick Sherwood Dunn and the Yale Institute of International Studies, see Fox, *The American Study of International Relations,* pp. 36–56.

72. Frederick S. Dunn, "The Scope of International Relations," *World Politics* (Vol. 1, No. 1, 1948): p. 143.

73. *Ibid.,* p. 144.

74. *Ibid.,* p. 144.

75. *Ibid.,* pp. 144–145.

76. *Ibid.,* p. 145.

77. William C. Olson, "Growth of a Discipline," in Brian Porter, ed., *The Aberystwyth Papers: International Politics 1919–1969* (London: Oxford University Press, 1972), p. 23.

78. For an analysis of Carr's contribution, see Paul Howe, "The Utopian Realism of E.H. Carr," *Review of International Studies* (Vol. 20, No. 3, 1994); Hedley Bull, "The Twenty Years' Crisis Thirty Years On," *International Journal* (Vol. 24, 1969); William T.R. Fox, "E.H. Carr and Political Realism: Vision and Revision," *Review of International Studies* (Vol. 11, No. 1, 1985); and Smith, *Realist Thought from Weber to Kissenger,* pp. 68–98.

79. E.H.Carr, *The Twenty Years' Crisis, 1919–1939: An Introduction to the Study of International Relations,* 2nd ed. (New York: Harper & Row, 1964), p. 8.

80. *Ibid.,* pp. 11–21.

81. *Ibid.,* p. 10.

82. *Ibid.,* p. 27.

83. *Ibid.,* p. 10.

84. *Ibid.,* p. 87.

85 Georg Schwarzenberger, *Power Politics: An Introduction to the Study of International Relations and Post-War Planning* (London: Jonathan Cape, 1941), p. 25.

86. Carr, *The Twenty Years' Crisis, 1919–1939,* p. 93.

87. Frederick Sherwood Dunn, *Peaceful Change: A Study of International Procedures* (New York: Council on Foreign Relations, 1937), p. 2.

88. Carr, *The Twenty Years' Crisis,1919–1939,* p. 222.

89. E.H. Carr, *The Twenty Years' Crisis, 1919–1939,* 1st ed. (London: Macmillan, 1939), p. 282.

90. Hans Morgenthau, "The Political Science of E. H. Carr," *World Politics* (Vol. 1, No. 1, 1948): pp. 133–134.

91. Hans J. Morgenthau, "An Intellectual Autobiography," *Transaction: Social Science and Modern Society* (Vol. 15, No. 2, 1978): p. 65.

92. Hans J. Morgenthau, *Politics Among Nations: The Struggle for Power and Peace,* 2nd ed. (New York: Alfred A. Knopf, 1955), p. 25.

93. *Ibid.*, p. 4.

94. Hans J. Morgenthau, *Scientific Man Versus Power Politics* (Chicago: University of Chicago Press, 1946), p. 85.

95. Many of the articles that shaped the second debate are included in Klaus Knorr and James N. Rosenau, eds., *Contending Approaches to International Politics* (Princeton: Princeton University Press, 1969). This entire episode of the field's history has also been greatly misrepresented. One effort to clarify the real history of this period is provided by Miles Kahler, "Inventing International Relations: International Relations Theory After 1945," in Michael W. Doyle and G. John Ikenberry, eds., *New Directions in International Relations Theory* (Boulder: Westview Press, forthcoming).

96. Morgenthau, *Politics Among Nations*, pp. 25–34.

97. *Ibid.*, p. 205.

98. Morgenthau, *Scientific Man Versus Power Politics*, p. vi.

99. Quincy Wright, "Realism and Idealism in International Politics," *World Politics* (Vol. 5, No. 1, 1952): p. 119.

100. *Ibid.*, p. 120.

101. Leonard Woolf, "Utopia and Reality," *The Political Quarterly* (Vol. 11, No. 2, 1940): pp. 171–172.

Conclusion

1. Michael Banks, "The International Relations Discipline: Asset or Liability for Conflict Resolution?" in Edward E. Azar and John W. Burton, eds., *International Conflict Resolution* (Sussex: Wheatsheaf Books, 1986), p. 11.

2. Charles W. Kegley Jr., "The Neoidealist Moment in International Studies? Realist Myths and the New International Realities," *International Studies Quarterly* (Vol. 37, No. 2, 1993): p. 131.

3. For a general overview of the theory of the democratic peace, see Bruce Russett, *Grasping the Democratic Peace: Principles for a Post–Cold War World* (Princeton: Princeton University Press, 1993); Michael W. Doyle, "Liberalism and World Politics," *American Political Science Review* (Vol. 80, No. 4, 1986); and David Lake, "Powerful Pacifists: Democratic States and War," *American Political Science Review* (Vol. 86, No. 1, 1992).

4. Russett, *Grasping the Democratic Peace*, p. 24.

5. For a general introduction to this controversy, see David A. Baldwin, ed., *Neorealism and Neoliberalism: The Contemporary Debate* (New York: Columbia University Press, 1993), and Charles W. Kegley Jr., ed., *Controversies in International Relations Theory: Realism and the Neoliberal Challenge* (New York: St. Martin's Press, 1995).

6. Charles W. Kegley Jr., "The Neoliberal Challenge to Realist Theories of World Politics: An Introduction," in Kegley, ed., *Controversies in International Relations Theory*, p. 1.

7. David A. Baldwin, "Neoliberalism, Neorealism, and World Politics," in Baldwin, ed., *Neorealism and Neoliberalism*, p. 11.

8. Miles Kahler, "Inventing International Relations: International Relations Theory After 1945," in Michael W. Doyle and G. John Ikenberry, eds., *New Directions in International Relations Theory* (Boulder: Westview Press, forthcoming).

9. Ken Booth, "75 Years On: Rewriting the Subject's Past—Reinventing its Future," in Steve Smith, Ken Booth, and Marysia Zalewski, eds., *International Theory: Positivism and Beyond* (Cambridge: Cambridge University Press, 1996), pp. 328–329.

10. David A. Baldwin, "Security Studies and the End of the Cold War," *World Politics* (Vol. 48, No. 1, 1995): p. 119.

11. See, for example, Alexander Wendt, "Anarchy is What State Make of it: The Social Construction of Power Politics," *International Organization* (Vol. 46, No. 2, 1992); Jonathan Mercer, "Anarchy and Identity," *International Organization* (Vol. 49, No. 2, 1995); and Nicholas Onuf, *World of Our Making: Rules and Rule in Social Theory and International Relations* (Columbia: University of South Carolina Press, 1989).

12. Ronen P. Palan and Brook M. Blair, "On the Idealist Origins of the Realist Theory of International Relations," *Review of International Studies* (Vol. 19, No. 4, 1993): p. 388.

13. G. Lowes Dickinson, *The International Anarchy, 1904–1914* (New York: The Century Co., 1926), p. v.

14. John H. Herz, "Idealist Internationalism and the Security Dilemma," *World Politics* (Vol. 2, No. 2, 1950): p. 157.

15. *Ibid.,* p. 158.

16. *Ibid.,* p. 159.

17. See John H. Herz, *Political Realism and Political Idealism: A Study in Theories and Realities* (Chicago: University of Chicago Press, 1951).

18. For example, see Richard Ashley, "Untying the Sovereign State: A Double Reading of the Anarchy Problematique," *Millennium: Journal of International Studies* (Vol. 17, No. 2, 1988); Helen Milner, "The Assumption of Anarchy in International Relations Theory: A Critique," *Review of International Studies* (Vol. 17, No. 1, 1991); John Gerard Ruggie, "Continuity and Transformation in the World Polity: Toward a Neorealist Synthesis," in Robert O. Keohane, ed., *Neorealism and its Critics* (New York: Columbia University Press, 1986); and Barry Buzan, Charles Jones, and Richard Little, *The Logic of Anarchy: Neorealism to Structural Realism* (New York: Columbia University Press, 1993).

19. For an introduction to this topic, see Marysia Zalewski and Cynthia Enloe, "Questions about Identity in International Relations," in Ken Booth and Steve Smith, eds., *International Relations Theory Today* (University Park: Pennsylvania State University Press, 1995).

20. For a discussion of pluralism and the various schools of thought that are often included under this heading, see Richard Little, "The Growing Relevance of Pluralism?" in Steve Smith, Ken Booth, and Marysia Zalewski, eds., *International Theory: Positivism and Beyond;* Ole Waever, "The Rise and Fall of the Inter-paradigm Debate," in Steve Smith, Ken Booth, and Marysia Zalewski, eds., *International Theory: Positivism and Beyond;* and William C. Olson and A.J.R. Groom, *International Relations Then and Now: Origins and Trends in Interpretation* (London: HarperCollins, 1991).

21. This is an important avenue of research that currently is being pursued. For example, see James N. Rosenau, *Turbulence in World Politics: A Theory of Change and Continuity* (Princeton: Princeton University Press, 1990); David Held, *Political Theory and the Modern State: Essays on State, Power, and Democracy* (Standford: Standford University Press, 1989); and Peter B. Evans, Harold K. Jacobson, and Robert D. Putnam, *Double-Edged Diplomacy: International Bargaining and Domestic Politics* (Berkeley: University of California Press, 1993).

22. See Kenneth N. Waltz, *Theory of International Politics* (New York: Random House, 1979), pp. 93–97.

23. For examples of this practice, see Robert Jervis, "Realism, Game Theory, and Cooperation," *World Politics* (Vol. 40, No. 3, 1988), and Kenneth Oye, ed., *Cooperation Under Anarchy* (Princeton: Princeton University Press, 1986).

24. See Robert O. Keohane and Joseph S. Nye, *Power and Interdependence: World Politics in Transition* (Boston: Little, Brown, 1977).

25. Examples include Jens Bartelson, *A Genealogy of Sovereignty* (Cambridge: Cambridge University Press, 1995); Michael Ross Fowler and Julie Marie Bunck, *Law, Power, and the Sovereign State: The Evolution and Application of the Concept of Sovereignty* (University Park: Pennsylvania State University Press, 1995); Janice E. Thomson, "State Sovereignty in International Relations: Bridging the Gap Between Theory and Empirical Research," *International Studies Quarterly* (Vol. 39, No. 2, 1995); Stephen D. Krasner, "Compromising Westphalia," *International Security* (Vol. 20, No. 3, 1996).

BIBLIOGRAPHY

Alker, Hayward R., and Thomas J. Biersteker. "The Dialectics of World Order: Notes for a Future Archeologist of International Savoir Faire." *International Studies Quarterly* 28 (June 1984): 121–142.

Alker, Hayward R. "The Humanistic Moment in International Studies: Reflections on Machiavelli and las Casas." *International Studies Quarterly* 36 (December 1992): 347–371.

Allen, Steven H. *International Relations.* Princeton: Princeton University Press, 1920.

Angell, Norman. *The Great Illusion: A Study of the Relation of Military Power in Nations to their Economic and Social Advantage,* 3rd ed. New York: G.P. Putnam's Sons, 1911.

Art, Robert J., and Robert Jervis. *International Politics: Anarchy, Force, Political Economy, and Decision–Making,* 2nd ed. Boston: Little, Brown and Co., 1985.

Ashley, Richard K. "Untying the Sovereign State: A Double Reading of the Anarchy Problematique." *Millennium: Journal of International Studies* 17 (Summer 1988):227–262.

Ashley, Richard K., and R.B.J. Walker. "Speaking the Language of Exile: Dissident Thought in International Studies." *International Studies Quarterly* 34 (September 1990): 259–268.

Austin, John. *The Province of Jurisprudence Determined and the Uses of the Study of Jurisprudence.* New York: The Noonday Press, 1954.

Baer, Michael A., Malcolm E. Jewell, and Lee Seligman, eds. *Political Science in America: Oral Histories of a Discipline.* Lexington: University Press of Kentucky, 1991.

Bailey, Stanley H. *The Framework of International Society.* New York: Longmans, Green, and Co., 1932.

———. *International Studies in Modern Education.* London: Oxford University Press, 1938.

Baldwin, David A. "Neoliberalism, Neorealism, and World Politics." In *Neorealism and Neoliberalism: The Contemporary Debate* ed., David A. Baldwin. New York: Columbia University Press, 1993.

———. "Security Studies and the End of the Cold War." *World Politics* 48 (October 1995): 117–141.

Baldwin, David A., ed. *Neorealism and Neoliberalism: The Contemporary Debate.* New York: Columbia University Press, 1993.

Ball, Terence, ed. *Idioms of Inquiry: Critique and Renewal in Political Science.* Albany: State University of New York Press, 1987.

Ball, Terence, James Farr, and Russell L. Hanson, eds. *Political Innovation and Conceptual Change.* Cambridge: Cambridge University Press, 1989.

Banks, Michael. "The Inter-Paradigm Debate." In *International Relations a Handbook of Current Theory* eds., Margot Light and A.J.R. Groom. London: Francis Pinter Publishers, 1985.

———. "The International Relations Discipline: Asset or Liability for Conflict Resolution?" In *International Conflict Resolution* eds., Edward E. Azar and John W. Burton. Sussex: Wheatsheaf Books, 1986.

Barnes, Harry Elmer. "Some Contributions of Sociology to Modern Political Theory." *American Political Science Review* 15 (November 1921): 487–533.

Beard, Charles A. *The Idea of the National Interest: An Analytical Study in American Foreign Policy.* New York: Macmillan Co., 1934.

———. *The Devil Theory of War: An Inquiry into the Nature of History and the Possibility of Keeping Out of War.* New York: Vanguard Press, 1936.

———. "Politics." In *Discipline and History: Political Science in the United States* eds., James Farr and Raymond Seidelman. Ann Arbor: University of Michigan Press, 1993.

Bluntschli, Johann Casper. *The Theory of the State,* 3rd ed. Oxford: Clarendon Press, 1921.

Borchard, Edwin M. "Political Theory and International Law." In *A History of Political Theories: Recent Times* eds., Charles E. Merriam and Harry Elmer Barnes. New York: Macmillan Co., 1924.

Booth, Ken. "75 Years On: Rewriting the Subject's Past—Reinventing its Future." In *International Theory: Positivism and Beyond* eds., Steve Smith, Ken Booth, and Marysia Zalewski. Cambridge: Cambridge University Press, 1996.

Booth, Ken, and Steve Smith, eds. *International Relations Theory Today.* University Park: Pennsylvania State University Press, 1995.

Boyle, Francis Anthony. *World Politics and International Law.* Durham: Duke University Press, 1985.

Bridgman, Raymond L. *World Organization.* Boston: Ginn and Company, 1905.

———. "World-Sovereignty Already a Fact." *The Advocate of Peace* LXIX (April 1907).

Brown, Francis James, Charles Hodges, and Joseph Slabey Roucek. *Contemporary World Politics: An Introduction to the Problems of International Relations.* New York: John Wiley & Sons, 1939.

Brown, Philip Marshall. "The Theory of the Independence and Equality of States." *American Journal of International Law* 9 (April 1915): 305–335.

———. "War and Law." *American Journal of International Law* 12 (January 1918): 162–165.

———. *International Society: Its Nature and Interests.* New York: Macmillan Company, 1923.

Bryce, James. "The Relations of Political Science to History and to Practice." *American Political Science Review* 3 (February 1909): 1–16.

———. *International Relations.* London: Macmillan, 1922.

Bryson, Gladys. "The Emergence of the Social Sciences from Moral Philosophy." *The International Journal of Ethics* XLII (April 1932): 304–323.

Bull, Hedley. "International Theory: The Case of the Classical Approach." In *Contending Approaches to International Politics* eds., Klauss Knorr and James N. Rosenau. Princeton: Princeton University Press, 1969.

———. "The Twenty Years' Crisis Thirty Years On." *International Journal* 24 (1969): 625–638.

———. "The Theory of International Politics, 1919–1969." In *The Aberystwyth Papers: International Politics, 1919–1969* ed. Brian Porter. London: Oxford University Press, 1972.

———. *The Anarchical Society: A Study of Order in World Politics.* New York: Columbia University Press, 1977.

Burgess, John W. *Political Science and Comparative Constitutional Law,* 2 vols. Boston: Ginn and Company, 1890.

———. "The Ideal of the American Commonwealth." *Political Science Quarterly* 10 (1895): 386–406.

———. "Political Science and History." *American Historical Review* 2 (April 1897): 401–408.

———. *The European War of 1914: Its Causes, Purposes and Probable Results.* Chicago: A.C. McClung, 1915.

———. "The Founding of the School of Political Science." *Columbia University Quarterly* 22 (December 1930): 351–379.

———. *The Foundations of Political Science.* New York: Columbia University Press, 1933.

———. *The Reminiscences of an American Scholar.* New York: Columbia University Press, 1934.

Butler, Nicholas Murray. *The International Mind: An Argument for the Judicial Settlement of International Disputes.* New York: Charles Scribner's Sons, 1912.

————. *The Basis of Durable Peace*. New York: Charles Scribner's Sons, 1917.

Butterfield, Herbert. *The Whig Interpretation of History*. London: G. Bell and Sons, LTD, 1959.

Butterfield, Herbert, and Martin Wight, eds. *Diplomatic Investigations: Essays in the Theory of International Politics*. London: George Allen and Unwin, 1966.

Buzan, Barry, Charles Jones, and Richard Little. *The Logic of Anarchy: Neorealism to Structural Realism*. New York: Columbia University Press, 1993.

Buzan, Barry, and Richard Little. "The Idea of 'International System': Theory Meets History." *International Political Science Review* 15 (July 1994): 231–255.

Carr, Edward Hallett. *The Twenty Years' Crisis, 1919–1939: An Introduction to the Study of International Relations*, 2nd ed. New York: Harper & Row Publishers, 1964.

Clark, Ian. *The Hierarchy of States: Reform and Resistance in the International Order*. Cambridge: Cambridge Univesity Press, 1989.

Coker, Francis W. "Pluralistic Theories and the Attack Upon State Sovereignty." In *A History of Political Theories: Recent Times* eds., Charles E. Merriam and Harry Elmer Barnes. New York: Macmillan Co., 1924.

Collini, Stefan, Donald Winch, and John Burrow. *That Noble Science of Politics: A Study in Nineteenth Century Intellectual History*. Cambridge: Cambridge University Press, 1983.

Coser, Lewis A. *Refugee Scholars in America*. New Haven: Yale University Press, 1984.

Crick, Bernard. *The American Science of Politics*. Berkeley: University of California Press, 1959.

Curti, Merle, and Vernon Carstensen, *The University of Wisconsin: A History, 1848–1925*, Vol. I. Madison: University of Wisconsin Press, 1949.

Cutler, A. Claire. "The 'Grotian Tradition' in International Relations." *Review of International Studies* 17 (January 1991): 41–65.

Davis, George B. "Doctor Francis Lieber's Instructions for the Government of Armies in the Field." *The American Journal of International Law* I (January 1907): 13–25.

Der Derian, James. "Introducing Philosophical Traditions." *Millennium: Journal of International Studies* 17 (Summer 1988): 189–193.

Der Derian, James, and Michael J. Shapiro, eds. *International/Intertextual Relations: Postmodern Readings of World Politics*. Lexington, Mass.: Lexington Books, 1989.

Dewey, John. "Austin's Theory of Sovereignty." *Political Science Quarterly* 9 (1894): 31–52.

————. *The Public and its Problems*. Boston: Holt, 1927.

Dickinson, Edwin DeWitt. *The Equality of States in International Law.* Cambridge: Harvard University Press, 1920.

Dickinson, G. Lowes. *The Greek View of Life.* London: Methuem, 1896.

———. *The European Anarchy.* New York: The Macmillan Co., 1916.

———. *The Choice Before Us.* New York: Dodd, Mead and Co., 1917.

———. *International Anarchy, 1904–1914.* New York: The Century Co., 1926.

———. *Causes of International War.* New York: Garland Publishing, Inc., 1972.

Donnelly, Jack. "Realism and the Academic Study of International Relations." In *Political Science in History: Research Programs and Political Traditions* eds. James Farr, John S. Dryzek, and Stephen T. Leonard. Cambridge: Cambridge University Press, 1995.

Doyle, Michael W. "Liberalism and World Politics." *American Political Science Review* 80 (December 1986): 1151–1169.

———. "Thucydidean Realism." *Review of International Studies* 16 (July 1990): 223–237.

Dryzek, John S., and Stephen T. Leonard. "History and Discipline in Political Science." *American Political Science Review* 82 (December 1988): 1245–1260.

Duggan, Stephen Pierce, ed. *The League of Nations: The Principle and the Practice.* Boston: The Atlantic Monthly Press, 1919.

Dunn, David J. "On Perspectives and Approaches: British, American and Others." *Review of International Studies* 13 (January 1987): 69–80.

Dunn, Frederick S. *Peaceful Change: A Study of International Procedures.* New York: Council on Foreign Relations, 1937.

———. "The Scope of International Relations." *World Politics* 1 (October 1948): 142–146.

Dunne, Timothy. "Mythology or Methodology? Traditions in International Theory." *Review of International Studies* 19 (July 1993): 305–318.

Dunning, William A. "The Fundamental Conceptions of Nineteenth-Century Politics." In *Congress of Arts and Sciences* ed. Howard J. Rogers. Boston: Houghton Mifflin and Co., 1906.

———. "Liberty and Equality in International Relations." *American Political Science Review* 17 (February 1923): 1–16.

Dykhuizen, George. *The Life and Mind of John Dewey.* Carbondale: Southern Illinois University Press, 1973.

Easton, David, John G. Gunnell, and Luigi Graziano, eds. *The Development of Political Science: A Comparative Study.* London: Routledge, 1991.

Easton, David, Michael Stein, and John G. Gunnell eds. *Regime and Discipline: Democracy and the Development of Political Science.* Ann Arbor: University of Michigan Press, 1995.

Ellis, Ellen Deborah. "The Pluralist State." *American Political Science Review* 14 (August 1920): 393–407.

Enforced Peace: Proceedings of the First Annual National Assemblage of the League to Enforce Peace, Washington, May 26–27, 1916. New York: League to Enforce Peace, 1916.

Evans Peter B., Harold K. Jacobson, and Robert D. Putnam, eds. *Double-Edged Diplomacy: International Bargaining and Domestic Politics.* Berkeley: University of California Press, 1993.

Farr, James. "The History of Political Science." *American Journal of Political Science* 32 (November 1988): 1175–95.

———. "Francis Lieber and the Interpretation of American Political Science." *Journal of Politics* 52 (November 1990): 1027–1049.

Farr, James, Raymond Seidelman, John G. Gunnell, Stephen T. Leonard, and John S. Dryzek. "Can Political Science History Be Neutral?" *American Political Science Review* 84 (June 1990): 587–607.

Farr, James, and Raymond Seidelman, eds. *Discipline and History: Political Science in the United States.* Ann Arbor: University of Michigan Press, 1993.

Farr, James, John S. Dryzek, and Stephen T. Leonard, eds. *Political Science in History: Research Programs and Political Traditions.* Cambridge: Cambridge University Press, 1995.

Fenwick, Charles G. *International Law.* New York: The Century Co., 1924.

Ferguson, Yale H., and Richard W. Mansbach. *The Elusive Quest: Theory and International Politics.* Columbia: University of South Carolina Press, 1988.

Ferguson, Yale H., and Richard W. Mansbach. "Between Celebration and Despair: Constructive Suggestions for Future International Theory." *International Studies Quarterly* 35 (December 1991): 363–386.

Finch, George. "The Effect of the War on International Law." *American Journal of International Law* 9 (April 1915): 475–478.

Finifter, Ada W., ed. *Political Science: The State of the Discipline.* Washington, D.C.: American Political Science Association, 1983.

Finifter, Ada W. ed. *Political Science: The State of the Discipline II.* Washington, D.C.: American Political Science Association, 1993.

Follett, Mary Parker. *The New State: Group Organization the Solution of Popular Sovereignty.* London: Longmans, Green and Co., 1934.

Ford, Henry Jones. "The Scope of Political Science." *Proceedings of the American Political Science Association* 1 (1905): 198–206.

Forsyth, M.G., ed. *The Theory of International Relations: Selected Texts from Gentili to Treitschke.* New York: Atherton Press, 1970.

Foucault, Michel. *The Archaeology of Knowledge.* Trans. by A.M. Sheridan Smith. London: Tavistock, 1972.

———. *The Order of Things: An Archaeology of the Human Sciences.* Trans. by A.M. Sheridan Smith. New York: Vintage Books, 1973.

———. *Discipline and Punish: The Birth of the Prison.* Trans. by Alan Sheridan. New York: Vintage Books, 1979.

Fox, William T.R. *The American Study of International Relations.* Columbia: Institute of International Studies, University of South Carolina, 1968.

———. "E.H. Carr and Political Realism: Vision and Revision." *Review of International Studies* (January 1985): 1–16.

Furner, Mary O. *Advocacy and Objectivity: A Crisis in the Professionalization of American Social Science, 1865–1905.* Lexington: University Press of Kentucky, 1975.

Garner, James Wilford. *Introduction to Political Science: A Treatise on the Origin, Nature, Functions, and Organization of the State.* New York: American Book Co., 1910.

———. "Limitations on National Sovereignty in International Relations." *American Political Science Review* 19 (February 1925): 1–24.

Garst, Daniel. "Thucydides and Neorealism." *International Studies Quarterly* 33 (March 1989): 3–27.

Gellman, Peter. "Hans J. Morgenthau and the Legacy of Political Realism." *Review of International Studies* 14 (October 1988): 247–266.

George, Jim. "International Relations and the Search for Thinking Space: Another View of the Third Debate." *International Studies Quarterly* 33 (September 1989): 269–279.

———.*Discourses of Global Politics: A Critical (Re)Introduction to International Relations.* Boulder: Lynne Rienner Publishers, 1994.

George, Jim, and David Campbell. "Patterns of Dissent and the Celebration of Difference: Critical Social Theory and International Relations." *International Studies Quarterly* 34 (September 1990): 269–294.

Gettell, Raymond Garfield. *Introduction to Political Science.* New York: Ginn and Co., 1910.

———. "Nature and Scope of Present Political Theory." *Proceedings of the American Political Science Association* 10 (1914): 47–60.

———. *History of Political Thought.* New York: Century Co., 1924.

Giddings, Franklin H. "Imperialism?" *Political Science Quarterly* 13 (December 1898): 585–605.

———. *The Responsible State: A Re-examination of Fundamental Political Doctrines in the Light of the World War and the Menace of Anarchism.* New York: Houghton Mufflin Co., 1918.

Gilpin, Robert G. "The Richness of the Tradition of Political Realism." In *Neorealism and its Critics* ed., Robert O. Keohane. New York: Columbia University Press, 1986.

Goldman, Kjell. "The Concept of 'Realism' as a Source of Confusion." *Cooperation and Conflict* 23 (1988): 1–14.

Goodnow, Frank J. *Politics and Administration: A Study in Government.* New York: Macmillan and Co., 1900.

——. "The Work of the American Political Science Association." *Proceedings of the American Political Science Association* 1 (1904): 35–46.

Gourevitch, Peter. "The Second Image Reversed: The International Sources of Domestic Politics." *International Organization* 32 (Autumn 1978): 881–912.

Griffiths, Martin. "Order and International Society: The Real Realism?" *Review of International Studies* 18 (July 1992): 217–240.

Groom, A.J.R. "The World Beyond: The European Dimension." In *Contemporary International Relations: A Guide to Theory* eds., A.J.R. Groom and Margot Light. London: Pinter Publishers, 1994.

Groom, A.J.R., and Margot Light, eds. *Contemporary International Relations: A Guide to Theory.* London: Pinter Publishers, 1994.

Gunnell, John G. *Philosophy, Science and Political Inquiry.* Morristown: General Learning Press, 1975.

——. "The Myth of the Tradition." *American Political Science Review* 72 (March 1978): 122–134.

——. *Tradition and Interpretation.* New York: University Press of America, 1979.

——. "Political Theory: The Evolution of a Sub-Field." In *Political Science: The State of the Discipline* ed., Ada W. Finifter. Washington: APSA, 1983.

——. *Between Philosophy and Politics: The Alienation of Political Theory.* Amherst: University of Massachusetts Press, 1986.

——. "In Search of the State: Political Science as an Emerging Discipline in the U.S." In *Discourses on Society: The Shaping of the Social Science Disciplines* eds., Peter Wagner, Bjorn Wittrock, and Richard Whitleys. Boston: Kluwer Academic, 1990.

——. "Disciplinary History: The Case of Political Science." *Strategies: A Journal of Theory, Culture and Politics* 4/5 (1991): 182–227.

——. "The Historiography of American Political Science." In *The Development of Political Science* eds., David Easton, John G. Gunnell, and Luigi Graziano. London: Routledge, 1991.

——. *The Descent of Political Theory: The Genealogy of an American Vocation.* Chicago: University of Chicago Press, 1993.

——. "The Declination of the 'State' and the Origins of American 'Pluralism.'" In *Political Science in History: Research Programs and Political Traditions* eds., James Farr, John S. Dryzek, and Stephen T. Leonard. Cambridge: Cambridge University Press, 1995.

Gurian, Waldemar. "On the Study of International Relations." *The Review of Politics* 8 (July 1946): 275–282.

Haddow, Anna. *Political Science in American Colleges and Universities, 1636–1900.* New York: Octagon Books, 1969.

Harley, Lewis R. *Francis Lieber: His Life and Political Philosophy.* New York: Columbia University Press, 1899.

Haskel, Thomas. *The Emergence of Professional Social Science: The American Social Science Association and the Nineteenth Century Crisis of Authority.* Urbana: University of Illinois Press, 1977.

Heatley, David P. *Diplomacy and the Study of International Relations.* Oxford: Clarendon Press, 1919.

Hershey, Amos S. *The Essentials of International Public Law and Organization.* New York: Macmillan Company, 1929.

Herz, John. "Idealist Internationalism and the Security Dilemma." *World Politics* 2 (January 1950): 157–180.

———. *Political Realism and Political Idealism: A Study in Theories and Realities.* Chicago: University of Chicago Press, 1951.

Hesse, Mary. *Revolutions and Reconstructions in the Philosophy of Science.* Bloomington: Indiana University Press, 1980.

Hicks, Frederick Charles. *The New World Order: International Organization, International Law, International Cooperation.* New York: Doubleday, Page & Co., 1920.

Higgins, Pearce. *Studies in International Law.* Cambridge: Cambridge University Press, 1928.

Hill, David Jayne. "International Justice." *Yale Law Journal* 6 (1896): 1–19.

———. "The Second Peace Conference at the Hague." *American Journal of International Law* 1 (1907): 671–691.

———. *World Organization As Affected by the Nature of the Modern State.* New York: Columbia University Press, 1911.

———. *The People's Government.* New York: D. Appleton and Co., 1915.

———. *The Rebuilding of Europe: A Survey of Forces and Conditions.* New York: Century and Co., 1917.

———. *Present Problems in Foreign Policy.* New York: D. Appleton and Co., 1919.

Hinsley, F.H. *Power and the Pursuit of Peace.* Cambridge: Cambridge University Press, 1963.

———. *Sovereignty,* 2nd ed. Cambridge: Cambridge Univesity Press, 1986.

Hobbes, Thomas. *Leviathan.* With an Introduction by C.B. Macpherson. New York: Penguin Books, 1985.

Hobhouse, L.T. *The Metaphysical Theory of the State: A Criticism*. New York: Macmillan Co., 1918.

Hobsbawm, Eric. "Introduction: Inventing Traditions." In *The Invention of Tradition* eds., Eric Hobsbawm and Terence Ranger. Cambridge: Cambridge University Press, 1983.

Hobsbawm, Eric, and Terence Ranger, eds. *The Invention of Tradition*. Cambridge: Cambridge Univeristy Press, 1983.

Hobson, John A. "The Scientific Basis of Imperialism." *Political Science Quarterly* 17 (1902): 460–489.

———. *Towards International Government*. New York: Macmillan Co., 1916.

———. *Imperialism: A Study*. Ann Arbor: University of Michigan Press, 1965.

Hoffman, Mark. "Critical Theory and the Inter-Paradigm Debate." *Millennium: Journal of International Studies* 16 (1987): 231–249.

Hoffmann, Stanley. *The State of War: Essays in the Theory and Practice of International Politics*. New York: Frederick A. Praeger, 1965.

———. "An American Social Science: International Relations." *Daedalus: Proceedings of the American Academy of Arts and Sciences* 106 (Summer 1977): 41–59.

Holsti, Kal J. *The Dividing Discipline: Hegemony and Diversity in International Theory*. Boston: Allen & Unwin, 1985.

———. "Mirror, Mirror on the Wall, Which Are the Fairest Theories of All?" *International Studies Quarterly* 33 (1989): 255–261.

Howe, Paul. "The Utopian Realism of E.H. Carr." *Review of International Studies* 20 (July 1994): 277–297.

Hoxie, Ralph Gordon, ed. *A History of the Faculty of Political Science, Columbia University*. New York: Columbia University Press, 1955.

Hull, William I. *The Two Hague Conferences and their Contributions to International Law*. Boston: Ginn & Co., 1908.

Hurrell, Andrew. "Kant and the Kantian Paradigm in International Relations." *Review of International Studies* 16 (July 1990): 183–205.

Ireland, Alleyne. *Tropical Colonization: An Introduction to the Study of the Subject*. New York: Macmillan and Co., 1899.

———. "On the Need for a Scientific Understanding of Colonial Administration." *Proceedings of the American Political Science Association* 3 (1906): 210–221.

Jervis, Robert. "Cooperation Under the Security Dilemma." *World Politics* 30 (January 1978): 167–214.

John, Ieuan, Moorhead Wright, and John Garnett. "International Politics at Aberystwyth, 1919–1969." In *The Aberystwyth Papers: International Politics, 1919–1969* ed., Brian Porter. London: Oxford University Press, 1972.

Josephson, Harold. *James T. Shotwell and the Rise of Internationalism in America.* London: Associated University Presses, 1975.

Kahler, Miles. "International Relations: Still an American Social Science?" In *Ideas and Ideals: Essays on Politics in Honor of Stanley Hoffmann* eds., Linda B. Miller and Michael Joseph Smith. Boulder: Westview Press, 1993.

———. "Inventing International Relations: International Relations Theory After 1945." In *New Directions in International Relations Theory* eds., Michael W. Doyle and G. John Ikenberry. Boulder: Westview Press, forthcoming.

Kaplan, Morton A. "Is International Relations a Discipline?" *The Journal of Politics* 23 (August 1961): 462–476.

Kant, Immanuel. *Perpetual Peace and Other Essays on Politics, History, and Morals.* Translated by Ted Humphrey. Indianapolis: Hackett Publishing Co., 1983.

Kauppi, Mark V., and Paul R. Viotti. *International Relations Theory: Realism, Pluralism, Globalism.* New York: Macmillan, 1987.

———. *The Global Philosophers: World Politics in Western Thought.* New York: Lexington Books, 1992.

Kegley, Charles W., Jr., and Eugene R. Wittkopf. *World Politics: Trend and Transformation,* 3rd ed. New York: St. Martin's Press, 1989.

Kegley, Charles W., Jr. "The Neoidealist Moment in International Studies? Realist Myths and the New International Realities." *International Studies Quarterly* 37 (June 1993): 131–146.

———. "The Neoliberal Challenge to Realist Theories of World Politics: An Introduction." In *Controversies in International Relations Theory: Realism and the Neoliberal Challenge* ed., Charles W. Kegley. New York: St. Martin's Press, 1995.

Kegley, Charles W., Jr., ed. *Controversies in International Relations Theory: Realism and the Neoliberal Challenge.* New York: St. Martin's Press, 1995.

Keller, Albert. *Colonization: A Study of the Founding of New Societies.* Boston: Ginn and Co., 1908.

Kent, James. *Commentaries on American Law.* New York: O. Halsted, 1826.

Kent, R.C., and G.P. Nielsson, eds. *The Study and Teaching of International Relations.* London: Pinter Publishers, 1980.

Keohane, Robert O. "Theory of World Politics: Structural Realism and Beyond." In *Political Science: The State of the Discipline* ed., Ada W. Finifter. Washington, D.C.: American Political Science Association, 1983.

———. "International Institutions: Two Approaches." *International Studies Quarterly* 32 (December 1988): 379–396.

Keohane, Robert O., ed. *Neorealism and its Critics.* New York: Columbia University Press, 1986.

Keohane, Robert O., and Joseph S. Nye, *Power and Interdependence,* 2nd ed. Boston: Scott, Foresman and Co., 1989.

Kerr, P.H. "Political Relations Between Advanced and Backward Peoples." In *An Introduction to the Study of International Relations* eds., A.J. Grant, Arthur Greenwood, J.D.I. Hughes, P.H. Kerr, and F.F. Urquhart. London: Macmillan and Co., 1916.

Kidd, Benjamin. *Social Evolution.* New York: Macmillan and Co., 1894.

———. *The Control of the Tropics.* New York: Macmillan and Co., 1898.

Kirk, Grayson. *The Study of International Relations in American Colleges and Universities.* New York: Council on Foreign Relations, 1947.

Klein, Bradley S. *Strategic Studies and World Order: The Global Politics of Deterrence.* Cambridge: Cambridge University Press, 1994.

Knorr, Klauss, and James N. Rosenau, eds. *Contending Approaches to International Politics.* Princeton: Princeton University Press, 1969.

Knutsen, Torbjorn L. *A History of International Relations Theory: An Introduction.* Manchester: Manchester University Press, 1992.

Krabbe, Hugo. *The Modern Idea of the State.* New York: D. Appleton and Co., 1922.

Krasner, Stephen D., ed. *International Regimes.* Ithaca: Cornell University Press, 1983.

———. "Compromising Westphalia." *International Security* 20 (Winter 1995/1996): 115–151.

Kratochwill, Friedrich, and John Gerard Ruggie. "International Organization: A State of the Art on an Art of the State." *International Organization* 40 (Autumn 1986): 753–775.

Kratochwill, Friedrich, and Edward D. Mansfield, eds. *International Organization: A Reader.* New York: HarperCollins, 1994.

Krippendorf, Ekkehart. "The Dominance of American Approaches in International Relations." *Millennium: Journal of International Studies* 16 (1987): 207–214.

Kuehl, Warren F. *Seeking World Order: The United States and International Organization to 1920.* Nashville: Vanderbilt University Press, 1969.

Kugler, Jacek. "Political Conflict, War and Peace." In *Political Science: The State of the Discipline II* ed., Ada W. Finifter. Washington, D.C.: American Political Science Association, 1993.

Kuhn, Thomas S. *The Structure of Scientific Revolutions,* 2nd ed. Chicago: University of Chicago Press, 1970.

Lakatos, Imre, and Alan Musgrave, eds. *Criticism and the Growth of Knowledge.* Cambridge: Cambridge University Press, 1970.

Lansing, Robert. "Notes On Sovereignty in a State." *American Journal of International Law* 1 (January 1907): 105–128.

Lapid, Yosef. "Quo Vadis International Relations? Further Reflections on the Next Stage of International Theory." *Millennium: Journal of International Studies* 18 (Spring 1989): 77–88.

———. "The Third Debate: On the Prospects of International Theory in a Post-Postivist Era." *International Studies Quarterly* (September 1989): 235–254.

Laski, Harold J. *Studies in the Problem of Sovereignty.* New Haven: Yale University Press, 1917.

———. *Authority in the Modern State.* New Haven: Yale University Press, 1919.

———. *The Foundations of Sovereignty and Other Essays.* New York: Harcourt, Brace and Co., 1921.

———. "International Government and National Sovereignty." In *The Problems of Peace: Lectures Delivered at the Geneva Institute of International Relations.* London: Oxford University Press, 1927.

Laswell, Harold D. "The Problem of World-Unity: In Quest of a Myth." *International Journal of Ethics* 44 (1933): 68–93.

———. *World Politics and Personal Insecurity.* New York: McGraw-Hill, 1935.

Laudan, Larry. *Progress and its Problems: Towards a Theory of Scientific Growth.* Berkeley: University of California Press, 1977.

Lawrence, T.J. *The Society of Nations: Its Past, Present, and Possible Future.* New York: Oxford University Press, 1919.

———. *The Principles of International Law,* 7th ed. Boston: D.C. Heath & Co., 1923.

Leacock, Stephen. *Elements of Political Science.* Boston: Houghton, Mifflin and Co., 1906.

Lebow, Richard Ned, and Thomas Risse-Kappen, eds. *International Relations Theory and the End of the Cold War.* New York: Columbia University Press, 1995.

Lenin, V.I. *Imperialism: The Highest Stage of Capitalism.* New York: International Publishers, 1939.

Lepawsky, Albert. "The Politics of Epistemology." *The Western Political Quarterly* 17 (1964): 21–52.

Levin, N. Gordon, Jr. *Woodrow Wilson and World Politics: America's Response to War and Revolution.* New York: Oxford University Press, 1968.

Lieber, Francis, ed. *Encyclopedia Americana.* Philadelphia: Thomas Desilver and Company, 1835.

———. *Civil Liberty and Self-Government.* Philadelphia: J. B. Lippincott Company, 1853.

————. *Miscellaneous Writings.* Philadelphia: J. B. Lippincott Company, 1880.

————. *Manual of Political Ethics,* 2nd ed. Philadelphia: J. B. Lippincott Company, 1885.

Lijphart, Arend. "International Relations Theory: Great Debates and Lesser Debates." *International Social Science Journal* 26 (1974): 11–21.

————. "The Structure of the Theoretical Revolution in International Relations." *International Studies Quarterly* 18 (March 1974): 41–74.

Lippmann, Walter. *The Stakes of Diplomacy.* New York: Henry Holt and Co., 1915.

————. *The Phantom Public.* New York: Harcourt Brace, 1925.

Little, Richard. "The Evolution of International Relations as a Social Science." In *The Study and Teaching of International Relations* eds., R.C. Kent and G.P. Nielsson. London: Francis Pinter, 1980.

————. "The Growing Relevance of Pluralism?" In *International Theory: Positivism and Beyond* eds., Steve Smith, Ken Booth, and Marysia Zalewski. Cambridge: Cambridge University Press, 1996.

Lyotard, Jean-Francois. *The Postmodern Condition: A Report on Knowledge.* Minnesota: University of Minnesota Press, 1989.

Maine, Henry Sumner. *Ancient Law, Its Connection with Early History and Its Relation to Modern Ideas,* 4th ed. London: Murray, 1930.

Maghroori, Ray, and Bennet Ramberg, eds. *Globalism Versus Realism: International Relations' Third Debate.* Boulder: Westview Press, 1982.

Markwell, D.J. "Sir Alfred Zimmern Revisited: Fifty Years On." *Review of International Studies* 12 (1986): 279–292.

Mathews, John Mamby, and James Hart, eds. *Essays in Political Science in Honor of Westel Woodbury Willoughby.* Freeport: Books for Libraries Press, 1937.

McDougall, Derek. *Harold D. Laswell and the Study of International Relations.* Lanham: University Press of America, 1984.

Merriam, Charles E. "The Present State of the Study of Politics." *American Political Science Review* 15 (May 1921): 173–185.

————. "Progress Report of the Committee on Political Research." *American Political Science Review* 17 (1923): 274–295.

————. "Recent Tendencies in Political Thought." In *A History of Political Theories: Recent Times* eds., Charles E. Merriam and Harry Elmer Barnes. New York: Macmillan Co., 1924.

————. *New Aspects of Politics.* Chicago: University of Chicago Press, 1925.

————. "Progress in Political Research." *American Political Science Review* 20 (February 1926): 1–13.

Merriam, Charles E., and Harry Elmer Barnes, eds. *A History of Political Theories: Recent Times.* New York: Macmillan Co., 1924.

Milner, Helen. "The Assumption of Anarchy in International Relations Theory: A Critique." *Review of International Studies* 17 (January 1991): 67–85.

Mitchell, C.R. "Analysing the 'Great Debates': Teaching Methodology in a Decade of Change." In *The Study and Teaching of International Relations* eds., R.C. Kent and G.P. Nielsson. London: Pinter Publishers, 1980.

Moon, Parker T. *Syllabus On International Relations.* New York: Macmillan Co., 1925.

Moore, John Bassett. *History and Digest of the International Arbitration to Which the United States Has Been a Party.* 6 vols. Washington, D.C.: Government Printing Office, 1898.

———. "Law and Organization." *American Political Science Review* 9 (February 1915): 1–15.

Morgenthau, Hans J. *Scientific Man Versus Power Politics.* Chicago: University of Chicago Press, 1946.

———. "The Political Science of E.H. Carr." *World Politics* 1 (October 1948): 127–134.

———. *Politics Among Nations: The Struggle for Power and Peace,* 2nd. ed. New York: Alfred A. Knopf, 1955.

———. "An Intellectual Autobiography." *Transaction: Social Science and Modern Society* 15 (January/February 1978): 63–68.

Morely, Felix. *The Society of Nations: Its Organization and Constitutional Development.* Washington, D.C.: The Brookings Institute, 1932.

Morris, Henry C. "Some Effects of Outlying Dependencies Upon the People of the United States." *Proceedings of the American Political Science Association* 3 (1906): 194–211.

Moses, Bernard. "The Control of Dependencies Inhabited by the Less Developed Races." In *Congress of Arts and Sciences* ed., Howard J. Rogers. Boston: Houghton, Mifflin and Co., 1906.

Munro, William Bennett. *Invisible Government.* New York: Macmillan Co., 1928.

Murphy, Craig N. *International Organization and Industrial Change: Global Governance Since 1850.* Oxford: Oxford University Press, 1994.

Neal, Fred Warner, and Bruce D. Hamlet. "The Never-Never Land of International Relations." *International Studies Quarterly* 13 (September 1969): 281–305.

Nicholls, David. *The Pluralist State: The Political Ideas of J.N. Figgis and His Contemporaries,* 2nd ed. New York: St. Martin's Press, 1994.

Odum, Howard W., ed. *American Masters' of Social Science.* Port Washington, N.Y.: Kennikat Press, Inc., 1965.

Olson, William C. "The Growth of a Discipline." In *The Aberystwyth Papers: International Politics 1919–1969* ed., Brian Porter. London: Oxford University Press, 1972.

Olson, William C., and Nicholas Onuf. "The Growth of a Discipline: Reviewed." In *International Relations: British and American Perspectives* ed., Steve Smith. Oxford: Basil Blackwell, 1985.

Olson, William C., and A.J.R. Groom. *International Relations Then and Now: Origins and Trends in Interpretation.* London: HarperCollins, 1991.

Onuf, Nicholas Greenwood. *World of Our Making: Rules and Rule in Social Theory and International Relations.* Columbia: University of South Carolina Press, 1989.

Oppenheim, Lassa. *International Law.* 2 vols. London: Longmans, Green & Co., 1905.

———. "The Science of International Law: Its Task and Method." *American Journal of International Law* 2 (April 1908): 313–356.

Oren, Ido. "The Subjectivity of the 'Democratic' Peace: Changing U.S. Perceptions of Imperial Germany." *International Security* 20 (Fall 1995): 147–184.

Oye, Kenneth, ed. *Cooperation Under Anarchy.* Princeton: Princeton University Press, 1986.

Palan, Ronen P., and Brook M. Blair. "On the Idealist Origins of the Realist Theory of International Relations." *Review of International Studies* 19 (October 1993): 385–399.

Palmer, Norman D. "The Study of International Relations in the United States." *International Studies Quarterly* 24 (September 1980): 343–364.

Parkman, Aubrey. *David Jayne Hill and the Problem of World Peace.* Lewisburg: Bucknell University Press, 1911.

Peterson, V. Spike. "Transgressing Boundaries: Theories of Knowledge, Gender and International Relations." *Millennium: Journal of International Studies* 21 (Summer 1992): 183–206.

Pocock, J.G.A. *Politics, Language, and Time.* London: Methuen, 1972.

Porter, Brian, ed. *The Aberystwyth Papers: International Politics 1919–1969.* London: Oxford University Press, 1972.

———. "David Davies: A Hunter After Peace." *Review of International Studies* 15 (1989): 27–36.

Potter, Pitman B. "Political Science in the International Field." *American Political Science Review* 27 (August 1923): 381–391.

———. *An Introduction to the Study of International Organization.* New York: Century Co., 1925.

———. *This World of Nations: Foundations, Institutions, Practices.* New York: Macmillan Co., 1929.

———. "International Organization." In *Encyclopaedia of the Social Sciences*, Vol. 7. New York: Macmillan Co., 1933.

———. "The Classification of International Organizations, II." *American Political Science Review* 29 (1935): 403–417.

Pound, Roscoe. "Philosophical Theory and International Law." In Bib*liotheca Visseriana.* Leyden, 1923.

Problems of Readjustment After the War. New York: D. Appleton and Co., 1915.

Pugach, Noel H. *Paul S. Reinsch: Open Door Diplomat in Action.* Millwood: KTO Press, 1979.

Ransom, Harry Howe. "International Relations." *The Journal of Politics* 30 (May 1968): 345–371.

Rappard, William E. *The Geneva Experiment.* Oxford: Oxford University Press, 1931.

Read, Elizabeth F. *International Law and International Relations.* New York: The American Foundation, 1925.

Reeves, Jesse S. "The Justicability of International Disputes." *American Political Science Review* 10 (February 1916): 70–79.

Reinsch, Paul S. *World Politics At the End of the Nineteenth Century, As Influenced by the Oriental Situation.* New York: Macmillan, 1900.

———. *Colonial Government: An Introduction to the Study of Colonial Institutions.* New York: Macmillan, 1902.

———. "The American Political Science Association." *The Iowa Journal of History and Politics* 2 (1904): 157–161.

———. "Colonial Autonomy, With Special Reference to the Government of the Philippine Islands." *Proceedings of the American Political Science Association* 1 (1904): 116–139.

———. *Colonial Administration.* New York: Macmillan, 1905.

———. "International Unions and their Administration." *American Journal of International Law* 3 (January 1909): 1–45.

———. *Public International Unions Their Work and Organization: A Study in International Administrative Law.* Boston: Ginn and Company, 1911.

Robertson, David Brian. "The Return to History and the New Institutionalism in American Political Science." *Social Science History* 17 (Spring 1993): 1–36.

Rochester, J. Martin. "The Rise and Fall of International Organization as a Field of Study." *International Organization* 40 (Autumn 1986): 687–721.

Rogers, Howard J., ed. *Congress of Arts and Science.* Boston: Houghton, Mifflin and Co., 1906.

Root, Elihu. "The Sanction of International Law." *American Journal of International Law* 2 (July 1908): 451–457.

———. "The Outlook of International Law." *American Journal of International Law* 10 (January 1916): 1–11.

Rosenau, James N. *Turbulence in World Politics: A Theory of Change and Continuity.* Princeton: Princeton University Press, 1990.

Rosenau, Pauline. "Once Again Into the Fray: International Relations Confronts the Humanities." *Millennium: Journal of International Studies* 19 (Spring 1990): 83–110.

Rosenthal, Joel H. *Righteous Realists: Political Realism, Responsible Power, and American Culture in the Nuclear Age.* Baton Rouge: Louisiana State University Press, 1991.

Ross, Dorothy. *The Origins of American Social Science.* Cambridge: Cambridge University Press, 1991.

Rothstein, Robert L. "On the Costs of Realism." *Political Science Quarterly* 87 (September 1972): 347–362.

Russell, Frank M. *Theories of International Relations.* New York: Appleton-Century-Crofts, Inc., 1936.

Russell, Greg. *Hans J. Morgenthau and the Ethics of American Statecraft.* Baton Rouge: Louisiana State University Press, 1990.

Russett, Bruce. *Grasping the Democratic Peace: Principles for a Post–Cold War World.* Princeton: Princeton University Press, 1993.

Sabine, George. "Pluralism: A Point of View." *American Political Science Review* 17 (February 1923): 34–50.

Sandelius, Walter. "National Sovereignty Versus the Rule of Law." *American Political Science Review* (February 1931): 1–20.

Schram, Sanford F. *Words of Welfare: The Poverty of Social Science and the Social Science of Poverty.* Minneapolis: University of Minnesota Press, 1995.

Schuman, Frederick L. *International Politics: An Introduction to the Western State System,* 2nd. ed. New York: McGraw-Hill Book Co., 1937.

Schwarzenberger, Georg. *Power Politics: An Introduction to the Study of International Relations and Post-War Planning.* London: Jonathan Cape, 1941.

Scott, James Brown. "The Legal Nature of International Law." *American Journal of International Law* 1 (October 1907): 831–866.

———. *The Hague Peace Conferences of 1899 and 1907,* 2 Vols. Baltimore: Johns Hopkins University Press, 1909.

Seidelman, Raymond, with the assistance of Edward J. Harpham. *Disenchanted Realists: Political Science and the American Crisis, 1884–1984.* Albany: State University of New York Press, 1985.

Seligman, Edwin R.A.. *The Economic Interpretation of History.* New York: Macmillan and Co., 1902.

———. "An Economic Interpretation of the War." In *Problems of Readjustment After the War.* New York: D. Appleton and Co., 1915.

Sharp, Walter R., and Grayson Kirk. *Contemporary International Politics.* New York: Rinehart & Co., 1944.

Shotwell, James T. *War as an Instrument of National Policy and its Renunciation in the Pact of Paris.* New York: Harcourt, Brace and Co., 1929.

———. *On the Rim of the Abyss.* New York: Macmillan Co., 1937.

———. *The Autobiography of James T. Shotwell.* New York: Bobbs-Merrill Co., 1961.

Singer, J. David. "The Level-of-Analysis Problem in International Relations." In *International Politics and Foreign Policy* ed., James N. Rosenau. New York: Free Press, 1969.

Sked, Alan. "The Study of International Relations: A Historian's View." In *The Study of International Relations: The State of the Art* eds., Hugh C. Dyer and Leon Mangasarian. New York: St. Martin's Press, 1989.

Smith, Michael Joseph. *Realist Thought from Weber to Kissenger.* Baton Rouge: Louisiana State University Press, 1986.

Smith, Munroe. "Introduction: The Domain of Political Science." *Political Science Quarterly* 1 (March 1886): 1–8.

Smith, Steve, ed. *International Relations: British and American Perspectives.* Oxford: Basil Blackwell, 1985.

———. "Paradigm Dominance in International Relations: The Development of International Relations as a Social Science." *Millennium: Journal of International Studies* 16 (1987): 189–206.

———. "The Forty Years' Detour: The Resurgence of Normative Theory in International Relations." *Millennium: Journal of International Studies* 21 (Winter 1992): 489–506.

Smith, Steve, Ken Booth, and Marysia Zalewski, eds. *International Theory: Positivism and Beyond.* Cambridge: Cambridge University Press, 1996.

Snow, Alpheus Henry. *The Administration of Dependencies: A Study of the Evolution of the Federal Empire, With Special Reference to American Colonial Problems.* New York: G.P. Putnam's Sons, 1902.

———. "The Question of Terminology." *Proceedings of the American Political Science Association* 3 (1906): 224–239.

———. "Neutralization Versus Imperialism." *American Journal of International Law* 2 (July 1908): 562–590.

———. "The Law of Nations." *American Journal of International Law* 6 (July 1912): 890–900.

———. "International Law and Political Science." *American Journal of International Law* 7 (April 1913): 315–328.

Somit, Albert, and Joseph Tanenhaus. *The Development of American Political Science: From Burgess to Behavioralism.* New York: Irvington Publishers, 1982.

Stawell, F. Melian. *The Growth of International Thought*. New York: Henry Holt and Co., 1930.

Steigerwald, David. *Wilsonian Idealism in America*. Cornell: Cornell University Press, 1994.

Stocking, George W. "On the Limits of 'Presentism' and 'Historicism' in the Historiography of the Behavioral Sciences." *Journal of the History of the Behavioral Sciences* 1 (July 1965): 211–217.

Strauss, Leo. *What is Political Philosophy?* Glencoe, Ill.: Free Press, 1959.

Suganami, Hidemi. *The Domestic Analogy and Word Order Proposals*. Cambridge: Cambridge University Press, 1989.

Sylvester, Christine. *Feminist Theory and International Relations in a Postmodern Era*. Cambridge: Cambridge University Press, 1994.

Symons, Farrell. *Courses On International Affairs in American Colleges, 1930–31*. Boston: World Peace Foundation, 1931.

Thompson, Kenneth W. *Political Realism and the Crisis of World Politics*. Princeton: Princeton University Press, 1960.

———. *Masters of International Thought: Major Twentieth Century Theorists and the World in Crisis*. Baton Rouge: Louisiana State University Press, 1980.

Thomson, Janice E. "State Sovereignty in International Relations: Bridging the Gap Between Theory and Empirical Research." *International Studies Quarterly* 39 (June 1995): 213–233.

Thorsen, Niels Aage. *The Political Thought of Woodrow Wilson*. Princeton: Princeton University Press, 1988.

Tickner, J. Ann. *Gender in International Relations: Feminist Perspectives On Achieving Global Security*. New York: Columbia University Press, 1992.

Treitschke, Heinrich von. *Politics*. Trans. by Blanche Dugdale and Torben de Bille. New York: Macmillan Co., 1916.

Trueblood, Benjamin F. *The Federation of the World*. Boston: Houghton, Mifflin and Co., 1899.

Tully, James, ed. *Meaning and Context: Quentin Skinner and His Critics*. Princeton: Princeton University Press, 1988.

Turner, Edward Raymond. "The Causes of the Great War." *American Political Science Review* 9 (February 1915): 16–35.

Turner, Frederick Jackson. "The Significance of the Frontier in American History." American Historical Association, *Annual Report for the Year 1893* (1894).

Vasquez, John A. *The Power of Power Politics: A Critique*. New Brunswick: Rutgers University Press, 1983.

———. "The Post-Positivist Debate: Reconstructing Scientific Enquiry and International Relations After Enlightenment's Fall." In *International Relations Theory Today* eds., Ken Booth and Steve Smith. University Park: Pennsylvania State University Press, 1995.

Vasquez, John A., ed. *Classics of International Relations.* Englewood Cliffs, N.J.: Prentice-Hall, 1986.

Vattell, Emmerich de. *The Law of Nations or the Principles of Natural Law.* In *The Theory of International Relations: Selected Texts from Gentili to Treitschke* ed., M.G. Forsyth. New York: Atherton Press, 1970.

Waldo, Dwight. "Political Science: Tradition, Discipline, Profession, Science, Enterprise." In *Handbook of Political Science,* Vol. I eds., Fred I. Greenstein and Nelson W. Polsby. Reading, Mass.: Addison-Wesley, 1975.

Walker, R.B.J. "History and Structure in the Theory of International Relations." *Millennium: Journal of International Studies* 18 (Summer 1989): 163–183.

———. "The Prince and the 'Pauper': Tradition, Modernity, and Practice in the Theory of International Relations." In *International/Intertextual Relations: Postmodern Readings of World Politics* eds., James Der Derian and Michael Shapiro. Lexington: Lexington Books, 1989.

———. *Inside/Outside: International Relations as Political Theory.* Cambridge: Cambridge Press, 1993.

Waltz, Kenneth N. *Man, the State, and War: A Theoretical Analysis.* New York: Columbia University Press, 1959.

———. *Theory of International Politics.* Reading: Addison-Wesley, 1979.

Ware, Edith. *The Study of International Relations in the United States: Survey for 1937.* New York: Columbia University Press, 1938.

Weber, Max. "Science As A Vocation." In *From Max Weber: Essays in Sociology* ed., G.H. Gerth and C. Wright Mills. New York: Oxford University Press, 1948.

Webster, Charles K. *The Study of International Politics.* Cardiff: The University of Wales Press Board, 1923.

Wendt, Alexander. "Anarchy is What States Make of it: The Social Construction of Power Politics." *International Organization* 46 (Spring 1992): 391–425.

Wendt, Alexander, and Daniel Friedheim. "Hierarchy Under Anarchy." *International Organization* 49 (Autumn 1995): 689–721.

Wheaton, Henry. *Elements of International Law.* In *The Classics of International Law* ed., George Grafton Wilson. Oxford: Claredon Press, 1936.

Whitworth, Sandra. "Gender in the Inter-Paradigm Debate." *Millennium: Journal of International Studies* 18 (Spring 1989): 265–272.

Wight, Martin. "Why is There No International Theory?" In *Diplomatic Investigations: Essays in the Theory of International Politics* eds., Herbert Butterfield and Martin Wight. London: George Allen and Unwin, 1966.

———. "Western Values in International Relations." In *Diplomatic Investigations: Essays in the Theory of International Politics* eds., Herbert Butterfield and Martin Wight. London: George Allen and Unwin, 1966.

———. "An Anatomy of International Thought." *Review of International Studies* 13 (July 1987): 221–227.

———. *International Theory: The Three Traditions.* Edited by Gabriel Wight and Brian Porter. New York: Holmes & Meir, 1992.

Williams, Bruce. "State Morality in International Relations." *American Political Science Review* 17 (February 1923): 17–33.

Williams, Michael C. "Hobbes and International Relations." *International Organization* 50 (Spring 1996): 213–236.

Willoughby, Westel Woodbury. *An Examination of the Nature of the State.* New York: Macmillan Co., 1896.

———. "The American Political Science Association." *Political Science Quarterly* 15 (1904): 107–111.

———. "Political Science as a University Study." *Sewanee Review* 14 (1906): 257–258.

———. "Relation of the Individual to the State." In *Problems of Readjustment After the War.* New York: D. Appleton and Co., 1915.

———. "The Juristic Conception of the State." *American Political Science Review* 12 (1918): 192–208.

———. "The Prussian Theory of the State." *American Journal of International Law* 12 (April 1918): 251–265.

Wilson, George Grafton. "The War and International Law." In *Problems of Readjustment After the War.* New York: D. Appleton and Co., 1915.

———. "The Modernization of International Law." *American Political Science Review* 19 (April 1926): 268–276.

———. *International Law,* 9th ed. New York: Silver, Burdett and Co., 1935.

Wilson, Woodrow. "The Study of Administration." *Political Science Quarterly* 2 (1887): 202–217.

———. "The Fourteen Points." In *Classics of International Relations* ed., John A. Vasquez. Englewood Cliffs, Prentice-Hall, 1986.

Wolin, Sheldon S. "Political Theory as a Vocation." *American Political Science Review* 63 (December 1969): 1062–1082.

Woolf, Leonard. "Utopia and Reality." *The Political Quarterly* 11 (April/June 1940): 167–182.

Woolsey, Theodore D. *Political Science, or the State Theoretically and Practically Considered.* New York: Scribner, Armstrong and Co., 1877.

————. *Introduction to the Study of International Law Designed As An Aid in Teaching, and Historical Studies,* 4th ed. Littletin, Colo.: Fred B. Rothman and Company, 1981.

Wright, Quincy. *Research in International Law Since the War.* Washington: Carnegie Endowment for International Peace, 1930.

————. *A Study of War,* 2 Vols. Chicago: University of Chicago Press, 1942.

————. "Realism and Idealism in International Politics." *World Politics* 5 (October 1952): 116–128.

————. *The Study of International Relations.* New York: Appleton-Century-Crofts, 1955.

Zalewski, Marysia and Cynthia Enloe. "Questions About Identity in International Relations." In *International Relations Theory Today* eds., Ken Booth and Steve Smith. University Park: Pennsylvania State University Press, 1995.

Zimmern, Alfred. *The League of Nations and the Rule of Law.* London: Macmillan and Co., 1936.

————. *University Teaching of International Relations.* Paris: International Institute of Intellectual Co-operation, 1939.

INDEX